T0300665

CHURCHILL'S CITADEL

CHURCHILL'S CITADEL

Chartwell and the Gatherings
Before the Storm

KATHERINE CARTER

YALE UNIVERSITY PRESS
NEW HAVEN AND LONDON

For information about this and other Yale University Press publications, please contact:
U.S. Office: sales.press@yale.edu   yalebooks.com
Europe Office: sales@yaleup.co.uk   yalebooks.co.uk

Set in Adobe Caslon Pro by IDSUK (DataConnection) Ltd
Printed in the United States of America.

Library of Congress Control Number: 2024941986

ISBN 978-0-300-27019-8

A catalogue record for this book is available from the British Library.

10 9 8 7 6 5 4 3

For Iain,
with love and gratitude

'I send this token, but how little can it express my gratitude to you for making my life & any work I have done possible, and for giving me so much happiness in a world of accident & storm.'
Winston Churchill to Clementine Churchill

12 September 1948

CONTENTS

CONTENTS

ILLUSTRATIONS

THE NEAR MISS

Adolf Hitler, Munich, 30 August 1932

The guest of honour was running late. The Churchills' table in the dining room of Munich's Grand Hotel Continental was ready, but Adolf Hitler was nowhere to be seen. In his absence, the Nazi Party's Harvard-educated foreign press secretary, Ernst 'Putzi' Hanfstaengl, entertained the group. He placed himself in the chair between the Churchills, with Winston to his right and Clementine on his left. He knew that the National Socialist Party could only benefit from a new and well-placed champion in Westminster. Though Churchill's political stock had fallen in recent years, he was still well connected and influential. The evening wore on but there was still no sign of Hitler. In one of the most astonishing 'sliding doors' moments in history, the Nazi leader questioned whether it was worth attending. After all, he was the rising star of German politics, and surely a British politician whose career was widely thought to be in a state of rapid decline was hardly worthy of his time.

Churchill knew things had changed for the worse in Germany. During his time in the country he became deeply troubled by what he soon called a 'war mentality', and no amount of charm offensives from senior Nazi figures could allay his concerns.[1] Upon his return to Chartwell, the house-on-a-hill that had captured his heart a decade before, he began to transform it from a rural idyll to a campaign headquarters; or, as his secretary later called it, his 'citadel'.[2] It was here that Churchill began the greatest fight of his life. Supported by

1

those around him at Chartwell, he met with friends, allies and acquaintances to influence, persuade and glean vital information to support his cause, away from the prying eyes of Westminster and London society. In the seven years that followed, he did everything in his power to sound the alarm about the evils of the Nazi regime, and the need for Britain to prepare for war. Chartwell was his centre of intelligence and his war room, with every corner a witness to events that changed the course of history.

During the summer of 1932, Churchill was on the backbenches of the House of Commons. He was the Conservative Member of Parliament for Epping in Essex, as he had been since he returned to the Conservative Party from the Liberals in 1924. But the Labour Party's election victory in 1929 toppled him from the great office of Chancellor of the Exchequer, where he had, for five years, shaped and managed the economic policies of the British Government. Though his political party now sat on the opposition benches, Churchill initially remained influential. He served in the Conservative 'Business Committee', the equivalent of the modern shadow cabinet, as Chairman of the Conservative Finance Committee. He was tasked with leading the Conservative criticism of his Labour Party opponent, Philip Snowden, and relished the chance to flex his strongest political-attack muscles in opposition. Some colleagues, however, began to question his performance, as well as the causes he championed. He wrote to Stanley Baldwin, the Leader of the Conservative Party, in September 1930 saying he cared about India 'more than anything else in public life',[3] amidst a growing debate about proposals for increased Indian self-government. The same letter included an invitation for Baldwin to join him at Chartwell for lunch to discuss the subject further. 'I have many works of construction to show you', he declared proudly of the extensive brick walls he had been building since 1925. He concluded, 'When the sun shines I would rather be here than anywhere in the world.'[4] Just a few weeks later, sensing that a split between the two men could lead to a schism in the Conservative Party, Baldwin penned a heartfelt, handwritten note to Churchill, reaffirming their friendship despite their differences. He wrote, 'I cannot have many more years before me, and it would be a joy to feel that I had kept the leaders of our party together until the end.'[5]

Despite the warm words, the pair both knew that Churchill was increasingly swimming against the tide of party opinion by remaining in opposition to Indian independence. One fellow Conservative MP noted in his diary that Churchill seemed to be making 'one blunder after another'.[6] As 1930 drew to a close, Churchill had come to realise that his working relationship with Baldwin had become 'sensibly altered'.[7] In January 1931, writing from Chartwell, Churchill composed a letter to him, citing their 'divergences of view upon Indian policy'[8] as his reason for no longer attending Business Committee meetings. His letter was accepted graciously and, having loosened the shackles of party loyalty, Churchill then followed his own political compass, and quickly became bolder in his remarks in parliamentary debates. The day after he sent his letter to Baldwin, he delivered a speech calling the Labour Prime Minister, Ramsay MacDonald, a 'Boneless Wonder', referring to a circus act he had seen as a child. Some praised the attack, with one ally calling it 'the wittiest speech of his life'.[9] Others, however, thought it offensive and an indication of poor political judgement. One letter from his fellow Conservative MP Nancy Astor declared that his personal attacks on individuals had broken 'the ordinary decencies & relationships of public life'.[10] Churchill replied saying that any attack he had made was because he was provoked, and that the 'very bad sore throat' from which he was suffering was as much to blame as anything else.[11]

During Parliament's break for Easter, Churchill returned to Chartwell and reflected on his diminishing political status. He had discovered that Baldwin wanted Neville Chamberlain, another former Chancellor of the Exchequer, to take the lead in battling the Labour Party's economic policies. On Maundy Thursday he wrote yet another letter of resignation, this time resigning from the Conservative Party's Finance Committee. Convinced that he still had much to offer, he concluded, 'Let me add that I shall always be ready to help you or Mr Neville Chamberlain in debate, whether on finance or other topics.'[12] Despite the supportive words, Churchill's decision to send the full wording of his letter to *The Times* for publication two days later irked Baldwin. 'I do not intend to send a letter to the press,' Baldwin replied, 'it is rather ridiculous our writing to each other through that medium.'[13]

When a general election was called in October 1931, the result saw Labour's majority fall, and a National Government was formed. Political representatives from all the major parties made up the new Cabinet. Churchill's boldness had proven to be terribly timed. His position and influence had fallen, he had distanced himself from the Conservative leadership, and he had been in overt opposition to the Labour Party both personally and politically. Reflecting on this time later, he described himself as being 'awkwardly placed in the political scene',[14] and it was these elements combined that saw him excluded from the new coalition Government.

For the first time since 1905, Winston Churchill did not sit on the front benches of the governing party or the opposition. He began to adopt the pose of an 'elder statesman' and, though he continued to attend parliamentary debates, his attendance became less frequent. Instead, he shifted his energy and attention to pursuits outside of politics. He spent an increasing amount of time writing at Chartwell, including newspaper and magazine articles, which he referred to as his 'pot-boilers'.[15] His primary focus, however, was always the writing of history books, which were his main source of income throughout his adult life. Having finished writing his history of the First World War, *The World Crisis*, in August 1931, he could then apply his literary focus to a biography of his ancestor, the Duke of Marlborough, whose defeat over the previously invincible French army of King Louis XIV secured his place in history. Progress, however, was delayed by a lecture tour of the United States.

It was during this trip when, in mid-December, while visiting New York, he began to cross Fifth Avenue, which was a two-way street at the time, and looked the wrong way as he stepped into the road. He was struck down by a car travelling at around 35mph and was severely injured. He suffered a scalp wound, a fractured nose, two cracked ribs, lots of bruising, inflammation of his right lung and shock. The accident became a sensational news story. Eleven days later he was offered a sizeable fee by the *Daily Mail* to write an article entitled 'My New York Misadventure',[16] after which he journeyed to

1. Winston and Clementine Churchill in the Bahamas, 1932.

the Bahamas to recuperate. After three weeks of rest, he resumed his tour, spanning much of the United States, before setting sail for Southampton in March to return to his literary labours. Working with his literary assistant Maurice Ashley, day and night, he drafted hundreds of thousands of words in the study at Chartwell. 'The great thing is to have a large volume of words behind us upon which every kind of pruning can be made', he wrote to Ashley. 'These beginnings are always difficult. Once the tale begins to burn, it glows.'[17]

A major step in the creation of what would become his 1,000,000-word homage to his ancestor was his trip to see the battlefield sites of the Duke of Marlborough's victories in France, Flanders, the Rhineland and Bavaria. Churchill set off from Chartwell on the afternoon of Saturday 27 August 1932. In what Churchill later called a 'family expedition',[18] he was accompanied by his wife Clementine, their 17-year-old daughter Sarah, and his close friend Frederick Lindemann, known to the family as 'the Prof'. The group was led by

Colonel Pakenham-Walsh, the War Office's expert on the Marlborough period. His in-situ verbal recreations of the battles enabled Churchill to 're-people them with ghostly but glittering armies'. It was only then, as he declared to friends, that he could truly interpret the battles for the first time.[19] Sarah, meanwhile, itched to move on from Belgium to Germany. She called the latter 'a lovely country' in a letter to a friend, but pondered, of the Germans, 'Why for goodness sake they could not be content with the wonderful bit of land allotted to them, instead of making hell by fighting for more.'[20] In a moment of astonishing prophecy, she noted that the Germans seemed 'revengeful and proud', adding that she was sure they would 'go for France the first moment they can'.[21] As the group travelled through Germany, Churchill found himself intrigued by political events, writing later that he 'naturally asked questions about the Hitler movement, and found it the prime topic in every German mind'.[22]

The German parliamentary election results were announced in Germany days after Britain's Parliament had broken for the summer. Support for the Nazis had soared and they went from 12 seats in the Reichstag in 1928, to 107 in 1930, then to 230 in July 1932. As a result, they had 37 per cent of the vote, making them the largest political party. The Churchills' 21-year-old son Randolph had already been in Germany for much of the summer, as one of six approved foreign journalists who accompanied Adolf Hitler on his election campaign. He was writing for the *Sunday Graphic* and boldly warned about the likely consequences of the Nazi Party's success as early as July 1932. 'The success of the Nazi party sooner or later means war', he observed, noting that they 'burn for revenge' and 'within three years at most Europe will be confronted with a deadly situation'.[23]

When Churchill told his son that he intended to spend time in southern Germany in September, Randolph strongly felt that his father should meet Hitler during his stay. After the last of their three days spent retracing Marlborough's manoeuvres on the battlefield, Churchill and his party drove to Munich. There they reunited with Randolph and checked in to the Grand Hotel Continental.[24] There he was introduced by his son to Ernst 'Putzi' Hanfstaengl, a half-American giant of a man, towering over those around him at 6 feet 5 inches, whom Randolph knew from his time covering the election. Hanfstaengl had been an ever-present figure in Hitler's inner circle and was tasked with introducing him to members of Munich's high society. He became Hitler's unofficial social secretary as well as his foreign press secretary, the combination of which saw him tasked with, among other things, ensuring he met the right influential figures. This included the likes of Diana and Unity Mitford, cousins of Clementine Churchill's, who would go on to become close friends of Hitler's. Unity became such an ardent champion of the Nazi regime that it was said she developed an 'almost hysterical devotion to Hitler'.[25]

To Churchill, the idea of Hanfstaengl and Hitler joining his family and friends for dinner appeared to be a last-minute and relatively impromptu arrangement, but this was not the case. It was in fact a carefully choreographed meeting instigated by Hanfstaengl and Randolph, for which planning had been under way for some time. Each of the two men felt that Winston Churchill and Adolf Hitler should meet, though with very different motives. The timing was ideal for Churchill, who sought an evening of entertaining debate and discussion after three long days of touring battlefields. The same could not be said for Hitler. According to Hanfstaengl's recollections, he had been with Hitler in the days beforehand, where he spoke at a series of mass demonstrations. As their plane landed into Oberwiesenfeld, a military airfield near Munich, Hitler's mood had darkened. After landing, Hanfstaengl received a call from Randolph to tell him that he, his father and other family and friends were at the Grand Hotel Continental. He said he hoped Hanfstaengl could join them all for supper, and wondered if it would be the optimal moment for him to bring Hitler too. Hanfstaengl agreed to try to persuade Hitler, but was keen to manage expectations. He declared that both he and Hitler were unwashed and unshaven, but would see what he could do.[26]

Hanfstaengl realised that Hitler had driven to the Brown House, the Nazi Party's headquarters in Munich, fashioned from a three-storey, neoclassical palace, dating from 1828.[27] He entered Hitler's office unannounced, declaring:

'Excuse me, Herr Hitler, for barging in here, but the message I'm bringing is so delicious that I want to serve it to you warm right away. Mr Churchill, the old man of course, is in Munich, as his son Randolph has just informed me, and would like to meet you. I've been asked to take you to the Continental for an informal dinner.'[28]

But Hitler's foul mood remained. 'What should come of it? Can't you see how busy I am?', he snapped, while seeming distracted as he leafed through files. 'What am I supposed to talk about with this Churchill anyway?', he added, saying that his English wouldn't be good enough to sustain any real conversation. Hanfstaengl objected, replying 'there's no other person in the world that is easier to talk to than him – art, politics, architecture, whatever you want to talk about. And you have me to interpret. Churchill is one of the most influential men in England and will be back in government. You absolutely have to see him.'[29]

Despite Hanfstaengl's pleas, Hitler remained stubborn and determined not to attend the meeting, voicing one objection after another. This was a common response of Hitler's when faced with the prospect of meeting someone who might make him feel inferior, either socially or intellectually. According to a pen portrait in the *Sunday Express* a month earlier, when confronted by any sudden event or unexpected information, Hitler would become 'all worry and uncertainty'. It was for this reason that 'although often challenged to debate, he habitually declines or ignores the challenge'.[30] A captivated crowd of thousands was one thing, but a highly intelligent political figure, who could easily out-manoeuvre him, was quite another. Hanfstaengl made one last attempt, saying he would dine with the Churchills anyway, and he hoped Hitler might join them later. Hanfstaengl recalled that Hitler 'squirmed like an eel', and declared that he needed to be fresh for a lengthy journey the following day, before remarking, 'Besides, this Mr Churchill is supposed to be an ardent Francophile.'[31]

Hanfstaengl then telephoned Randolph Churchill, trying to conceal his disappointment, and said that he was hopeful that Hitler might appear later. He went to the Grand Hotel Continental where he found Churchill's party. A table for ten had been booked to seat the group that included Winston and Clementine Churchill, Randolph, Sarah, Churchill's close friend Professor Lindemann, the owner of the *Daily Telegraph* Lord Camrose, and Colonel Pakenham-Walsh and his wife. The ninth place was Hanfstaengl's. The tenth remained empty.

'In Lady Clementine Churchill I met a lovely, cheerful and charming hostess,' Hanfstaengl later recalled but, enjoyable as her company was, it was Churchill with whom he wanted to speak.[32] The conversation moved on to the political situation in Germany and it was at this point that Churchill asked Hanfstaengl, 'Why is your chief so violent about the Jews? . . . What is the sense of being against a man simply because of his birth?'[33] Hanfstaengl thought carefully, and decided to give as mild a response as he could. He focused on what he regarded as the problems resulting from the influx of Eastern European Jews, and the 'excessive representation' in the professions. Churchill listened, but had no intention of nodding along. 'Tell your boss from me that anti-Semitism may be a good starter, but it is a bad sticker', he replied.[34] The wording, however, confused Hanfstaengl, whose attempt to fathom the phrase 'bad sticker' led to amusement among the group, and they laughed as what it actually meant was explained to him.[35]

At the end of the dinner, the gentlemen of the group were relaxing and enjoying brandy and cigars as they discussed the international situation in Europe. Hanfstaengl's frustration that Hitler had not appeared became more than he could bear. He decided it was worth one more shot and made his excuses to leave the table, claiming that he needed to make a quick telephone call to his wife. 'But of course, ask your wife to join us', Clementine kindly offered, as Hanfstaengl hastily made his way towards a telephone in the hotel lobby.[36] He quickly dialled the number for the Brown House but, according to his long-standing secretary, Fräulein Johanna Wolf, Hitler had left a while earlier.[37] Hanfstaengl called Hitler's apartment in Prinzregentenstrasse and spoke to Frau Winter, the housekeeper of his modest five-roomed home,[38] but she too could not say where he was. Putting down the receiver, Hanfstaengl turned to go back towards the dining room, only to see Hitler, in a trench coat and green hat, and still unshaven, there in the hotel, standing on the stairs in front of him. Hanfstaengl watched as Hitler chatted to a Dutch gentleman whom he recognised as a friend of Hermann Göring's and a donor to the Nazi Party. The two men were saying goodbye and, as Hitler turned to leave, Hanfstaengl ran over to him. 'Herr Hitler, what are you doing here? You declined Churchill's invitation and now you are standing here when Churchill or his son may appear at any moment.' Given that Randolph knew about the plan for the dinner, if he saw Hitler there but with no intention of dining with them, it would be seen as a deliberate snub. It even crossed Hanfstaengl's mind that a member of Churchill's party might over-hear chatter among the hotel's staff about Hitler having been there that evening.[39] For Hanfstaengl, there was one solution, and perhaps the evening could still be salvaged. 'Now that you are here, I sincerely ask that you come in as you are and say hello to the Churchills and their friends. The Churchills and the others are in the best spirits.'[40] But Hitler refused again, citing his unkempt appearance as his reason. Hanfstaengl began to plead, saying he would be happy to carry on entertaining the group, and keep them in the dining room, if Hitler could hurry home, change, shave and return. Hitler, however, could not be persuaded. 'Hanfstaengl, you know very well that I have a lot to do at the moment and that we want to start very early tomorrow. So good night.'[41] With that, Hitler disappeared.

Winston Churchill and Adolf Hitler never met in person, and Churchill's own account of that dinner shows that he never knew just how close a near miss it actually was. By not meeting Churchill, Hitler had made the mistake that countless others would over the next seven years: writing Churchill off as an irrelevance. For those who saw otherwise, and met with Churchill at Chartwell during those years, they added strength to a force which would one day be strong enough to take on Hitler and his tyrannical regime.

As I write this, I am aware of a rather striking parallel as, like Churchill in 1932, it is ten years since I too first walked through the grand oak doors of Chartwell. I was tasked with managing the house and the truly astonishing collections within its walls, from his mono-grammed slippers to his Nobel Prize. As Chartwell's first ever dedi-cated Curator, my role also came with the once-in-a-lifetime chance to live in the attic rooms of the house which, I hasten to add, were servants' quarters and far more modest than the rooms occupied by the Churchills. Over the years I called those rooms in the rafters of Chartwell my home, I came to know every creak the building made, and saw the Churchills' home in a light, quite literally, that few others had seen, or will ever get to see.

My decade at Chartwell, immersed in its history both day and night, has given me a unique first-hand understanding of how the house would have worked and what it was truly like to live there. Combining this experience with extensive research over the last ten years has enabled me to understand the role the house played, not just in the lives of the Churchills and their family, but also for the army of staff who supported them there, and whose lives also orbited around Chartwell. Their recollections offer a fascinating lens through which life at Chartwell can be seen, from the everyday to the extraor-dinary, and it has been a pleasure to unearth their stories of life at Chartwell between the wars.

As well as looking at the broader story of Chartwell during the crucial years leading up to the Second World War, I intend to reposi-tion it in the historical narrative, from scenic backdrop to centre-stage. For years, Chartwell has been described by many as the place to which Churchill escaped when the frustrations and pressures of political life became too much to bear. It has been said that the quiet and solitude gave him focus to write. That he would calmly feed his fish, and paint his landscapes of the gardens and the Kent countryside beyond. It was, according to many histories of Churchill in the 1930s, the place where he could relax in a place of relative serenity and solitude, but there are ample sources to contradict this tranquil vision. You only need to look at Chartwell's visitors' book, which was typically only signed by overnight guests, to see how untrue such a portrayal is. Even with the book's omissions of anyone who popped in for just a few hours (with a handful of high-profile exceptions), there are still more than 700 different individuals who signed it. When including all those who didn't sign the book, the number of individuals who visited the Churchills at Chartwell is likely to number in the thousands.

There were the 'shooting stars', as Churchill's youngest daughter Mary used to call the household names that came to Chartwell:[42] the likes of Charlie Chaplin, Albert Einstein or Lawrence of Arabia; but most of these visits have yet to be thought of by historians as worthy of in-depth historical analysis and study in their own right. They tend to be included simply as part of a longer list of interesting characters and noteworthy individuals. But why were they visiting? What was the context, political or personal, of the meetings they had with Churchill? Was he forging an alliance, gleaning information, or doing all he could to influence and persuade his guests to come around to his way of thinking? Lesser-known visitors also played their part, becoming vital and relied-upon sources of information to Churchill. It was they who, according to Mary, 'came and went ... telling grim stories and all bearing witness that time was running short'.[43]

Some visited to sound the alarm about Nazi Germany. Others came to strengthen diplomatic relations, putting their hopes in a man who they felt, even in the depths of political isolation, still held power and influence. There were informants, political allies, messengers and spies, bringing top secret information straight to the Churchills' door. Churchill's secretary, Grace Hamblin, who witnessed the comings and goings from October 1932 onwards, described Chartwell as his 'private world', into which came 'peers and potentates as well as ordinary men, to discuss the threat of war'.[44]

Chartwell became the headquarters from which Churchill mounted his campaign against Nazi Germany. The gatherings at Chartwell strengthened Churchill's resolve and added to the evidence, accounts and testimonies he was painstakingly accumulating at his country home. His possession of this information, and his skilful use of it in private discussions and public speeches in the 1930s, armed him with the knowledge and authority that ultimately helped lead to his appointment as Prime Minister in May 1940.

In 1932, however, no one, not even Churchill, could have imagined the fate that awaited him, and few could see the threat that Adolf Hitler and Nazism posed. Within days of the almost-meeting in Munich, Churchill became seriously ill and found himself 'laid up with paratyphoid' in a hospital in Salzburg.[45] By the time he got back to Chartwell he was desperate to return to normal, but he overexerted himself and set back his recovery. 'He tried to do too much in his weakened condition,' his secretary Violet Pearman wrote to a friend of his, 'and of course this is the unhappy result.'[46] The news soon broke of his condition, with reports in the press noting that he would be confined to his bed for some time.[47] Churchill, meanwhile, gave a mixed picture to enquiring friends and family. 'I am now recovering decidedly,' he wrote in October, 'but I lost an awful lot of blood.'[48]

It was during his convalescence at Chartwell that Stanley Baldwin, then Lord President of the Council in Ramsay MacDonald's government and his de facto second in command, made an address in the House of Commons which publicly supported Germany's demand to be allowed to rearm, on condition that it pledge to renounce the use of force. Churchill refused to let such an opinion go uncontested and insisted on speaking in the Commons at the next possible opportunity, to respond to Baldwin's address. Still weak from his illness and resting in his four-poster bed, he dictated a speech to his secretary, known affectionately to the Churchills as 'Mrs P'.[49] Her shorthand notes were typed in the format used for all of Churchill's speeches, with the lines double-spaced and the pages held together by a treasury tag through a single hole punch in the top left corner. Less than two weeks after Baldwin's speech, on Wednesday 23 November, Churchill had recovered enough to return to Parliament, and took his place in the debating chamber, clutching his speech notes, and readying himself to take on the Government.

He rose to his feet and declared that there would be another war with Germany if steps were not taken immediately, especially given that Germany's parliamentary system was now under the control of those he described as 'military men'.[50] Germany did not want equal status as Baldwin believed, but instead a rearmed Germany would soon demand the return of lost territories and lost colonies. Describing scenes he had witnessed in Munich that summer, he reflected on the 'bands of sturdy Teutonic youths, marching along the streets and roads of Germany, with the light in their eyes of desire to suffer for their Fatherland'.[51] He also lamented the naivety of those who championed Britain's disarmament as a means of avoiding war, and those who believed other nations were doing the same. 'All over Europe, except here, there is hardly a factory which is not prepared for its alternative war service; every detail worked out for its immediate transformation upon a signal.'[52]

Churchill's speech went largely unheeded at the time, but has since been considered, including by President John F. Kennedy, as 'the opening gun' of Churchill's campaign for the need to prepare for war. That weekend he returned to Chartwell, and Winston Churchill's countdown to war began.

2. *Randolph and Winston Churchill in Munich, Germany, during the Churchills' battlefields tour, summer 1932.*

CHAPTER 1

SOUNDING THE ALARM

Albert Einstein, 22 July 1933

Albert Einstein is among the most famous visitors to Chartwell. When he travelled to meet with Winston Churchill at his Kent home, more than a decade had passed since he received his Nobel Prize in Physics. He had become the most famous scientist in the world, and his unique image made him universally recognisable. During his visits to England in the summer of 1933, however, he hoped to attend a series of covert meetings with influential individuals. The nature of the discussions meant he had to do so away from the limelight and without drawing attention to himself. Though not an easy task for someone like Einstein, his mission was too important not to undertake. With fear of the growing persecution of German Jews, and with a price on his head, he knew he could never return to his homeland. As Churchill was one of the few public figures at the time to have openly voiced concern about Nazi Germany, Einstein travelled to Chartwell to tell him what he had experienced, and to describe the hardships his friends, colleagues and family continued to endure. The need for secrecy at the time is why so little information about this visit survives. But a pair of photographs of Churchill and Einstein standing together in the garden at Chartwell shows that Churchill knew this was a vital and historic moment, even if the visit was to remain a closely guarded secret for years to come.

When Churchill came back to Chartwell after his Marlborough research trip to Belgium and Germany, the gardens looked particularly beautiful. 'I adore autumn in England', his daughter Sarah wrote upon her return to their country home in September. 'Everything carries a crystallised dew drop.'[1] She continued to delight as the season progressed, exclaiming that 'the bog beech on the bank below my window has lost nearly all its leaves and through its bare branches I get a glimpse of even more of the view'.[2] Her relief at their return was shared by her father, who first fell in love with Chartwell's setting, and the landscape that fell away into distant woodlands, in 1921. Clementine had loved it too at first, writing that its hilltop position was 'like a view from an aeroplane'.[3] A subsequent viewing, however, quickly changed her mind. Beyond the ancient manor house's red-brick facade was a dark and gloomy house that faced the wrong way, had a leaking roof and a frontage just a few metres away from a public road. Furthermore, according to their architect Philip Tilden, the house was 'weary of its own ugliness so that the walls ran with moisture, and creeping fungus tracked down the cracks and crevices'.[4]

For Clementine, it simply was not what she wanted in a forever home. 'She would have liked a lovely low house,' her secretary later revealed, 'so that you could step out into the garden easily, but you see at Chartwell you had to come right down the stairs before you were anywhere near the garden.'[5] The final nail in the coffin came when she realised how difficult it would be to find and keep staff, as it was miles from the nearest village and off the local bus routes. Yes, the views were lovely, she agreed, but it simply wasn't practical or affordable and so, in her mind, it wasn't for them. Winston however was, and always would be, 'blind to drawbacks and deaf to reason' on the subject of Chartwell.[6] There were too many things that seemed perfect for him. He had always wanted to buy a house in Kent, ever since his Kent-born childhood nanny, Mrs Everest, had planted an early seed that it was the garden of England. Given that it was in the northernmost corner of the county, it was possible to drive to Westminster in under an hour. It was a stone's throw from Quebec House, the former home of General James Wolfe, victor of the Battle of Quebec and a hero of Churchill's. Last but not least, there was the breathtaking and unrivalled view.

When, a year later, the house was still on the market, and his love for it hadn't diminished, he made arguably the boldest move of his marriage. With Clementine heavily pregnant, and despite knowing she had soured on the idea, he bought the house without telling her. 'I am certain we can make ourselves a permanent resting place', he said to Clementine, trying to convince her to have faith in the endeavour. 'But if you set yourself against Chartwell, or lose heart . . . it only means further instability.'[7]

The glorious views proved poor compensation when, having spent £5,000 on buying Chartwell, it was another two years and a further £20,000 of repairs and remodelling before they could move in. The core of the house was Tudor, and the building's expansion over the following centuries was piecemeal and of varied quality. Dry rot, damp and water ingress led to serious concerns about its structural stability and the safety of its electrics. Entire sections of the building had to be removed and reconstructed, but even then some of the problems would remain long after the builders had gone. Churchill continually had to evacuate the 'nursery wing' when driving rain led to water running down the walls of his daughters' bedrooms.[8] He then found dry rot in a beam that held up an entire wing.[9] Most alarmingly of all, entire sections of cornice would randomly crash down from the drawing room's ceiling, including on one occasion over the fireplace, where the children had reportedly been playing moments earlier. The finished design of the house also left something to be desired for certain members of the family. 'The house is hideous', the Churchills' teenage daughter Sarah once abruptly wrote to a friend, though she conceded 'I do think the surroundings beautiful'.[10]

Beyond fixing, or trying to fix, the building's defects, was Churchill's insistence that the rooms be flooded with light, as required by his artist's eye. Trees were felled to give a greater sense of light and air, although Winston couldn't bear to watch. 'Winston hates to see a tree damaged or destroyed,' an early biographer of Clementine's noted, saying that she, on the other hand, 'is fascinated to see one fall. Whenever a tree has to be felled, Clementine will stand watching until the job is done.'[11] Sarah later recalled the felling of a cedar tree at this time to make room for the east wing, with Churchill remarking, 'If you go on like this, Clemmie, we had better rename the house One Tree Hill.'[12]

That same east wing, which Churchill called his 'promontory', offered triple-aspect views and projected out toward the lakes. Clementine got the best room in the house at the top of this wing, as well as her say over most of the house's decor. Her favourite colour, duck-egg blue, would feature heavily in several rooms including her bedroom, which she juxtaposed with her tomato-coloured moiré silk bed covers and complementary floral prints for the other soft furnishings. Otherwise, much of the house featured 'acres of the palest cream paint', as her daughter Mary later recalled, 'which went very well with the old beams'.[13] This included Churchill's study which, in the 1920s and early 1930s, also served as his bedroom. It was arguably the greatest triumph of the 1922–24 renovations. The Victorian ceilings were removed, only to reveal roof timbers dating to the early sixteenth century. The historian in Churchill delighted in this feature and so kept the beams exposed. He then added narrow floorboards designed to resemble the deck of a ship, harking back to his time as First Lord of the Admiralty when he was in charge of the navy. He would stride up and down the room, through clouds of his own cigar smoke, feeling in command as he dictated to a secretary until the early hours of the morning. This room became the beating heart of Chartwell, and was the hub of Churchill's astonishing political and literary output for the latter half of his life.

On his return from his 1932 *Marlborough* research trip, however, the panoramic views, resplendent in their autumn colours, could sadly only be seen by Churchill from his bed. 'Papa is back here now and we push him about in an invalid chair,' his daughter Sarah remarked, 'which annoys him considerably!'[14] Two months after his return from his travels, he wrote to a friend with palpable frustration, saying 'I am gradually recovering my normal strength, but on the whole I have passed a pretty large portion of this year as an invalid.'[15]

For much of his convalescence, Churchill had relied heavily on the household staff at Chartwell, which at that time still ran like an Edwardian country house. In the early 1930s the Churchills typically had a butler, a head housemaid, an underhousemaid, a 'tweeny' (a between stairs maid), a footman, a cook, a kitchenmaid or two, a scullerymaid, a parlourmaid, a valet for Winston and a lady's maid for

Clementine. There were also the gardeners, the odd-job man, two or three secretaries, a research assistant, the nanny and the chauffeur.[16] The nature of Chartwell meant that the staff often had to contribute in ways beyond what many employers might ask. One example of this arose when Churchill needed to get into his painting studio but found it locked and the odd-job man was off for the afternoon. He thought carefully and decided that the only solution was to climb through a window from the adjoining cottage which, at that time, was occupied by the chauffeur, Samuel Howes, and his wife Olive, Clementine's former lady's maid. The effects of paratyphoid quickly became apparent when Howes successfully lifted Churchill up and helped him climb through the 12-inch-wide window. 'Sir, you would not have got through that window before your illness', Howes remarked.[17] For a moment Churchill looked concerned, before turning away and walking somewhat despondently towards his awaiting canvases and oil paints.

While Churchill recuperated at home, he continued to reflect on his time in Germany and the dangers posed by the political situation there. 'The different parties in Germany,' Churchill wrote in an article for the *Daily Mail* in October 1932, 'are all vying with each other to win votes by putting up the boldest front against the foreigner.'[18] In an earlier draft, he noted that there needed to be greater awareness in Britain of 'the internal stresses of Germany' and 'the cries and counter-cries raised by the various parties struggling for power',[19] but Churchill struck through this line in his notes with his red-inked pen and so it did not make the final article. At the same time, he knew all too well that the British public were still traumatised from the First World War. Few were willing to consider the possibility of another global conflict and so he watched with alarm from Chartwell as pacifist sentiment in Britain grew.

A speech by Stanley Baldwin in the House of Commons on 10 November sought to promote international disarmament as a means of preventing war. He warned that it was nearly impossible to defend civilian populations against air attack. Furthermore, he wanted 'the man in the street to realise that there is no power on earth that can protect him from being bombed, whatever people may tell him. The bomber will always get through.'[20] An indication of how much this fearful perspective and accompanying pacifism permeated the British psyche can be seen in a debate at the Oxford Union the following February. A motion that 'This House will in no circumstances fight for its King and Country' was carried with 275 votes in favour, compared to just 153 against.[21] The debate garnered considerable coverage at the time and infuriated Churchill. He called the vote 'squalid' and 'shameless', and declared that 'One can almost feel the curl of contempt upon the lips of the manhood of all these people when they read this message sent out by Oxford University in the name of young England.'[22] A week later, Randolph Churchill, who had been a member of the Oxford Union before quitting his studies in 1930, tried to reverse the verdict. He was defeated even more resoundingly, this time by 750 votes to 138.

This mood among the youth of Britain was in stark contrast with young people in Germany, 3 million of whom joined Hitler's *Sturmabteilung* (SA), the Nazis' paramilitary wing, by the end of 1933. Festering resentment towards established political leaders and financial hardship drove the young people of Germany to radical alternatives. Hitler promised them strong leadership and a national rebirth, which were particularly appealing to that disaffected generation, and many undertook direct action as a result.

On 10 May 1933, university students in 34 towns across Germany began burning books deemed 'undesirable' to the new governing regime with such fervour that over 25,000 were incinerated in one night. In Berlin alone, over 5,000 students bearing the swastika created an inferno of destruction outside the opera house, consisting of 2,000 books deemed to be 'un-German'. They burned books by Jewish, left-wing and liberal authors and those by critics of Nazism. Those thrown into the fires included works by Karl Marx, Helen Keller, H. G. Wells, Ernest Hemingway and Albert Einstein. These almost ritualistic spectacles were accompanied by the chanting of oaths and the wielding of flaming torches. Einstein heard of this devastating cultural destruction while staying in Belgium. He then wrote of it in a letter to his and Churchill's mutual friend, Professor Lindemann, with whom Churchill had travelled to Munich the previous year. 'I am sitting here in my very pleasant exile', Einstein wrote, with a palpable sense of relief at being far from such scenes.[23] His choice of wording was perhaps surprising given the £1,000 reward advertised by a German newspaper for anyone who could successfully take his life. Lindemann replied, 'It seems that the Nazis have got their hands on the machine and they will probably be there for a long time.'[24]

Albert Einstein was among those who had initially underestimated the Nazis. In an interview for the *New York Times* in December 1930, he said that Hitler was 'living on the empty stomach of Germany' and 'As soon as economic conditions improve, he will no longer be important.'[25] Two years later, Einstein was once again in America, this time in California, when Hitler was appointed Chancellor of Germany. Within weeks of the Nazis' seizure of power, his property and possessions were confiscated. 'I dare not enter Germany because of Hitler', he wrote to his close friend and rumoured lover, Margarete Lenbach, on 27 February 1933.[26] On his return to Europe, he visited the German Embassy in Brussels to surrender his German citizenship. He told a journalist before his departure from the United States that 'Humanity is more important than national citizenship.'[27] Einstein had to decide his next move quickly. It was then that he received an invitation from Commander Oliver Locker-Lampson, a maverick Member of Parliament with an adventurous spirit, who was also a long-time friend of Churchill's. While offering sympathy for Einstein's plight, he said 'That even Einstein should be without a home has moved me deeply' and offered Einstein and his wife the use of his London home for a year.[28] This was a surprisingly generous offer given that the pair had only met once and even then only in passing. Einstein politely declined, choosing to remain in Belgium and stay instead in Le Coq-sur-Mer, a small resort near Ostend. However, a seed had been planted, and it was not the last time that the great physicist would hear from the MP for Birmingham Handsworth.

Writing at the end of May 1933 to fellow physicist Max Born, who had also recently escaped from Germany, Einstein said of his reputation there, 'I've been promoted to an "evil monster".' He added, 'all my money has been taken away from me. But I console myself with the thought that the latter would soon be gone anyway.'[29] By that time, Nazi policies had forced the abrupt retirement or removal from office of all Jewish state employees, including those working in Germany's universities. When it was pointed out to Hitler that this could have catastrophic consequences on the development of scientific understanding and application in his country, he replied, 'Then we shall do without physics and chemistry for 100 years.'[30] Sensing the inevitable, Einstein wrote to Lindemann, saying, 'I shall never see the land of my birth again.'[31]

Churchill had known Professor Lindemann since the latter months of the First World War, when he 'distinguished himself by conducting, in the air, a number of experiments, hitherto reserved for daring pilots, to overcome the almost mortal dangers of "spin".'[32] The pair became much closer from 1932 onwards, and Lindemann frequently travelled from Oxford to visit the Churchills at Chartwell. He went on to become the most frequent signatory in the house's visitors' book, and by the summer of 1933, with the Churchills having lived in the house for nine years, he had signed it 40 times. He became Churchill's chief advisor on scientific aspects of modern warfare, especially air defence, and the pair often talked on the subject until the early hours of the morning. His insights were more than compensation for any difficulties his hosts faced in accommodating his strict vegetarian diet. Churchill's literary assistant, Maurice Ashley, later recalled his dietary requirements as consisting of just 'whites of egg and stewed apple', both of which fortunately could be found in plentiful supply in Chartwell's kitchen garden.[33] Lindemann was also teetotal, and so couldn't partake in the ever-present champagne at Chartwell, which was almost always Pol Roger and was in plentiful supply in the early months of 1933 as the family had much to celebrate.

The Churchills' eldest daughter Diana had recently married John Milner Bailey at St Margaret's Westminster, the same church that Winston and Clementine had married in 25 years before. Any wedding costs were quickly offset when Churchill agreed to write *A History of the English-Speaking Peoples* for £100,000, spread over five years. At the time, the advance was the largest ever paid, to any author, for a single book.[34] Though still immersed in *Marlborough*, it was not unusual for him to be working on one book with the next already agreed. Ashley later recalled that in the years he worked at Chartwell, from 1929 to 1933, Churchill produced three books in addition to his biography of Marlborough: *The Aftermath*, *My Early Life* and *The Eastern Front*.[35] A biography of Churchill written at the time, entitled *Battle*, went to great lengths to tell of the joy and consolation that Churchill found in writing, describing how he in fact needed the pursuit as 'a vent for the ceaseless activity of his brain'.[36]

Politically, however, he became increasingly isolated. From Chartwell he continued his campaign against giving India dominion status, which he regarded as 'tantamount to the abdication of an Imperial trust' and certain to 'bring measureless misfortune upon both the British and Indian peoples'.[37] Loyal friends tried to persuade Churchill that it wasn't in his best political interests to take this stance. One such note came from Lord Linlithgow, the Chairman of the Parliamentary Joint Select Committee on Indian constitutional reform. In a letter headed 'Secret', Linlithgow warned Churchill 'you are in the process of working yourself into a very poor tactical position' and 'it seems to me that, in pursuing your present course, you are gravely prejudicing your own position, now and for the future.'[38] On 20 April 1933, Mrs Pearman made notes of a telephone call from Lord Lloyd, a former Governor of Bombay who was strongly opposed to Indian independence. She was asked to pass the note on to Churchill as soon as possible, which she did upon finding him in the grounds of Chartwell.[39] Lloyd proposed a meeting, with the intention of forming a group led by him, Churchill and Henry Page Croft, the MP for Bournemouth. A month later, Churchill drafted a constitution for what became known as the India Defence League, firmly allying himself to a cause which would remain at the forefront of his mind for the next two years.

It was around this time that Einstein travelled from Belgium to Oxford to deliver a series of lectures, as he had done numerous times before. On this occasion, however, it was clear to attendees that the campaign against him in Germany had deeply affected him. An undergraduate student who saw him speak at an event on 2 June later recalled that he appeared nervous and uncertain as to how he would be received. The enthusiastic applause when he finished was said to result in 'a wonderful change in Einstein's face' in which he seemed 'transfigured with joy and delight'. The onlooker described how he clearly realised that 'no matter how bad he was treated by the Nazis, both he himself and his undoubted genius were at any rate greatly appreciated at Oxford.'[40]

His concern was understandable. The passing of the Enabling Act in Germany on 23 March had given Hitler dictatorial powers. Soon after, Churchill made a prescient speech in the House of Commons in which he referenced the 'odious conditions' now ruling in Germany, which he prophetically argued could be 'extended by conquest to Poland'.[41] He also berated the Government for their blind faith in disarmament as a means of preventing war. Churchill's warnings, however, came at a time when there was growing resentment towards him in Parliament. Many MPs were convinced that his criticisms of Government policy were simply the result of bitterness at having been excluded from high office, rather than genuine conviction about the state of Britain's defences, or the likelihood of war with Germany. Back at Chartwell, those around him noticed that his mood began to darken. His secretary, Miss Hamblin, later remembered what she called his 'gloom and doom days'.[42] They were often those when he had spoken in the House of Commons and his words had been mocked or ignored. She admitted, though, that she hadn't fully understood the reason for his frustration at the time, saying 'I thought he was just being a bear very often.'[43]

By mid-summer, with all other political parties banned, Germany ceased to be a democracy, and Hitler became the country's supreme ruler. By this time, the first concentration camps had been established as weapons of domestic political terror and were being used to incarcerate those opposed to Nazi rule. For Einstein, the greatest moment of dread came when Hitler declared that he, a Nobel Prize-winning physicist, was now an enemy of Germany. The *Völkischer Beobachter*, the Nazi Party's newspaper, soon published a series of attacks on him. This was followed by the release of an anti-Semitic publication, approved by the Nazis' Minister for Propaganda Joseph

Goebbels, which listed the enemies of Nazi Germany. It included a picture of Albert Einstein, alongside the caption *'BIS JETZT UNGEHAENGT'*, meaning 'Not Yet Hanged'.[44]

After another brief visit to Belgium, Einstein returned to England in July. This time, rather than lecturing undergraduates, his mission was to speak to as many influential people as he could about the treatment of Jews in Germany. He had to do so covertly, leaning on the influence of those he felt he could trust with his life. 'If I appear publicly as a prosecutor of the German government,' he wrote to a friend, 'it will have terrifying consequences for the German Jews. Even those who definitely have a right to talk to me, based on their demeanour so far, are begging me to stay in the background.'[45]

Professor Lindemann, who had first met Einstein when he was studying aeronautical physics in Berlin, was one of those trusted few in England and the pair frequently corresponded during these turbulent months, typically in German. The small world of academia had brought the two men into regular contact over the years, and they developed an easy and genuine friendship. Einstein once said of Lindemann that, though he wasn't necessarily a pioneer of new ideas, if something new came up, Lindemann could rapidly assess its significance for physics as a whole and there were very few people in the world who could do that.[46] Their relaxed manner is illustrated by an account of Einstein having mentioned a mathematical proposition that he believed, but for which he had never been able to find mathematical proof. The next day Lindemann sought Einstein out to let him know that he'd solved the problem while relaxing in the bath.[47] His skill of being able to relay complex theories in layman's terms was a big part of his appeal to Churchill. Sarah recalled one occasion over lunch at Chartwell when Churchill asked Lindemann to explain quantum theory in less than five minutes and using words of only one syllable. Timed by Churchill on his pocket watch, Lindemann not only succeeded but did so in such an engaging way that the party burst into spontaneous applause when he finished.[48] He was such a constant presence at the Churchills' country home that they thought of him as 'part of our Chartwell life'.[49] It was for this reason that, when Oliver Locker-Lampson was asked to host

Einstein, despite the rejection of his offer earlier in the year, his first thought was to contact Churchill, and his second was to tell Lindemann, whom he also knew well. 'Someone has seen Einstein and is bringing him to England,' Locker-Lampson's covert note to Lindemann read, 'and has asked me to put him up at my cottage this weekend.' He added, 'I have, therefore, arranged to do this and am taking him to Winston's on Saturday. I do hope you are likely to be there.'[50]

Oliver Locker-Lampson was virtually the opposite of Lindemann, but had much in common with Churchill. He was an upper-class, Conservative MP who first met Winston Churchill in 1911. At the time, he was the Conservative MP for North Huntingdonshire, while Churchill was the Liberal Party's MP for Dundee, serving in Government as Home Secretary. The following year, Locker-Lampson invited Churchill to visit his ancestral home of Newhaven Court in Cromer. Handily, Churchill was already due to be in the area, as his new role of First Lord of the Admiralty required him to inspect nearby naval establishments along the east coast. The pair dined in splendour and developed a rewarding friendship, despite being political opponents at the time. When war was declared in 1914, Locker-Lampson joined the Royal Navy Volunteer Reserve as a Lieutenant Commander, with his position having been vouched for by Churchill. He was also among the small group that fiercely defended Churchill against criticisms of his role in the ill-fated Dardanelles campaign the following year. Furthermore, Locker-Lampson and fellow officers of the armoured car squadrons, a unit of the Royal Naval Air Service that Churchill had helped to create, decided to show their gratitude to him. They clubbed together and bought a portrait of Churchill by the acclaimed artist Sir John Lavery. It shows Churchill in his First World War uniform as a Lieutenant Colonel of the 6th Battalion of the Royal Scots Fusiliers, and is considered to be among his finest portraits. To this day, this treasured gift hangs on the main stairs at Chartwell.

Locker-Lampson was seen by many as a self-promoter who welcomed any opportunity to feature in the British press. Perhaps it was for this reason that he contacted Einstein out of the blue just two days after the Nazis' Enabling Act was passed. The worsening of his situation by July made Einstein suddenly more appreciative of Locker-Lampson's offer of help. He wrote to his ex-wife Mileva saying that the Germans had taken his money and, while the Swiss authorities had intervened, they had done so weakly and he had little hope of success. Furthermore, his American income had been devalued by the Wall Street Crash, concluding 'the whole family has been reduced to the status of beggars'.[51]

On the same day that Locker-Lampson wrote to 'the Prof' about the Chartwell visit, Einstein was also making arrangements. 'I am going to England tomorrow, where I'll speak to the most notable Conservatives', he wrote to Lionel Ettlinger, a fellow German Jewish, anti-Nazi activist, before adding, 'I will present the plan to them.'[52] This plan was in fact a political mission with the goal of saving as many Jewish academics from Nazi persecution as possible. He intended to use the power and influence of his name to secure opportunities for them outside Germany and needed to get influential political figures on side. Given Churchill's public warnings about the Nazis, it is perhaps unsurprising that he was on Einstein's must-see list. For Churchill, the possibility of meeting one of the finest minds of his generation would certainly have been reason enough to agree. But he very likely also wanted to gather as much information from Einstein as he could about the Nazi regime, and any insights that could support his belief that they were preparing for war.

The problem Churchill faced in convincing others, was that Hitler was successfully preaching disarmament, as were other world leaders. On 16 May 1933, a pamphlet entitled *Elimination of Weapons of Offensive Warfare: Message from the President of the United States* was published. It outlined President Roosevelt's hopes for the abolition of all offensive weapons, including tanks and heavy artillery. The next day Hitler called Roosevelt's proposal 'a ray of comfort for us all who wish to co-operate in the maintenance of peace'.[53] In what has since become known as his 'Peace Speech', Hitler declared that war would be 'unlimited madness' and the German Government knew 'that in any military action in Europe, even if completely successful, the sacrifice would be out of all proportion to any possible gains'.[54]

The world seemed reassured and rather enchanted by the Nazi dictator, and the British press widely proclaimed a belief that Hitler should be taken at his word. This was the climate in which Churchill, ensconced at Chartwell, sought information and first-hand accounts from those who could counter this prevailing view. What Churchill needed most were trustworthy individuals who would testify to what they had witnessed in Germany. Einstein had already written to Lindemann saying, 'I think the Nazis have got the whip hand in Berlin. I am reliably informed they are collecting war material and in particular aeroplanes in a great hurry.' He continued, 'If they are given another year or two the world will have another fine experience at the hands of the Germans.'[55] The meeting was so important to Churchill that any obstacles arising from the short notice were immediately overcome. Locker-Lampson's alert to Lindemann was sent on Thursday 20 July, and the meeting took place just two days later.

The summer of 1933 was far from a quiet one for the Churchill family. They had been away from Chartwell for lengthy periods, and the house hadn't hosted guests, according to the visitors' book, since 23 May. Since Parliament had risen for its summer recess, the Churchills had visited their friends Henry Rainald and his wife Imogen at Firle Place in Sussex. Clementine and Sarah then headed to London, staying in their penthouse flat in Morpeth Mansions, and attending the glittering array of social and sporting occasions that the London season had to offer: from watching tennis in the royal box at Wimbledon to attending the Henley rowing regatta. Clementine's engagement diaries, however, were dominated by her role as chaperone for Sarah, who was being presented as a debutante at court that summer. It was an exciting time for the whole family as it marked Sarah's coming out into society and her transition into adulthood. Clementine's letters, however, indicate that she would probably rather have been at Chartwell. She wrote to a friend saying that her fellow mothers-of-debutantes were 'a depressing back-biting tribe & I have to sit for hours with them ... I'm thinking of taking a cookery book to balls. I could be hunting up tasty dishes to try, instead of listening to their gossip.'[56] It was this whirl of dinners, parties and balls that kept her away from Chartwell at the time of Einstein's visit.

Fortunately for Churchill, he was firmly ensconced at Chartwell, spending virtually every moment working on *Marlborough*. A week before Einstein's visit he had been to Blenheim Palace to research and seek the input of his cousin, the 9th Duke of Marlborough. After the visit, Churchill wrote to him, 'I am very much indebted to you for your help in my task, in the success of which we have an equal ancestral interest.'[57] With writing deadlines looming, not even the announcement of an impromptu visit from Albert Einstein could derail his labours on the book for more than a few hours. At the very time that Locker-Lampson was motoring to Chartwell, with Einstein in the passenger seat, Churchill was dictating a letter to his secretary, to be sent to his researcher, Maurice Ashley. The fact that it was a Saturday made no difference to Churchill, especially as any alterations to the current chapter's text had to be made before the end of Sunday so printing could begin on Monday. 'Do not delay', he urged Ashley.

Locker-Lampson found himself driving one of the world's most famous men to the Churchills' Kent home. The winding, tree-lined roads from the nearby village of Westerham would have been familiar to him, having been a regular visitor to Chartwell since the family moved there in 1924. The leafy canopies overhead cast down streams of dappled sunlight through which the pair sped before arriving at Chartwell's sizeable wooden double gates. As they made their way onto the semi-circular drive, they parked alongside Lindemann's Mercedes-Benz, a car the Churchills' son Randolph later remembered fondly, saying it made Lindemann the envy of his fellow professors at Oxford.[58] The Churchills' Daimler, a gift from more than 140 sympathetic friends after his 'unfortunate intercourse with a taxi in New York',[59] was usually parked in the garages by the chauffeur's cottage. There, too, was their old Wolseley, the car in which Churchill had driven Sarah and Randolph to see Chartwell for the first time in 1922 while Clementine was still resting after the birth of their youngest daughter Mary.[60] The excitement of that first glimpse of Chartwell reportedly led to Churchill neglecting to fully release the handbrake as he set off, a fact that wasn't realised until a band of willing helpers had kindly pushed the car several hundred yards.[61]

The gardens that lay before Einstein and Locker-Lampson were bathed in the midday sun. The exceptional weather led to a report at the time stating 'the summer of 1933 may fail to secure adequate mention because it was mainly "pleasant"'.[62] Sarah described Chartwell at that time, saying it had 'plenty of sun, slight breeze' and in the distance a 'blue smoky mist which promises more heat'.[63] Clementine, meanwhile, wrote to a former secretary of hers saying, 'This year the garden has really been rather lovely – Everything is looking more established.'[64] At that time there were just two gardeners: Albert Hill, the head gardener, and Victor Trowbridge, the under-gardener. Both had been at Chartwell since the mid-1920s and so knew the annual rhythms of the gardens well, from the butterfly walk, planted especially with buddleia and lavender to attract butterflies, to the productive garden providing food for the table and flowers for the arrangements in the house. The heat had led to a particularly fruitful summer for the kitchen garden. The 15 peach trees were a particular source of pride, with the Churchills boasting to guests that they had yielded 600 peaches, which Clementine had preserved in over a hundred bottles.[65] The wilder parts of the garden weren't so much to Clementine's tastes. Speaking of the planting around the ponds, she remarked, 'So far it looks like a craggy wilderness, but I think that if Mr Pug [a pet name for Churchill] is not too wilful about certain details it may in time be beautiful.'[66] Then there was the meticulously kept terrace lawn where the Churchills often had 'picnic tea', as their daughter Mary later recalled, on sunny summer days.[67] This part of the garden, behind the house, afforded views down toward the lakes and across the Weald of Kent. It also benefited from being almost entirely in the sunshine until early afternoon, except for a spot under the great yew tree, which provided shade and relief from the midsummer heat.

Locker-Lampson had dined at Chartwell several times before, with Lindemann often present, so he had an idea of what might await. Lunch was usually served at 1.30pm, with invitations for guests suggesting an arrival time 15 minutes beforehand. Meanwhile, the food was being prepared by the kitchen's double-act of Margaret and Elizabeth. The cook had recently left and the two kitchenmaids were muddling through, having been practising over the weeks that the family were away. The Churchills typically hired young girls in their late teens or early twenties, who didn't have a great deal of experience and who Clementine would then 'train up'.[68] She herself was fascinated by food, collecting recipes and ensuring that those who visited Chartwell always had delicious meals. 'Although she didn't cook herself,' Miss Hamblin later recalled, 'she knew exactly what ingredients were to every dish and how it was made.'[69] The girls' cooking was, therefore, acceptable when it was just the family and the household who needed feeding. When there were important visitors, the Churchills often hired a cook to supplement the kitchen's staffing for the weekend, but the short notice of Einstein's visit meant there wasn't time to make such arrangements. A picnic tea, however, was manageable, and perfect for Einstein who famously ate and drank very little. In the sweltering kitchen, amidst midsummer heat, they prepared all the food for the picnic. Typically, this would include sandwiches, for which Clementine left astonishingly specific instructions. 'Get hold of a large loaf and don't cut the slices too thin or too thick,' she insisted, before adding, 'Trim the crusts off the edges and put plenty of butter on the bread.' For Churchill's favourite, beef sandwiches, she insisted that the beef came clear to the edge of the bread as 'He doesn't like to bite twice into a sandwich before he can tell what's inside it.'[70] Jam tarts also featured frequently in picnic teas. They were Churchill's favourite pastry, and were relatively simple to make, 'but it had to be perfect if it was to be made for him' as 'the next best would never do.'[71] Margaret was focused on the task in hand, but Elizabeth's mind was almost certainly on other things, as this culinary team was about to be separated. She had become engaged, with the wedding scheduled for 3 September and, knowing that she had to give a month's notice before leaving, she was aware that she didn't have long. When she did summon the courage, Clementine despaired at yet another change of staffing and how she would once again have to find another 'young cook', who she would have to train herself. 'Margaret (Thank God) is still with us', she wrote with relief to a friend, as at least one half of the duo would remain.[72] Margaret turned out to be one of the longer-lasting kitchenmaids. Two years later,

Churchill reflected on how yet another cook had given her notice, writing to Clementine, 'She sent in her spoon and ladle on her own account. I am very glad. She had the knack to the highest degree of making all food taste the same . . . I subsist on soup which Margaret makes for me secretly in London and is delicious.'[73]

Unlike his travelling companion, Einstein could only guess what a meeting with Churchill at his country home might entail. He was probably mindful of the considerable differences between him and his host. Einstein had revelled in the liberal culture of the years of the Weimar Republic, and probably assumed he would have little in common with the grandson of a duke. He also had little apparent interest in politics, but their shared recognition of the threats posed by Nazi Germany would soon eclipse any differences between them.

The pair were greeted at the door by the Churchills' valet-cum-butler, David Inches, who was addressed by the children and other

3. The west-facing front facade of Chartwell, 1930s.

staff at Chartwell as 'Mr'.[74] Churchill, meanwhile, simply referred to him as 'my man'.[75] He was said to be a 'tremendous character' and was described as 'always overworked, always perspiring, sometimes drunk!'[76] They walked through Chartwell's great oak doors and under the grand Corsican pine doorframe: a remarkable piece of architectural salvage acquired in 1923, which was thought to be from the interior of a much grander house. Upon entering, the pair may have been taken by Inches to the library, which often served as a waiting room for the Churchills' guests when Clementine wasn't present to greet them in the drawing room. Churchill himself was notoriously unpunctual. On the day of Einstein's visit, he eventually appeared in one of his boilersuits, a garment similar to a workman's overalls, which were dubbed his 'rompers' by the family.[77] Churchill owned them in various colours and materials from charcoal pinstripe to burgundy velvet. Often, they were accompanied by his monogrammed slippers and a large ten-gallon Stetson, which he had bought years earlier in California as a way of protecting his pale, pinkish skin when he was likely to spend any length of time outdoors.

Einstein, meanwhile, appeared wearing a rather crumpled white linen suit, which was perhaps understandable given his recent journeys. Having travelled by ferry to England from Belgium the day before, he caught a train to London where he was picked up at Victoria Station by Locker-Lampson and driven to Winterdown Cottage, the small farmhouse near Esher in Surrey which he had rented for the summer. Einstein's accommodation, however, was not in the house itself but rather a small thatched wooden hut in the garden. Despite his assurances of privacy, Locker-Lampson also invited journalists and photographers to visit. Pictures were published in several national newspapers, including the *Daily Mirror* which included a posed picture of the two in Locker-Lampson's garden, accompanied by text describing Einstein's presence as 'unnoticed'.[78]

Churchill was still working when the group arrived. His urgent *Marlborough* deadlines made it one of the mornings when he worked up until their arrival. 'He was very naughty about staying and dictating for too long', his secretary recalled. 'Quite often there were guests to lunch and he wouldn't get up until they were here, or nearly here, and there would be a last-minute scramble.'[79] With Professor Lindemann already at Chartwell, Churchill descended the stairs, met the group, and the four of them walked through the glass terrace doors and down the curving stone steps that led onto the terrace lawn. Each took their seat in one of the family's wicker chairs, with Churchill selecting the one offering the best possible view. 'He would sit facing South,' his secretary later recalled, 'so that he could see all around the garden.'[80] It was at this point that the Churchills' ten-year-old daughter Mary appeared from the Marycot, the play cottage Churchill had built on the far edge of the walled garden for his two youngest daughters. With Sarah having quickly outgrown it, the single-roomed structure with check curtains and small chandelier became Mary's domain. It also contained a miniature Aga which she had previously used to bake drop scones for Charlie Chaplin, using a recipe taught to her by her nanny 'Moppet', Maryott Whyte, a cousin of Clementine's. The scones were deemed such a success that she repeated the honour for subsequent guests, and so she strolled merrily across the garden bringing a basket full of freshly baked treats for Albert Einstein.[81]

Knowing that they only had limited time together, the conversation turned quickly to the growing threat posed by German rearmament. Having been a lifelong pacifist, Einstein had recently and publicly made a remarkable shift in his views. Just two days earlier, he had declared, 'Were I a Belgian, I should not, in the present circumstances, refuse military service: rather I should enter such service cheerfully in the belief that I would thereby be helping to save European civilisation.'[82] Many of his former colleagues in Germany criticised this as 'atrocity-mongering'. The Prussian Academy of Sciences published a note that they were 'distressed by Einstein's activities as an agitator in foreign countries'.[83] Germany's public institutions had begun to align themselves with the Nazi government and against the world-famous physicist.

Lindemann acted as interpreter for the group, since Churchill spoke little German and Einstein's English, though good, was still relatively limited in 1933.[84] Einstein described how he had watched the rise of Nazism from his home in Berlin over the last decade and the hardships he had personally faced since Hitler became Chancellor of Germany. He described his recent change in opinion, and agreed with Churchill about the need for an armed response to Nazi militarism. Lastly, he stressed the urgent need for support for German Jewish academics. He argued that they were currently in real peril, and needed to find alternative roles in universities outside Germany as soon as humanly possible. Lindemann, whom Einstein later described as 'untiring' during the meeting, listened intently, but translating throughout. Of everyone present, he was the one able to offer the most immediate practical assistance to Einstein's colleagues. Locker-Lampson offered comfort, which Einstein described later that afternoon as 'touching'. His response seemed genuine. Einstein wrote to his wife, with a hint of surprise, that Locker-Lampson 'seems to have no egoistical motives for his undertaking'.[85] Churchill, meanwhile, responded with his thoughts on the geopolitical situation. As was often the case, he dominated the scene, but with insights and analysis that left Einstein of the opinion that he was 'an eminently clever man'.[86]

When they had finished their afternoon tea, the group stood up from the table and began to walk across the garden, with Churchill showing off his completed projects and those works that were ongoing. They walked past the loggia, a roofed structure which was open on two sides in the north-eastern corner of the terrace lawn. Churchill had begun to think it a little plain and a few months later he commissioned his nephew, John Spencer Churchill, to decorate the interior with a mural depicting the victorious battles of their shared ancestor, the Duke of Marlborough. The painting arrangement was reportedly made more difficult by Churchill's constant corrections. This was not regarding accuracy of the scenes, but the way in which John chose to approach the task, by starting at the top of the loggia and working downwards. 'I always survey the whole scene with greater clarity if I attack the white areas first,' Churchill replied, 'and afterward concentrate on the pockets of resistance.'[87]

The four men continued along the path, underneath the vine-covered pergola, towards Clementine's walled rose garden. Clementine often tended this part of the garden herself, dressed in a blouse and trousers with gloves. She loved being immersed in the delicious scent of that part of the garden, which mirrored her preference for rose-scented perfumes.[88] She took particular pride in it that summer, writing to her former secretary that the roses had been 'glorious'.[89] It was in this spot that the group decided to capture the moment on camera. The photographer was almost certainly Lindemann, who was himself rather camera-shy and much preferred to be behind the lens. Special family moments at Chartwell were often captured by him, including when the Churchills' youngest daughter Mary laid the foundation stone of the Marycot.[90]

A few seconds of that universally awkward 'how shall we stand then?' moment transpired, during which Churchill removed his hat and began to light a cigar. Even in 1933, these were synonymous with the image of Winston Churchill. His caricatures, with features selected to ensure he was instantly recognisable, had included cigars since before the First World War. Einstein clasped his hands behind his back and stood upright. The camera flashed, but Churchill wasn't ready. He then changed his mind. After all, this wasn't a photograph for public consumption. It was for him and his family to keep and treasure, immortalising the moment Papa met Albert Einstein. He didn't need to rely on his cigar or any other props of image. He and Einstein were, in his mind, equals after all. He put the hat back on to shade his eyes from the sun and held the cigar low by his left side. The pair turned to face the camera and, with muted smiles reflecting the gravity of their discussion, the meeting of two icons of the twentieth century was immortalised.

As the group said their goodbyes, Einstein felt both understood and relieved. He wrote to his wife just a few hours later that 'these people have made good preparations and will act resolutely soon'.[91] Each of the three men may have been offering more reassurance than they could guarantee at that point, but they all felt their resolve had been strengthened, and felt compelled to do all they could for him.

The task of seeking out opportunities for German Jewish academics, especially those working in the sciences, fell to Lindemann. As the plight of Jewish intellectuals in Germany worsened over the following years, Lindemann created and found funding for numerous

4a&b. Winston Churchill with Albert Einstein in the rose garden at Chartwell, July 1933.

new positions and research fellowships at Oxford, and recruited a remarkable group of refugee physicists to fill the roles. This group, including Erwin Schrödinger and Fritz London, contributed to Oxford becoming the world-class centre of physics that it is today. His efforts did not end there. He quickly became an ever-present contributor to Churchill's campaign against Hitler and would take on an increasingly risky role for Churchill as the 1930s wore on.

Einstein continued his tour of notable Englishmen's houses with Locker-Lampson in the days that followed. They spent two hours with H. G. Wells, had tea with the former Foreign Secretary Austen Chamberlain, and visited the Surrey home of the former Prime Minister, David Lloyd George. A particularly moving moment occurred during the latter visit when Einstein went to sign Lloyd George's visitors' book. Seeing a column entitled 'address', Einstein reportedly hesitated before putting pen to paper and simply writing '*Ohne*', meaning 'without any'.

Four days after the Chartwell meeting, Oliver Locker-Lampson invited Einstein to watch him speak in Parliament. He used the '10-minute rule', a mechanism by which Members of Parliament can raise issues they personally care about in the House of Commons. Locker-Lampson's proposed motion was entitled 'That leave be given to bring in a bill to promote and extend opportunities of citizenship for Jews resident outside the British Empire'. Einstein watched from above, wearing the same white suit he had worn to Chartwell the previous Saturday, and with his cloud of white hair making him instantly recognisable, and noticeable, to all in attendance. 'I am not personally a Jew,' Locker-Lampson began his speech, '... but I hope that I do not require to be a Jew to hate tyranny anywhere in the world.' He singled out Einstein, remarking that Germany had 'turned upon her most glorious citizen', and gestured upwards to his guest, before continuing, 'to-day Einstein is without a home'. His speech came on what was the hottest day of the year so far, which had created a sweltering atmosphere in the debating chamber. 'The Huns have stolen his savings,' he added, before proclaiming that 'the road hog and racketeer of Europe have plundered his place.'[92]

From newspaper coverage in the following days, it was clear that Einstein's appearance in the Commons had helped shine a spotlight on their shared cause. Einstein was touched by the support he had received during his visit and was, according to a journalist from the *Daily Telegraph*, in 'the gayest of moods' at lunch on 27 July. He had been impressed by the English summer, calling it a 'revelation', and said that everything about his visit had been pleasant. 'But what seems to have impressed him the most,' the journalist continued, 'was the discovery that there is so much serious thought in England.'[93]

Einstein returned to Belgium for the last weeks of summer and continued to use every ounce of influence he could towards his mission. He made it a condition of acceptance of any positions offered to him that the institution should offer further professorships to German scientists. He contacted Lindemann asking about an advisory role that had been offered to the Nobel-Prize-winning physicist, at Christ Church, Oxford. Einstein wrote to ask if that role could be given to another German theoretical physicist instead of him. 'That agreement was made in better times,' he wrote to Lindemann, 'when the German colleagues were not yet at a loss. I therefore hereby ask you whether there is no possibility of allowing another specialist to take part in this beautiful privilege in my place.'[94]

While Locker-Lampson led the initial charge in Parliament, Churchill's campaign grew more gradually. Always wanting to be armed with evidence for his arguments, he sought out first-hand accounts, pamphlets and newspaper cuttings illustrating Germany's military preparedness, and began to fill the filing cabinets of the secretaries' office at Chartwell. He began to weave the threat of Nazi Germany into his speeches at every possible opportunity, from the House of Commons to village fêtes. One such speech, composed in the study at Chartwell shortly after Einstein's visit, was entitled 'Europe's Hour of Danger' and was given on 12 August 1933 in Theydon Bois, a village in his constituency. The speech contrasted the glorious summer of a country at peace with those other nations that had 'fallen prey to anarchy or tyranny or are devoured by ferocious hatreds of race, class or faction'. He ominously warned of 'evil dangerous storm clouds which either overhang or lie on the horizon'.[95] He continued:

39

I hope our National government and especially the Cabinet Ministers in charge of the Navy and Army and the Air Force will realise how grave is their responsibility ... I trust they will make sure that the forces of the Crown are kept in a proper state of efficiency, with the supplies and munition factories which they require, and that they will be strong enough to enable us to count for something when we work for peace, and strong enough if war should come in Europe ... Always remember that Britain's hour of weakness is Europe's hour of danger.[96]

In giving this speech, and others in the same vein, in the aftermath of Einstein's visit, Churchill began to declare his opposition to anyone who wanted to pursue a British policy of unilateral disarmament or diplomatic friendship with the Nazi regime. Chartwell rapidly became the political command-centre for this campaign.

As early autumn came, Einstein made his last visit to England and, once again, chose to stay with Commander Locker-Lampson, not knowing that a series of bizarre publicity stunts awaited him. The famous sculptor Jacob Epstein was invited to visit to create a bust of Einstein, the announcement of which featured in several national newspapers. A photoshoot was arranged, which showed Einstein with a local gamekeeper hired to provide personal protection and Locker-Lampson's gun-wielding secretaries Margery Howard and Barbara Goodall, posed as if they were somehow assisting the physicist with his work. Locker-Lampson also featured in each of the photographs, either astride a horse, listening attentively to Einstein or gazing out across the Norfolk countryside with him. All this seemed to be in stark contrast with the low profile Einstein hoped to have, having reassured his wife beforehand, 'I am going to the countryside, where nobody will recognise me. I have a good feeling in anticipation.'[97] Einstein's desire for privacy and solitude during this trip had one notable exception: a speech given to a sold-out Royal Albert Hall on 'Science and Civilisation' on 3 October. A diary clash unfortunately prevented the Churchills from attending. However, names familiar to them were among the high-profile speakers announced in *The Times* as supporting Einstein at the event, including Sir Austen Chamberlain and, of course, Commander Locker-Lampson.[98]

The news coverage of Einstein's lecture unfortunately created a new threat to his safety, with rumours of an assassination plot resulting in a need for protective cordons around the Hall and a significant police presence at the event. Some newspapers suggested that Einstein was himself the threat to peace. The *Daily Mail* menacingly warned that Einstein 'would be wise to stop this injudicious agitation in this country against the Nazi regime in Germany.'[99] Meanwhile, the *Evening News* declared before the lecture that it would be 'a piece of alien agitation on British soil designed to make bad blood between this country and Germany'. They concluded their article by saying that 'Intelligent and patriotic people will stay carefully away'.[100]

Though Einstein chose not to mention either the Nazi Party or Adolf Hitler by name in his speech, there could be no doubt who he was speaking about. He thanked those in attendance for the 'well-organised work of relief', which had 'done a great service not only to innocent scholars who have been persecuted, but to the traditions of tolerance and justice which for centuries you have upheld with pride'. He hoped for a future where historians could reflect that 'in our days, the liberty and honour of this Continent was saved by its Western nations, which stood fast in hard times against the temptations of hatred and oppression'.[101]

Four days after speaking at the Royal Albert Hall, Einstein was driven in great secrecy, and amid continuing fears for his safety, to Southampton, where he embarked for New York. His view from the ship as it pulled away from the south coast of England was Einstein's last ever glimpse of Europe. Less than two weeks later, German officials at the World Disarmament Conference announced that Germany intended to withdraw from the League of Nations, which proved to be one of the Nazis' first steps towards readying Germany for war.

CHAPTER 2

DEFENCE AGAINST THE SKY

T. E. Lawrence, 25–26 February 1934

In the interwar years there was one sound which could bring an unrivalled level of excitement at Chartwell to both family and household staff alike. The roar of a Brough motorbike on the driveway could only mean one thing: Lawrence of Arabia had arrived. He went by the name 'T. E. Shaw' by the 1930s, and lived a far more modest existence than his fame and notoriety could otherwise have allowed him. He depended on the few close friends he could rely on to help sustain the anonymity he craved. For Churchill, the arrival of his old friend to his country home was always far more than an opportunity to reminisce about old times. Alongside the 'shadowy messengers from Europe',[1] as his daughter Mary called those informants from across the Channel, Churchill sought the expertise of those already in his circle. The man whom he frequently described as a genius could now bring first-hand insights into the newest of Britain's three armed forces, the Royal Air Force, at a time when Churchill was increasingly preoccupied by the risk posed to Britain by war in the skies.

By the early weeks of 1934, Churchill was pouring his energy into developments across both the house and gardens of his home. 'There was always work going on', one secretary later recalled, and costly work at that.[2] The construction of a new swimming pool required 11 labourers, with Churchill ever-present at the building site. 'Mr Pug is in his element with troops of workmen', Clementine remarked, though she jokingly questioned his motives for the project. 'I believe he made the swimming pool solely for the pleasure of having one of those machines which he has been craving for ages', she wrote of her husband's inexplicable excitement about hiring a cement mixer.[3]

The heated and filtered pool became a focal point for the family. Archive footage survives, thought to have been filmed by Lindemann, which shows Churchill and his son Randolph bobbing up and down in the water, before the camera shifts to Mary precariously balanced as she attempts to stand on her older brother's shoulders.[4] The three older Churchill children were all young adults by this time, leaving only Mary of school age, but all came back to Chartwell often. Unfortunately, Diana's recent marriage to John Milner Bailey had quickly started to show cracks and so she frequently returned to Chartwell without her husband, distracting herself from her unhappiness with the familiarity of family life. Her sister Sarah, on the other hand, was blossoming. Having been a clumsy child, it was suggested by Churchill's friend and artist mentor, William Nicholson, that dance lessons might be beneficial. He had once seen her listening to the gramophone Diana had left behind when she left home, and suggested that Clementine might let Sarah go to the dance school his granddaughter was already attending. Though she was 19 and attended a class of mostly ten-year-olds, she fell in love with dance, and would devote the rest of her life to the pastime.[5] Even then, however, she still had a touch of the teenager about her, with Clementine once saying 'sometimes she looks absolutely lovely – but on the other hand she can look like a moping raven.'[6]

Mary, who later called herself the 'Chartwell child', was seven years younger than her closest sibling, Sarah, and 13 years younger than the eldest sibling, Diana. As a result, she was often excluded from the older children's adolescent adventures. From high above in the treehouse Churchill had built for his children, they would shout 'go and find Nana', suggesting that she play with the household's nanny, known as Moppet, instead. Fortunately for Mary, Moppet was kind, attentive and loyal. She had been recruited following the distrust the Churchills developed of unfamiliar nannies after the devastating loss of their daughter Marigold, who had become ill

5. *Diana Churchill seated with Maryott 'Moppet' Whyte, also known as 'Nana', Mary's childhood nanny. They are joined by Puppy, one of the many resident dogs at Chartwell, on the wall of the pink terrace at Chartwell, summer 1934.*

while in the care of inexperienced hands. 'She brought up Mary really,' Grace Hamblin later recalled of Moppet, and when Clementine was away from Chartwell in the 1930s, 'Moppet was left in charge.'[7] It was reportedly Moppet's warmth and care that made Mary develop quite differently to her brother and sisters. According to one biographer, it was Moppet's influence which led to her becoming 'a sunny, uncomplicated, well-behaved small girl who loved her pony, learned her lessons, and adored her parents'.[8]

Meanwhile, the Churchills' only son Randolph benefited from a freedom and independence which was wholly unknown to his sisters. Churchill especially indulged him and, as a result, he became bold and ambitious. He felt certain that a stellar political career awaited him, and predicted that he would be an MP by the time he was 21 and a member of the Cabinet by 23. By 1934, and as yet unelected at the age of 23, he was already well behind schedule. He had, however, made great strides in the field of journalism. His regular Sunday column in London's *Weekly Dispatch*, entitled 'Searchlight on Politics', aided both his'and his father's agendas. In a column in early February he reflected on a recent House of Commons debate and positioned his father as having won the day. He chose not to mention rather telling events in the debating chamber the day before. On that occasion, Clement Attlee, the soon-to-be Leader of the Labour Party, quoted a recent remark of Churchill's calling for the Royal Air Force to have parity with other countries but had to pause afterwards because of the extent of the laughter among the assembled Members of Parliament.[9]

Britain's vulnerability to air attack played heavily on Churchill's mind in 1934 and there were many who agreed with him. The Chiefs of Staff, the most senior military personnel in the British Armed Forces, presented an annual review on Imperial Defence policy at this time, declaring 'The expansion programme with the Royal Air Force should be continued without further delay.'[10] There was, however, reluctance among some members of the Cabinet to heed this advice. Within weeks of Churchill's plea in Parliament, the Secretary of State for Air, an office Churchill himself held just 13 years earlier, acknowledged that other countries were pursuing a more active policy than Britain. While he was 'greatly perturbed at this situation', he felt that, due to the ongoing Disarmament Convention, 'it would not be advisable to consider any more extensive measures this coming year.'[11] If the decision-makers in Westminster were deaf to Churchill's concerns, he needed more evidence to support his stance and a greater understanding of what was happening in the rank and file of the RAF, but it needed to happen away from his Westminster colleagues, and so he invited the most notable airman he knew to Chartwell.

T. E. Lawrence gained worldwide renown following his extraordinary role in the Arab Revolt during the First World War. His knowledge of the Middle East and fluency in Arabic made him a key figure in coordinating military actions. As a result, he led Arab tribes in guerrilla warfare against the Ottoman Empire. His story became legendary and by the 1920s he was a household name. The relationship between Churchill and Thomas Edward Lawrence was born out of the ashes of the First World War, with the pair first meeting at the Versailles Conference in 1919.

Three years later, on Armistice Day in November 1922, Lawrence called Churchill 'a great man . . . as brave as six, as good-humoured, shrewd, self-confident & considerate as a statesman can be'.[12] Churchill's view of Lawrence was similarly admiring, and he later recalled, 'Here was a man in whom there existed not only an immense capacity for service, but that touch of genius.'[13] Despite their mutual admiration, the two men could not have been more different in demeanour. Lawrence was modest to the point of awkwardness, with a complete indifference to the fame and honours that were readily available to him, including, as was widely believed at the time, the crown of Arabia. While both men were romantic adventurers at heart, Churchill, unlike Lawrence, always revelled in the publicity and acclaim that inevitably followed his escapades.

Despite their contrasting characters, an opportunity for the pair to work closely together came in 1921 when Churchill was offered the role of Secretary of State for the Dominions and Colonies, with a newly expanded ministry set to include a Middle East Department. Churchill felt that if he could deliver in this office, perhaps he might find himself one step closer to the ministerial role he coveted more than any other: Chancellor of the Exchequer. This was the office previously held by his late father and whose heavy black robes, with their glistening gilt threads, Churchill had kept on standby since his father's early death, aged just 45, in January 1895. The team for this new department, therefore, had to be carefully chosen by Churchill himself to best execute the role and aid his political ascent. Aware of Lawrence's knowledge of the region, and skills in diplomacy, he immediately offered him the role of Political Advisor. Writing to his friend Robert Graves, Lawrence described how 'Winston Churchill in his third effort to get me to join his new Middle Eastern Department used arguments which I could not resist.'[14] When discussions of salary arose, Lawrence asked for £1,000, which Churchill said was the most modest thing he had ever been asked, and insisted he take £1,600.[15] Churchill wrote to his wife Clementine that he had 'got Lawrence to put on a bridle and collar'.[16] Clementine cooed, 'How clever of you to get Lawrence', in reply.[17]

Unfortunately, for Churchill, it was after just a year of service, in April 1922, that Lawrence asked to be released from his position at the Colonial Office. Churchill refused to accept the inevitable. Lawrence submitted his resignation ten times, each of which was rejected, but Lawrence was keen to leave Westminster life. 'I'd rather be a chimney sweep than a politician. Their job makes them second-rate. Too much necessity for compromise ... I have finished with them.'[18] He then uncompromisingly announced his departure in June 1922.

Despite no longer working together, the pair remained on good terms. 'I need hardly say that I'm always at [Churchill's] disposal if ever there is a crisis', he wrote to Sir John Shuckburgh, the head of the Eastern Department of the Colonial Office.[19] After several aimless weeks in London, Lawrence joined the RAF as an aircraftman, initially under the alias John Hume Ross, in the hope of achieving some sort of anonymity at the outset of this new chapter. According to his earliest biographer, he 'went into the Air Force for the same reason that some of the most thoughtful men of the Middle Ages went into a monastery'.[20] Lawrence himself, however, had more practical ambitions, saying that the utilisation of the air was 'the one big thing left for our generation to do'.[21] A few months later his identity was discovered by the press, resulting in front-page coverage in various newspapers. He found himself swiftly dismissed and joined the Tank Corps as T. E. Shaw, but soon missed the air force and returned to it in 1925. He joined the Marine Branch at RAF Mountbatten in Plymouth, where he worked largely on the development of the air force's rescue boats, and became known for his marine knowledge and practical application. He remained there until 1933 when he took up duties at the Marine Aircraft Experimental Establishment at RAF Felixstowe.

Despite his interest and aptitude, there were those who questioned Lawrence's motives for joining the RAF, and his friendship with Churchill raised further eyebrows. On one occasion he went out at lunchtime and was challenged by his superiors when he arrived back late. He replied that he had been detained at a lunch party, citing both Winston Churchill and the Archbishop of Canterbury among attendees. The response was one of disbelief and Lawrence found himself subject to disciplinary procedures. That quickly

6. *Aircraftman T. E. Shaw,
known as 'Lawrence of
Arabia', circa 1930.*

changed when the party's host called his superiors, confirmed the
guest list as Lawrence had stated, and so he was released from all
punishments.[22] The problems arising from such friendships were
soon brought to the attention of the most senior figures in the RAF.
At one point, Hugh Trenchard, often referred to as 'the father of the
Royal Air Force', informed Lawrence that his continuing contract of
service was dependent on him no longer visiting, or even speaking
with, any 'great men', including, mentioned by name, Winston
Churchill.[23] Six months later, he was still subject to this restriction,
which he described as having been asked to 'drop Winston'.[24]

The problem was that Lawrence was wholly unrelatable to those
around him in the RAF, and nobody knew who the 'Somebody in
high authority' was who ordered the Royal Air Force to accept him
in the first place. Given Churchill's former role as Secretary of State
for Air, he seemed a prime candidate for this act of altruistic nepo-
tism. Lawrence also showed considerable loyalty to Churchill. On

one occasion, Churchill fell out with a friend of Lawrence's. Leaping to the defence of his former employer, Lawrence called Churchill 'my most considerate chief, and for whom I have personal affection, as well as admiration'.[25] When, in December 1926, Lawrence presented Churchill with a first edition of his *Seven Pillars of Wisdom*, an autobiographical account of his experiences during the Arab Revolt, he read the inscription with delight: 'Winston Churchill, who made a happy ending to this show. 1.12.26.' A further note was added in 1932, recognising their enduring friendship, and proclaiming how 'eleven years after we set our own hands to making an honest settlement, all our work still stands ... To have flamed for eleven years is statesmanship. I should have given you two copies of this work.'[26] Churchill later said his book ranked with the greatest ever written in the English language.[27]

By the early 1930s Lawrence's increasingly reclusive nature, and chastisement by senior military personnel for the friendships he held dear, led him to cut himself off and retreat into his work or to Clouds Hill, the former forester's cottage in Dorset that he called home. He had bought it in 1923 but only began to invest in it, and make a permanent home, a decade later. 'I have no dependents, no sense of public spirit, or of duty to my neighbour. I like to live alone for 80% of my days,' he wrote to a friend. 'The golden rule seems to direct me to live peacefully in my cottage.'[28] It therefore took a very special invitation to lure him out from his increasingly monastic lifestyle, but one such invitation arrived just before Christmas.

The prompt for the gathering at Chartwell in February 1934 was a seemingly unremarkable one. In November of the previous year, Churchill had sent Lawrence a copy of the first volume of *Marlborough*. Lawrence replied with a note in mid-December saying that it had taken longer to read than he had hoped. The reason for the delay was in part because Clouds Hill, which he called 'the "Chart-well" where I want to retire next year',[29] was so cold in the winter that he had to go to bed early each evening to try to counter the effects of the chill. As soon as he had finished reading it, he sent Churchill a glowing review, saying that beyond 'the humour, the irony and understanding of your normal writing', it went one step further and 'shows more discipline, strength and great dignity'.[30] For this reason, Lawrence thought it was his finest work to date.

It is, however, in the latter half of this letter that we see the particular catalyst for his visit to Chartwell. Signed copies of Churchill's multi-volume *The World Crisis* had been cherished possessions of Lawrence's. He had them while in India in 1927 and then they, along with other precious volumes, had been stored in a friend's house for safekeeping. It was from this location that they were 'exposed to borrowers', almost certainly having been stolen, including his inscribed copies of Churchill's *Crisis*. 'I am so sad at having lost them', Lawrence wrote, offering to source another set of first editions if Churchill might consider signing them for him. 'They are such good books, and essentially bettered by showing you have touched them.'[31]

Churchill's reply, most likely dictated from his bed at Chartwell, was written three days later. It was typical of him to start each day by reading the day's newspapers and letters, which were brought to him as soon as he awoke by his faithful butler, Inches. Breakfast arrived at 8am and then, shortly after that, one of his two secretaries, at that point either Mrs Pearman or Miss Hamblin, would check in on him to see if he was ready to compose his replies. The volume of post coming to Chartwell often meant there was a backlog of letters and so the secretaries had to work quickly to ensure the urgent letters were responded to, with either 'ac', indicating a simple acknowledgement, or 'thank' written on the top corner. Grace later recalled that she found the whole process 'very bewildering' when she first started at Chartwell in 1932.[32] There were two shifts: either 8.30am until around 7.30pm, or a late morning start until 2 to 3am. They typically worked seven days a week, and any time off had to be when Churchill's schedule meant he could cope with just one secretary, which wasn't often. 'Our holidays were very erratic,' Miss Hamblin later recalled, 'but I didn't seem to mind.'[33] Their dedication was unquestioned, as reflected in an interview Mrs Pearman did for the *Sunday Express* in March 1934 as part of a series called 'Secretaries of Famous Men'. When asked what was the chief value in being a secretary, she replied 'in taking burdens from her employer's shoulders', before adding that she hoped to see Churchill made Prime Minister one day.[34]

The response Churchill dictated to Lawrence's letter was heart-felt, saying that he would treasure the note and inviting him to visit. 'Now why not mount your bicycle and come spend a day or two here in the near future. Drop me a line if you can come, but anyhow come.'[35] Clementine, meanwhile, paid particular attention to Lawrence's note about the freezing conditions in his cottage and, in an act of festive kindness, invited him to spend the Christmas of 1933 with them at Chartwell.

The magic of Christmas at Chartwell was its constancy. The same group returned to the Churchills' corner of Kent most years, reuniting on Christmas Eve. Clementine, who had been one of four siblings but had sadly lost two by the time she was in her mid-thirties, welcomed her sister Nellie and her family, the Romillys. Winston's brother Jack was another constant, with his wife Gwendoline, known as 'Goonie', and their three children. The noise of a cacophony of cousins filled the house at Christmas. The dining room provided the stage for amateur performances, with make-up kindly provided by Mr Gurnell, the chemist in the nearby village of Westerham. For Churchill, however, even Christmas Day was a working day. His secretaries had to be on hand too, and later recalled 'he was never terribly good tempered because he couldn't get anyone on the telephone and it made him so cross'. There was no good time to be doing nothing in Churchill's mind. 'He liked the world to be busy and something happening all the time.'[36] On the upside, the secretaries, and a number of the household staff were invited to take part in the festivities, from decorating the house with natural festive foliage to playing Father Christmas on Christmas Eve night, a role usually assigned to Moppet, but which Randolph did too on occasion. The gifts were retrieved from the 'Genie's cupboard',[37] a strictly out-of-bounds closet, before they were laid beneath the Christmas tree, which took pride of place in the library. Its positioning meant that, when the doors were open to the drawing room, an 80-foot-long vista was afforded of the glittering spectacle. It was lit with flickering candles which, on one occasion, set the tree alight, but fortunately Randolph heroically saved the day and put out the fire. The gifts underneath the tree, always wrapped in brown paper and tied with a red ribbon, were of a plentiful supply.

Christmas was looked forward to by the staff at Chartwell as much as the Churchills. Every year, they held a big party in the servants' hall on the lower ground floor, next to the kitchen. Each member of staff, and the family members of those who lived in cottages on the estate, were given presents. 'At one time my sister and I were the only children on the estate so we fared better than most', the daughter of head gardener Mr Hill later recalled. Unfortunately her gift that year of 'a large baby doll with a china head' proved too fragile, and after it was dropped, sadly the doll was no more.[38]

A handful of 'lonely bachelors' were offered invitations to join the Churchills for Christmas over the years. Lindemann was one of the fortunate few to be granted this honour, as was Eddie Marsh, a trusted aide of Churchill's of more than 20 years. For Lawrence, to receive such a coveted invitation said a great deal about how much he had come to mean to both Churchills.

An early meeting of Lawrence and Clementine took place in Egypt in 1921 when the pair enjoyed each other's company as part of a larger excursion group on camels to see the Pyramids. It was during this adventure that Churchill, according to fellow camel-rider Gertrude Bell, fell off his camel like 'a mass of sliding gelatin'.[39] Clementine joked unsympathetically, remarking, 'How easily the mighty are fallen!' Lawrence, however, chose to offer Churchill's ego some comfort. He insisted that the camel was clearly so delighted to be escorting Churchill that he 'blew himself up with pride'. As a result it must have been the later letting out of that air that loosened the saddle girth, 'and off you came'.[40] From this moment, Clementine could see that Lawrence was a true friend to her husband, an assumption she didn't always make of Churchill's closest companions. As a result, Lawrence was always given the warmest of welcomes at Chartwell, but 1933's Christmas plan was not to be, as Lawrence declined the invitation. Instead, he wanted to be at his cottage, which he had only camped out in up until then, but the Christmas break would give him three consecutive days to test his new home. 'That does not lessen your kindness in asking me to Chartwell,' he reassured Clementine, before remarking, 'Chartwell is a nice name, but my cottage is called Clouds Hill. Good, don't you think, for an airman's retirement?'[41]

Once the festivities of 1933 had passed, and the new year dawned, a conciliatory Churchill decided to send an olive branch to Stanley Baldwin, the Leader of the Conservative Party. 'India apart,' he wrote, 'you have my earnest good wishes.' Even so, he couldn't resist reminding Baldwin of his stance on Germany. 'After all,' he added, 'it is the European quarrel that will shape our lives.'[42]

Two weeks later, Lawrence found himself startled when, dining in Southampton, he suddenly heard Churchill's voice. 'I've never heard the place quiet before', Lawrence remarked of the hall he described as usually being 'a bus drivers' and troops' eating home'.[43] With the room listening intently, Churchill proceeded to give a speech, of which Lawrence had one criticism, which he disclosed in a letter to Clementine that evening. 'He let his heart come out too often', Lawrence wrote. 'In England now-a-days it isn't done to always be sincere.' Then, in a rather noncommittal note, he added, 'Please warn Winston of the probability of my turning up on a doorstep before many weeks are passed, with two fat books for him, for his signing.'[44]

Such vagueness was far from ideal for Clementine. Her skills as hostess relied on her having a full understanding of who would be at Chartwell and when. She needed to know at least the day before. She wrote back to Lawrence seeking clarity and suggested 24 February as Archie Sinclair and his wife, among others, were already due to visit and perhaps he might like to join. Lawrence, however, was away from his cottage, in Wolverhampton, Nottingham and then London, and didn't see the letter for two weeks. 'Please realise that wherever and whenever you write to me,' he pleaded on 10 February, 'you address an absent man!' Lawrence thought her proposed date was possible, but again he was unable to commit, saying 'a fortnight is almost eternity in a nomadic life. I may be anywhere, or very deep in my work.' Knowing Clementine as he did, he tried to offer some level of certainty, but could only give it nearer the time. 'Let me send you a wire, about the 21st, saying "possible" or "impossible". Please read delight into the first and grief into the second, whichever comes.'[45] He added that he liked Archie Sinclair and joked that he had always wondered what happened to him, knowing full well he was a senior member of the Liberal Party. Clementine and Lawrence finally agreed that he would visit Chartwell on Sunday 25 February, but, while they had been comparing diaries, events on the world stage had moved apace.

On 26 January 1934 Hitler had announced a 10-year non-aggression pact with Poland, yet another calculated move to convey to fellow world leaders that he had peaceful intentions. But Churchill saw through this move. He had begun collecting documents at Chartwell related to the Nazi Party's aims, many of which were stored in a large lockable wooden box which he kept in the study. These included translated excerpts from *Mein Kampf*, Hitler's personal manifesto, which had been published nine years earlier and made it only too clear where his ambitions lay. The translated notes included one by Hitler asking, 'To solve the question of the re-establishment of the power of Germany, it is not enough to ask "How shall we manufacture arms? How shall we create the spirit which renders a nation capable of bearing arms?"'[46]

With Hitler's ambitions of territorial expansion laid bare in his own writings, his peaceful overtures of January 1934 were most likely met with disbelief by Churchill. As an historian, he couldn't help but see the countless parallels between Hitler and aggressors of the past. He was acutely aware of the number of tyrants throughout history who had made and then broken such pacts, with the long sunken shelves of Chartwell's study filled with histories and books testifying to this fact. If he was right in his increasing belief that a future conflict would very likely involve attack from the air, it seemed that aerial assaults on cities would be so overwhelming that any victim would soon surrender. For Britain, the way to defend itself against such a fate was continuing investment in the development of technology and growth of manufacture at the same rate as, or faster than, the other great powers.

On 7 February, a three-hour debate took place in the House of Commons, which had opened with Sir Reginald Clarry highlighting that 'we are, unfortunately, at least the fourth, the fifth, or, as some say, the sixth on the list of Powers in the world in relative strength in the air.' He then went on to pose the question, 'How much longer are we going to drift into trouble because we take undue notice of political doctrinaires and ignore the warnings of practical men?'[47]

Churchill waited patiently, clutching his meticulously prepared speech. He then rose to his feet, and delivered what was the opening barrage of his five-year political offensive, calling for Britain to rearm in the face of the threat from Nazi Germany. 'Wars come very suddenly', he began, recalling the lead-up to the outbreak of war in 1914. He described how, at that point, the navy was their shield, as there was no air menace to speak of. The current situation was incomparably more dangerous. 'This cursed, hellish invention and development of war from the air has revolutionised our position', he said, before imagining scenes of future wars. He described 'the crash of bombs exploding in London and the cataracts of masonry and fire and smoke' which, he said, 'will warn us of any inadequacy which has been permitted in our aerial defences'. Finally, he urged the National Government to ensure that Britain's Air Force was as strong as that of France or Germany, 'whichever is the stronger'.[48]

Despite this prophetic speech, Churchill was no nearer to any official political role beyond that of MP for his own constituency. There had been increasing pressure from MPs that the Government should set up a new Ministry of Defence, which would then coordinate the work of the army, the navy and the air force. The leader of this campaign, the influential military theorist Basil Liddell Hart, favoured Churchill for the post. So, too, did the former Foreign Secretary Austen Chamberlain, who wrote to his sister on 15 February, saying 'there is only one man who by his studies & his special abilities & aptitudes is marked out for it, & that man is Winston Churchill!'[49]

Yet another of the National Government's Cabinet reshuffles took place that month, with representatives of the Labour, Liberal and Conservative parties manoeuvred into place, but still there was no ministerial role for Churchill. As a result, his warnings of the dangers Germany posed were still largely ignored by the Government. In his continuing political isolation, he was especially keen to hear Lawrence's insights, as his former advisor, but also in his new capacity as someone working at the forefront of developments in RAF technology. As February wore on, few other visitors were invited to Chartwell as Churchill focused steadfastly on writing the next volume of *Marlborough*. The only visitors' book signatories before Lawrence's visit that month were: Lindemann; Clementine Waring, who had been a friend of Churchill's mother; the artist William Nicholson, who was painting a conversation-piece portrait for the Churchills' silver wedding anniversary; and the Churchills' nephew Johnny who was busy painting the pavilion. It was at this time that Johnny later recalled, 'as often as not, lunch was devoted to unrelieved gloom about the international situation. Even in those early days of German military renaissance my uncle was convinced that war was inevitable.'[50] One alternative topic of conversation Johnny recalled was his uncle asking those around him, 'What do people say?', as he was keen to have insights into public opinion and used his wider family as informants on the general consensus regarding current affairs.[51]

There was one notable event immediately prior to Lawrence's visit to Chartwell. On Friday 23 February, two days before the gathering, Churchill travelled to Oxford to speak at the university's Conservative Association, with more than 500 undergraduates present. A series of questions was put to him, with subjects ranging from the threat posed by Japan's foreign policy to the British Empire, to the question of the President of the United States' increasingly isolationist policies. One of the most telling questions from the students was posed by John Crighton, who asked whether Churchill 'admits that any rearmament by Great Britain would induce an arms race and impede international co-operation'.[52] Churchill calmly answered that no, there was no danger created by an arms race unto itself. A more dramatic moment arose when a German student, Adolf Schlepegrell, asked Churchill whether he agreed 'that the immediate return of the Saar territory to Germany would bring about an improvement in Franco-German relations and is therefore in the interests of European peace'. Churchill rejected the idea. It would be in contravention of the Treaty of Versailles, the terms of which reflected that Germany had taken the leading part in 'plunging the whole world to ruins'.[53] Things became heated as the student, determined to push as far as he could, asked, 'Does Mr Churchill believe that the German people, the men and women who live there today, are responsible for the war?' With increased tension in the air, Churchill looked him directly in the eye and replied, 'Yes'. Schlepegrell stood up, gave a parting bow to Churchill, and silently walked out of the room, to a mixture of applause and disapproval.

Lawrence, meanwhile, prepared for the journey to the Churchills' country home. He had already warned Clementine that his journey would be by motorbike and he would therefore arrive 'in a disreputable state', but was confident that his hosts would be understanding. A week before Lawrence's visit, he wrote to a friend saying, 'On Saturday midday I proceed to Caterham, to stay that night with Mrs. Winston Churchill – my annual and very-much-looked-forward-to visit.'[54] A further, much briefer note regarding the upcoming visit was a telegram Lawrence sent to Nancy Astor, the American-born English socialite who became the first woman to sit in the House of Commons. Clearly sent to decline an invitation to an alternative gathering, the note simply read 'Promised this weekend Winston. Shaw.'[55]

Despite his high regard for his hosts, he may well have been wary at the thought of being part of a larger gathering. One close friend of his later recalled, 'Usually he shunned all social occasions, even the simplest, and never took the initiative in arranging them.'[56] Within days of receiving Churchill's invitation to Chartwell, for example, he declined another invitation from a fellow veteran of the Arab Revolt, for dinner in London. 'I have no dress clothes, no money for them or railway fares, no leave this year, no leisure, and a distaste for dining well', he wrote to his friend. 'Perfection is fish and chips in a newspaper. Fourpence, and no sitting down.'[57] A dinner at Chartwell couldn't be further from this modest idea of 'perfection'. Lawrence knew from previous visits that a Chartwell dinner was often a platform for Churchill to perform, as well as relish the discussion and debate that arose. Having such an iconic figure as 'Lawrence of Arabia' in attendance, however, was among the few instances when Churchill would let another have the floor, but Lawrence had grown to hate the limelight. At least at Chartwell he was among friends, and the Churchills' fellow guests that weekend were a carefully selected group.

The first of the signatures that follow T. E. Shaw's in Chartwell's visitors' book for that weekend were Archibald Sinclair, the Liberal MP for Caithness and Sutherland, and his wife Marigold. Sinclair, or 'Archie' to his friends, had known Churchill for almost 20 years, including having served under him on the Western Front during the First World War. The pair had much in common, with their American mothers, unhappy childhoods, shared history as cavalry officers and similar political views. It was perhaps these parallels that led some to the conclusion that the handsome Sinclair at one point could have been a possible match for Clementine's younger sister, Nellie, though each found love elsewhere and they were married to others by the end of the Great War. Sinclair also knew Lawrence from his time in the Colonial Office, including having been a fellow participant in the notorious camel-based excursion in Egypt a decade earlier. Consequently, he was a familiar face for the Churchills' shyest guest. Not only that, but the Sinclairs always enjoyed their visits to their country home, with Archie once writing, 'We enjoyed our visit to Chartwell quite inexpressibly – I have never left anywhere except my own home more sadly.'[58]

The next name in the list of that weekend's signatories is that of Sylvia Henley (née Stanley), Clementine's cousin. 'They told me once they've been friends since they were three years old', Miss Hamblin later recalled. 'She came very, very often and she was a very good guest because she liked to play cards with [Churchill].'[59] After Sylvia's husband's death in 1925, her presence at Chartwell became near-constant. She signed the visitors' book more than a hundred times, a total second only to Lindemann's. A further guest was Colonel Pakenham-Walsh, the historian who had accompanied the Churchill family to Munich two years prior. He didn't sign the visitors' book as he only stayed for lunch.

The final name in the visitors' book list was Diana, the Churchills' eldest child. She tried to put on a brave face for her family following the breakdown of her marriage but her regret was evident. She later admitted that she got married because she could not face the succession of huge meals at Chartwell, only to then find herself tied to a man who had a drink problem.[60] Clementine once said of her eldest daughter's sensitivity, 'she is a lovely fragile little flower which droops when neglected',[61] a sentiment captured in chalk in a portrait of Diana by Charles Louis Geoffroy-Dechaume from 1930 which Clementine hung on her bedroom wall at Chartwell. Even Diana's striking red finger-waved hair in the portrait can scarcely distract from her sad aquamarine eyes, and their distant forlorn gaze.

Of all the excitement ahead of a visit by Aircraftman Shaw, the greatest was reserved for the Churchills' youngest daughters. Sarah considered Lawrence one of her favourite guests at Chartwell because he was especially considerate to the younger children and very fond of their mother. For Mary, one particular visit stood out in her memory from the previous summer when she was ten years old. Having been down to the stables looking after her goats, a constant in her morning routine, she came across Lawrence strolling across the lawn. 'Together we walked up and down, making footprints in the dew-drenched grass', she remarked. 'I wish I could remember what he said, I'm sure I prattled away about my animals.'[62]

As Lawrence's Brough Superior SS100 motorbike roared onto the driveway, staff and family members alike dashed to the windows to see the world-famous hero of Arabia. 'He would arrive, dressed in his air force uniform, with a great roar on his motorcycle,' Mary later recalled, 'and I always tried to be round to greet him; I liked him very much, and noticed his piercing blue eyes and intense manner.'[63] On that particular February day, Lawrence had travelled from Southampton to Westerham, a journey totalling approximately 100 miles. Though bitterly cold, it was one of those bright cloudless winter days, and so Lawrence made good time on his journey, arriving at the Churchills' house by early afternoon. He pulled up just in time for lunch and, unlike the more formal meetings, Inches wasn't sent to answer the door. Instead, Churchill dashed to the door to meet 'Lurens', his phonetically pronounced nickname for his old friend. As Lawrence dismounted, the pair hailed each other with great enthusiasm.[64] They then headed for the drawing room, where Clementine and the other guests were already assembled. Lawrence was given his usual warm welcome by the family, before the group descended the lower half of the house's main stairs and made their way to the dining room.

With the scent of that afternoon's freshly prepared meal drifting in from the kitchen, which was just a short corridor away, each member of the lunch party took their seat. The fire had already been lit, as the house's fires had been for much of the month owing to bitingly cold winds, and temperatures commonly around freezing. Lawrence was very likely relieved that his journey to Chartwell was now complete, and he could settle down to a good meal, with fine company, in the warmth of the dining room. As a low-ceilinged room in the newly created wing, it had the potential to be a gloomy space, but the five almost floor-to-ceiling arched windows, in their neoclassical style, brought in light as well as the views across the garden and beyond. Then on winter nights, with the curtains drawn, and the warm light from the room's orange-shaded lamps, it felt intimate, secluded, and an optimal setting for secret discussions between close personal friends.

One of the most remarkable features of meals during Lawrence's visits was how he was one of a very small number of people whom Churchill would allow to eclipse him conversationally. His soft voice, combined with everyone else's desire to hang on his every word, often prompted silence from those around him. The often loud and extroverted Churchill family were rendered virtually mute, as he spoke slowly and gently. Recalling one weekend visit, the Churchills' teenage daughter Sarah later wrote, 'we would all listen in pin drop silence to what he had to say. I remember my father sitting back watching him with half a smile, and letting him run the conversation.'[65] This may well have been a concession afforded to Lawrence because his conversation with Churchill involved 'interlarding his remarks with a suitable amount of flattery', in which Churchill reportedly revelled.[66] According to one acquaintance, he had a frequent and expressive habit of simply agreeing with his hosts, saying slowly, ruminating: 'Yes, yes: oh, yes.'[67]

On this occasion, however, there was little time for pleasantries. Less than an hour after his arrival, Churchill wanted to know Lawrence's thoughts on how Britain might defend itself in the event of aerial bombardment by enemy forces. Given Churchill's borderline obsession by that time with defence against attack from the air, it's a wonder that he waited that long before probing his guest. Sylvia Henley, who had witnessed the Churchills' table chat countless times before, noted that this conversational pivot seemed 'out of the blue'. After all, a lunch at Chartwell was typically a light and entertaining affair. But Churchill was hungry for information and so he turned to Lawrence and posed the question that he had been longing to ask: 'In the event of an air attack what would be our best defence?'

Lawrence hesitated before answering, reflecting on his own experience, his own opinion and how best to frame his answer for his kind host and old friend. He was most likely prepared for the subject to arise, as he had been probed on it numerous times in recent weeks by those acquaintances with far less riding on his answer than Churchill. On 7 February, a friend of Lawrence's asked him for his views on modern developments in air power for an upcoming pro-war book he was writing. 'It is ridiculous to spend £117,000,000 p.a. on defence weapons about as useful as the broad-sword and busby, when we might have a really powerful force', the friend exclaimed.[68] Lawrence's replies to this and other similar enquiries show him awake to the possibility of German aggression in the near future. In a telling letter to Lionel Curtis, a sought-after advisor on international questions and friend of Churchill's, Lawrence reflected that he wouldn't want RAF expenditure to increase at that moment in time, but 'When Germany wings herself – ah that will be another matter, and our signal to reinforce.'[69]

In that moment around the lunch table, Lawrence chose not to reply with comments about Germany specifically. He also didn't take the pessimistic Baldwin line of admitting defeat as soon as that point of an attack had been reached. After giving the question due consideration, he turned to his host and simply replied, 'Multiple air force defence stations to intercept.'[70] Churchill acknowledged the answer and, according to Sylvia, 'seemed satisfied' with Lawrence's reply. The reason for Lawrence's brevity might well have been because of the known opinion of Archie Sinclair, who at the time was highly critical of rearmament, and felt that disarmament was the best way of securing peace. Lawrence's quiet nature meant he wouldn't have wanted to stoke an impassioned debate across the table, and Churchill, being mindful of his friend's inclinations, probably thought it best to continue the conversation later in private. The seven-word answer was enough in that moment to indicate to Churchill that Lawrence had already given the subject some thought, and that he wasn't taking the defeatist line that so many parliamentarians had adopted by that time. Churchill now knew that, in Lawrence, he had an ally who was as alive to the threat of aerial bombardment as he was.

As the group finished their lunch, they rose from their seats and each readied themselves for the afternoon's intended activity: swimming. It may have been a surprise to their guests, at a time of almost Arctic conditions outside, but their host was too excited about his new swimming pool for any of their guests to avoid the inevitable invitation to join him for a dip.[71]

The latest addition to Chartwell's landscape was one in which Churchill took great pride. It was 12 feet deep at its deepest point and had diving boards to allow family and guests to show off their skills. The conditions of the cold February day were mitigated by the pool's heating mechanism, which could raise the temperature of the water to 75°F (24°C), which prompted friends to joke that it used as much energy to heat as would heat the entire Ritz Hotel in London. That weekend's gathering was one of many where antics in the pool stood out in the Churchills' friends' recollections. Diana Cooper described an afternoon of fun in Chartwell's pool a few months later, with the Churchills and Freda Dudley Ward, the former mistress of the future King Edward VIII.[72]

> Forty winks in the afternoon and then (unexpectedly) bathing at 7 in pouring rain, intensely cold with a grey half-light of approaching night, yet curiously enough, very enjoyable in its oddness … the whole party were splashing about with gleeful screams in this sad crepuscule.[73]

Churchill's childlike sense of fun was similarly remembered by friends of the Churchill children. A friend of Sarah's from adolescence later recalled one occasion when she was standing at the edge of the pool, admiring her friend's superb swallow dives, when suddenly . . . splash! As she spluttered and made her way out of the water, she realised that Churchill had crept up behind her and pushed her in. 'Just as I was recovering and wiping the water from my eyes . . . splash . . . he had pushed me in again.'[74] Mary looked on, apparently 'gurgling with delight' as Churchill chortled cheekily.[75]

Perhaps wisely, Lawrence chose not to join the Churchills in the pool on this occasion, as he was still thawing from the ride over to Chartwell and couldn't face the prospect of disrobing in sub-zero temperatures, no matter how warm the water was. In declining the invitation, he told the family that he wasn't a great swimmer, though this contradicts the recollections of others who knew him well, who said that he 'loved swimming'.[76] He clearly regretted his excuse afterwards. In his thank you note to Clementine he asked, 'If I take a course of swimming lessons . . . will I qualify to visit you once more in the summer?'[77] Churchill, meanwhile, took the plunge with gusto. Having already had his first bath of the day, with his second one to follow later in the afternoon, he relished the opportunity to swim whenever he could. When the party had all exhausted themselves, they exited the pool, wrapped up in their towels and dressing gowns and dashed back towards the warmth of the house.

It was almost certainly after the group's swim that Churchill and Lawrence broke away from the rest of the group to continue the discussion from lunch in private, with Lawrence disclosing his grave concerns about the direction of the RAF by the spring of 1934. To close friends he had admitted that the RAF urgently needed to construct at least 15 more aerodromes with 'useful' planes therein, as opposed to those military aircraft he said were 'like Christmas trees, all hung with protruding gadgets'.[78] He was also, privately, very critical of senior personnel, calling the air marshals 'rather wooden headed', including those in the Aeronautical Inspection Department whom he deemed 'hopeless'. Perhaps most damning, he said that the Air Ministry's air tactics and strategy were 'infantile'.[79] Lawrence also privately despaired at the Government's response to the international situation at the time, as can be seen in his letter to a friend where he remarked, 'Balance of power (post-war edition) means that nobody dare do anything.'[80] On this subject, he and Churchill were of one mind.

The break in proceedings provided an ideal opportunity for all those gathered to disperse and ready themselves for dinner. In Churchill's case, this involved returning to bed for an afternoon nap. 'He would go off for 20 minutes and awake quite refreshed and ready for anything', Miss Hamblin later reflected on Churchill's lifelong habit.[81] Typically, his naps would be followed by his second bath of the day before dressing for dinner. Upon awakening, Inches would have laid out Churchill's evening attire, before helping him dress. He would then descend down the heavy oak stairs to the drawing room to meet his guests who, owing to his notorious lack of punctuality, were usually all there before him. First came the sherry, which was followed by dinner with champagne, likely Pol Roger's 1928 vintage, and then brandy, and finally port. On one occasion, after consuming all these elements over the course of an evening, Churchill's researcher Maurice Ashley became violently sick in the night and refused the port the following evening. 'Ah!', said Churchill, 'I have some excellent Madeira.' Not wanting to admit the reason for his refusal, Ashley reluctantly accepted the alternative. From then on, whenever he dined at Chartwell, Churchill declared, 'Ashley likes Madeira.'[82]

Lawrence had been allocated the 'Henry VIII' room, the principal guest room of the house, always reserved for the most special guests. It was in the oldest part of the house, next to Churchill's study, with impressive historic beams overhead. Its only downside was that it looked onto the front driveway, and therefore lacked the panoramic vistas afforded on the other side of the house. It may well have been on this occasion that he changed into his ivory silk robes with gold embroidery that he had worn during the time of the Arab Revolt. He rarely wore them by the 1930s, but an exception was made at Chartwell to delight the Churchill children. 'My father told me to come down to the drawing room in my dressing gown before dinner, as there was a surprise for me', Mary later described with glee. 'And indeed there was – for sitting there was my friend, attired in the robes of a Prince of Arabia!'[83] She wouldn't have been able to stay for long, however, and, as was typical at the time, she soon retreated with Moppet to the southern wing of the house for her 'nursery supper'. On another occasion, a friend of Sarah's described a Chartwell gathering where Lawrence had neglected to bring anything to change into for dinner. He announced that he had no dinner jacket, at which point he was reportedly loaned one of Churchill's. 'He made a marvellous sight, looking so very small and lost', Sarah's friend recalled. 'His hands and feet could not be seen, the trousers tripping him up at every step and the cuffs dangling in his soup.'[84]

Upon reuniting on that cold February evening in 1934, the party then returned to the dining room. Dinner typically started at 8.15pm and would usually go on until after 10pm.[85] The menu, always carefully curated by Clementine, was shaped to put their best foot forward, as Churchill knew the power of food in dinner-table diplomacy. The chilled champagne was brought to the table and the dinner was then served by either Inches or one of the maids.

One of the ways in which Lawrence and Churchill's tastes differed most was in their ideal dinners. Lawrence never smoked or drank. He also wasn't especially interested in food, although there were a few simple treats that he enjoyed, including 'oranges and coffee with cream'.[86] The contents of his home at Clouds Hill reflected his lack of interest in fine dining or cuisine. He wrote to Clementine once describing his cottage as having 'no cooking place, no grates, no pots or pans'.[87] So depleted were his resources that on Christmas Day, having turned down Clementine's invitation, he instead 'dinnered off a tinned chicken'.[88] The Churchills, meanwhile, had two distinct approaches when dining at Chartwell. When it was just the family, they ate far more modestly. 'His taste in food was in fact very simple', his secretary Miss Hamblin later recalled.[89] Even then, the Churchills were used to quality ingredients, supplemented by fresh fruit, vegetables and eggs from Chartwell's kitchen garden. With guests, however, the cuisine became more decadent. The family-only dinners of roast chicken, grilled fish and lamb cutlets were replaced by the likes of pan-seared filet mignon, roast guinea fowl, and lobster salad. The choices were often inspired by the menu cards Clementine had kept from dinners out at hotels and restaurants that she had particularly enjoyed.

When all the courses were finished, the ladies withdrew and the gentlemen remained around the table. From Sylvia Henley's account it is clear the subject of war preparations didn't arise while the whole group were together. Accounts of Chartwell visits at that time, however, indicate that the subject was unlikely to have been ignored, and so likely came up again when the gentlemen were alone. Churchill's nephew later recalled those guests who could not handle Churchill's all-consuming focus on the subject of defence at the time. 'Johnny, I'm going to leave the table on an excuse. I cannot stand it anymore', uttered the artist William Nicholson to him, behind his napkin.[90] After an hour or so's discussion with Lawrence and Sinclair, Churchill then bid goodnight to guests and ascended to his study, where the late-shift secretary was ready for three to four hours of dictation, at that time mostly on *Marlborough*. On the whole, the evening was deemed a great success, and Lawrence himself remarked afterwards that 'Chartwell's inhabitants are as exciting as mixed drinks and much better in taste'.[91]

The only moment of disappointment in the weekend came with Lawrence's hasty departure on the Monday morning, so as to be on the road before forecast snowstorms arrived. He went to say goodbye to Churchill, who was asleep when he poked his head around the door, though was soon awoken by its loud creak. Lawrence then looked around to say goodbye to anyone else he could find. He was especially disappointed that this didn't include Mary. 'Please tell her I'm sorry about it', he wrote to Clementine afterwards, clearly fearing a bridge with his young friend may have been burned by not having given her a proper farewell.[92] He did the right thing leaving when he did, however, as he faced half an hour of blizzard conditions on his motorbike towards the end of his journey back to Dorset. As the other guests bid more leisurely farewells on that snowy Monday morning, the household staff had to quickly turn the house around for yet more guests. That evening the Churchills welcomed their American friends Otto Pickhardt and his wife Helen. The pair secured their place in Churchill's affection when Pickhardt prescribed 'the use of alcoholic spirits', of a minimum of 250 cubic centimetres, following Churchill's accident in New York in 1932, despite America being in the grip of Prohibition at the time.[93]

As Lawrence rode away from Chartwell, with his freshly signed copies of *The World Crisis*, his thoughts very likely returned to events of the weekend, and his concern about Germany quickly grew in light of discussions with Churchill. Soon after the visit, he wrote to their mutual friend, Lionel Curtis, saying that technological developments under Hitler would mean that any new aircraft developed by the Germans would be 'formidable'.[94] He then said the priority for defence in the air should be research and development including, as he disclosed to Churchill at Chartwell, into anti-aircraft gunnery and developing the art of sound ranging (the practice of locating the positions of enemy forces). This view mirrored Churchill's own, that investment of funds and resources into technological developments would be vital in securing future victories.

On Wednesday 28 February, just two days after Lawrence rode away from Chartwell, the Cabinet accepted the 1934 Air Estimates, which were £1 million less than in 1931. A debate on the subject was scheduled for Thursday of the following week. Churchill was determined to voice his opposition to what appeared to be a step backwards in terms of military preparedness. When the time came, he rose to his feet and began by acknowledging that a pro-disarmament stance was understandable. The preservation of peace had been a noble ambition, and he too hoped that no such continental struggle as they had known in 1914 would arise. This, however, should not be a question of pacifism against militarism. In his opinion, Britain should be able to have a sound system of defence no matter what. He declared:

> We must not despair, we must not for a moment pretend that we cannot face these things. Dangers come upon the world; other nations face them ... and there is not the slightest reason why, with our ability and our resources, and our peaceful intentions, our desire only to live quietly here in our island, we should not raise up for ourselves a security in the air above us which will make us as free from serious molestation as did our control of blue water through bygone centuries.[95]

Churchill's speech was masterful in explaining that rearming was not by definition a signal of preparations for war, but could also be a deterrent. He explicitly highlighted the danger posed by the Nazis by stating 'Germany is arming fast, and no one is going to stop her . . . I have not any knowledge of the details, but everyone is well aware that those very gifted people with their science and with their factories, with what they call their air sports, are capable of developing with great rapidity a most powerful air force for all purposes, offensive and defensive, within a very short period of time.'[96] The Achilles heel Churchill revealed in that speech was his lack of details, or enough empirical evidence about Germany's preparations for war to draw firm conclusions. Until he could be in possession of such materials, he relied entirely on his powers of persuasion, both in the House of Commons chamber and in private. Three days after the Air Estimates debate, sensing no change in the tide, he wrote to the Conservative MP Sir Samuel Hoare. At that time he was serving as the Secretary of State for India, but he had previously been Air Secretary and so Churchill pleaded to him that 'no time should be lost in doubling the air force'.[97]

As the year went on, Lawrence became increasingly desolate. In November 1934 his role was changed to work on RAF boats in Bridlington, which led to him complaining to friends of 'the foulness of the North Sea in Winter'.[98] He had also heard of a plan to make a film called 'Lawrence of Arabia'. 'Presumably he means me,' Lawrence said of the proposed director, 'and I have strong views as to the indesirability of any such film.'[99] He began to count down to his retirement from the RAF in February 1935, and when the time came, and Aircraftman Shaw became Mr Shaw, he made the 300-mile journey from Bridlington to his beloved cottage. But his return to Clouds Hill did not give him the peace and solitude he so desired. He soon found his home subject to a deluge of 'press hounds' who subjected him to levels of harassment that forced Lawrence, on one occasion, to jump over the fence at the end of his garden to escape. This prompted one further, and final, visit to Chartwell, following three weeks of brutal press intrusion. This time it was not documented in the visitors' book, a possible reflection of Lawrence's desperation to be undiscoverable. Lawrence had previously written asking if Churchill could introduce him to Lord Rothermere, the chairman of Associated Newspapers, to whom he would plead for clemency and privacy. Churchill was only too happy to help his old friend, and he suggested a lunch between the three men at Chartwell on Sunday 24 March. Lawrence simply replied 'Splendid. Will arrive Sunday morning independently. Shaw.'[100]

When Sunday came, Lawrence climbed on his motorbike and sped to Chartwell, keen to plead with Lord Rothermere that journalists and photographers should be instructed to leave him alone. Rothermere gave his word and two days later, without a journalist or photographer in sight, Lawrence happily returned to his cottage. From that point on, he revelled in his surroundings and turned down almost all the invitations he received. This included one from Lady Astor inviting him to Cliveden, where she believed the reorganisation of the national Defence Forces would see him offered a senior role, especially as Stanley Baldwin was due to be in attendance. He, however, had no intention to venture back into any kind of public role and replied, 'No: wild mares would not at present take me away from Clouds Hill.'[101]

The following week, on 13 May 1935, Lawrence was riding his beloved motorbike near his home and swerved to avoid a collision with two young boys on bicycles. Lawrence flew forward over the handlebars of his bike and landed about ten yards away. He died after six days in a coma, just after 8am on Sunday 19 May, aged 46. The death certificate read, 'Congestion of the lungs and heart failure following a fracture of the skull and laceration of the brain sustained on being thrown from his motorcycle when colliding with a pedal cyclist.'[102] The funeral was arranged by Lawrence's brother Arnold. Among the 100 invitees were Winston and Clementine Churchill. On the previous day, *The Times* had included a tribute to Lawrence written by Churchill:

In Colonel Lawrence we have lost one of the greatest beings of our time. I had the honour of his friendship. I knew him well. I hoped to see him quit his retirement and take a commanding part in facing the dangers which now threaten the country. No such blow has befallen the Empire for many years as his untimely death.[103]

When, after Lawrence's death, his belongings at Clouds Hill were inventoried, it was recorded that a copy of *The World Crisis* featured in the collection. Inside the front cover was a handwritten note saying, 'Inscribed by Winston S. Churchill for Lurens to replace stolen property, February 1934.'[104]

CHAPTER 3

THE ANGLO-AMERICAN DISAGREEMENT

Joseph P. Kennedy, 5 October 1935

Winston Churchill's belief in the importance of what he called 'the Special Relationship', between the United Kingdom and the United States, had its roots in his very existence. The son of an English aristocrat and an American heiress had a unique perspective on Anglo-American cooperation. As 1935 wore on, however, he despaired, writing in September, 'Germany arming at breakneck speed, England lost in a pacifist dream, France corrupt and torn by dissension', and 'America remote and indifferent'.[1] As his concern deepened, he looked towards the United States in hope of joining forces in defence of freedom and democracy. By inviting a highly influential figure in American politics to his country home just a few weeks later, Churchill hoped to create a friendship and alliance, in which the pair would campaign for shared resources to defend the world from tyranny. What he could not have known at the time was that he was making his case to a man who would later come to be known as one of the most notorious American appeasers.

The meeting between Joseph P. Kennedy and Winston Churchill has been the subject of much confusion. Conflicting accounts pinpoint their first encounter at Chartwell as being on different dates from 1933 to 1937. Confirmation of this remarkable meeting can be found in the depths of Clementine Churchill's engagement diaries, a meticulous and constantly updated record of the comings and goings of the matriarch of Chartwell. On 5 October 1935, in the 1 o'clock

71

window, the word 'Kennedys' appears hastily written in pencil. The lunch that took place was among the smaller gatherings at the Churchills' home, with Joe and his wife Rose as their only guests. Churchill's intention was to pitch an Anglo-American naval force. Rose later recalled Churchill's belief that such an endeavour would 'dominate the world and police it and keep the other nations in their present status quo' and was his way of 'solving the conquest of the rising Nazi strength'.[2] Churchill knew, however, that America's isolationism in the mid-1930s would be a barrier, and hoped Kennedy might be an ally in helping him persuade Americans of the threat posed by Hitler's Germany.

In November 1934, Churchill gave a broadcast on the BBC, which by that point had become a rare occurrence due to his increasingly tense relationship with the broadcaster.[3] In what proved to be a prophetic address, Churchill made the startling case that a time of danger had fallen upon Britain. 'We are no longer safe in our island home,' he began, before describing how 'a group of ruthless men preaching a gospel of intolerance and racial pride' had taken hold in Germany.[4] He also stressed that the Royal Navy, which had been Britain's surest defence for centuries, could not defend against weaponry from the air. He added that, though he prayed it wouldn't be the case, Britain might be dragged into another war, just as the United States had been in 1917. The speech was widely admired at the time, including by a fellow Member of Parliament who described it as 'solemn, clear, logical and impressive . . . the finest wireless address I have ever heard'.[5]

The positive response to his speech gave a moment of relief in what had otherwise been a frustrating few months for Churchill, the effects of which began to take their toll on those around him. His secretaries, who often saw him at his most raw, were starting to struggle with the demands of the role, and Mrs Pearman soon contacted an agency about finding alternative work. She noted that both she and Miss Hamblin were 'fed-up with the hours of work'.[6] For £5 a week, plus bus fares, and all their meals while at Chartwell, the secretaries worked 12 to 14 hours every day, with no weekends, and only the occasional days off when it happened to suit Churchill himself. 'He pays very badly in every department of house and estate life', Mrs Pearman continued, complaining that the nature of her work at Chartwell resulted in a 'drain to my health and the absolute cutting off from all my friends'.[7] The eccentricities of their employer also made for an unusual working environment. Joyce Cutting, who worked as a secretary at Chartwell in 1931, remarked that Mr Churchill sometimes worked while half-dressed, wearing what she described as 'pink Celanese underwear' (later identified as silk).[8]

Despite their apparent disgruntlement in 1934–35, both secretaries continued in their roles at Chartwell. They worked on book chapters, articles, household accounts, speeches and constituency work, all of which flowed from Chartwell. They travelled with him to the House of Commons, weekends at country houses with friends, research trips, electioneering and holidays abroad.[9] Wherever he went in 1935, either Mrs Pearman or Miss Hamblin would be by his side. 'In time we all realised that in full return for the stress and strain, we had the rare privilege of getting to know closely all the beauty of this dynamic but gentle character', Miss Hamblin later recalled.[10] It wasn't just the secretaries, though, that struggled at this time. The local newspapers constantly featured adverts for staff for Chartwell – from weekend help in the kitchen, with the specific requirement that they always work from 10am on Saturdays until Monday morning, to the unusual request that two friends were needed for the role of pantrymaid and third housemaid. The latter request for applicants in pairs was in part because of Chartwell's isolation. The domestic staff who lived on-site could rarely drive and so, if they were far from home, they would often get homesick and lonely. 'She used to engage maids from Wales,' remembered Miss Hamblin, remarking on how they were 'quite raw, in their first post, you know, poor little things.' She was acutely aware that Chartwell was these girls' new home and so she tried to help them settle in to their new surroundings. 'I remember I used to bring them to dances in Westerham sometimes,' she recalled, 'and sometimes they got back very late and had to climb through a window.'[11]

Almost certainly unaware of the high jinks going on among his staff, Churchill had other things on his mind. On 26 November

1934, six days after receiving the news that Germany's air force, the Luftwaffe, would be as large as Britain's within a year, the Cabinet decided to speed up the process of air rearmament from four years to two. Two days later, Churchill moved for an amendment to the vote of thanks for the King's Speech, with the wording:

In the present circumstances of the world, the strength of our national defences, and especially of our air defences, is no longer adequate to secure the peace, safety and freedom of Your Majesty's faithful subjects.[12]

With a week's notice before the motion was due to be debated, the discussion as to how to deal with Churchill's proposed motion dominated proceedings at three Cabinet meetings. The Prime Minister responded by denying that the Luftwaffe was nearing equality, saying Germany's air force wasn't half of that of the RAF. Two days later was Churchill's sixtieth birthday, which was celebrated with a party in his honour, though it fell in the midst of an unfortunate political climate.

Shortly after his birthday, Churchill hosted a journalist from Birmingham's *Sunday Mercury* at Chartwell, as part of his campaign to strengthen his standing among the general public. 'For rather too long now,' the article began, 'he has been submerged at his desk at Chartwell Manor.' The journalist described his arrival at Chartwell, saying 'You ring the bell and a maid garbed in the old-fashioned large cap and apron answers', before describing the scene that awaited him. 'Lamps gleam on ivory walls – books rest on a chest of polished oak – down a staircase lovely ladies are descending to dinner.'[13] The description then continued to Churchill's appearance, including his 'happy fat chin' and the breadth of his forehead, described as being 'as remarkable as his energy'. The conclusion of the piece is perhaps the most striking, in which the young writer declared 'India may now provide the highway to the Premiership. At 60, as politicians go, Winston Churchill is still young enough.'[14]

A week later, with his mind far from any parliamentary debates, Churchill stood with his children on a platform at Victoria railway station and waved farewell to Clementine. She was embarking on an adventure across the world in search of Komodo dragons for London Zoo, the planning for which had been underway for just over a month.[15] 'You all looked so sweet and beautiful standing there,' she wrote to Winston after her train pulled away, 'and I thought how fortunate I am to have such a family.'[16] Shortly after her departure she sent a telegram to Mrs Pearman asking her to make arrangements for maps marking the route of her voyage to be made for Churchill.[17] That way he and Mary could track her far-off progress during the cold winter months at Chartwell.

Churchill ended the year with a message to her saying all was quiet on the Chartwell front.[18] The image of a lonely man, at the outset of a new decade of his life, comes across in messages to his friends too. 'I am nearly always alone', he dictated in reply to Lord Londonderry, as he asked his old friend to come to discuss the situation regarding air defence. He concluded with an interesting note, reflecting on the handwritten letter to which he was replying. 'I have almost lost the art of thinking with a pen in my hand, but you retain the agreeable aptitudes of our ancestors.'[19]

The Churchills' separation lasted four months, during which time Churchill channelled his restless energy into his campaigns, his writing and his home. Writing frequently to Clementine in his 'Chartwell Bulletins', he would regale his wife with tales of the mechanical digger working on the lakes, the mating black swans, the chauffeur's damp cottage and ongoing work on the brick wall in front of the house, with its ball-finials intended to mirror the design of those at General Wolfe's former home nearby. Another common feature were the tales of Mary Smith, the widow of Jack Smith, known as 'Donkey Jack'. They had lived in a hut on common land near to Chartwell until Jack died. As Jack was facing a pauper's grave, Churchill stepped in to pay for the funeral, as well as letting Mrs Smith move onto his land at Chartwell for the rest of her life. 'Mr Churchill has been my good friend through all my troubles', she told a journalist from the Evening Standard.[20]

Most alarming was the note on 21 January in which Churchill casually mentioned, 'The house was nearly burnt down yesterday.' He

7. *The hired mechanical digger used to modify the lower lake at Chartwell, including transforming the peninsula into an island, 1934. Winston Churchill is the figure to the right of the digger. He wrote to Clementine on 18 January 1934 saying, 'The mechanical digger has arrived. He moves about on his caterpillars only with the greatest difficulty on the wet ground. But when he gets to work he is simply marvellous.'*

described how the maids had been packing Clementine's bedding away and put two electric light globes under the cushions and covered them with folded blankets. Moppet happened to go into Clementine's room to turn off the main lights, not knowing about those under the blankets. An hour later, a strong smell of burning led Inches to rush to the scene, finding her mattress badly burned and the cushions about to burst into flames. In words unlikely to have reassured his wife, he added, 'imagine if it had happened in the middle of the night. No one can tell if the whole house would not have burned to the ground.'[21] Fortunately for all involved, Chartwell remained standing.

Just a few days before Chartwell's near miss, a vote was held in the Saar, a coal-rich region of 730 square miles on the French and Belgian border with a population of 800,000.[22] The Treaty of Versailles of 1919 had put the region under control of the League of Nations, and it was governed by a commission which was run firstly by a Frenchman, then a Canadian, and finally a Briton. Throughout this time, the proceeds of the coal mines were given to the French as part of Germany's reparations. Furthermore, it had become a place of refuge for a number of Hitler's opponents. The Saar plebiscite, as it is generally termed, was to decide who should control the region – Germany or France. The result was an astounding victory for Germany, which won with a 90 per cent majority. The Nazis' victory gained worldwide attention. Coverage of the vote in the *China Weekly Review* made the front page but, in damning terms for the Nazi regime, the paper called it the first time in history that a people enjoying the benefits of democracy had 'thrown these over and decided to bend their heads under the yoke of dictatorship'.[23] Despite negative coverage in some publications, Hitler was able to use this resounding success to bolster his image domestically and internationally. He could now argue that German-speaking peoples unequivocally wanted to be reunited under Nazi rule. A young British journalist, Shiela Grant Duff, covered the vote for *The Observer* and described the aftermath: 'The million swastikas which hang on the walls in the Saar give the impression that a plague of spiders have descended.'[24] Her accounts include the testimonies of those she met, including one woman whose mother, a woman in her sixties, 'had her face wiped in a muck heap because she did not celebrate the triumph of the plebiscite'.[25] Meanwhile, panic was setting in in certain quarters, as stories of concentration camps and prisons in Germany began to spread.

The region quickly became a vital resource for the Nazis in terms of both industrial production and the manufacture of weaponry. From the other side of the Atlantic, Albert Einstein looked on with horror at events in Europe. Just a week after the plebiscite, he wrote to Lindemann about the threat that now faced the world. 'It seems to be that people are gradually recognising the full import of this danger', he wrote to Churchill's closest friend. Reflecting on his time in England with the two of them in 1933, he added, 'Two years ago it could so easily have been stopped, but at that time no one wanted to hear about it.'[26]

The views of those in the United States had been of interest to Churchill for the entirety of his political career. In the 1930s, in his new role as elder-statesman-cum-journalist, he was able to write opinion pieces about current affairs in America. 'I meet a great many American politicians and have friendly relations with them which I hope to renew and cultivate', he wrote to the managing editor of *Collier's Weekly* during his time in the United States in 1932.[27] Of the people of the United States more generally, he reflected, 'I have become a great admirer of your people, and have developed many extremely cordial sentiments towards them during my travels.'[28] The high regard was mutual and Churchill had a considerable following in the United States, with his broadcasts to the country in the 1930s typically attracting audiences in the tens of millions.

The inauguration of a new President, Franklin Delano Roosevelt, took place in March 1933. The following year, Churchill published an article entitled 'While the World Watches', in which he described the new President's policies as being from 'a narrow view of American self-interest'.[29] He was, however, quick to compliment Roosevelt by, interestingly, comparing him favourably to Adolf Hitler. 'The petty persecutions and Old World assertions of brutality in which the German idol has indulged,' he wrote, 'only show their smallness and squalor compared with the renaissance of creative effort with which the name of Roosevelt will always be associated.'[30] It was, therefore, with great interest that Churchill watched events in the United States. It was hardly a new-found interest, however, as indicated by a visit to Chartwell by a different Roosevelt just two years earlier, when the President's son James met with Churchill at his country home. Though it was not recorded in Chartwell's visitors' book, Kay Halle, a close friend of Randolph's, later recalled the dinner of 8 October 1933. After everyone had finished their meal, Churchill initiated a game by which each guest had to disclose a confession or their fondest wish. When the question was put to him, he answered without hesitation, 'I wish to be Prime Minister and in close and daily communication by telephone with the President of the United States.' He then asked a secretary to bring a piece of paper to the table, onto which he drew a symbol showing the pound and the dollar signs intertwined. 'Pray, bear this to your father for me', he said, handing the piece of paper to James Roosevelt. 'Tell him this must be the currency of the future.'[31]

The early months of 1935 were the last of those that Churchill described as 'apart from my anxiety on public affairs, were very pleasant to me'. He described how the situation in Europe was on his mind constantly, in particular the rearming of Germany. 'I lived mainly at Chartwell, where I had much to amuse me', he reflected on this time. 'I never had a dull or idle moment from morning till midnight and with my happy family around me dwelt at peace within my habitation.'[32] This began to change that summer, when his daughter Sarah later recalled 'a shadow was growing over the former sunlit scene'.[33] 'The German situation is increasingly sombre', he wrote to Clementine in early March. He reflected on diplomatic discussions taking place with Russia and France, and their desire to live in peace, which had the potential to be a catalyst for joint action towards mutual security. 'There is safety in numbers. There is only safety in numbers', he told Clementine.[34] It was around this time that he wrote a pamphlet on behalf of the India Defence League entitled 'India "The Great Betrayal": A Broadcast Address'. In it he wrote, 'the benefits which Britain derives from India are only a frac-tion of the blessings we have given India in return.' He also described the India Home Rule Bill as 'a gigantic quilt of jumbled crochet work' before adding, 'By this deed we abandon our mission in the East, the faithful discharge of which has been our greatest glory.'[35] Even in this pamphlet, however, he couldn't resist highlighting the storm clouds gathering over Europe, and pleaded that it was the wrong time to disrupt and destabilise the British Empire.

The toll of his rapidly increasing political schedule began to show. He confessed himself tired and his family, for different reasons, were beginning to feel the strain. All the Churchill sisters, plus Moppet, had been roped into supporting Randolph's election campaigns, firstly when he stood as an independent Conservative candidate for Wavertree in Liverpool, when he apparently became accustomed to women singing 'Randolph, hope and glory' at him.[36] He then backed an Independent candidate at a by-election in Norwood in March who received so few votes that he lost his deposit. Defeated and exhausted from the frantic electioneering, the family started to succumb to illness: Mary with whooping cough and Randolph with jaundice-like symptoms. Even their pets staged a rebellion of sorts. 'I have banished all the dogs from our part of the house', Churchill wrote to Clementine. 'I really think you will have to buy a new strip of carpet outside my landing.'[37]

The first signature of Ralph Wigram, a man considered 'the genius of the place' at the Foreign Office,[38] appears in Chartwell's visitors' book on Sunday 7 April. Churchill could no longer bear having to admit in Parliament that he was without specifics or detail, and informants who shared his fears began to make their way to Chartwell. Ralph Wigram became a key source of insider informa-tion, and Churchill later said it was he who 'helped me to form and fortify my opinion about the Hitler movement'.[39]

Wigram had expressed grave concerns about Nazi Germany for some months, writing in October 1934 that they were 'working for an army of offensive strength'.[40] He was proved right when Adolf Hitler reintroduced conscription, with compulsory military service announced on 16 March 1935. This was followed soon after by a statement announcing that Germany's air force equalled Britain's in strength. The measures taken, Hitler declared, had simply been towards the goal of 'moral rehabilitation and construction of the German people' which 'need be of no interest to the outside world'.[41] Furthermore, Hitler argued that Germany was more vulnerable than other countries due to its densely populated industrial areas, compared to other nations with larger open spaces. This risk, according to him, made Germany 95 per cent more vulnerable than those countries. This was why it was necessary for Germany to have an air force but, at the same time, why, according to Hitler, 'Germany was the country most interested in the preservation of peace'.[42] After Wigram's visit to Chartwell, he and Churchill remained in covert contact and arranged for a second meeting three weeks later to help Churchill to prepare his 'air memorandum'. His concerns, however, went beyond the subject of air parity. In the House of Commons, Sir Herbert Samuel, the Leader of the Liberal Party, called Churchill 'the most strenuous and uncompromising of the advocates for an expansion of our forces on the sea and in the air'.[43]

Churchill's comfort at this time was the return of Clementine from her voyage. He was so excited for her return that he went to Dover pier to meet her straight off her boat. 'I have not grudged your long excursion,' he had previously written to her, 'but now I do want you back.'[44] At the bottom of the page he drew a picture of a pig, Clementine's pet name for her husband, with the word 'expectant' alongside.

Still imbued with the sense of relief at being reunited with his beloved wife, Churchill opened an astonishing letter, sent to him on 12 May. It was from Lord Rothermere, the chairman of Associated Newspapers for whom Churchill had recently brokered the meeting with T. E. Lawrence just a few weeks earlier. Rothermere was forwarding a letter he had received from Adolf Hitler, which Churchill perused, as usual with his letters, while eating his breakfast in bed but, as it was written in German, he most likely sought the help of his German-speaking friend, Frederick Lindemann. Written on 3 May 1935, on swastika-headed paper, the letter sought greater Anglo-German understanding. 'I believe that a methodical scientific examination of European history over the last 300 years will reveal that 9/10 of the blood sacrificed on battlefields was completely in vain', Hitler wrote. He also praised England's ability to avoid becoming embroiled in continental wars of recent centuries, and said that such avoidance was what had created the conditions that allowed Britain to build 'the greatest empire in history'. He lamented the impact of the First World War, for having robbed both countries of a generation of young men but, worse than that, in his opinion, it left 'a legacy of prejudice and passion', which strengthened the case of 'those who aim at the sabotaging of the consolidation of Europe and to those who are inwardly hostile to the strengthening of White supremacy in the world'.[45] Finally, Hitler reiterated his vision for an alliance, saying:

England's historically unique colonial activity and naval power would unite with one of the first soldier nations in the world. If this understanding were to be supplemented by the addition of the American nation, then it would be absolutely impossible to see who in the world could disrupt a peace that consciously and intentionally does not neglect the interest of white peoples.[46]

Churchill considered the contents of the letter, but had to play his hand carefully in his reply to Rothermere. Instead of a response of fire and fury, Churchill described how an alliance with Germany would be contrary to Britain's approach to foreign affairs throughout history. 'We have on all occasions been the friend of the second strongest power in Europe,' he wrote to Rothermere, 'and have never yielded ourselves to the strongest power.' He calmly concluded, 'I see no reason myself to change from this traditional view.'[47] Though he had no intention of any kind of rapprochement with Nazi Germany, he kept the letter. It had given him a direct understanding of what precisely was on Hitler's mind at the time, including the might of Britain's navy, and how strongly he wanted to avoid being in opposition to such a powerful force.

It was on 8 May 1935 that the truth about Germany's preparations for war became undeniable to the British political establishment. Cabinet were informed that the RAF was now inferior to the Luftwaffe by 370 aircraft. Then, on 22 May, Stanley Baldwin admitted that he had been incorrect in his response to Churchill's motion the previous November, uttering the devastating words, 'There I was completely wrong.'[48] There was, at least, a clear response to this alarming news, and Cabinet soon authorised the expansion of the home defence force of the RAF to 1,512 aircraft.

While he was relieved to see immediate action taken to strengthen Britain's air defences, the matter of Germany's navy increasingly dominated Churchill's thoughts, as shown in a speech he gave less than three weeks after reading Hitler's proposal. Reflecting on his time as First Lord of the Admiralty in the First World War, his 31 May speech in the House of Commons recalled the speed at which submarines were manufactured by the end of 1914, at a rate of 20 in six months. He felt certain that Germany was exceeding this pace, since they were doing so in peacetime, and especially given that 'the whole of their industry is woven into an immediate readiness for war'.[49] He also questioned relations between Germany and Japan, and Hitler's pursuit of 'power diplomacy'. He concluded with a mari-time metaphor, remarking that 'it would be folly for us to act as if we were swimming in a halcyon sea, as if nothing but balmy breezes and calm weather were to be expected', saying instead that Britain was 'entering a corridor of deepening and darkening danger'.[50]

As the question of Germany's military might raged on over the summer, a change at the top of Government took place, with the Conservative Party's Leader Stanley Baldwin appointed as Prime Minister. This gave Churchill a small glimmer of hope that he might return to high office. However, he felt that an appointment was unlikely, especially given that only a limited number of places in the new administration could be assigned to Conservatives, and he was duly proved right. Not only that but his position suddenly became more difficult. It was one thing to oppose the stance of the National Government when it had a Labour Prime Minister, Ramsay MacDonald, at the helm. The succession of Stanley Baldwin on 7 June meant that, for the first time since the formation of the three-party coalition in 1931, any attacks by Conservative backbenchers were now aimed at the leader of their party. Churchill's campaigns – whether marshalling opposition to greater self-government for India or criti-cising disarmament policies as a way of securing peace – now meant going directly against his party's leadership.

At the same time as Baldwin took over, talks were ongoing between Samuel Hoare, who had newly moved from Secretary of State for India to the Foreign Office, and Joachim von Ribbentrop, Hitler's foreign affairs advisor. As a result of these discussions, on 18 June 1935 the Anglo-German Naval Pact was signed, in which the British Government accepted a proposal from Germany that their naval strength, in terms of total tonnage, was allowed to be 35 per cent of that of Britain and the wider Commonwealth combined. Furthermore, in terms of submarines specifically, Germany was henceforth, if an 'exceptional situation' arose, allowed to possess equal tonnage. The agreement effectively freed the German Government from the naval restrictions of the Treaty of Versailles, and the outcome was deemed to be such a success for the Führer that it was subsequently referenced by one German historian as 'the happiest day' of Hitler's life.[51] On the signing of this agreement, there was instant concern among Churchill's allies, not only about the likely strengthening of Germany's navy, but also about the potential impact on relations with France. 'I fear the French are going to get excited about a naval agreement with Germany', Ralph Wigram wrote to Churchill from his desk in the Foreign Office on the day the pact was signed.[52]

As the summer recess neared, Churchill's increased focus on naval security can be seen in a secret memorandum written on 23 July 1935. Though entitled 'Air Defence', it includes his predictions as to what might await following an outbreak of war if Germany attacked Britain, France and Belgium, including consideration of Germany's navy. This was followed the next day by a speech given in Harlow. With a general election due to take place that autumn, he was already making it a key narrative within his speeches that a wrong electoral outcome could have disastrous, and potentially fatal, consequences for national security. 'Both in the air and in the Navy we will have to make substantial preparations to put ourselves in a state of security', he said while expressing significant concern that, of 17 ships featured as part of a recent naval review, 14 dated back to the First World War.[53] Action was required urgently in terms of both scale and modernity of the British fleet.

Ensconced at Chartwell for much of the summer, his frustrations at the European situation became all-consuming. He wrote to Ava Wigram, the wife of his Foreign Office informant, 'things are going from bad to worse in Europe and I feel the greatest anxiety about them'.[54] Fortunately, the glorious weather at his Kent home provided some consolation, and he continued to invite guests to discuss political matters or simply share in the sunshine-laden views and sense of escape that Chartwell offered. Weekend parties took place almost every week between 1 June and 7 August with a spectacular array of guests, with 39 signatures of mostly overnight-stayers in the house's visitors' book. As well as the usual close family and Chartwell regulars, they included the likes of Edwardian aristocratic A-Lister Ettie Desborough, who had been a close friend of Churchill's mother for almost 40 years and was a lady-in-waiting to Queen Mary. She thought very highly of her friend's son, whom she first met in 1891

8. *Mary Churchill with her two goats, Molly and Milly, in the walled garden at Chartwell, mid-1930s.*

when he was just 16 years old. She once remarked, 'I love his stead-fast undubious massive intellect, his independence and scorn, his devotion to high things, his humour – above all his heart.'[55]

Another guest that summer was Pamela Lytton, formerly Pamela Plowden, one of Churchill's early loves, who remained strikingly beautiful 30 years on from their courtship. His aunt Leonie came too, the last of the Jerome sisters who had included his mother Jennie, who had passed away in 1921, and his aunt Clara, who died in January 1935. She was joined by the fabulous Comtesse Phyllis de Janzé, a friend of the Churchills who had holidayed with them a year earlier and took her pet monkey Rodrigo with her. She was said to be one of the first women to ever wear a short skirt, and was immedi-ately recognisable with, as Cecil Beaton later described, 'the face of a puma' and 'the fastidious walk of a crane'.[56] Her signature in the visi-tors' book is followed by that of Major General Frederick Peake. He had served in the First World War under T. E. Lawrence, to whom he was often compared, and was described in his obituary as 'one of the most colourful figures in the turbulent Middle East'.[57] Churchill's secretary at the time later recalled these 'lovely weekend parties where all of the family gathered together'.[58] Mary too remembered the buzz and excitement of such gatherings during the parliamen-tary holidays, reflecting that 'Chartwell throbbed with life'.[59] And so they, and many more, made up the parade of influential, charismatic and fascinating individuals who made their way to Chartwell in the long hot summer of 1935.

Despite the weekend parties and frivolities at the Churchills' family home, that summer was also one of ignominious defeat for Churchill and the further decline of his influence over foreign affairs. The Government of India Act became law on 2 August 1935, which saw the end of one of his most impassioned and sustained political campaigns. The 'revolt' against the Government's India policy had, at its height in February 1935, provoked opposition from 85 Conservative MPs, all of whom voted against the bill, with another 20 abstaining. When combined, the number of rebels and abstainers was less than a quarter of the party, and while Churchill had led the Conservative attack on the policy, no other Conservative former ministers on the backbenches followed his lead. By the time the act had passed, Churchill had spent considerable political capital on the campaign, but was accepting of the outcome. Three weeks later, one of the most remarkable visits to Chartwell took place when Ghanshyam Das Birla, a close associate of Mahatma Gandhi's, joined the Churchills for lunch at their country home.

Churchill was in the garden when Birla arrived, wearing a workman's apron and a large hat with a feather in it. 'I found him no fire-eater', Birla later wrote in a report of the meeting for Gandhi. He described Churchill as: 'A most remarkable man. As eloquent in private talk as he is in public speech.'[60] Clementine joined the pair for lunch, and Birla called her 'very interesting',[61] but observed that when Churchill spoke, she simply listened quietly. Birla's report then describes the usual tour that Churchill gave his guests. First the brick walls, then the studio, then the swimming pool, where he described how the water was heated and filtered. 'The cost of this luxury must be enormous', Birla said to himself, though Churchill quickly added that he only spent £3 a week on it.[62]

When the subject of India arose, Churchill remarked, 'I do not like the Bill but it is now on the Statute Book ... so make it a success.' He also asked about Gandhi, before adding, 'I should like to meet him now. I would love to go to India before I die. If I went there I would stay for six months.'[63] He then paused and asked Birla whether he would be well received in India, to which Birla reassured him that he would be. Their conversation, which Birla reflected had been dominated by Churchill speaking for 75 per cent of the time, concluded with Churchill offering his outlook on what might await for India. 'I would be only too delighted if the Reforms are a success. I have all along felt that there are fifty Indias. But you have got the things now; make it a success and if you do I will advocate your getting much more.'[64]

The resumption of activity in Parliament in September saw a quieting of Chartwell. One exception was the arrival of Bernard Baruch on 15 September. Baruch was a wealthy American financier, an advisor to Presidents, and an old friend of Churchill's. The Churchills' daughter Mary later called him 'a regular transatlantic summer visitor in the 1930s', as well as recalling his significant stature. At 6 foot 5, he used to tower over those around him, including Mary who called him 'certainly the tallest person I had ever seen'.[65] The pair first met in 1918 when Churchill was Minister of Munitions and Baruch was a Commissioner on the American War Industries Board. Known to Churchill as 'Barney', Baruch introduced Churchill to many in his extensive network of connections during his visit to the US in 1929. His kindness included escorting Churchill in his private railroad car from Chicago to New York. Their time together inspired Churchill, having gained further insights into Baruch's financial acumen, and he became alive to the possibilities that might await by speculating on the stock market. The timing, however, could not have been worse and proved disastrous for the Churchills' finances. The Wall Street Crash resulted in losses for Churchill equivalent to roughly $1,000,000 in today's money. Baruch felt partly responsible and compensated Churchill almost a tenth of that amount from his own personal finances. Churchill, however, had been bitten by the bug, and continued to invest in stocks. He instigated a practice at Chartwell where his secretaries were instructed to find him every hour and to tell him the prices of his stocks. 'We had to keep a sort of graph of the prices that went up and down', Miss Hamblin later recalled, before describing the lengths they went to to ensure he was always kept abreast. 'If he was painting one had to go down to the Studio with them,' she continued, 'or if he was out doing something on the lake we had to go through the mud and take the prices to him wherever he was.'[66]

It was at this time that fortune began to favour the elder Churchill children, who had long since moved out from Chartwell, but were finding long-overdue happiness. Diana had met Duncan Sandys, the Conservative candidate, while campaigning with her brother at the Norwood by-election earlier in the year. Within weeks of the announcement of her divorce from John Milner Bailey, a relationship blossomed between the pair, and he was invited to Chartwell for the first time for a weekend in mid-June. 'Mr Pug & I were rather staggered at first,' Clementine wrote to a friend when the engagement was announced that summer, 'but now we rather like him (no money) & HOPE all is for the best.'[67]

Despite the happy family life and long-standing friendships that sustained him at Chartwell, Churchill remained frustrated politically. Writing to Clementine from the Ritz in Paris, he relayed a conversation with fellow politician Sir Robert Horne, who had said, 'B[aldwin] does not mean on any account to get into war. Rather it seems they will use the humiliation to rebuild the Fleet & Air F[orce].'[68] By this time, the situation with Britain's navy had become as much a concern to Churchill as air policy and air strength. 'We must rebuild the fleet', he wrote to his old friend Lord Winterton on 30 September. 'But that I believe is generally conceded, though I suppose there will be endless procrastination.'[69]

Amidst this backdrop of apparent lethargy on the subject of naval matters, Churchill knew that, as merely a private individual, he could still enter into discussions with those with influence, and potential allies, to make his case for decisive action. It was at this point that he received an intriguing telegram from his old friend Baruch on the evening of 25 September 1935:

JOSEPH KENNEDY FORMER CHAIRMAN SECURITIES COMMISSION SAILING NORMANDIE TODAY WITH LETTERS YOUR MOST IMPORTANT PEOPLE [STOP] SUGGEST YOUR WIRING HIM MAKING APPOINTMENT TO SEE HIM AS HE IS IMPORTANT

AND GOOD RELATIONSHIP BETWEEN YOU TWO MIGHT HAVE FAR REACHING RESULTS.[70]

Knowing and trusting the wisdom of his friend, Churchill swiftly dictated a telegram to his secretary, to be cabled to the ship on which Kennedy was sailing across the Atlantic. 'Trust I may have pleasure of meeting you over here', the brief note read. 'Please cable your movements. Winston Churchill, Chartwell, Westerham, Kent. 27.9.35.'[71]

The suggestion by Baruch was, at first glance, a politically astute one. By the mid-1930s, Kennedy was not only a close advisor to President Roosevelt, he was also a personal friend. An account of a visit that summer by the President to Marwood, a large estate near Washington DC leased by the Kennedys, described a merry party. The group reportedly drank mint juleps, watched movies on the lawn and sang along to an accordion, with the President showcasing his 'rather nice tenor-baritone'.[72] The year before, Roosevelt had not only pushed for Kennedy to be appointed a Commissioner of the newly created Securities and Exchange Commission, but insisted that Kennedy be made Chairman also. Despite the efforts by his friend, Kennedy gave written notice for this role on 6 September 1935, asking to be relieved by 23 September ahead of his travels to Europe. 'I am now through with public life forever', he wrote to well-placed friends, though those who knew him well thought this unlikely to be the case.[73] Even upon his arrival in Britain, he was sending regular telegrams to Roosevelt updating him on his popularity on the far side of the Atlantic. 'Don't worry about election in America you could be elected anything in England', he gushed to his friend. 'If the papers and business men of America gave you ten percent of the deal that they give you here, you would be president for the rest of your life.'[74]

A meeting was swiftly scheduled between the Churchills and the Kennedys for the following week at Chartwell. It was only prevented from happening sooner by Churchill's obligation to attend the Conservative Party Conference in Bournemouth from Wednesday 2 October until the morning of Saturday 5 October. This was a major event in the British political calendar; Churchill had been painstakingly preparing for it, and planned to speak on 'the Naval resolution', on Thursday morning.[75]

The Churchills departed for the Burlington Hotel in Bournemouth the evening before, where they dined with Lord Lloyd, a long-standing political ally of Churchill's who was President of the Navy League and who lobbied the government to spend more on the Royal Navy. Churchill and Lloyd planned to support a resolution by their friend and colleague Sir Edward Grigg, on the Government's duty to provide adequate armed forces for defence. Churchill's amendment to Grigg's resolution included the following:

(1) To repair the serious deficiencies in the defence forces of the Crown, and in particular, first, to organise our industry for speedy conversion to defence purposes, if need be.

(2) To make a renewed effort to establish equality in the air with the strongest foreign Air Force within striking distance of our shores.

(3) To rebuild the British Fleet and strengthen the Royal Navy, so as to safeguard our food and livelihood and preserve the coherence of the British Empire.[76]

To Churchill's delight, the resolution was carried unanimously and gave him a taste of the influence he hoped might await. With a general election looming, he understood that the role of First Lord of the Admiralty might soon be vacant. 'I wished very much to go there should the Conservatives return to power', he later remarked, though he knew there were allies of the Prime Minister who did not wish to see him occupy his old post. He tried not to make assumptions and instead focused on the international situation, noting: 'The growing German menace made me anxious to lay my hands upon our military machine.'[77]

As the conference came to an end, the Churchills were driven at breakneck speed back to Chartwell. 'We had close calls on the road', the Churchills' chauffeur Samuel Howes later recalled. 'The kind of driving he demanded made this inevitable.'[78] The car was also filled with cigar smoke, papers and boxes and one of the two secretaries was crammed in also. 'You would feel awfully crushed and taking your poor dictation and in a wobbly hand', Miss Hamblin later remembered.[79] As they swiftly travelled back to Kent in order to be at home before the Kennedys arrived, Churchill read an account of Baldwin's reception and speech at the conference. He was proclaimed as the leader 'who all his life has preferred the unobtrusive paths of steadiness and of peace, and who by sheer force of character has gained support extending far beyond his own party'.[80] The article underneath, entitled 'American Foreign Policy', very likely also caught Churchill's eye that morning. Stressing the 'isolationist tendencies of Congress', the article quoted a speech recently given by President Roosevelt in San Diego in which he assured his audience 'most earnestly' that the United States' Government intended and expected to remain at peace with all the world, as he went on to reaffirm the doctrine of neutrality and the 'good neighbour'.[81]

As the Churchills' car swept around the country roads near Chartwell, he became increasingly overjoyed as they neared his family home. 'When he entered the precincts of Chartwell along the road, he would say "Ah! Chartwell!",' Miss Hamblin once said, 'and he would throw all the things to one side.'[82] With the car finally parked on the driveway, Churchill dashed inside, quickly changed his clothes and then dictated a handful of telegrams to his secretary, including one to Baruch. 'Kennedy lunches Chartwell today', he noted, before changing the subject and seeking Baruch's advice on the purchase of yet more shares.[83]

Meanwhile, the Kennedys were motoring through the heavy October rain from London. Rose Kennedy later wrote of the pair's excitement as they travelled through the English countryside and arrived at Chartwell where Clementine welcomed them at the front door. 'Mrs Churchill met us clad in her tweeds, topped by a most becoming shade of rose sweater which heightened the color of her fresh English complexion.'[84] The garments were most likely part of an extensive wardrobe update Clementine had made upon her return from her cruise. She had lost weight while on the voyage and had to rapidly replenish her wardrobe in time for King George V's jubilee and the many related events which she was due to attend. Fortunately, her 5 foot 8 figure had become that of many shops' sample sizes. 'I was able to step into the models,' she excitedly wrote from Chartwell to a friend, 'as by the time I got home I weighed (in a state of Nature) 8 stone 9lbs!'[85]

Mirroring his wife's attire, Churchill also greeted the Kennedys clad in his tweeds, which Rose thought made him look more like a country squire than an English statesman. The group walked into the house together, across the entrance hall with its cream walls and black tiled floor and then descended the main stairs to the dining room. They made their way across the cold stone floor towards the large rush mats, on each of which was a circular table made from scrubbed oak. The slightly larger of the two tables was the one at the far end of the long, narrow room. Its positioning meant it was surrounded by windows, which perfectly showcased Chartwell's gardens and grounds. It was also flooded with light, even on grey days. Churchill directed the group to the larger table and each pulled out their chair to take a seat.

Churchill had a particular strength of feeling about dining room chairs, so much so that he wrote a dissertation on what the ideal one should be like. It should 'be comfortable and give support to the body when sitting up straight' and 'it should certainly have arms which are an enormous comfort when sitting at meals'. He also disliked it when arms and legs spread, 'as if it were a plant'. By being narrow in their design, 'this enables the chairs to be put close together if need be, which is often more sociable'.[86] He presented his dissertation to Clementine, with a suggestion that all their existing dining chairs be sold, along with those of a similar purpose for around the house. Instead, they should have 20 new ones made to his specifications. The 12 intended for the dining room could then be covered with a fabric of Clementine's choosing. She selected Warner's 'Arum Lily' design in ivory and green, which complemented the cream walls and emerald green curtains perfectly.

With Churchill having much to say, and little time, the group skipped the pleasantries that often dominate first meetings. Instead, Churchill quickly made his case to Kennedy that Britain and the USA should develop a shared naval force. If they could do so, it would create a force of such strength that they would be able to police the world's waters and use their combined might for the purpose of collective security. 'That idea dominated Churchill's mind,' Rose later wrote, 'and was his way of solving the conquest of the rising Nazi strength.'[87] Churchill acknowledged, however, that this would be a very difficult idea to sell in America, as there were too many isolationists, especially in the Midwest. He also told the Kennedys that he thought that the number of those of Irish descent who hated the English would be a barrier to acceptance of the idea. This was perhaps an ill-advised remark, given that Kennedy was the grandson of Irish immigrants, who had arrived in the United States less than a century before, and he was fiercely proud of his heritage.[88]

Unfortunately for Churchill, his manner of persuasion wasn't terribly appealing to the Kennedys. Afterwards, they compared their time at Chartwell with a dinner they had with Churchill's friend Lord Beaverbrook, who had been inquisitive, curious and seemed captivated by his guests. Churchill, however, simply held court. Rose said that he 'talked expansively, narrating, explaining and trying to convince us of the wisdom of his points'.[89]

One area of interest, particularly for Clementine, was around public perceptions of the President's wife, Eleanor Roosevelt. She had heard rumours that the First Lady was an 'exhibitionist' who was 'using her husband's high office to court publicity for herself', and was keen to know whether Rose thought this was true.[90] 'I tried to convince her that I thought Mrs Roosevelt was sincere,' Rose later recalled, 'and I felt people would accept her in her self-appointed role, would value her sincerity and unselfish devotion to the common man.'[91]

After lunch, during a break in the rain, the group made the journey down the garden path towards Churchill's painting studio. He showed his guests several unfinished paintings, amidst those completed canvases that adorned the walls. The ones he was working on were still lifes of flowers and fruits, since he was unable to do his preferred painting *en plein air* during the autumnal downpours. By the early 1930s Churchill had painted more than 300 oil-on-canvas landscapes, seascapes, still lifes and portraits, most of which were at Chartwell, with the exception of those he gave to friends as gifts. His love of bright colours meant that walking into his studio was like entering a kaleidoscope. Churchill, the keen-to-impress amateur artist, would stand by, hopeful of praise from his guests, but could be very critical of his paintings, often uttering to guests that a particular work was 'Not one of the best'. His painting was probably the only area of his life where he felt like he was forever the student, so much so that he once wrote, 'When I get to heaven I mean to spend a considerable portion of my first million years in painting, and so get to the bottom of the subject.'[92] From the Studio, the group went to see the walls that Churchill had built. 'It seemed a queer avocation for a man to have,' Rose reflected, 'but there was his hobby and there was the wall to bear mute testimony.'

Following the group's farewells, the Kennedys drove away from Chartwell and back towards London. The Churchills continued with their afternoon ahead of the arrival of Professor Lindmann, who was due at 5pm. Churchill headed upstairs for his usual afternoon nap and felt positive about the meeting, having decided to introduce Joe to a number of his friends and political allies. He was confident that he had forged a new transatlantic alliance with Kennedy, who had appeared interested in his idea for joint action against Nazi Germany. His belief was reinforced by the follow-up note Kennedy sent to Baruch, which read 'rose and i had most pleasant time we have ever had at churchills thank you appreciate it more than i can tell you back here in a couple of weeks seeing him again.'[93] It appeared that the meeting had made an impact on Kennedy, and the hope was that their discussions would resume later in the month.

After a week in England, the Kennedys crossed the Channel for meetings in France, Switzerland and Holland, following which they would return to England before travelling back to the United States early in November. Before they left London, Churchill followed up, as promised, with an enthusiastic letter confirming, 'I have invited a distinguished company to meet you on the 28th and have already a great many acceptances.'[94] Unfortunately, Kennedy's son John Fitzgerald Kennedy, known to the family as Jack but whom history would later know as 'JFK', had become seriously ill in London with hepatitis. He was swiftly hospitalised, and so the European tour was cut short. Kennedy returned to London, cabled Jack's doctors in the States, and was advised that he was probably suffering from a relapse of the 'agranulocytosis' which had left him hospitalised on a previous occasion.[95] 'I am deeply grieved about your son,' Churchill's letter continued, 'and earnestly trust it will soon be relieved.' He continued, 'Of course you must not think of being at all hampered by this engagement. On the whole however I think it would be well to carry on.'[96] A week later, Kennedy replied but not as Churchill had hoped. 'After a week of great concern and anxiety, I have sent my boy back to America,' he wrote, concluding, 'I propose to follow him on Wednesday.'[97]

The disappointment Churchill felt was considerable, as he was denied the opportunity to cement this new and exciting political alliance, but he had other ideas of how he could further his plans for a transatlantic naval agreement. He began working on his campaign material ahead of the General Election on 14 November 1935, including a printed manifesto which was distributed to his constituents. The four-sided pamphlet, adorned on the front with a smiling photograph of Churchill, and written at Chartwell, opened with achievements of the last four years under the National Government, comprising Conservative, Liberal and Labour representatives. In it he briefly acknowledged the Government's policy on India, which he called 'unwise'. He did, however, concede, 'The India question has now passed from debate into experiment', before adding, 'It is our duty to give that experiment a fair chance.'[98] The bulk of the message with which he hoped to win the votes of his constituents was on the subject of national defence, with most of the focus on the Navy. 'We have still a powerful navy, and our officers and seamen are of the highest quality. But the ships are wearing out,' the pamphlet read, 'and many are outclassed by the new ships which other countries have already built and are rapidly building.'

Perhaps most telling, in this vital piece of campaign literature, which he knew was one of the few ways he could share his views with all his constituents, is the reference he made to the USA. Writing it in his study at Chartwell just days after the afternoon he spent with Joseph P. Kennedy, and ahead of a crucial election, he declared:

It would be shameful to send our men to sea in vessels which will soon be no match for foreign ships. We must rebuild our Fleet

*9. Joseph P. Kennedy
on board the* Queen
Mary, *June 1938.*

and fit it with all the appliances which modern science can devise. In this – and not in this only – we must keep in the closest touch with the United States of America, whose Navy is as important to the peace of the world as our own.[99]

In inviting Joe Kennedy and his wife to Chartwell, Churchill assumed that he had the optimal setting and situation to charm the pair. He felt confident that he had successfully argued the case for 'the Special Relationship' and how it could be applied to the cause of freedom from tyranny. But this meeting was one where Churchill ultimately failed in his mission. Reflecting on this time years later, Churchill wrote, 'All this while the United States remained intensely preoccupied with its own vehement internal affairs and economic problems.'[100] This wider political context, and Churchill's failure to build a rapport with Kennedy in their few hours together at Chartwell, meant that their relationship never quite recovered from this initial wrong-footing. The pair became wary of each other over the coming years, especially once it became apparent that Kennedy had no intention of supporting Churchill's stance against Hitler and Nazi Germany. 'Maybe I do him an injustice,' Kennedy later wrote of Churchill, 'but I just don't trust him.'[101]

CHAPTER 4

THE CASE FOR FRANCE

Pierre-Étienne Flandin, 21–22 November 1936

In the year that followed the Conservative Party's victory in the 1935 General Election, and with no ministerial post having been offered, Winston Churchill despaired at his continuing political isolation. With little influence in Parliament, his country home became a meeting place for fellow parliamentarians who opposed the policies of the National Government. As the year wore on, he also sought to strengthen alliances across his international networks. His reputation for being a 'Francophile', as Adolf Hitler once called him, was cemented in the increasingly close relationship he had with Pierre-Étienne Flandin, the Prime Minister of France from November 1934 to May 1935. Later calling him 'the French statesman with whom I had the closest personal contacts before the war',[1] Churchill became reliant on Flandin in the mid-1930s as a fellow believer in the power of Franco-British joint action against Hitler's increasingly aggressive foreign policy. It was their genuine friendship and rapport that meant Churchill was the first political figure that Flandin went to after Germany's invasion of the Rhineland, despite still being in the depths of his political wilderness.

The decision by the Prime Minister, Stanley Baldwin, to call a General Election was made on 18 October 1935. Two weeks earlier, the Italian army under Benito Mussolini had invaded Ethiopia, then known as Abyssinia, and forced the country's Emperor Haile Selassie into exile. The chosen timing of the election was heavily influenced by

10. Pierre-Étienne Flandin, former Prime Minister of France, 1937.

the worsening international situation. British public opinion demanded action against Italy and the Government knew that if it failed to participate in collective action, a wave of ill feeling could sweep it from power. Baldwin reportedly consulted no one beforehand about the decision, and announced his call for an election the next day.[2]

A complicating factor was the Government's anxieties over Anglo-French relations at this time. A Franco-Italian Accord had been signed earlier that year, as Italian support in the event of war with Germany was seen as vital for France. As a result, on 7 October, Pierre-Étienne Flandin, now no longer Prime Minister, attended a secret meeting with Hugh Lloyd Thomas, the deputy to the British Ambassador in Paris. There, Flandin explained that the French Government would do little beyond modest economic sanctions against Italy following the invasion.[3] The British Foreign Office took Flandin's disclosure as confirmation that France might not give

Britain an unequivocal promise of armed assistance. A week later, the French Prime Minister, Pierre Laval, said that France could only aid Britain if Italy attacked a British naval force in the Mediterranean. Meanwhile, private offers of armed assistance were made by the French on 18 October, but only if Britain publicly disavowed the heftier sanctions advocated by the League of Nations. Torn between British public opinion, national security and international diplomacy, it is perhaps little wonder that Baldwin, on that very day, decided that there had to be an election.

As a result, Churchill suddenly found himself with an election to contest. Despite needing to give additional time and energy to his constituency, he continued his campaign against Nazi Germany through his articles, including the boldly titled 'The Truth about Hitler'.[4] It described how Adolf Hitler had turned the German spirit of despair, in the aftermath of the First World War, to one of revenge. 'At the same time,' he argued, 'the English pacifists, aided from a safe distance by their American prototypes, forced the process of disarmament into the utmost prominence.'[5] He also described how Germany's efforts to regain armed power had actually begun under the previous government of Heinrich Brüning, who had been Chancellor of Germany from 1930 to 1932. But Churchill was keen to separate Brüning from any association with the Nazi Government, and stressed that he had been driven out by them 'under threat of murder, from German soil'.[6] The German Ambassador in London was outraged by what Churchill had written, especially the derogatory remarks and direct attacks on Hitler.[7] Newspaper reports about the Nazi Government's reaction to the article appeared in publications all over the world, and the magazine in which it had featured was banned in Germany indefinitely as a result.

Meanwhile, back in his own constituency, Churchill was very likely nervous of the outcome when the votes were counted. The campaign had not been an easy one, and there were several local meetings where he faced considerable hostility, but he needn't have worried. Not only did he win, but he did so with the largest majority of his career, securing 59 per cent of the vote. But any hopes that such a resounding victory would lead to a return to government were soon disappointed. 'Clemmie tells me that Winston has not yet been approached', Harold Nicolson wrote in his diary on 21 November. 'He has got tickets for Bali, where, if not offered a Cabinet job, he proposes to spend the winter.'[8]

Life at Chartwell remained eventful during this time. Randolph appeared in newspaper headlines for a speeding fine he received on a drive between Chartwell and London.[9] Sarah, meanwhile, had begun her career on the stage, taking part as a member of the chorus in a revue called *Follow the Sun*. After seeing the first show in Manchester, Clementine wrote to her former secretary with a rather mixed review, saying, 'I'm really very proud of her tho I would rather she were not on the stage.'[10] Despite the remark to Harold Nicolson, no Bali trip materialised that winter, but the Churchills did travel, nonetheless. Their holiday would take them across Europe instead, but first, Churchill arranged to meet Pierre-Étienne Flandin for lunch in Paris on 10 December.

The relationship between Churchill and the former French Prime Minister was something of a slow burn. The pair most likely first met when Churchill was Secretary of State for War and Air between 1919 and 1921, with Flandin holding the government office in charge of French aviation for much of that time. Flandin had been considered a rising star in French politics, with headlines such as 'M. Flandin the Next Premier?' featuring in English newspapers since 1933.[11] Churchill equally had his eyes cast to the other side of the English Channel, famously exclaiming, 'Thank God for the French Army' in March of that year.[12] He returned to the same theme a month later, declaring, 'France is not only the sole great surviving democracy in Europe; she is also the strongest military power, I am glad to say, and she is the head of a system of States and nations.'[13]

It was upon the announcement of his appointment as Prime Minister in 1934 that a telegram was sent to Flandin from both Winston and Clementine Churchill. 'We beg of you to accept our sincere congratulations on the great task you have so bravely assumed',[14] the couple wrote, which was soon followed by an in-person meeting at a Foreign Office banquet in February 1935. Nicknamed 'the Skyscraper', Flandin was a difficult person to miss at any party, given that he was 6 feet 4 inches tall and broadly built. He was also the youngest Prime Minister in the history of France and brought a fresh approach to his office. He reportedly avoided newspapers, much preferring to hear the news on the radio while shaving each morning.[15] Churchill deemed Flandin a man of 'calm strength',[16] but his premiership proved short-lived and by the summer of 1935 his Government was defeated as a result of a financial crisis. Churchill wrote to Flandin a month after the defeat, emphasising his personal faith in the Anglo-French entente, especially given the growing threat from Germany to both nations. 'I feel greatly the dangers which menace both our countries, and indeed what is still called civilisation', Churchill wrote of the rise of Nazi Germany. 'But I cannot shake off that feeling which I have always had for the last quarter of a century, namely that England and France will somehow or other come through them together.'[17]

His stirring words might well have been inspired by a letter he had received from Ava Wigram, a friend of his, and the wife of his loyal informant Ralph Wigram. She had contacted Churchill at the end of June, telling him that Flandin was due to visit England soon, and perhaps he should invite the former French Prime Minister for a meeting. Reading her note at Chartwell, he agreed that it was a good idea. 'I think I could make a small agreeable circle around him,' Churchill wrote to Ava on 2 July 1935, 'of which I hope you and your husband would form an invaluable link.'[18] It was agreed that Ava would act as the intermediary, and pass the invitation on to Flandin.

It was from his home in Yonne, in the countryside south-east of Paris, that Flandin opened the invitation to Chartwell. He did so in some pain, as he had recently broken his arm in a car accident, and so feared this might delay any meeting between the two men. A trip to England in October or November seemed much more realistic. 'I would be even more desirous to meet you as events seem to evolve quite rapidly and unpleasantly in regards to peace and Franco-British relations', Flandin wrote to Churchill. He also noted that he had been closely watching the progress of Churchill's campaign against disarmament, and done so with much admiration. 'I have followed constantly your courageous political action. The facts alone show that you are right.'[19] Having to wait until the autumn, however, was far from ideal, and perhaps if Churchill was in France over the summer, Flandin suggested the pair might be able to meet then. When Flandin heard of Churchill's re-election in November 1935, he penned a note of congratulations. 'We read here, in the newspapers, with great hope that you will get into government at the occasion of its reshuffle', Flandin wrote, noting too that many of his own political allies were hopeful of him being offered a role in Cabinet very soon.[20] However, the newly re-elected Prime Minister, Stanley Baldwin, faced a difficult task in choosing his new ministerial colleagues. 'Every member of the gov'mt has come back with the exception of two of our labour colleagues', he remarked to his old friend, Edward Winterton. 'I am therefore much in the position of the President of a University Boat Club who finds his crew all coming into residence for a second year!'[21]

Suspecting that there was likely to be little movement in the new Cabinet, Churchill wrote to Flandin, saying, 'I do not think it likely that Mr Baldwin will require my help now he has got so good a majority.' He reflected on his continuing place, out of high political office, and remarked, 'I think I can perhaps do some useful work from my corner seat below the gangway and am very content with that position.'[22] Churchill then recognised that a visit by Flandin to England was unlikely to happen soon owing to ongoing difficulties with his arm injury. He wrote, 'I hope your health will be so far restored that you can visit us in the Spring,' adding that a visit to Chartwell in the new year 'will do far more justice to my landscape than this sombre season.'[23]

Given that Churchill was planning a winter trip, which involved a stop in Paris on the way, he suggested the pair meet then. 'I would come over by the early morning aeroplane (or possibly the night before) in the hopes that you could spare me an hour.'[24] Unfortunately, Flandin wasn't available, but he too hoped to arrange a meeting as soon as possible. If there was any chance Churchill could postpone his visit by a day or two, Flandin said he could pick him up from Le Bourget airport and then the pair could go for lunch. 'Also, should you want to meet other politicians, you would just have to tell me which ones and I will ask them to join us', Flandin kindly offered.[25]

With this added incentive, Churchill quickly changed his plans. The date was set and the pair would meet for lunch on 10 December, at Flandin's home, at 139 Boulevard Malesherbes in Paris.

While Churchill arranged his meeting with the former French Prime Minister, the dust continued to settle on the outcome of the general election. While Churchill managed to convey an air of contentment to those around him, Clementine showed due annoyance on her husband's behalf. 'I think Mr Baldwin is revengeful over the Indian controversy and now that <u>he</u> has this enormous majority in the country, does not mean to put him in the Government', Clementine wrote to her former secretary. Resigned to their fate for the foreseeable future, she simply remarked, 'Let's hope that they will really set about getting modern aeroplanes and getting the fleet ship-shape.'[26]

The Churchills travelled firstly to Paris, then Barcelona. While he was there, Randolph sent his father an urgent telegram declaring, 'Heavy rearmament inevitable and this your best reentry card. Earnestly beg you stay Barcelona.'[27] The reason for the urgent plea to stay away was a scheduled debate in the House of Commons on the League of Nations and Abyssinia. 'You will be in a unique position of strength,' Randolph wrote more calmly the next day, 'since you will neither have supported the Government, compromised yourself by hostility, nor taken the negative though semi-hostile line of abstention.'[28] The Churchills then boarded a ship from Barcelona to Mallorca, before parting ways. Winston continued on to Morocco, joined later by Randolph, Diana and her new husband Duncan. 'They are so happy', he wrote of his eldest daughter and new son-in-law. 'They say it is a second honeymoon.'[29]

Clementine returned to England for Christmas at Blenheim Palace, before swiftly departing again for a skiing holiday in Austria with her daughter Mary and her niece Clarissa. Churchill, meanwhile, stayed at Hotel Mamounia in Marrakesh, calling it 'one of the best I have ever used'.[30] He marvelled at the 12-foot-deep balcony which gave him plenty of room to paint the glorious views and also a beautiful spot to read the French newspapers and thereby keep abreast of all the goings-on in politics there. 'The French have come a long way with us against Mussolini and they will expect a similar service when the far greater peril of Hitler becomes active', he told Clementine at the end of December.[31] Underneath the section of the letter typed by his secretary was a handwritten note penned by Churchill to his wife on New Year's Eve. In it he wrote that he had been offered a bet of £2,000 by his friend Lord Rothermere if he went teetotal in 1936. Churchill had first refused, telling Clementine that 'life would not be worth living'.[32] He had, however, accepted the next best bet, not to drink any brandy or undiluted spirits in 1936, for a mere £600.

'I miss my Pig very much', Clementine wrote to her husband a week later from her hotel in Zürs in Austria. Her letter continued and she began to reflect on the political situation. 'I really would not like you to serve under Baldwin,' she wrote, 'unless he really gave you a great deal of power.'[33] In a letter to Clementine the next day, Churchill seemed at peace, for now at least, with his political fate. He reflected on the words of his ancestor, the Duke of Marlborough, from 1708: 'As I think most things are settled by destiny, when one has done one's best, the only thing is to await the result with patience.'[34]

For a time, Chartwell remained quiet, and a stillness fell upon the house. 'When he was in a place, the whole place seemed to vibrate with life,' Kathleen Hill, another secretary of Churchill's later recalled, 'but when he was away it was as still as death.'[35] This soon changed with the news on 20 January of the death of King George V. Churchill had thought he would travel back via Paris, where he had been invited to the Paris Chamber of Commerce to speak at their annual dinner on 30 January.[36] He had been urged by the Ambassador to attend, but the period of national mourning had begun, and so he dashed back to Chartwell. All his plans to strengthen his relations with French political counterparts had to wait. This proved to be a wise decision, as the day after he arrived back to Chartwell, the Prime Minister's Principal Private Secretary wrote to him asking him to be one of the MPs present for the Address of the House, to the King, at Buckingham Palace. Despite the appearance of favour from the Prime Minister, Churchill remained uncertain of what awaited him. Just a few days after returning to England, he wrote to a friend, 'I have no idea what the future has in store for me, but you will find me vigorously advocating our rearmament while time remains by every channel that is open.'[37]

For the last week of January, the week of the state funeral itself, Churchill's engagement diary showed a packed schedule of official engagements, alongside dinners and lunches with close friends and confidants. That weekend he returned to Chartwell, and it was from his bitterly cold study at Chartwell that he wrote to the new King, Edward VIII, sending his condolences. The heartfelt note promised his faithful service, and declared that 'in the long swing of events Your Majesty's name will shine in history as the bravest and best beloved of all the sovereigns who have worn the island Crown'.[38]

Meanwhile, Churchill once again felt downhearted about the political situation. In declining an invitation to speak at a constituency fête later in the year, he wrote: 'I do not know where I shall be in August, or how I shall feel about politics – or indeed where we shall any of us be!'[39] As Churchill despaired, he called into his confidence a group that he had come to rely on, who were known at the time as 'the Churchill Group'. According to Churchill, they 'met regularly and to a large extent pooled our information'.[40] Each of them had known Churchill for years and, though not always in agreement, there was a foundation of trust and a shared belief by 1936 that urgent action against Germany was necessary. 'All of us were obsessed with the German peril and the nakedness of our country to meet it,' one of the group later wrote, 'and Winston was galvanic in collecting the latest information to place before us.'[41] It was this coalescing and sharing of records, documents, statistics and intelligence which meant the meetings had to be far from prying eyes. Despite efforts to undermine and discredit the group, they met a dozen times over the course of two years, each taking their turn to host dinners at their homes, or in the private rooms of London hotels and restaurants. Invitations for the first meeting of 1936 were sent out on Monday 17 February, with the urgency made apparent by the fact it was scheduled to take place just five days later, at Chartwell.

Not all of the invitees were able to join, but the final list included some of Churchill's most trusted allies. They hadn't all shared his stance on India, but were united in fear of the Nazi threat. Previous cabinet ministers were among those who journeyed to Chartwell that weekend, including Austen Chamberlain, the former Foreign Secretary, and Robert Horne, former Chancellor of the Exchequer. Edward Grigg, the former Governor of Kenya, joined the group, as well as two Members of Parliament who had yet to hold ministerial roles but had shown sufficient loyalty to Churchill to date. Henry Page Croft, the MP for Bournemouth, was invited, having been one of Churchill's staunchest supporters throughout the India debate. 'Thanks for your invite', Page Croft's hastily written note replied. 'Will arrive about 6pm Saturday and stay till Monday.'[42] Bob Boothby, Churchill's former Parliamentary Private Secretary during his years as Chancellor, was the youngest attendee, having just turned 36. The last person on the list was the ever-present Professor Lindemann. Clementine was still skiing in Zürs, and so it truly was 'a man's party', as Austen Chamberlain later described it.

In his element as host, Churchill ushered the group of friends to the dining table. The possible creation of a new Minister of Defence role in Government was at the forefront of all the attendees' minds. Austen Chamberlain had spoken on the subject in Parliament that week and received much praise for his speech. Churchill was said to have 'showed study, genius, power of drive and imagination' over the course of their discussions that night at Chartwell which, in his guests' eyes, positioned him as a Minister of Defence in waiting.[43] 'Winston Churchill, whose speech in private conversation is like Niagara, a ceaseless torrent', Henry Page Croft later remarked. 'The man who would "butt in" must be very agile with Winston, but as the stuff is so good Winston can always be forgiven.'[44]

There was also agreement among those present that a dangerous year awaited for Europe. They complained of the lacklustre approach of those in power, which meant it would be difficult to ensure adequate preparedness before action needed to be taken. The next morning, Austen Chamberlain was sat at the writing desk in Chartwell's drawing room and penned a note to his sister, saying: 'Committees grind & grind but their wheels move very slowly.' He added that he might write a book on the subject one day, and would title one chapter 'Baldwin – the Idle Man'.[45] All of the group stayed overnight except for Edward Grigg, and so he was the only one not to sign Chartwell's visitors' book. 'I enjoyed it immensely,' Grigg wrote to Churchill afterwards, 'talk, food, drink, setting – all equally delightful and stimulating.'[46] The other attendees all later reflected fondly on their time at Churchill's Kent home, including Bob Boothby, who remarked, 'I couldn't have enjoyed it more'.[47] Churchill too seemed positive about the meeting. 'All enjoyed themselves', he told Clementine. 'The house was warm, the food good, the beds soft, & the cat made herself most agreeable to Austen.'[48] Meanwhile, Austen reflected, 'there were almost as many opinions as men, but on one thing we were all agreed – that Germany was a danger, the one danger that might be fatal to us, & that that danger had been too long neglected.'[49] Despite the pessimism of the group, Churchill did have reason for optimism. His emerging ally, Pierre-Étienne Flandin, had recently been appointed as France's Foreign Minister. Not only that, but the Franco-Soviet Mutual Assistance Pact, which had been signed by Flandin in May 1935, was then ratified on 27 February 1936. This became the spark that ignited Hitler's next move, and consequently there were few people Churchill wanted to speak to more than Flandin, but first, he had to speak to the man who hoped to win his approval to marry his daughter, the pair having met just a few months earlier.

When Sarah began performing on the stage at the age of 21, she later reflected that 'suddenly my life had meaning'.[50] Her years of practising at Chartwell had led her to a successful career, one which Churchill had played his part to help with. When Sarah had her first audition, she was forced to admit that she was there without her parents' permission. When this proved to be a deal-breaker to the casting director, she told her father, who immediately wrote to him saying that she had studied with perseverance and determination for two years and he would be especially grateful if she could be given another chance.[51]

A friend of hers from the time remarked that 'She had a ferocious singleness of purpose – her love for the stage was intense.'[52] But little known to Churchill, part of the reason for her zeal was the star of the

*11. Sarah Churchill emerging
from the ground floor of the
nursery wing at Chartwell to
greet her chocolate-coloured
spaniel, Trouble, mid-1930s. Her
bedroom was the south-facing,
bay-windowed room above.*

show, Vic Oliver, with whom she quickly fell in love. He too became
devoted to her, but Sarah feared that her desire to marry Oliver would
affect her relationship with her parents, 'which had hitherto been
cloudless and happy'.[53] She was right to suspect things wouldn't go
smoothly. A meeting between Churchill and Oliver took place in
February 1936 and he took an instant dislike to the 'common as dirt'
36-year-old who arrived at his door.[54] Churchill wrote to Clementine
afterwards in his own hand, which was a rare sign of something too
personal for the secretaries to type. He remarked of Oliver's 'foul
austro-yankee drawl', and mocked how he called Sarah the 'brainiest
& sweetest gurl'.[55] Churchill made his feelings clear to Oliver. 'I told
him that if there was an engagement, it would force me to make an
immediate public statement in terms which would be painful to them
both', he told Clementine, at which point Oliver apparently got up
and left, followed by Sarah. Churchill asked Diana to reason with her

sister, following which Sarah told her family that the engagement was off. 'In my talks to her on the telephone she seems calm & in fairly good spirits', Churchill reflected after the dust seemed to have settled. 'I don't think there is any immediate cause to worry.'[56] For now at least, all seemed well with the Churchills' middle daughter. Clementine was relieved that the issue had passed, remarking that 'Sarah must have been more than stage struck – in the middle ages it would be thought she was bewitched.'[57]

At the same time as his ill-fated meeting with Oliver, Churchill became resigned to his continuing place on the backbenches of Westminster. 'Evidently B[aldwin] desires above all things to avoid bringing me in . . . But his own position is much shaken, & the storm clouds gather', he wrote to Clementine.[58] Fortunately, the tide had begun to turn in terms of military preparedness. On 25 February 1936, the Cabinet approved a report that called for expansion of the Royal Navy, as well as the re-equipping of the British Army.

At Chartwell, the return of Clementine and Mary from Austria created a sense of a full house again, though frustrations resulting from their staffing difficulties continued. Another of the kitchen-maids handed in her notice and Mrs Black, the new cook, was already advertising again for weekend help.[59] Meanwhile, more bad luck struck when Churchill discovered that one of his black swans, Jupiter, had died.[60] She had been at Chartwell for ten years and great efforts had been made to keep her and her companions safe. This included a contraption Churchill had made himself to keep the foxes away, which consisted of a light on a wheel that would then circle round throughout the night.[61] There was some good news, however. Senior political figures had begun to consider a return of Churchill to the government, in the newly created role of Minister of Defence. A friend of his quoted a conversation she had with Neville Chamberlain, the Chancellor of the Exchequer, where he said, 'Of course if it is a question of military efficiency, Winston is no doubt the man.'[62] His hopes began to rise that he might be brought back into the fold, and on 3 March he wrote to Clementine, 'If I get it, I will work faithfully before God & man for Peace, & not allow pride or excitement to sway my spirit.'[63] Events, however, moved quickly in Europe.

The ratification by France of the Franco-Russian mutual assistance pact gave Germany the excuse it needed to break the terms of the Locarno Pact, an agreement signed by France, Great Britain, Germany, Belgium and Italy in 1925. All signatories had given mutual guarantees of the territorial status quo, including the demilitarisation of the Rhineland, an area of land intended to act as a buffer between France and Belgium on one side, and Germany on the other. On the morning of Saturday 7 March 1936, Germany's Foreign Minister informed the Ambassadors of Great Britain, France, Belgium and Italy that the Locarno Pact was now considered invalid and that German troops were in the process of occupying the Rhineland as a symbol of their sovereignty, a decision which Adolf Hitler said had followed 'a difficult internal struggle'.[64]

Hitler made a speech at midday in the Reichstag, which attacked the Treaty of Versailles and 'the unreal connection which appeared to exist between the discrimination of the German Volk by Versailles and the interests of the French'.[65] He then described how he had tried in vain to build 'a bridge of understanding to the people of France' and, referencing the Locarno Pact, added 'Germany's contribution to this Pact presented the greatest sacrifice. While France fortified its border with steel, cement and arms, and equipped it with numerous garrisons, we were made to bear the burden of permanently maintaining total defencelessness in the West.'[66] It was, therefore, according to Hitler, for Germany's 'primal right of a people to safeguard its borders and maintain its possibilities of defence' that the German Reich Government had 're-established the full and unlimited sovereignty of the Reich in the demilitarised zone of the Rhineland.'[67] Upon hearing that German forces had entered the Rhineland, Churchill immediately wrote to Pierre-Étienne Flandin.

The letter to France's Foreign Minister was dictated by Churchill to his secretary and marked 'Confidential'. There were no pleasantries, and instead he sent a simple request for information with two main lines of enquiry. The first was to ask for confirmation of the French estimates around the present strength of the German Air Force. Churchill's own estimates were that the Nazis had 1,200 machines at that point in time, and that this would increase to 1,500 by June and reach 2,000 by the end of the year. The second was an enquiry around French expenditure on aviation in 1935. 'I wish to check my information on both these points for the purpose of the debates about to take place in Parliament', Churchill confided in Flandin, revealing that he was due to speak on 10 March.[68] He promised he would not disclose the source of the information, and suggested that a cipher message through the French Embassy would probably be the best way of answering him. He then reassured Flandin that he hoped he wasn't creating any difficulty in sending those requests, and that if it wasn't possible, he would understand completely. Flandin replied the very next day, enclosing all the information Churchill had requested.[69] What Churchill may not have realised was that preparations were already under way for the newly appointed Foreign Secretary Anthony Eden, the Lord Privy Seal Lord Halifax and Churchill's confidant Ralph Wigram to fly to France on 9 March for an urgent meeting with French officials, including Flandin.

While these talks took place in Paris, Churchill gave his speech in Parliament on Tuesday 10 March regarding his proposal for the establishment of a Ministry of Supply. 'This work should have begun in vigour three years ago', Churchill pleaded. 'All I urge is, Do it now.'[70] Churchill was due to be in London for the next few days, but Wigram's return from Paris on 11 March resulted in the urgent suggestion that the pair speak in private, where there was no possibility of them being overheard. As a result, Wigram travelled out to Churchill's country home that evening. Seated together at Chartwell's dining table, Wigram said that Flandin wanted immediate action, including, if necessary, the immediate ejection of German troops from the Rhineland by force, as well as sanctions towards Germany. He continued, telling Churchill that Eden had opposed the use of force, but agreed to reconvene in London a few days later for further talks. The next morning Flandin was in London, and Churchill drove up from Chartwell first thing so the pair could meet at his flat in Morpeth Mansions. Flandin told him that he proposed to demand from the British Government simultaneous mobilisation of the land, sea and air forces of both countries.[71] Churchill was impressed by

Flandin's determination, but felt that there was little he could do from his detached, private position. All he could do was to wish Flandin 'all success' for his mission over the coming days.

Another meeting was quickly arranged for 13 March in order that Flandin could update Churchill on his progress. 'Flandin is dining with me Friday night at 8.15pm,' Churchill wrote to Austen Chamberlain, 'Pls do come.'[72] It was on that same day that the Prime Minister, Stanley Baldwin, created the new office of Minister for Co-ordination of Defence. Any hopes Churchill had held that the appointment might be his were immediately dashed when Sir Thomas Inskip, a lawyer with no military experience, was appointed.

At the dinner between Churchill, Flandin and Austen Chamberlain, the three men came up with a strategy. Churchill urged Flandin to demand an interview with Stanley Baldwin. Meanwhile, he and Chamberlain were due to speak at an event in Birmingham the next day, which they felt certain would garner media coverage. In his speech, Churchill declared that the triumph of the Nazi regime in the Rhineland meant that 'events would continue to roll and slide remorselessly downhill towards the pit in which Western civilisation might be fatally engulfed'.[73] Austen Chamberlain, meanwhile, championed his old friend by publicly saying, 'Mr Churchill has great courage and infinite energy, and great and wide experience of the matters of defence, and there will be many of the House of Commons who regret that Mr Baldwin has not thought fit to call him to that new office, for which he has greater qualifications than any living politician.'[74] Their thinking had been correct and both speeches received coverage in national newspapers. Unfortunately, Flandin's efforts with the Prime Minister had not gone so well. His pleas fell on deaf ears, with Baldwin stressing that public opinion was against any kind of Anglo-French intervention, and reportedly declaring 'England is not in a state to go to war'.[75]

At a meeting on 17 March of the December Club, a group of around 20 political figures who regularly met for dinner in the House of Commons, Flandin was invited as the guest of honour. 'He has got all his thoughts perfectly in the right order,' Harold Nicolson wrote to his wife, Vita Sackville-West, 'and he deploys his procession of argument quite gently but firmly, like a nun escorting a crocodile of foundlings to church.[76] His boldest remark of the evening was that if the British Government broke its word, 'the world will be shown that violence is the only political factor which counts, and Germany, as the most powerful single force on the Continent, will become the mistress of Europe'.[77]

Churchill had dined elsewhere with Lord Winterton but joined some of the group later in the smoking room. There he described the duty they all had to generations yet unborn in deciding what future awaited between Britain and Germany.[78] Unfortunately for his French ally, much of the discussion in the days and weeks that followed accused France of 'warmongering'. There were those who thought that any state of crisis that had arisen was due to France's response to Germany's remilitarisation of the Rhineland. Members of Parliament had used the time to test the water in their constituencies and ascertained that there was little appetite for another war. As a result, the campaign by the French was seen as one of coercion. 'A pro-French policy hasn't a hope,' one MP remarked at the time, 'the whole country is pro-German.'[79]

Flandin returned to France, Churchill returned to Chartwell, and the crisis seemed averted in the short term, with the likes of Lord Lothian declaring that Germany had simply walked into her own backyard.[80] Sarah Churchill recalled her father's mood darkening further at this time. He would stand at the edge of the terrace lawn and shout, 'In twenty short minutes the enemy, on leaving the coast of France, can be overhead, menacing, in a way never before contemplated, the security of our island!', which she said caused a fear to grip her heart.[81] But life at Chartwell carried on, as it always did. Another parlourmaid came and went.[82] The dogs, including the well-named 'Trouble', Sarah's chocolate-coloured spaniel, remained troublesome. Arguably the greatest impact came when Churchill's long-standing secretary Mrs Pearman suffered a nasty fall at Chartwell, which required her to stay in bed until she had recovered. 'If you are not insured I will pay for any necessary scientific treatment that is required,' Churchill reassured her, 'and your salary of course will continue during this illness.'[83] This put extra pressure on his second secretary, Miss Hamblin. 'I remember when Mrs Pearman had been ill for about six weeks and I'd been struggling on alone, and I felt awfully tired', she later recalled. She asked if she could seek support from an agency secretary until Mrs Pearman was back at Chartwell. Churchill initially agreed but appeared to have misunderstood what she proposed. When she bid him goodnight and said the temporary secretary would be with him the following day, he had forgotten and was horrified. 'He did feel that he was in the wilderness,' Miss Hamblin said, 'and in Chartwell he felt that it was a very enclosed circle somehow, and he didn't want intruders.'[84]

Miss Hamblin's exhaustion was justified: she worked seven days a week from 8.30am until the early hours of the morning. The Churchills' Kent home was rapidly becoming a repository of military intelligence, housing secret estimates of German air strength. In June 1936 this included Flandin's notes, which Churchill sent to Sir Thomas Inskip, the newly appointed Minister of Defence.[85] Chartwell also continued to host Ralph and Ava Wigram, who brought with them Ralph's own observations and notes as well as confidential Foreign Office memorandums, white papers about disarmament, examples of Nazi political propaganda, extracts from speeches by German ministers, copies of despatches by ambassadors, and much more. Often, as soon as these secret documents reached Chartwell, Churchill would give them to Professor Lindemann, who would drive them immediately to Oxford, photograph them, develop copies in his own dark room, and then drive them at great speed back to Chartwell so the originals could be returned to the Foreign Office before certain parties noticed their absence.[86] 'It is such a privilege and encouragement for me to hear your views,' Wigram wrote to Churchill. 'I wish and wish they were the views of the Government.'[87] It was this wealth of information that Churchill wove into numerous powerful speeches over the spring and summer of 1936, espousing the need for continuing Anglo-French understanding as well as campaigning to media outlets and newspaper proprietors to carry his campaign as far as possible.

When Clementine Churchill travelled to France in May 1936, she wrote to her husband with a full report of the insights she had gleaned.

Having spent much of her adolescence in Dieppe, she spoke fluent French and so was able to have in-depth conversations about current affairs with those around her. She told Churchill that moderate French opinion of him was that he was 'too gloomy and uncompromising'.[88] She described others' unpopularity as well, including in her note, 'No one likes Flandin.'[89] She also reported that there were many who agreed with the Nazis' position that the Franco-Soviet Pact was indeed a breach of the Locarno treaty and so felt that Hitler was entitled to send troops into the Rhineland as a result. Churchill despaired at not only the inaction by those he felt should be Britain's allies but also their support of Nazi Germany's actions. The day after receiving Clementine's letter, he spoke in the House of Commons on the subject of German rearmament, declaring that it was 'proceeding upon a colossal scale, and at a desperate break-neck speed'.[90] He went on to attack the Government and its lack of leadership, saying: 'Is there no grip, no driving force, no mental energy, no power of decision or design?'[91]

The next day, Stanley Baldwin privately discussed the subject of Winston Churchill with his confidant Thomas Jones, the former Deputy-Secretary to the Cabinet, showing his true feelings of his former close colleague:

One of these days I'll make a few casual remarks about Winston. Not a speech – no oratory – just a few words in passing. I've got it all ready. I am going to say that when Winston was born lots of fairies swooped down on his cradle gifts – imagination, eloquence, industry, ability, and then came a fairy who said 'No one person has a right to so many gifts', picked him up and gave him such a shake and twist that with all these gifts he was denied judgement and wisdom. And that is why while we delight to listen to him in this House we do not take his advice.[92]

A quieter summer awaited the Churchills at Chartwell that year, with half the number of signatories in the visitors' book compared to the equivalent months in 1935. Instead of hosting visitors, he immersed himself in the factory of words that was his study. He continued to work on *Marlborough* and had recently appointed his third research assistant in three years. Bill Deakin would join Churchill in the study at around 10.30pm most nights. He was afforded a break in the drawing room with a whisky and soda at around 1am, before resuming his work with Churchill for another hour or two.[93] As well as his ongoing efforts with his biography of his ancestor, Churchill continued to write countless articles to try to sway public opinion. 'How to Stop War' was published in the *Evening Standard* on 12 June, championing the cause of collective security as a means of averting another conflict. In it he stated that an aggressor who attacks another country 'will be resisted by all, and resisted with such wrath and apparatus, with such comradeship and hearty zeal, that the very prospect may by its formidable majesty perhaps avert the crime'.[94] The speeches continued too, including one in Rolls Park in Chigwell where he declared that 'What our country needs, especially in Foreign Affairs, is leadership ... Without it the cause of Parliamentary Government will be at a woeful and perhaps fatal disadvantage compared with the glittering and formidable dictatorships which have arisen in so many powerful countries.'[95] This speech underwent a number of revisions during its creation, with the text struck through numerous times, including the original wording of 'new and horrible dictatorships', which he quickly replaced with more majestic language.

There was one particular parliamentary encounter that Churchill singled out as being of vital importance that summer, a deputation of Privy Councillors who went to Baldwin on 28 and 29 July to lay before him the facts so far as they knew them. The group, consisting of 18 men across both the House of Commons and the House of Lords, spent three to four hours across two successive days. Churchill's statement lasted 75 minutes, and concluded that 'we are facing the greatest danger and emergency of our history', before adding, 'we have no hope of solving our problem except in conjunction with the French republic'. This, he argued, 'is the best hope'.[96]

Less than a month after this impassioned plea, Churchill was in France with his butler Inches, where he remained for four weeks. 'I have been painting all day and every day',[97] he wrote to Clementine, having discovered the crystal-clear waters of the River Loup, which he delighted in studying and attempting to recreate on canvas. A friend who joined Churchill at a lunch party during the holiday described him arriving 'in an enormous Texan hat, the car full of easels & painting appliances'.[98] He also arranged a number of military visits, including watching manoeuvres at Aix-en-Provence with his old friends General Georges and General Gamelin, the Commander-in-Chief of the French Army. He then visited the Maginot Line, an underground fortification system intended to protect the eastern border of France from Germany, after which he returned to Paris and stayed at the Embassy. 'The officers of the French army are impressive by their gravity and competence', Churchill wrote to Clementine. 'One feels the strength of the nation resides in its army.'[99]

It was while he was in France that Pierre-Étienne Flandin reached out to him, having heard from Ava Wigram that he was nearby. 'If a stay in my humble country house could tempt you, I would be delighted,' Flandin wrote to Churchill on 5 September 1936.[100] Churchill accepted the invitation, and arrangements were made for Flandin's car to pick him up in Dijon on Sunday 13 September.[101] Churchill later gave an account of a meeting earlier that day with Mrs Goldsmith Rothschild, the only child of Berlin's 'coal king' Fritz von Friedländer-Fuld. She told Churchill of the terrible treatment of Jews in Germany since the passing of the Nuremberg laws a year before. She described how she defiantly wore a Star of David made of yellow diamonds, in response to which Churchill, in awe of her bravery, called her 'a remarkable woman'.[102]

Clementine, meanwhile, was at Chartwell and made a number of appearances in Churchill's constituency in his absence. 'I went over to Woodford & opened a fête & was made to bowl in a cricket match', she wrote to Winston. 'I find I can't bowl straight – at least not over arm – it's very annoying.'[103] The rest of the family were spread far and wide. Randolph was in Brussels, Mary in Brittany, and only Sarah of the younger siblings was nearby to keep her mother company, as Diana was heavily pregnant and busy preparing for the birth of her first child.

Upon arriving at Flandin's house, Churchill marvelled at his charming home, idyllically placed in the middle of a valley in the heart of France. 'We have exhausted the formalities of conversation on politics,' he wrote that night to Clementine, '& I have retired to bed to write to you.'[104] The pair had much in common and discussed the similarities in their families, as Flandin too had one married daughter, two unmarried daughters and a son. One striking difference, however, was the modifications made to Flandin's home so he could be readily accessible to his constituents. 'He has a special office & waiting room at the gate', Churchill wrote, '& once a month about eighty come to a levée.'[105] Churchill could hardly imagine such a situation, and outlined to Flandin the advantages of not having a home in one's constituency.

Unknown to Churchill, there was about to be a seismic shock to his family life. While cleaning the Churchills' London flat at Morpeth Mansions, where Sarah had been staying, one of the housemaids found a telegram in the waste-paper basket. It was to Sarah from Vic Oliver, who by then had returned to America. The maid couldn't resist the temptation to see what Sarah had thrown away, and so she pulled the telegram out of the basket to find just four words: 'Do nothing precipitate darling.'[106] Sarah had thrown it away as she was determined to ignore anyone urging caution, even Oliver himself. On 15 September, coinciding with Mary's 14th birthday, she bolted to New York. 'Please make Papa understand that I did not just wait til he was out of the country – it was a last minute decision,' Sarah wrote to Clementine, 'I just have to go – I'm sorry.'[107] Randolph immediately followed in pursuit of his sister, garnering headlines such as 'Churchill's Son Chases Sister across Atlantic' in newspapers around the world.[108] Mary later recalled that it was the first time she had seen Clementine cry. 'It had a very painful effect on me,' she remembered; 'I realised then how much Sarah had hurt them.'[109] Churchill tried to put on a brave face while among friends, remarking a month later, 'I believe she inherited the adventurous spirit of her father.'[110] The maid who had found the telegram only realised what it meant after Sarah had gone, by which time it was too late. It was amid this upset and upheaval that a source of much-needed joy arrived when, on 19 September, Diana gave birth to the Churchills' first grandchild, a boy called Julian.

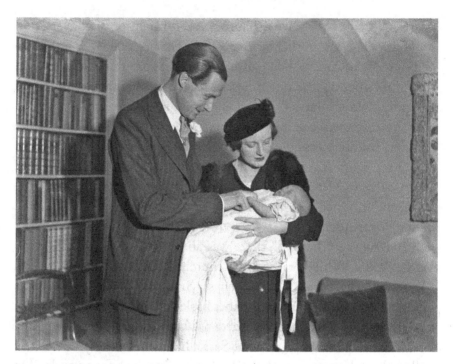

*12. Diana Sandys (née Churchill) with her husband Duncan Sandys
on the occasion of their son Julian's christening, November 1936.*

Amid the difficulties in his family life, on 21 October Churchill found himself under direct attack from Germany's Foreign Office. According to the *Diplomatische Korrespondenz*, 'The method of the "Churchill Group" consists in regarding every removal by Germany, of a danger spot, as a preparation for unfriendly acts elsewhere and as confirmation of the "German Danger".'[111] Churchill carefully crafted his response to the accusation in his study at Chartwell, in which he stated that any nation which was the victim of unprovoked aggression, including Germany, would find guarantees of assistance forthcoming. At the same time, however, he reinforced his argument, saying: 'The German people are being subjected during this winter to many privations and are making many sacrifices in order to perfect their terrible war machine.'[112] The next day an agreement of cooperation was signed between Nazi Germany and Mussolini's Italy, which soon after became known as the Rome–Berlin Axis. In a powerful speech in the House of Commons, Churchill declared that 'the era of procrastination, of half-measures, of soothing and baffling expedients, of delays, is coming to its close' and declared that they were now 'entering a period of consequences'.[113]

Urgent action was now necessary, and the need for a firm agreement of joint action between Britain and France became more vital than ever. Churchill wrote to Flandin, who remained the French Foreign Minister, and invited him to Chartwell on Saturday 21 November. It was hoped that he could join as part of a larger party, alongside Churchill's younger brother Jack and his wife Goonie, and Eddie Marsh, a former private secretary of Churchill's and long-time ally. Professor Lindemann would join too, but couldn't get to Chartwell before Sunday.

Knowing the importance of the success of this meeting, Clementine hired a cook especially to prepare the meals, whom the Churchills had first used in 1933. Georgina Landemare had been a kitchenmaid but then trained under a French chef whom she later married. Miss Hamblin later recalled how Mrs Landemare would arrive at Chartwell 'rather grandly on Friday afternoon, when all the shopping was done and ready for her, and she would go back on Monday morning'.[114] She would travel by train from London, be collected from the nearest station at Westerham and brought to Chartwell. Upon arriving at the house, she met with Clementine to create a menu for that weekend's guests, typically serving exquisite French food. For the weekend of Flandin's visit, the chosen menu was in sharp contrast with the beans on toast, and the fish and chips, that had been served at Chartwell earlier in the week, both of which were served on evenings when Winston and Clementine Churchill were in London.[115]

The menu created by Georgina for Flandin began with a lunch upon Flandin's arrival of *gigot d'agneau et légumes*, a leg of lamb with vegetables, that she then served with soubise sauce, a classic cream sauce made by sautéeing onions and adding them to a béchamel sauce. For dessert Mrs Landemare proposed *gâteau de riz*, a French style of rice pudding that was poured into a caramel-lined dish and baked. She intended to serve it with apple sauce, but Clementine struck through this line in the house's menu book, writing 'Apricot sauce' instead, and added a note that it should be served with 'iced whipped cream'. Dinner that evening included the diplomatically chosen *filets de sole murat*, a dish named after Joachim Murat, one of Napoleon's most famous marshals. This course was followed by pheasant, ice cream and savoury canapés. The menu on Sunday was equally decadent, including the likes of chicken chasseur for lunch and partridge 'italienne' for dinner, with yet more cakes and ice creams for dessert.[116]

The culinary efforts had the desired effect of impressing their guest and making him feel at ease in the Churchills' company at their country home. 'I would like again to thank you for your so charming hospitality at Chartwell', Flandin wrote on 28 November, having returned by then to France.[117] He was particularly charmed by the Churchills' 14-year-old daughter Mary, who a family friend later recalled had become 'very intelligent with wide blue eyes' and 'a great sense of fun'.[118] She had taken the trouble of showing their guest the numerous animals in her care, including dogs, cats, orphan lambs, bantam chickens, goats, budgerigars and canaries.[119] Flandin offered suggestions as to how certain cannibalistic behaviours might be remedied, though no records survive as to which species was the culprit.

Alongside the delicious food and the unorthodox illustration of country life by Mary, serious matters were discussed. In the days before the meeting, Churchill had been collecting as much evidence as he could to confirm his understanding of both British and French preparedness in terms of their air forces. He had once again sought out French estimates of German air strength and met with Wing Commander Anderson at his Morpeth Mansions flat in London to capture the current numbers in terms of both machines and men of the Royal Air Force.[120] The meeting at Chartwell gave Churchill a final chance to confirm his current understanding of the calculations informing decision-making in France, and the conversation became a vital weapon in his arsenal of understanding, ahead of what would most likely be a tense and confrontational meeting with the Prime Minister the next day.

At 4pm on Monday 23 November Churchill met with Stanley Baldwin in his private room at the House of Commons. 'Mr Churchill's deputation', as the press branded the group accompanying him, also included Austen Chamberlain, Robert Horne and Henry Page Croft, all of whom had been at Chartwell for the meeting to discuss the state of Britain's defences in February. The *Daily Mirror* reported that morning that 'Secret service reports will be displayed and every Government card relating to foreign affairs laid on the Premier's table', before boldly adding that, if Churchill wasn't satisfied that the Government were doing their best to rearm, that he would very likely 'place himself at the head of a powerful non-party group pledged to re-arm against Fascist and Nazi aggression'.[121]

The meeting lasted for nearly two hours and began with a statement by the Minister for Defence. He pessimistically stated, 'We are basing our assumptions on the hypothesis that Germany will attempt to defeat the forces of Great Britain by a sustained and intensive air bombardment of London and other selected targets where vital industries or dense populations are concentrated.'[122] He went on to challenge the accuracy of figures used by Churchill in speeches that year comparing British and German air strengths, saying, 'the discrepancy is due to the difference between our way and the French way of estimating air strength.'[123] Churchill agreed that there was a difference. British calculations numbered German squadrons as 9, whereas the French counted the German total as 12, the additional 3 being because their estimates included reserve squadrons. Churchill, armed with the information gleaned from Flandin at Chartwell that weekend, doubled down on the reason for his belief in the French totals rather than the Air Ministry's. He argued that the extra 3 in France's calculations were 'every whit as good – pilots, crews to keep them in order, superiority of machines – as the 9 which you count'.[124]

The alliance between Flandin and Churchill, which was cemented by their time together at Chartwell, had given Churchill a reliable source of French intelligence to support his campaign for rearmament. In his letter of thanks for the Chartwell meeting, Flandin disclosed that there would soon be an announcement from the French Foreign Office declaring the reciprocity of French and British commitments to each other, which Churchill called 'the most important milestone in the conscious association of our two anxious peoples'.[125] Their attempts to build a coalition against Nazi Germany, however, were thwarted by wider circumstances, including the devastating effects on Churchill's prestige just a few weeks later, when he decided to intervene in Britain's greatest constitutional crisis of the twentieth century.

CHAPTER 5

AN ABDICATION FORMULA

Archibald Sinclair, 5–7 December 1936

In a document written by Churchill entitled 'The Abdication of King Edward VIII', tellingly marked 'Secret' in the top left corner, Churchill's sense of history, fierce loyalty to the Crown, friendship with the King, and romantic nature are all apparent. These factors all contributed to his decision to intervene in the 'great matter' as to whether the new monarch would choose love or duty. By positioning himself in direct opposition to the Government, he gambled his political reputation on a plan formed at his country home, which came to be known as 'the Chartwell formula'.[1] As the crisis escalated, he invited a group of trusted confidants to his home. Over the course of a wintry weekend, he concocted a plan which, if successful, would subvert Baldwin's plans to depose a rightfully anointed king, stabilise the monarchy and discredit the Government. Rather than returning Churchill to power and influence, it saw him booed from the House of Commons, caused immeasurable harm to his prestige and derailed his campaign to hasten Britain's readiness for war.

The death of King George V, the third monarch Churchill had served over the course of his political career, brought about a sense of deep sorrow that was felt throughout the country and across the world. Never before had such news spread so quickly, and responses ranging from weeping in the streets of Montreal, to spontaneous silence in Melbourne, were reported in the British press.[2] Churchill, too, had a strong sense of appreciation not just of the King, but the institution of monarchy itself. The collapse of other countries' royal dynasties over the previous 20 years, including those of Germany, Russia, Austria-Hungary and most recently Spain, made the stability of the British Crown all the more remarkable. Those countries which had lost their kings and queens had quickly lapsed into anarchy, dictatorship, civil war and revolution.[3] It was his belief in the stabilising influence of the British monarchy, and its role in what Churchill called 'the continuity and tradition of our national life',[4] that added to his own sense of loss upon the death of the King. In an obituary for the *News of the World* Churchill wrote, 'In a world of ruin and chaos King George V brought about a resplendent rebirth of the great office which fell to his lot.'[5]

Having hastily returned from Morocco to Chartwell, Churchill composed a letter of condolence to his old friend, who had transformed upon the death of his father from the Prince of Wales to King Edward VIII.[6] A genuine friendship existed between the two men, and so the words were truly meant when Churchill wrote, 'I have felt for Your Majesty in the sorrow of a father's death and in the ordeal of mounting a throne.'[7]

It was known at the time of his accession that Edward VIII was in a relationship with the American divorcée Wallis Simpson, though few at the time saw this as a cause for concern. She wasn't the first love of his life, after all. That was an honour held by Freda Dudley Ward, whom the young Prince Edward had first met in 1919 and with whom he quickly fell in love. Described as 'small, elegant and exceptionally pretty',[8] Freda was widely liked, including by the Churchills, whom she visited at Chartwell. Her relationship with the Prince was intense and his letters to her were near constant, totalling more than 2,000 during their 16-year relationship. Though he indulged in other fleeting romances, it was Freda to whom he was still writing in 1931: 'I love and adore *only you* my love.'[9] This was, however, the year that he was introduced to Mrs Wallis Simpson. Three years later, upon telephoning the Prince's residence at York House, the operator told Freda that she had been instructed to no longer put her calls through to the Prince. By January 1936 there was no room in the King's heart for anyone but Wallis.

The relationship was widely known in society circles, and though 'branded with the stigma of a guilty love', as Churchill later reflected on Wallis being married at the time, 'no companionship could have appeared more natural'.[10] Though not featured in newspapers for public consumption, the couple frequently attended dinners, soirées and parties together throughout the early months of the new King's reign. One such lavish gathering at Blenheim Palace, just a few days after the new monarch's forty-second birthday, took place during the last weekend of June. It included not only Edward and Wallis but, from the Blenheim Palace visitors' book, it is evident that Wallis's husband Ernest Simpson was in somewhat awkward attendance too.[11] The Churchills were also present, and the King took advantage of the opportunity to ask his old friend to help him write a speech for the upcoming occasion of presenting Colours to battalions of the three senior regiments of the Brigade Guards. Churchill duly obliged and, with only a few minor changes, the King used his old friend's wording. 'Only a few of us on parade this morning have known the awful weight of war,' the King declared; 'I pray that never again will our age and generation be called upon to face such stern and terrible days.'[12] The King wrote to Churchill afterwards offering his profuse thanks and noting how well the speech was received, 'not only as a suitable address for that occasion, but as introducing a peaceful note at this somewhat disturbed time'.[13]

Churchill was only too aware how disturbing things had become that summer. On 19 May 1936, Allan Clark, a contractor to the War Office, met with Churchill in secret. He had recently visited several munitions factories in Germany to see how their manufacturers produced forgings and shells. In a report of the visit, he observed in one factory that the rate of production of bombs was two a minute per machine. The factory he visited had a hundred of these machines, and had been at that level of productivity for more than two years. 'We were informed that we were the first foreigners ever to have seen this plant,' Clark wrote, 'and incidentally this is only one of many such plants in Germany.'[14] The next day he sent a copy of his report to Chartwell. That evening Churchill pored over the report with Desmond Morton, a friend of his who lived just a few miles from

Chartwell. To demonstrate Morton's value as an ally to Churchill, he has since been described as 'the driving spirit for the study of industrial intelligence in Britain and for its contribution to defence, rearmament and economic planning'.[15] When they had finished with the document for the night, Churchill wrote in pencil 'Put in Defence Box' on the top corner and handed it to his secretary, to add to the mountain of evidence of Germany's rapidly growing war production that he was accumulating at his country home. Those close to Churchill knew of this resource of intelligence, some of whom fed it with further observations and findings. 'He maintained a private bureau of information at Chartwell', his friend Cecil Roberts recalled.[16] Having visited Germany that summer, he too wrote a report for Churchill of the smiling assurances of peaceful intentions he had witnessed there, alongside the creation of a sinister war machine.

Meanwhile, Viscount Swinton, the Secretary of State for Air, wrote to Churchill on 15 June that he was 'deeply concerned by the inactivity of the Government' regarding the defence of London against air attack.[17] A year earlier he had requested that Churchill be invited to join the Air Defence Research sub-committee of the Committee for Imperial Defence. By the summer of 1936 Churchill was lamenting that: 'During the ten months I have sat upon the Committee I have been shocked at the slowness with which every investigation proceeds.'[18] The next day Churchill dined at the Savoy Grill with Albrecht Bernstorff, a German diplomat who had been forced to resign from the German Foreign Office, alongside several close political allies. Harold Nicolson, the Labour MP for Leicester West, noted that Bernstorff was 'extremely courageous and outspoken in his hatred of the Nazis, and I fear he is not long for this world'.[19] When Churchill asked how a second war with Germany might be prevented, Bernstorff simply replied, 'overwhelming encirclement'.[20]

With Churchill's attention immersed in Germany's preparations for war, he received an unexpected request from Walter Monckton, a legal advisor and close confidant of the King, to meet with him at the end of July. The pair met in private at Churchill's flat in Morpeth Mansions and Monckton proceeded to tell him that Mrs Simpson was considering divorcing her husband. Ernest Simpson was reportedly happy to acquiesce to his wife's request, especially as he too was already living with another woman. The King apparently had no plans to marry Mrs Simpson, though he was apparently relieved at the thought of her being free from the marriage, especially with his strong 'possessive sense'.[21] Monckton then asked Churchill what he thought of the idea of her getting a divorce. Churchill's first instinct was that it 'would be most dangerous'. Society gossip was one thing, but it was quite another to have a divorce play out in the courts which might well lead to accusations that an innocent man had been wronged 'on account of the King's intimacies with his wife'.[22] In the end he couldn't stomach the idea and urged Monckton that all possible efforts should be made to prevent such a course of action.

The conversation then shifted to the subject of Wallis being invited to Balmoral, the Scottish home of the Royal Family since the reign of Queen Victoria. Once again, Churchill strongly urged against it. He did not realise that his objections on both matters would soon be relayed to Wallis directly. She was astonished that Churchill had shown himself to be 'against her' and he found himself instantly side-lined in the King's esteem. It was another four months before the two men spoke again.

While the British press remained mute on the subject of the King's romantic life, the American press was flooded with stories about the couple. In October 1936 Wallis Simpson was granted a divorce from her husband and the headlines in the United States went into overdrive. 'King Edward to Wed Mrs Simpson in June', the *New York American* had as its front page lead on 26 October, declaring that a wedding would follow shortly after the King's coronation. 'He believes that the most important thing for the peace and welfare of the world is an intimate understanding and relationship between England and America', the article continued, before concluding that their marriage might very well be what brought about greater coop-eration between English-speaking nations.[23] Churchill was sent copies of this and numerous other similar articles, but the King's personal life was not yet a burning issue in Britain.

For much of the summer and autumn of 1936, Churchill had been working closely with a group known as 'Focus', short for Focus in

Defence of Freedom and Peace. The group had formed the year before, initially as a secretive and largely unstructured organisation that met to discuss the Nazi threat. By 1936 it had begun to publicly campaign to alert the public to the dangers of the Nazi regime, and to push the case for British rearmament. It hoped to achieve this by creating 'a source from which unbiased and objective information will constantly flow to the Government and to the whole country'.[24] The group's members knew they had a difficult task ahead of them, especially in light of, as Churchill called it, the 'regrettable pro-Nazi attitude of a considerable section of the National Press'.[25] The group was funded by Eugen Spier, a German Jewish financier who had been living in England since 1922, and whose properties included Claremont, a Palladian mansion which had been owned by Clive of India in the eighteenth century and the Crown in the nineteenth century.[26] His network gave Churchill access to royalty and senior political figures across Europe. Spier saw the Nazis as a threat not only to his fellow Jews, but also to every democrat and every democratic institution. 'We must organise public meetings in London and the provinces', Spier declared, before adding that Churchill must be the figurehead for their efforts. 'Churchill is the one man who is capable of putting our case for strengthening our military and spiritual forces to our own government and public, and to the governments and public of other countries.'[27]

Within days of the announcement of Wallis Simpson's intention to divorce, Churchill convened a lunch of about 30 members of Focus, now also known as the Anti-Nazi Council, in the Pinafore Room at the Savoy. Attendees included Sir Austen Chamberlain, Oliver Locker-Lampson and numerous other past visitors to Chartwell. Churchill began by expressing delight that so many distinguished individuals, representing every section of public life in Britain, had joined, and added that he was especially appreciative in light of him remaining in the political wilderness at that time. He then said how he was far from satisfied with what the Government was doing about rearmament. There had been some progress, but not enough and far too slow.[28] The Government's diplomatic response, meanwhile, was weak, in the face of Nazi aggression, and the group agreed to hold a public meeting at the Royal Albert Hall on 3 December for an anticipated audience of more than 5,000. The press would also be invited to attend, aided by the Anti-Nazi Council's Organising Secretary, Arthur Richards, who had been the Publicity Manager for the *Daily News* and *The Star* from 1924 to 1935. Finally, the group agreed to meet again on 5 November, to have one final meeting before the Royal Albert Hall event, after which Churchill returned to Chartwell.

One of the main topics of conversation at Chartwell at this time was Churchill's upcoming journey to America. His recent frenetic activity against the looming German threat had exhausted him and Clementine knew her husband was in need of rest. He had set upon Florida as the destination and decided to let his butler Inches take the time off too. This meant that only Miss Hamblin would accompany him. 'He said if I could look after his socks and so on he'd be quite happy', she later recalled. 'He was going to paint, and would I just look after his palette and that sort of thing, no serious work.'[29] Despite having said he wouldn't work, she knew her employer very well, and planned to take her portable typewriter with her just in case. The plan was to set sail on the *Normandie* on 18 December, and then arrive in New York on Christmas Eve. He would then head to Florida where he would stay until early January, and then be back in England by the time Parliament returned on 26 January. Miss Hamblin's excitement was palpable as, for her, it seemed the adventure of a lifetime. She bought new clothes especially for the trip and her family moved their festivities forward so she could celebrate with them before setting sail. Churchill also gave her £10 to spend on clothes, equivalent to about three weeks of her wages. 'I lived in a whirl for weeks', she later said, remembering the sense of anticipation as December drew near.[30] Little did she know that Mrs Pearman, the more senior of the Churchills' two secretaries at the time, had an eye on the door. She had been at Chartwell for eight years, but wrote to Sir James Hawkey, the Vice-Chairman of the Conservative Association in Churchill's constituency, that working for Churchill meant 'giving up my whole life to him, sacrificing my friends, seeing hardly anything of my children, and having no rest, recreation or anything else'.[31] She, like the King, had turned 42 that year, and had begun to despair of the life of

*13. Grace Hamblin, the Churchills' secretary, in the secretaries'
office at Chartwell, mid-1930s.*

duty that seemed to await her too. 'I have more than once tried to
make Mr Churchill understand the inexorable grip he has on my life',
she told Hawkey. While Churchill did occasionally offer concessions
to improve her work–life balance, 'he thoughtlessly drifts back into
the old ways before the week is out'.[32]

The household staff at Chartwell had one final gathering to
prepare for before the festive season. The party scheduled for the first
weekend of December was a gathering of six seemingly unconnected,
but nonetheless fascinating individuals. Firstly, there were Archie
and Marigold Sinclair, who were always welcome at Chartwell,
having been friends with the Churchills for 20 years. Then there was
Harcourt 'Crinks' Johnstone, a Liberal politician who was at that
point out of Parliament, but who Churchill had been in close touch

with about the Government's need to invest in mechanisms for defence against aerial bombardment. Crinks had contacts in France who were testing the use of balloon technology as a method of defence. He had been updating Churchill on their progress, and he in turn had been lobbying the British Government to invest in trials of this technology.[33] Churchill, Sinclair and Crinks were all connected by their active involvement in Focus, and so the timing of the Chartwell meeting, scheduled for just two days after the Royal Albert Hall event, was very likely intended to involve a post-event analysis of sorts. The next name of that weekend's signatories in the visitors' book was Christine Churchill, who had holidayed with Clementine in France in the spring. She married Viscount Churchill, a distant relative of Churchill's, in 1927 but his death from pneumonia in January 1934 left her a widow with a young daughter, and pregnant with their second child. The last name in the list of those who dined and stayed was Christopher Hassall. He was a friend of Eddie Marsh, Churchill's first private secretary upon being appointed Under-Secretary of State for the Colonies in 1905. Hassall was a successful writer and, at 24 years old, the youngest member of the party. Had circumstances been different he would most likely have been seated next to Sarah. She had not yet returned from New York, but missed her family and her home. 'I think of you all and Chartwell often', she wrote to her father in November.[34] The final invitee was Bob Boothby, Churchill's parliamentary private secretary from his time as Chancellor of the Exchequer, who was also due to appear on the platform at the Royal Albert Hall event. He joined the group for Sunday 6 December but did not stay overnight. The group was one the Churchills were keen to impress, as can be seen by Clementine having once again hired Mrs Landemare to prepare all their meals that weekend. As usual, all of the arrangements were Clementine's responsibility, as Winston continued his campaign in Westminster.

The speeches Churchill had made in the House of Commons in November brought him widespread acclaim. A speech of his on 12 November was seen as a particular success, with even one usual detractor, Sir Henry 'Chips' Channon, so impressed that he wrote in his diary that Churchill 'had just delivered a smashing attack on the

Government's defence programme, or rather, the Government's neglect of our defences'.[35] Alongside his campaign for rearmament, there was a growing concern in Churchill's circle on the subject of the future of the King's relationship with Wallis Simpson. On Friday 20 November, Walter Monckton, the King's advisor, wrote to the Prime Minister, Stanley Baldwin. 'At present his ideas are a little fluid', Monckton wrote, before adding 'He will not do anything precipitate or selfish.'[36] By the following Monday, with the Churchills having bid farewell to Pierre-Étienne Flandin at Chartwell and journeyed to London, Winston was growing increasingly concerned. A fellow member of Focus, Lord Citrine, met the Churchills for lunch at their flat in Morpeth Mansions to discuss the meeting at the Royal Albert Hall, but Churchill soon changed the topic of conversation to the King and Mrs Simpson. 'He stressed that the King was deeply in love with her and would not give her up', Citrine later recalled in his memoir.[37] 'Winston looked grave, and, putting his hands on his breast, he said with emotion "He feels it here", at which I looked at Mrs Churchill's thoughtful face, but said nothing more.'[38]

By 25 November it was becoming increasingly difficult to prevent speculation in the British press of an upcoming royal wedding, and the possibility of Wallis becoming Queen. 'If so, the leakage will soon become a flood and burst the dam', the Archbishop of Canterbury wrote to the Prime Minister.[39] The escalating panic of the looming constitutional crisis effectively distracted from events taking place in Berlin on the same day. At the Reich Chancellery, Joachim von Ribbentrop, the German Ambassador to Great Britain, and the Japanese Ambassador to Germany, Kintomo Mushanokōji, signed the Anti-Comintern Pact. The agreement was rooted in the two countries' shared hatred of communism, but also reflected other commonalities between Germany and Japan. Both had strong authoritarian traditions, with Japan said to be 'the very model of the divinely inspired autocratic military nation to which Hitler aspired'.[40] By the 1930s, both countries' leaders were in total opposition to democratic ideals and basked in aggressive nationalism. They also both considered themselves 'have-not' nations, who felt they had been unfairly treated by Western democracies. In London there was confusion as to why Germany's signatory was von Ribbentrop, rather than the more obvious choice of Germany's Foreign Minister, Konstantin von Neurath. An article soon after speculated what the reason might be: 'Is it, as suggested in some quarters, a gentle hint to us to take serious notice of what has been happening between the Nazis and our former allies? . . . On the face of it there seems no reason for such an extraordinary departure from diplomatic practice.'[41]

Later that day, at the Dorchester Hotel, Churchill gave a speech for the New Commonwealth Society Luncheon. He began by warning that 'Europe, and it might well be the world, is now approaching the most dangerous moment in history.' He continued in this alarming vein by declaring, 'It is this conjunction of new air power with the rise of dictatorships that has brought all countries into a peril unknown in barbarous times, or even in the most brutal periods of human history.'[42] Even with a looming constitutional crisis, and burgeoning alliances between dictatorial regimes, the fate of his country home was ever-present in his thoughts. 'We must get Chartwell down to a smaller scale if we are to keep it', he wrote to Clementine on 27 November, as he began to question whether they could afford to continue living in the home he so loved.[43] On the day Churchill shared his fears for their finances with his wife, Stanley Baldwin summoned an urgent Cabinet meeting to discuss the subject of the King and Mrs Simpson.

With the American press discussing the prospect of Wallis Simpson becoming Queen of England, and rumours spreading across the globe, Stanley Baldwin had asked the King what his intentions were on 18 October. The King had expressed a desire to marry Wallis, and understood that this would very likely mean having to abdicate. Things, however, had evolved by the time of a subsequent meeting between them on 25 November. The King believed that many would support him marrying the woman he loved if he was willing to accept a morganatic marriage, with Wallis becoming the Duchess of Cornwall rather than Queen. Baldwin then pointed out to his Cabinet that the Government might need to resign over the matter, creating a constitutional crisis in the form of the King vs the

Government. Not only that, but the King had been encouraged by someone to believe that Winston Churchill would in these circumstances be prepared to form an alternative Government. It was in the aftermath of this extraordinary discussion that one Cabinet Minister noted, 'we are faced with a problem compared with which even the international issues, grave as they assuredly are, pale into comparative significance.'[44] While this extraordinary meeting was under way, Churchill was at Chartwell, dictating the wording of the speech he would give at the Royal Albert Hall in a few days' time.

The news of the King's plan to marry Wallis finally broke to the British public on the day of the Royal Albert Hall event, and Churchill struggled to keep his focus on that evening's proceedings. When in the House of Commons that day, he stood up, with his voice cracking and tears in his eyes, saying he hoped nothing irrevocable would be done before reflection. Chips Channon noted in his diary that evening that, in response to his words, 'the din of the cheering was impressive'.[45] But Churchill needed to channel his energy for the speech he would give later that day. There was too much at stake for him not to. In his own account of the event, he wrote, 'We had the feeling that we were upon the threshold of not only gaining respect for our views but of making them dominant.'[46] When the evening came, Churchill was introduced by two of his friends and colleagues. Lady Violet Bonham Carter began by calling Churchill 'that brilliant political phenomenon who eludes all categories and defies classification'. Alfred Wall, Secretary of the London Trades Council, then spoke of the Prime Minister, saying he was 'a great politician and a true English gentleman', but added, as he very deliberately turned to Churchill, that Baldwin 'should now make room for stronger leadership'.[47] The cheers when Churchill rose to speak were deafening, and he began by declaring that he and all his fellow speakers were there because they were united in wanting to stop this war. A dangerous division was opening up all over the world, and the recent agreement between Germany and Japan was a manifestation of this rift. As a result, it was time for all the free nations, in Europe and across the Atlantic, to take the measures to place themselves in a state of security and adequate defence, adding that this was 'not only for their own safety but also that they might hold aloft the beacon-lights of freedom'.[48] Despite the undoubted success of the event in the eyes of those in attendance, the power of the royal news story totally eclipsed it. The 42-year-old MP for Stockton-on-Tees, Harold Macmillan, recorded in his memoirs that 'All the effect of the Albert Hall meeting was destroyed.'[49]

The lack of coverage for the event left Churchill feeling defeated but, in the matter of the King's relationship with Wallis Simpson, things began to move quickly. At 5pm the following day, on 4 December, Walter Monckton telephoned Churchill from Fort Belvedere, a royal residence in Windsor Great Park that had been a favourite of the King's since 1929. Monckton asked if Churchill was free that evening, as there might be the possibility of joining the King there for dinner. Two hours later the meeting was confirmed and Churchill was driven there at once. He later recalled that the King had appeared happy for the first 15 minutes, but soon the personal strain began to show and he appeared exhausted. Having not spoken to the King since July, Churchill thought it best to let the King express his thoughts first. 'I have not abdicated,' he announced, 'I never used the word abdication in my conversation with the Prime Minister.'[50] He also wanted to make a broadcast, but he had been forbidden from doing so. According to notes Churchill wrote after the conversation, the King said that he wanted two weeks to decide, and ideally somewhere far away, possibly Switzerland. He hoped to ask the Prime Minister to grant him that concession in their meeting the next day, but wondered if his not wanting to abdicate there and then would result in the Government resigning. 'Your Majesty need not have the slightest fear about time. If you require time there is no force in this country which would or could deny it to you,' Churchill reassuringly replied, 'Ministers could not possibly resign on such an issue as your request for time.'[51] He did, however, advise the King not to leave the country, as Mrs Simpson was in Cannes and the assumption would be that he had fled to see her. In the King's account of the conversation, there was also a moment when Churchill had seemed outraged.[52] He was astonished that Baldwin had secured promises from Clement Attlee, the Leader of the Labour Party, and Archie Sinclair, the

*14. Sir Archibald
Sinclair, Leader of the
Liberal Party in
Westminster, London,
September 1938.*

Leader of the Liberals, not to participate in the formation of a new Government, were he to resign. Given that Sinclair was among the list of invitees for his gathering at Chartwell that weekend, Churchill no doubt intended to grill his old friend in the privacy of his home within a matter of hours.

It was well after midnight when the two men said goodbye. Churchill promised to write to the Prime Minister, urging him to stop hurrying the King. His parting words for his monarch were, simply, 'Sir, it is a time for reflection. You must allow time for the battalions to march.'[53] Churchill returned to his flat at Morpeth Mansions that evening, and stayed all of the next day, Saturday 5 December, despite his guests beginning to gather at Chartwell. In the morning he penned a letter, in his own hand, to Baldwin as promised. The letter shared the nature of his conversation with the King, and added that he had concerns about the King's health, noting that he had two marked and prolonged blackouts during their meeting. 'It would be a most cruel & wrong thing to extort a decision from him in his present state.'[54] He then wrote a press statement, pleading for time and patience, stressing that 'every method should be exhausted which gives the hope of a happier solution'.[55] His conclusion, influenced by his skill as a writer of histories, read: 'If an abdication were to be hastily extorted, the outrage so committed would cast its shadow forward across many chapters of the history of the British Empire.'[56]

Given that Georgina Landemare's carefully chosen menu was being served from lunchtime that day, it was clear to all that Churchill had, for the time being at least, left his guests in the lurch. With Clementine channelling all her skills as hostess, those who had arrived earlier in the day were treated to a starter of gnocchi a la Romaine, chateaubriand for the main course, followed by a lemon soufflé. When it was just the family at home, the food would typically have been brought through by a parlourmaid, but with a larger group of guests, the task fell to Inches.[57]

That evening, still in London, Churchill wrote to the King, summarising that the day's events had led to 'Good advances on all parts giving prospects of gaining good positions and assembling large forces behind them.'[58] In a momentary lull in activity, he then dashed back to Chartwell to greet his guests. That evening the party dined on consommé de volaille, a poultry broth which was the perfect starter for a cold, wintry evening. This was followed by sole fillets 'pompadour', roast duck with vegetables, vanilla and fig ice cream with cherry sauce and finishing once again with savouries. This time there were no pencil amendments by Clementine in the menu book, as Mrs Landemare's recommendations were deemed perfect for their guests and for that occasion.[59] She was very likely delighted with this seal of approval, but some of the Churchills' permanent staff were feeling the strain of events on their day-to-day tasks. Their chauffeur, Howes, was starting to tire from the constant late nights of driving, and was close to breaking point.[60]

The next morning, in the Sunday papers, Churchill's press statement was published. The King later called it 'a magnificent plea'

139

but added 'through no fault of Mr Churchill's it came too late. There could be no turning back for me now.'[61] Furthermore, the mood among his fellow parliamentarians was solidifying in staunch opposition to any further delays. There were concerns about the formation of a 'King's party', with Churchill thought likely to be at the helm. Furthermore, the King himself was losing energy for the fight. On the morning of Sunday 6 December, after he had finished his breakfast, the King called Walter Monckton into his room. 'I want you to go to London immediately and warn the Prime Minister that when he comes to The Fort this afternoon I shall notify him formally that I have decided to abdicate', the King told his aide.[62] Churchill, however, not knowing of the King's changed position, refused to yield. He was convinced that another solution could be found and, with some of his closest friends and most long-standing advisors around him, he came up with a desperate scheme to buy time that night, known as 'the Chartwell formula'.

Knowing that Wallis Simpson's divorce would not become absolute for another five months, Churchill was convinced that a final decision could be delayed. Furthermore, he began to see notes of effusive support arriving at Chartwell. His friend and unofficial advisor, Desmond Morton, wrote that he thought Churchill's press statement was magnificent, and suggested that an abdication could strengthen support for extremist political parties. 'It will give an enormous impetus to those misguided persons who believe in Fascism or Communism,' he wrote, and 'before long, a Dictatorship of the "Right" or the "Left" will become a real possibility.'[63] Ironically, other notes of support came from the likes of Walter Newbold, a Member of the Executive of the Communist Party, who wrote: 'Count me all in once more with yourself in the line you are taking in respect of the King.'[64]

Soon the deluge of letters to Chartwell became unmanageable, with hundreds of people writing to Churchill to offer their opinions on the King's possible marriage. The secretaries had to start storing them in sacks, separating out those from his constituents, all of whom were acknowledged with a postcard.[65] There were also hundreds of telegrams. One notable feature of this collective response is the number of women who felt compelled to write to Churchill, and from across all elements of society. Dorothy Abram, the caretaker of Stokesay Castle, wrote to him saying, 'We are no longer living in the eighteenth century and surely it is possible to clear away all these hypocrisies & to pass a straight-forward Act so that the King is free to choose any woman he wishes for his Queen.'[66] Meanwhile, Marjorie Deans, a screenwriter and film director, wrote: 'I am terribly afraid of the weakening effect on the Monarchy likely to result from the present King's abdication.'[67] Other letters of support came from female academics, novelists, poets, composers, shopkeepers, house-wives and aspiring political figures. Ethel Scarborough, who had stood for election against Aneurin Bevan in Ebbw Vale in Wales the year before, telegrammed Churchill declaring: 'We rely on you to form a Government and prevent abdication.'[68] Chartwell quickly became the epicentre of a campaign against the King's abdication. It was at this point that Bob Boothby arrived at Chartwell to join the second day of that weekend's party.

It was on the evening of Sunday 6 December that the full party gathered in Chartwell's dining room where a veritable feast awaited them. Borscht to start, then red mullet, followed by sautéed chicken 'Stanley', served in a sauce of onions, tomatoes, mushrooms and cream, accompanying vegetables, and for dessert pineapple ice cream and a matching compote. Last but not least, a croque-monsieur was served to conclude the decadent meal.[69] Contrary to the original plan of discussing next steps after the Royal Albert Hall event, there was only one subject for discussion that night, but the serious task of developing a plan took place after dinner.

As the ladies withdrew for the evening, Churchill, Sinclair, Boothby, Crinks and Hassall remained at the table. With Churchill still adhering to the terms of his year-long bet to abstain from neat spirits, he had to settle for a glass of port with his cigar, while those around him indulged in brandy. The group remained at the table until close to midnight, with Sinclair, Boothby and Churchill domi-nating the conversation. The idea was that the King should accept, for the moment, the Government's advice on the subject of his marriage and, in doing so, buy some more time while a potential alternative solution might present itself. Churchill was already in talks with several academics to assess historical precedent, and he would collate their thoughts to see if anything could be done differently as a result. There was also the possibility that the King might in due course reconsider any thought of sacrificing the throne. Equally, the Government might well retreat from its insistence that he should abdicate. Their plan would be put forward as both Churchill's and Sinclair's, as the two most senior political figures at the meeting, and would be communicated to the King the next day.[70] Boothby then departed from Chartwell, later noting that, as he said goodbye, he was confident that Churchill was 'resolved to try and persuade the King to accept the formula which we had all helped to devise'.[71]

The next morning, when Churchill came down from his bedroom to join his guests, Archie Sinclair noticed that his 'mood had changed', and later disclosed this to Boothby.[72] A dramatic change had taken place overnight and as all their guests departed, having each signed the house's visitors' book, Churchill readied himself for what awaited in the House of Commons. Howes drove him to the Houses of Parliament, where he dictated a note to the King. In it, he said that the only possibility of him remaining on the throne was to give a declaration along the lines of: 'The King will not enter into any contract of marriage contrary to the advice of His Ministers.'[73] At this time, the Chartwell formula appeared to still be the plan of action. 'I reached the House on Monday rather prepared in my mind to be attacked for what I had written over the weekend,' Churchill later wrote, 'and addressing myself too attentively to that possibility.'[74] In anticipating a battle, Churchill went into the day's proceedings in attack mode. Boothby, for one, was struck by Churchill's odd behaviour. 'When I reached the House of Commons you would not speak to me', he later wrote to Churchill. 'I was dismayed and feared the worst.'[75] He later told his fellow parliamentarian Harold Nicolson that Churchill had appeared restless and was glancing into corners. He remarked, 'when a dog does that, you know that he is about to be sick on the carpet. It is the same with Winston. He managed to hold it for three days, and then comes up to the House and is sick right across the floor.'[76]

When Baldwin gave his update he was slow and measured, calmly revealing that nothing had yet been confirmed in relation to the King's chosen course of action. Churchill then rose to ask a supplementary question to get assurance that 'no irrevocable step would be taken before the House had received a full statement'.[77] However, he failed to do so in line with parliamentary protocol and was twice called to order by the Speaker of the House. 'He hesitated and waved his spectacles vaguely in the air', Harold Nicolson wrote in an update to his wife that evening. People began to shout 'Sit down!', and some reportedly booed him, and he was greeted with unanimous hostility, at which point Churchill 'waved his spectacles again and then collapsed'.[78] It was a painful spectacle for those who witnessed him seemingly crumble before their eyes. 'He tried to stand his ground, but lost the House,' Chips Channon noted in his diary that evening, 'and I fear did the King's cause harm.'[79]

Those involved in the creation of the Chartwell formula the evening before were especially shocked by the display. There had never been any agreement about protests being made in Parliament, and his decision to do so was seen as erratic and selfish. 'I understood last night that we had *agreed* upon a formula', Boothby wrote to him on the Monday night. 'But this afternoon you have delivered a blow to the King, both in the House and in the country, far harder than any that Baldwin ever conceived of.'[80] He continued saying that Churchill's actions had shrunk his supporter base in Parliament, and that he couldn't understand why Churchill would take such drastic action less than a day after agreeing a completely different approach. Boothby's concluding thought proved to be a hurtful blow to his old friend, in showing that even his most faithful supporters were beginning to question him:

What happened this afternoon makes me feel that it is almost impossible for those who are most devoted to you personally to follow you blindly (as they would like to do) in politics. Because they cannot be sure where the hell they are going to be landed next.[81]

It was during Churchill's time at Chartwell that weekend, while steadfastly focused on finding potential solutions, that he missed an imperceptible change that had taken place in public opinion. Many across the country were shocked at the notion that their King could be so hesitant in choosing between his duty to his people, and his affections for a woman who was twice-divorced. This view was then relayed by members of the public to their Members of Parliament, and so the views of British people and their representatives in the House of Commons had quickly coalesced. Even the King was by this time resigned to his fate, noting that, by Monday 7 December, any hint of support for a King's Party 'was a corpse'.[82] Churchill's rash and ultimately futile action, in contrast to the reasoned plan made at Chartwell, was said by an observer to have 'undone in five minutes the patient reconstruction work of two years'.[83] The King, however, never forgot Churchill's act of loyalty:

I have always regretted that incident, and would give much for the power to erase it from the records of that ancient assembly that owes him so much. Yet I am proud, also, that of all Englishmen it was Mr Churchill who spoke up to the last for the King, his friend.[84]

The abdication took place on 11 December 1936.[85] For each of the three last days of the reign of King Edward VIII, Churchill was driven from Chartwell to Fort Belvedere before lunch, and then brought back to Chartwell in the evening. Existing entries on Churchill's engagement cards were crossed out, as all other plans were cast aside in favour of time with the King. On the final night, Churchill's chauffeur Samuel Howes watched as the two men said goodbye at the front door. The King was taken in his Buick car to Windsor to make his abdication address and Churchill got in the back of his Daimler. Howes later recalled that, as he drove back to Chartwell, Churchill had tears flowing and the entire journey passed in silence.[86]

There was one further casualty of the abdication crisis for Churchill. 'The late nights with Mr C began to tell on me', Howes later recalled. At one point he was given a 'severe telling off' by Clementine, which proved to be the last straw, and he gave his notice as a result. Churchill was shocked and tried to persuade Howes, who had been with him since July 1928, to stay, but to no avail. In his reference for Howes, Churchill wrote: 'He is trustworthy, sober, a skilful mechanic, splendid driver, and a reliable man with whom I am sorry to part.'[87]

After all that had taken place in recent weeks, Churchill chose not to go to America for his holiday after all. Having been due to depart on 22 December, the ripple effect of the crisis meant that the trip was cancelled just 24 hours before they were due to set sail. Instead, plans were made for Diana, her husband Duncan and their baby Julian to come to Chartwell for Christmas. Randolph joined too, and Mary revelled in so many of her family being together. An unexpected additional pair joined them just before New Year, when the Churchills' newly wed daughter Sarah returned with her new husband Vic to her family home.[88] Little did they know that it would be the last time they would all be together at Chartwell for the festive season before the outbreak of war.

15. Sarah Oliver (née Churchill) with her husband Vic Oliver, arriving on board the Aquitania into Southampton following their recent wedding in New York, December 1936.

There was one disappointed member of the Churchills' household that Christmas. The cancellation of the America trip, which his secretary had anticipated as a once-in-a-lifetime adventure, instead became 'a terrible flop'. 'Are you very disappointed?', Churchill asked, perhaps not realising that her specially bought trousseau was packed and ready to go, and that she had already spent the money Churchill gave her to buy new dresses. 'Well, yes I am', she said downheartedly. Churchill paused, thought for a moment, and then replied, 'Well, you can keep the £10.'[89]

CHAPTER 6

HITLER'S PREDECESSOR

Heinrich Brüning, 4 August 1937

For insights and analysis of the political goings-on in Germany in the 1930s, there were few better-informed individuals who made the journey to Chartwell than Heinrich Brüning. As a leading politician during Germany's post-war Weimar Republic, and Chancellor of Germany from 1930 to 1932, he witnessed Hitler's political ascent from an uncomfortable front-row seat. By 1937 he had long since fled his country, out of fear for his life after the Nazis came to power. He travelled to Churchill's country home in August 1937, accompanied by Gottfried Treviranus, his former Transport Minister and close personal friend. Treviranus was lucky to be alive, having escaped an attempt on his life by the Nazis in June 1934. The two men visited Churchill, convinced that Hitler's regime could be overthrown. Their insights into potential opposition to Nazism within Germany planted a seed in Churchill's mind that there could be a bloodless way of averting yet another global war, though the two men's testimonials brought into sharp relief the extraordinary risks faced by anyone who opposed Adolf Hitler.

Churchill's keen interest in post-war politics in Germany had long pre-dated the rise of Hitler. Prince Bismarck, grandson of Kaiser Wilhelm II, remembered meeting Churchill in London in October 1930 where the pair discussed the latest political developments. Churchill had apparently been following recent newspaper reports and was 'extremely well informed' and 'pleased about the parliamentary

16. Heinrich Brüning, when Chancellor of Germany, January 1932.

victory of the Brüning government'.[1] This high opinion appeared to have diminished, however, when the Chancellor visited London in 1931. He met many of the British political establishment, but Churchill's presence was notably lacking. Brüning supposedly thought that this snub was because Churchill held him responsible for the German rearmament that began during his time as Chancellor.[2] Brüning's own position became increasingly precarious against a backdrop of rising unemployment and electoral success for the Nazi Party. He made one last attempt at redeeming himself in the eyes of the German electorate at the disarmament negotiations of April 1932, but when he returned to Berlin empty-handed, his fall swiftly began. On 30 May, in what has since been described as 'a pathetic interview', President Hindenburg told him to resign.[3]

Following the appointment of Hitler as Chancellor in 1933, Brüning became increasingly nervous about the constant surveillance he was subject to, and began to change his lodgings every two or three days. Fortunately, there were those who regarded him as one of Germany's greatest statesmen and were willing to provide refuge for him. The following spring, one acquaintance observed that he had begun to resemble 'a hunted animal, constantly startled and already exhausted, just waiting for the final bullet'.[4] In May 1934 Brüning burned what was left of his personal papers and fled Germany, initially crossing the border into Holland. Within a month, on 12 June, he was in London, lunching with British political figures, including Archie Sinclair and Bob Boothby.[5] His timing meant that he escaped one of the most terrifying ordeals faced by Hitler's opponents, the Night of the Long Knives, and one of his closest associates would see first-hand the terror this entailed.

It was a warm June afternoon and Gottfried Treviranus, a former minister in Brüning's Cabinet who was generally regarded as the ex-Chancellor's closest friend, had been playing tennis in his back garden. A lorry containing a dozen SS members stopped outside his house and, with drawn revolvers, came across his daughter Barbara. 'Where is Treviranus?', they shouted. The former minister's father was upstairs in the house, confused by the request and responded, 'Here I am'.[6] While the men rushed upstairs, Barbara dashed to the tennis court, calling out to him, 'Everything in front is swarming with Nazis!' Still in his tennis attire, he jumped over his garden wall, ran to his car and started the engine, with the SS shooting at him as he sped away from his home. They quickly returned to the truck and drove after him but couldn't shoot because of the heavy traffic and soon lost him. In his getaway, he raced through junctions, and later recalled that 'as the car shot through a three-way crossing, I heard two calls to stop and saw two SS boys with carbine guns on the left'.[7] They shot at him five times, missing each time. Once he was confident he was no longer being followed, he drove to the home of General von Schleicher, the penultimate Chancellor of Germany during the Weimar Republic. Unexpectedly coming across crowds of people, Treviranus asked what had happened, only to be told that both the General and his wife had been shot at around 12.30pm. Suddenly realising that he was the target of a methodical purge of former political leaders, he summoned a remarkable aura of calm, got back into his car and drove into the country where he smashed it against the edge of the road, to give the impression he had fled across nearby fields. He then caught a taxi to the house of a family member who loaned him a suit that was two sizes too big. Then he quickly began to plan his escape to London. That night, his family packed, and burned all their files and letters. There were 85 people recorded as having been killed that night, though some estimate that the total number was as high as 1,000. Two days later, a search warrant was released, announcing that Treviranus was wanted for high treason. 'He evaded arrest by escaping. Because of the dangerous nature of the criminal, firearms are to be used if he is detected.'[8]

Treviranus arrived into Harwich, having taken a night boat from Hoek van Holland, on 15 July. He was quickly reunited with Brüning who had been staying with friends in Weybridge in Surrey. Brüning had already successfully ingratiated himself with the political set in London, and was first invited to Chartwell on 9 September 1934. The first meeting had been arranged by Major Archibald Church, who had served as the Labour MP for Central Wandsworth in London from 1929 to 1931. Church and Brüning initially went to the home of Churchill's friend and political ally, Brendan Bracken. The three men were then driven by Bracken to Chartwell, where Churchill was waiting with Professor Lindemann and Edward Spears, another old friend whom he had known since the First World War and whose son was Churchill's godson. Clementine welcomed the group, but quickly made her excuses and left them to their gentlemen's dinner.

Churchill immediately began bombarding Brüning with questions, grilling him about the rise of the Nazi movement and the future of Germany and Europe, which left quite the impression on the former Chancellor. 'For anyone who, like me, enjoys pointed phrases, quick and imaginative deductions and answers, and loves directness and an easy natural style in conversation, his charm is inescapable.'[9] Brüning later recalled that this first meeting was among the first times in months that he had felt in good humour following the terrible ordeal he had experienced both in Germany and then as a political refugee. Churchill dominated the conversation, with Lindemann making the occasional remark, but Church, Bracken and Spears were left with little opportunity to speak. Instead, they found themselves simply witnessing their host engaged in debate with Brüning. Churchill also plied his guest with whisky, to which Brüning was not yet accustomed. He later admitted, 'I have never drunk so much again.'[10] Given his alcohol-induced haze at the time, Brüning struggled to remember specifics of the conversation that evening in the summer of 1934, with one exception: Churchill declared, 'Germany must be defeated again and this time finally. Otherwise France and England will have no peace.'[11]

By the summer of 1935, Brüning was predicting another military conflict in Europe would erupt by autumn 1936 or spring 1937 at the latest.[12] Unfortunately, he soon realised that his political influence in Westminster was limited, and it appeared that the British Government lacked the will to assert itself against the increasing military might of Germany. He began to consider alternative ways by which Britain could help bring about the downfall of the Nazi regime. In May 1936, shortly after the Nazis' occupation of the Rhineland, Brüning confided in Sir Arthur Salter, Professor of Political Theory at Oxford University, that he wanted Britain to liaise directly with German generals about what terms they would consider to overthrow Hitler. He admitted that the thought of British inaction was causing him to lose sleep, and added, 'there is not much time left, at most twelve months, to prevent a repetition of the tragedy of the last war on a much greater scale'.[13]

To those in whom he confided his concerns, and his proposed solutions, it was often suggested that he should speak to members of the Government. Brüning, however, had become increasingly paranoid, and was convinced that such conversations would then be leaked to Nazi informants, who could then frustrate any of his ideas. He was, however, certain of the likely success of his plan. 'I had no doubt that if only once the British were willing to look ahead and to say that they would act if Hitler became aggressive,' Brüning later reflected, 'that he could be stopped and then easily overthrown.'[14] Unfortunately, by then, he had come to believe that his own efforts were proving futile and, as 1936 drew to a close, he perceived a strange indolence in Britain's political circles towards the aggressive policies of Nazi Germany.

For Churchill, 1937 also began with his own sense of futility and loss. His daughter Mary later called this period 'probably the lowest point of Winston's political fortunes'.[15] Not only that, but his trusted Foreign Office informant, Ralph Wigram, had died on New Year's Eve, and Churchill lost a friend who had been willing to take considerable risks to help him. 'He was one of those – how few – who guard the life of Britain. Now he is gone – and on the eve of this fateful year', Churchill wrote to Wigram's widow. He also praised the role she had played in supporting her husband, adding: 'You shielded that bright steady flame that burned in the broken lamp. But for you, it would long ago have been extinguished.'[16] She in turn felt a great sense of gratitude to Churchill, saying: 'He adored you so – & always said you were the greatest Englishman alive.'[17] She even asked Churchill if he could arrive early to the funeral so he could be there to support her in her grief. Just two weeks later, another friend of Churchill's, Baron Islington, passed away. The letter Churchill sent to his widow Anne was particularly moving. 'What jolly times we had when our world was young! ... As one gets old – the scene contracts, and the colours fade,' he wrote, before concluding, 'I hope & pray that there will still be some mellow sunshine left for you.'[18]

With Clementine and Mary away skiing at the start of the new year, and Churchill left on his own, he threw himself back into Chartwell life and indulged in his favourite hobbies to try to lift his spirits. He moved much of his painting activity up to the house, though was always careful and ensured that nearby furniture was covered with dust sheets first. By painting in the warmth of the drawing room, he could avoid having to go down the meandering garden path in 'tremendous rain' and with the valley by then 'soaking'.[19] He would carefully stage still life scenes to recreate on canvas, particularly relishing the challenge of painting sparkling glass and gleaming metal surfaces when positioned in dramatic light. These paintings, which showcased his developing skills of capturing reflections and shadows, tended to use far more muted tones than the bold and brilliant shades of his outdoor scenes.

He also resumed his focus on writing, and Bill Deakin, his research assistant, stayed in a guest room for days on end to be constantly on hand. Churchill even extracted 15 golden orfe from the lake and relocated them to the largest and most beautiful of Chartwell's three ponds. 'They are wonderful fish,' he wrote to Clementine, 'I told them to eat whatever they wish.'[20] True to his word, Churchill arranged for the finest maggots available to be sent specially by train from Yorkshire. 'The tins were about a foot high and marked "Maggots Immediate" and smelt to high heaven!', Miss Hamblin later recalled. 'When they arrived at Westerham station the porter would ring and say "Is that the Secretary?", and you would say "Yes", and he would say "Your maggots are 'ere Miss!", so you'd have to whip off to Westerham or else send the chauffeur to collect the maggots.'[21]

The new chauffeur, Charles Cale, seemed to be able to withstand this and other unusual tasks asked of him, which were simply accepted as part of Chartwell life.[22] 'The young chauffeur is a very nice fellow,' Churchill remarked, 'and I am taking great pains with him.'[23] Other staffing changes were afoot, as Mr Arnold, the estate carpenter and odd-job man at Chartwell, left at the end of January. This was probably lamented most by the Churchills' children as Mr Arnold, alongside their nanny Moppet, was the staff member who featured most in their childhood photo albums capturing Chartwell life. He was replaced by Patrick Jackson, whose wife Mary was hired as Chartwell's head parlourmaid in October 1937.[24] Mr Arnold's departure was soon followed by Inches, who left Chartwell in the spring. Clementine wrote in his reference that the only reason for him being let go was because they were going to get a parlourmaid instead, and the salary would therefore be less costly to them.[25]

The subject of finances increasingly arose between Churchill and his wife in the early months of 1937. 'I think we have had a very cheap month here', Churchill proudly wrote to Clementine in February.[26] He told her that very little wine had been drunk and he was trying to get the fuel they required for heating to last as long as possible. What used to last two weeks now lasted three, despite the freezing cold weather. It was amid these privations that a potential buyer of Chartwell made themselves known. Churchill had £25,000 in mind as the minimum price he would consider, but thought that if such an offer was not forthcoming, they could carry on there for another year or two. 'No good offer should be refused,' Churchill told Clementine, 'having regard to the fact that our children are almost all flown, and my life is probably in its closing decade.'[27] Just a few weeks later, one of Churchill's most loyal political allies, Sir Austen Chamberlain, passed away, which only added to his sense that he too may not have much time left.

By this time Gottfried Treviranus had achieved celebrity status in London for having evaded SS forces in Berlin three years earlier, with the *Daily Telegraph* describing his escape as being 'in the best traditions of filmland'.[28] Meanwhile, Heinrich Brüning had relocated to the United States and secured a teaching position at Harvard University. His activities were frequently monitored, with the German Consulate in Boston regularly sending updates to the German Embassy in Washington, DC. One such report described a series of lectures Brüning gave at Dartmouth College, saying: 'He did not address current political issues and was cautious with his statements.'[29] It was also understood that Brüning hoped to return to England soon, a scenario most likely hastened by the nature of press coverage about his lectures. The *Boston Evening Transcript* began to quote news stories from Germany about Brüning, saying that his swift departure from Germany was due to 'a bad conscience' and described how, as Chancellor, he had 'forced himself and his policies on the German people by police terrorism and riot act decrees'.[30] Brüning remained tight-lipped in light of such press coverage, insisting that he wished to avoid any comment that might be regarded as antagonistic to the Reich Government.

Those in Germany who had been loyal to Hitler began to become nervous too. In May 1937 Ernst Hanfstaengl, the man who had tried to introduce Churchill to Hitler five years earlier, arrived in London.[31] On the eve of his 50th birthday, three months earlier, he was summoned by Hitler to fly to Spain, supposedly to assist German journalists who were reporting on the Spanish Civil War.[32] He had found himself in a dispute with Hitler and, though confused by the urgency, thought the mission might improve his standing with the

Führer and so he accepted the assignment. He was rushed to the airport, but became suspicious when he was handed a parachute and ordered to put it on. Worse still, the pilot had a completely different understanding to Hanfstaengl of the intended destination. He persuaded the pilot to return to Germany and then immediately fled to Switzerland. Hermann Göring, one of the most senior members of Hitler's inner circle, wrote to him there saying 'the whole affair was only intended as a harmless joke'.[33]

As Hanfstaengl's efforts to avoid assassination brought him from Zurich to London, Churchill continued to welcome guests to Chartwell who were willing to bring confidential information to his door. Among those who journeyed to Churchill's home was Pierre Cot, who visited mid-afternoon on a Monday in May. Cot was an anti-war activist who was President of the International Peace Conference and shared Churchill's support of collective security to prevent another global conflict. Following their meeting, Cot sent Churchill a detailed 19-page memorandum on German air strength. 'I am sending you this document through the intermediary of the British Embassy in Paris,' Cot wrote to Churchill, 'on the basis of its secret nature.'[34] Cot's report included 1936 and 1937 estimates, as well as a forecast of the continuing growth of Germany's air strength for the following year. These totals were then compared with likely projections for Britain and France. The report caused Churchill considerable alarm, and he wasted no time in making sure that Desmond Morton, his neighbour and contact in industrial intelligence, saw it too.[35]

The analysis of military intelligence at Chartwell briefly ground to a halt when the celebrations for the coronation of King George VI and Queen Elizabeth began. The ceremony at Westminster Abbey, on 12 May, was a magnificent occasion, though notably lacking the King's elder brother, the newly titled Duke of Windsor. Just a few days earlier, following a dinner with friends, one attendee noted that Churchill 'remained pro-Windsor to the end'.[36] If this was the case a week before, however, a change of opinion soon took place. During the coronation, he turned to his wife with eyes full of tears and said: 'You were right; I see now the other one wouldn't have done.'[37] Clementine had long since held the view that the King should have

155

sacrificed his own personal happiness for duty, and her daughter Mary later recalled how her parents argued fiercely about it at the time.[38]

In the months that followed, Churchill was able to maintain loyalty to both brothers. Writing to the former King after the coronation, Churchill said: 'The line I take is "I wish to see the King reign gloriously, and the Duke of Windsor live happily".'[39] Though he had found contentment in his relations with the former and current Kings, he was far less happy about how his attendance at the coronation was represented in the press. A telling letter to Percy Cudlipp, the editor of the *Evening Standard*, complained about 'the disgusting photograph you picked out to show how much older I am now than at the previous coronation'. Churchill added: 'I suggest you should give me a second chance with a real contemporary picture, instead of joining in the general campaign to make me an elder statesman and send me to the knackers!'[40]

In the weeks following the coronation, Churchill was invited to the newly renovated German Embassy in London on two occasions. First, there was a ball to celebrate the coronation a few days after the event, which reportedly had a 'sparking' guest list of royalty, diplomats and senior political figures.[41] That was followed by a lunch meeting request from Joachim von Ribbentrop, the German Ambassador, on 28 May. 'I had of course met him several times in society', Churchill later reflected. 'He now asked me whether I would come to see him and have a talk.'[42] By that time Ribbentrop had shown himself to be hugely ambitious, having negotiated both the Anglo-German Naval Agreement of 1935 and the German pact with Japan in 1936. He had reportedly been offered the role of Foreign Minister of Germany, but wanted to remain in his diplomatic post in London a while longer to make the case for an Anglo-German entente, or possibly even an alliance. Churchill's curiosity was most likely piqued by Ribbentrop's invitation and, with the possibility of gaining first-hand insights into Germany's intentions, it was too good an opportunity for Churchill to miss.

The two men met in the large drawing room of the German Embassy, where they remained in deep conversation for more than two hours. Hitler had instructed Ribbentrop to tell Churchill that he could guarantee the integrity and security of the British Empire. Churchill replied that the Royal Navy had been doing that for hundreds of years, and there would be no need to take Hitler up on his offer. Ribbentrop pushed the point further. This was an offer to shield and protect all nations within the British Empire, and that Germany would 'stand guard' over it. What was required in exchange, according to Churchill's account, 'was that Britain should give Germany a free hand in the East of Europe'.[43] All Britain had to do was to turn a blind eye.

For a moment, Churchill decided to halt his witty replies in favour of appearing curious, in order to find out how much of Eastern Europe Hitler actually wanted. Ribbentrop pointed to a nearby wall map, and casually went through the Nazis' hit list. Churchill, though only speaking for himself, felt that the British Government would be unlikely to stomach such overwhelming domination of Central Europe by Germany. 'In that case,' the Ambassador remarked, 'war is inevitable. There is no way out.'[44] Churchill suggested that Germany should not underestimate his country, and after the two men had parted ways he immediately reported the entire conversation to the Foreign Office.

Yet another dramatic change awaited those whose worlds revolved around Westminster, when the Prime Minister, Stanley Baldwin, retired at the end of May. He was succeeded by Neville Chamberlain, who gave a strangely prophetic speech upon becoming the new head of the British Government:

These next two years may well be critical in the history of Europe, and, whether they end in chaos or in a gradual appeasement of old enemies, and the restoration of confidence and stability, will depend very likely upon the part played by this country, which is bound to be important, and may well be decisive.[45]

Once again, any hopes of Churchill being brought back into the Government were soon dashed, and he spent much of the summer at Chartwell, in a state of unbridled frustration. 'There's no plan for any kind of anything. It is no good. They walk in fog', he uttered gloomily to the journalist Cecil Roberts who visited him at his country home. 'Everything is very black, very black', he said, looking out towards the swans on the lake.[46] Things were looking equally bleak for Heinrich Brüning in the summer of 1937. He was recorded in *Paris-Soir* as saying: 'I don't even want to have to care about the country of which I was, for two years, the Chancellor.'[47]

Though Churchill was not consumed with government affairs as he might have hoped, any available time was soon filled with his renewed focus on the next volume of *Marlborough*. His plan for its completion was so ambitious that, despite their financial difficulties, it was decided that an additional secretary was needed for Chartwell.

Kathleen Hill, or 'Mrs Hill' as she would always be known to the Churchills, was invited to an interview at Chartwell and found herself seated in the drawing room with Clementine. 'Now, would you be willing to work at night for Mr Churchill? Because he often stays up working at night until about three o'clock in the morning', Clementine asked. Mrs Hill said that she would, at which point Churchill himself appeared. He was 'in a boiler suit and looking all very pink and white. I was struck by the fairness of his skin', she later recalled. Having left the interview not quite sure whether she had the job or not, she received a letter from Mrs Pearman a few days later, asking if she could start the following week.[48] She became the Churchills' first resident secretary, with her own room in the house. 'I was captive you see', she joked, remembering how her proximity to her employers meant that she could do the longest days of the three secretaries. Though she was supposed to have a lengthy break before dinner, this was a rare occurrence. Having initially been engaged to help with Churchill's literary work, she soon became involved in all aspects of Chartwell, including the running of the household. This was always a time-consuming part of the secretaries' work since, by nature of Chartwell's remote location, and the Churchills not being the best-paying of employers, they saw consistently high turnover. As a result, there was a near constant need to recruit and train new staff. In addition to these tasks, Mrs Hill became increasingly involved in Churchill's political world. She later recalled the deluge of messages coming into Chartwell. Because Churchill was bricklaying for one of the cottages, she and the other secretaries used to have to go and find him each time an urgent letter or telegram arrived. 'We had to run all down those steps and up the ladder and take the message, and he would dictate what he wanted to say and I would run back', she remembered years later. 'I think we did quite a quarter of a mile on those occasions.'[49] Churchill's bricklaying in earlier years had often been spent accompanied by his younger daughters, Sarah and Mary, who acted as his 'bricklayer's mates'.[50] By the late 1930s, Churchill was likely to be found labouring alone, though there were times when the children of the Churchills' staff at Chartwell were invited to lend a hand. This included an occasion when one of the young daughters of Mr Hill, the head gardener, took on the task of carefully handing the bricks across, one at a time, after which Churchill gave her a sixpence as thanks for her assistance.[51]

The need for constant contact with his political network, even when in the relative seclusion of Chartwell, became even more acute

17. Winston Churchill bricklaying and building one of the garden walls at Chartwell, early-1930s.

in the summer of 1937. His opposition to Government policy regarding the European situation was now overt, and a stream of people were seeking him out, in the privacy of his country home. The former foreign minister of Romania, Nicolae Titulescu, was among those who made the journey, lunching at Chartwell with Winston and Clementine on 8 June. He felt the journey from the Ritz to rural Kent worthwhile in order to ascertain Churchill's view on whether Britain would be prepared to defend any states threatened by German aggression. Though still in his political exile, Churchill reassured Titulescu, and also invited him to join the Focus group for lunch at the Savoy the following Monday. According to Eugen Spier, the financial backer of Churchill's Anti-Nazi Council, Churchill paid tribute 'to the courage and energy with which Titulescu had faced difficult and trying years and maintained his policy of co-operation with Western democracies'.[52] Titulescu clearly enjoyed the kindness of his host and the company of those who were tirelessly campaigning against the Nazis, later saying that the gathering had been 'a most enjoyable affair'.[53]

Though Nazi aggression seemed to be in a temporary hiatus, the international crisis raged. In the summer of 1937, the conflict between China and Japan dramatically worsened, and discussions took place in the Foreign Office as to whether there should be joint action by the French, British and American governments in response to Japanese aggression. The Chinese Ambassador in London, Dr Quo Tai-chi, contacted the Foreign Secretary, Anthony Eden, to request that the British should intervene to help bring a halt to the fighting, and added that he was making the same request of the United States and Russia.[54] Churchill soon wrote of the 'lamentable events now taking place in the Far East', and 'the remorseless conquest and subjugation of parts of China by Japan'.[55] He did, however, surmise that Japan's strategy of entangling its troops in China most likely meant that a global war, in which Britain would play a part, was not anticipated that year, and the greatest immediate threat was still the one in the heart of Europe.

On the afternoon of 19 July 1937, Churchill was due to speak in a Foreign Office debate. Eden opened proceedings, updating those in attendance on the global situation. He began by saying that the situation in the Far East was 'confused and anxious and it is difficult even to describe it in precise terms'. He added that fortunately the British Government enjoyed very good relations with both the Chinese and the Japanese governments. When his turn came, Churchill rose to his feet and spoke mainly on the subject of the Spanish Civil War, which had been raging since the previous year. He then concluded with the subject of German supporters of Nazism who lived in Britain. He described how the Nazis had created a new ministerial role to 'direct and concert the action of Nazi Germans living abroad',[56] before noting that there were tens of thousands of such individuals in Britain at that time.

One fellow parliamentarian present for the speech was Brigadier-General Spears, who was very likely influenced by Churchill's thoughts on Germans in England, and wrote to him just a few hours later. 'Brüning is back in England for a few weeks', Spears wrote. 'Would you care to meet him again and hear his news?'[57] Churchill replied that he would be delighted to see Brüning again. As Parliament was no longer sitting, he was mostly at Chartwell, but he had visitors and engagements every day until 4 August, and so wondered if that date might work. On 28 July Spears left word with Mrs Pearman to pass on a message: 'General Spears says that Dr Brüning will be delighted to come to luncheon here on the 4th. Can he also bring Mr Trevanini [sic], who is with him and through whom he does everything.'[58] Mrs Pearman went out into the gardens in search of Churchill, who was taking advantage of the warm summer weather. Upon finding him, she handed him the note. Churchill simply wrote 'yes', following which Mrs Pearman went back to the secretaries' office to make the final arrangements with Spears. Understanding that Churchill seemed to be in a receptive mood, he wrote again a few days later, asking if he could bring his 16-year-old son, Churchill's godson, Michael. 'I should very much like you to see him again', Spears wrote.[59] Churchill replied that not only should he bring Michael, but that his wife May, the successful American author known to most as Mary Borden, was welcome to join too.[60]

The decision was then made to make this a bigger occasion. Professor Lindemann, who by this point seemed to be at Chartwell on almost a weekly basis, was invited too. Sir James Hawkey, the Vice-Chairman of the local Conservative Association in Churchill's constituency, was also invited, along with his daughter Dinah. Sir Roger Keyes, the former Admiral of the Fleet, was also present. The group seemed a rather random assortment, which Churchill himself recognised in a letter to Clementine, who was away at a spa resort in Austria at the time. 'What a pot pourri!' he noted of the group who would meet for lunch at Chartwell the next day, before adding, 'But I expect it will go all right.'[61]

With his wife May and son Michael already in the car, Edward Spears collected Brüning and Treviranus and the five of them drove together to Chartwell. Brüning was delighted to see Professor Lindemann there once again. To those who hadn't yet met Lindemann, Churchill introduced him to the group as a man who 'hears the language of the experts in the stars and can make it understandable to me!'[62] Upon taking their seats for lunch, there was the usual preamble about the weather and Chartwell's delightful setting. Treviranus later called the Churchills' home 'Chartwell Park',[63] which reflected the sheer scale of the landscape, and a belief that it must be Churchill's very own parkland.

After the initial pleasantries, both of the German guests briefly described their escapes from Germany, largely for the benefit of those attendees whom they were meeting for the first time. This included Treviranus's exploits, which undoubtedly appealed to Churchill's own sense of adventure, as someone who once said: 'Nothing in life is so exhilarating as to be shot at without result.'[64] The conversation then turned to the possibility of regime change in Germany. Brüning believed that the German Army commanders would consider a revolt if Hitler carried his foreign policy too far, and if they became aware of the danger of another conflict erupting across Europe. 'I tried to persuade Winston Churchill that it was imperative for the British Government to work out a maximum proposal of conditions, to which they would agree, should Hitler's regime be overthrown and an arms limitation agreement reached',[65] Brüning later recalled. The response from the group to this suggestion was described by Brüning as 'a somewhat emotional pro-French sentiment'. He was struck by the response of those around him who appeared not to be concerned about any imminent threat to Britain or the British Empire, and instead only discussed the possible threat to France. Furthermore, if France were defeated, and Nazi Germany victorious, the general opinion of those around the table was that this would simply result in a weakening of the British position in Europe, and so possibly around the world too.[66] Churchill, however, interjected, saying that war was inevitable in the foreseeable future, and Britain would very likely become embroiled.[67]

The idea presented by Brüning that the German generals could possibly be persuaded to revolt against Hitler seemed in sharp contrast to Churchill's understanding at that time. 'Only the generals want war!', he shouted, pushing his chair back before pacing up and down the dining room. Treviranus quickly replied, 'Only the amateurs in uniform!', meaning that he thought those with significant military leadership experience were not the ones in Germany who were spoiling for a fight. At this point General Spears gave Treviranus 'a furtive nod'. With Churchill still away from the table in a state of disgruntlement, Keyes tried to lighten the mood. 'He didn't say amateur admirals, Winnie!', he remarked to his friend.[68] Churchill snorted, returned to his chair, took a puff on his chewed cigar, and the discussion moved on. He then reportedly described how the Government was pandering to Hitler, leaving his two German guests with the impression that he had become a sort of Leader of the Opposition. Churchill then turned to Treviranus and asked, 'Couldn't you make it clear to the people that Hitler wants war? You've known him long enough!', to which Treviranus replied that he could not be expected to achieve something that even the great Churchill himself had so far failed to do.[69]

As Churchill and his guests finished their lunch, they took advantage of the sunshine and went for a stroll through the garden. As he so often did, Churchill made a point of showing off the brick walls that he had built. As some of the group went on ahead to admire their host's handiwork, Churchill hung back with Brüning and Treviranus, and apologised for his tendency to erupt when in disagreement. According to Treviranus's recollections, Churchill then confided in the two men that his temper was due to the trouble he had with nannies and governesses when he was very young, before he was brought under the care of his faithful and adoring nanny, Mrs Everest.[70]

Soon the group returned to the driveway in front of the house and as his guests got into their cars, Churchill most likely headed upstairs for his daily afternoon nap, before resuming work on *Marlborough*. 'I am working day and night and the progress on M is enormous – I have done nearly 20,000 words this week alone', Churchill wrote to Clementine. 'I am certainly not wasting the days.'[71]

Despite his unstinting focus on the next volume of his biography of his ancestor, Churchill did take a moment to write to Brüning just a few hours after he left Chartwell. The reason for the note was that Churchill was about to publish a series of his past essays together in a single volume called *Great Contemporaries*. The subjects included Adolf Hitler, President Hindenburg and Kaiser Wilhelm II. 'I should be grateful to you if you have the time to glance through them,' Churchill asked of Brüning, 'and entirely of course for my private information, make any comments which occur.'[72] He added that it had been 'very agreeable' to see him at Chartwell, which was a view reflected by his guests, including Treviranus who wrote of his enjoyment and appreciation of the hospitality at Chartwell. Brüning replied straight away, admitting: 'When talking to you personally about international relations, I felt I had to be very open, although I usually hold back, because despite the current mood of many in Germany that are more hostile to the regime than ever before, I cannot change the situation significantly.' All he could offer to Churchill was his own perspective, but he added an unusual request. He suggested that Churchill should travel to Germany 'and talk openly with the people'. Brüning then said that since he was now unable to influence the German people at large, perhaps Churchill might consider going and speaking directly to the people of Germany. 'That could actually affect the future because people realise the power you have in England', Brüning concluded.[73]

On 9 August Brüning left England for Holland, and it was almost three weeks before he was able to send a reply to Churchill about the chapters for his book.[74] Meanwhile, Churchill continued to host guests at Chartwell, including the writer H. G. Wells, the artist William Nicholson and the new Secretary of State for War, Leslie Hore-Belisha. 'I remember Hore Belisha asking Winston to let him have a painting,' Mrs Hill later recalled of that visit, to which Churchill replied, 'I'll give you a painting when you solve the army problem!'[75] But Hore-Belisha did not come away from Chartwell empty-handed. He later admitted to Clementine that he had unintentionally 'misappropriated that wonderful eye lotion which Winston lent me!'[76] The recent coronation photos that caused him such distress had perhaps triggered something of a self-care regime in the 62-year-old Churchill.

A few weeks later, Brüning replied to Churchill's chapter queries with a seven-page-long letter. He praised the chapters on Hindenburg and the Kaiser, but cautiously wrote, 'I do not know if I can say very much about your article: Hitler and his Choice.'[77] He then continued his line of thought from the lunch at Chartwell, and the matter of senior military figures in Germany being opposed to war. He was keen to stress that, after Hitler came to power, the *Reichswehr*, the German armed forces, were by no means the driving force behind German rearmament. From the contacts he still had in Germany, he understood that the rank and file of the army did not have a high opinion of Hitler, and gave the example of the army's Commander-in-Chief, General von Fritsch, who he said was not one of Hitler's supporters. 'I suppose it will always [be] amazing for later historians that the European Powers did not see this fact,' Brüning noted, 'and did not realise its importance.'[78]

By the end of 1937, Heinrich Brüning had settled into his exile in the United States, having begun teaching at Harvard that autumn. He continued to look for opportunities to discuss global politics with influential individuals and was keen to offer his insights to interested members of the general public. Meanwhile, Treviranus had bought a house in Surrey in the south-east of England, and his children were enrolled in local schools, though he was forced at one point to nervously plead to the Home Office for an extension to his family's permit to remain in Britain.[79] Churchill and Brüning stayed in touch, often discussing the deteriorating international situation as both watched on in horror as the Rome–Berlin Axis merged with the German–Japanese Anti-Comintern Pact on 6 November 1937.

Despite the glimmer of hope that Brüning had presented to Churchill, of a coup d'état which might oust Hitler and thereby avoid war, the Churchills suffered a devastating blow in the autumn of 1937. Their finances reached such a low point that they could no longer deny the imminent need to sell Chartwell. Photographs were taken of the house and its interiors and sent to the agents Knight, Frank & Rutley, though Churchill insisted these just be kept on file for enquiries rather than publicly advertised. Arrangements were made for Lady Maria St Just, an Anglo-Russian actress who counted Tennessee Williams among her closest friends, to view the house on 22 November. Churchill couldn't face the encounter and made himself scarce, spending the day with his researcher, Bill Deakin, at the London flat instead. With his continuing sense of helplessness, amid his ongoing political exile, and now at risk of losing his home, Churchill reached a low ebb. Despite their difficulties and the possibility of having to leave Chartwell, his wife Clementine never lost faith in him. She was certain that better days lay ahead, and on 30 November she sent him a birthday telegram, which prophetically read: 'Many Happy Returns, my Darling one, and may your star rise.'[80]

CHAPTER 7

THE PAN-EUROPEAN COUNT

Richard Coudenhove-Kalergi,
26–27 February 1938

It was perhaps inevitable that a man whom Adolf Hitler had nicknamed the 'Cosmopolitan Bastard' would get on well with Winston Churchill. Richard Coudenhove-Kalergi, whose parents were Austro-Hungarian and Japanese, was married to the Jewish Austrian actress Ida Roland, and had become a Czechoslovak citizen after the First World War. Having spent much of the 1920s and 1930s championing the idea of a Pan-European movement, he was therefore a particularly interesting dinner companion to Churchill at that time. The pair spent several hours together at Chartwell trying to fathom how countries threatened by Nazi Germany might form an alliance in an attempt to prevent war. Their discussion was so appreciated by Churchill that he gave his guest a copy of his most recent publication, *Great Contemporaries*, and agreed to speak again soon. Three weeks later, that very book, bearing Churchill's signature, was confiscated by the Gestapo, from Coudenhove-Kalergi's home in Vienna, as Nazi troops marched into Austria.

As 1937 drew to a close, the Churchills spent little time at Chartwell. Instead, they spent most days in London or visiting friends, so they could close down much of the house and reduce Chartwell's running costs. One rather welcome financial boost came in the form of a cheque, for the second year running, for having gone another year without drinking neat spirits, courtesy of Churchill's now long-standing bet with Lord Rothermere.[1] Over the course of two years, he won £1,100 from the wager, equivalent today to around £90,000. He also continued to write his articles for additional income, including his piece 'Britain Rearms' for the *Evening Standard*, which praised the efforts of Leslie Hore-Belisha, the Secretary of State for War, for his work in boosting recruitment into the British Army, but added that significant investment in equipment and supplies needed to follow.[2] Those close to Churchill may have noticed some subtle economies being made, as one invitee to his Morpeth Mansions flat noted in his diary that they had drunk sparkling moselle with their lunch instead of Churchill's usual champagne.[3] But the lobster they were served made clear that any economising was being done rather selectively.

In terms of his political focus, Churchill decided to change his approach for 1938. He paused his campaign to strengthen the Royal Air Force, noting that the Government had now realised the truth of his arguments on the subjects over recent years and was beginning to take action.[4] By that time he believed that Germany's air force had become stronger than the French and British air forces combined.[5] If this were true, and if Germany were able to utilise the power of the Italian air force also, Britain was not in a position to go to war at that time, unless perhaps they were given active Russian assistance. With this in mind, Churchill chose to turn his focus to strengthening Britain's international alliances.

Just a few days after New Year, Churchill journeyed to the British Embassy in Paris with his secretary Mrs Pearman, after which they spent most of January in the south of France. His diary was filled with reunions with old friends, including dinner with Pierre-Étienne Flandin on 8 January. Unfortunately, he found his old informant's account of the situation in France 'most pessimistic', which was even more disappointing to Churchill than that evening's cuisine, which he called 'lamentable'. Flandin made it clear that, by that time, many in France thought it likely that Germany would become the undisputed ruler of Europe in the near future. Churchill blamed those Prime Ministers and Foreign Secretaries who had been at the helm of international diplomacy between 1932 and 1935, and had failed to prevent Germany from rearming. 'A thousand years hence it will be incredible to historians that the victorious Allies delivered themselves over to the vengeance of the foe they had overcome', he wrote to Clementine, who was on holiday with Mary in Switzerland.[6]

Another scheduled meeting during his time in France was with the Duke of Windsor and his new wife Wallis. 'Whatever he suggests I shall have to do,' Churchill wrote to his friend Maxine Elliot, 'as I have not seen him since that dark day when he left our country, and as you know I am a devoted servant.'[7] He most likely had concerns over recent press coverage of the Windsors' tour of Germany, including the former British monarch being warmly greeted by Adolf Hitler. To his relief, the dinner was a great success, though it was clear that the Duke was no longer granted the deference to which he had been accustomed, and he had to fight for his place in the conversation with the other guests.[8]

Upon Churchill's return to Chartwell in early February, he discovered that Neville Chamberlain had moved one of his allies in the Foreign Office. Robert Vansittart, a key figure in anti-Nazi circles, was made Chief Diplomatic Advisor, which was seen by many as an empty post of reduced influence compared to his previous role as Foreign Office Permanent Secretary.[9] Meanwhile, Hitler had removed his Foreign Minister, replacing him with Joachim von Ribbentrop, the man who had tried to twist Churchill's arm at the Embassy in London. One report called him 'the most dangerous of the extremists Hitler had surrounded himself with on account of his stupidity'.[10] The Führer had also put himself at the head of the German armed forces. 'Now the whole place is in the hands of violent men,' Churchill wrote to a friend, 'and I fear very much lest something should happen in Central Europe.'[11]

An unexpected letter was awaiting him when he returned to Chartwell. It was from Count Richard Coudenhove-Kalergi and was addressed to 'His Excellency, Mr Winston Churchill'. 'I intend to come to London to discuss the problem of a closer cooperation between England and a Pan-European movement', the Count wrote from his home in Vienna.[12] He said that war in Europe was inevitable, and the danger could only be prevented by a pan-European Union group being established in England, with Churchill, ideally, as

18. Count Richard
Coudenhove-Kalergi,
founder of the
Pan-European Union,
1931.

the chairman. 'I am sure that there is no British statesman with whose ideas I sympathize as much as with yours. But of course we must talk over the whole problem.'[13] Showing his keenness to see Churchill, Coudenhove-Kalergi wrote again saying that he would be in London from 9 February. A pencil note, written by Churchill on this second letter reads 'Reminder. Try to see him'.[14]

The idea of a cross-European organisation was not new in 1938. It had been discussed, with various levels of seriousness, by statesmen, bankers, industrialists, academic economists and political scientists in the years since the First World War.[15] Coudenhove-Kalergi became President of the Pan-European Union in 1923, and it was for this reason that he was given a wrathful inclusion in Adolf Hitler's book, *Mein Kampf*, published in 1928. By 1930 the Union had established branches in almost every country in mainland Europe, and had its own periodical *Paneurope*, published in Paris and Vienna. Churchill was intrigued by Coudenhove-Kalergi's invitation. He asked Clementine whether they had enough time for lunch at the flat with him on 15 February, knowing that they needed to leave ample time to travel to an engagement that afternoon at Churchill's alma mater, Harrow School.[16] It was at this point that Leo Amery, the Liberal MP for Birmingham South and a contemporary of Churchill's from their time at Harrow, wrote to Churchill. Mentioning Coudenhove-Kalergi's arrival into England, Amery wrote, 'He is lunching with me on Tuesday and I am asking just three or four men to meet him. I think you would find him interesting and I believe he has the only real solution to the European problem.'[17] Amery had been impressed by a talk Coudenhove-Kalergi gave at Chatham House in London in April 1936. The pair dined together shortly after, with Amery writing in his diary, 'C to dinner, very anxious lest Hitler should jump Austria at any moment.'[18]

Churchill accepted Amery's invitation without hesitation, and telegrammed Coudenhove-Kalergi at Brown's Hotel in Mayfair to confirm that he would attend. The group met at 112 Eaton Square on 15 February. At this first meeting Coudenhove-Kalergi outlined his position. He felt confident that conflict in Europe could be avoided through governmental collaboration and arbitration treaties. He also discussed the political situation in Austria, and Amery noted that Coudenhove-Kalergi was 'not too pessimistic', and thought that Kurt von Schuschnigg, the Chancellor of Austria, may yet find a solution to quash any ambitions Hitler might have. He was, however, uncertain of the role Britain might play in the future of Austria.[19] Churchill was intrigued by his new acquaintance and, with Austria increasingly in his thoughts, noted Coudenhove-Kalergi's views and wondered if the pair might meet again.

Meanwhile, events began to quickly deteriorate. Late on the night of 20 February, Churchill was in his bedroom at Chartwell when he was alerted to a telephone message saying that Anthony Eden had resigned from his role as Foreign Secretary.[20] Churchill was shocked and deeply affected by this news. 'I must confess that my heart sank,' he later wrote of that moment, 'and for a while the dark waters of despair overwhelmed me.'[21] He lay awake all night, the only time in his life when sleep deserted him, and he became engulfed in a fear of what might await. Although the two men weren't always in agreement, Churchill wrote that Eden 'seemed to me at this moment to embody the life-hope of the British nation'.[22] He lay in his bed at Chartwell, and remained open-eyed until the light from that morning's sunrise slowly lit the room. 'I watched the daylight slowly creep in through the windows,' Churchill later recalled of that morning's dawn, 'and saw before me in mental gaze the vision of Death.'[23]

Upon Eden's resignation, Lord Halifax was appointed Foreign Secretary. Just three months earlier he had, at Hermann Göring's invitation, travelled to Germany under the pretext of attending a hunting exhibition in Berlin. A meeting between Halifax and Hitler was organised at Berchtesgaden, the Führer's holiday home in the Bavarian Alps. According to the recollections of General Beck, Chief of the German General Staff and a witness to the conversation, Hitler assured Halifax that any changes to Germany's borders would be done by peaceful means. In reply to this, and further reassurance from Göring, Halifax conceded that it would be difficult in that case for Britain to intervene.[24] Even the idea of Halifax's visit to Berlin had been strongly objected to by both Anthony Eden and his Under-Secretary of State, Sir Robert Vansittart, let alone a meeting with Hitler.[25] Eden had threatened to resign at that point in 1937, and Churchill, among others, shared his outrage.[26] By February 1938, matters had reached a point where Eden finally felt he had no other option. As the following day dawned, a sleep-deprived and broken Churchill prepared the speech he would give in Parliament the following day.

As he readied himself to be driven by Cale to Westminster, he sought out members of the household staff to alert them to his departure. This was a lifelong habit of Churchill's, as remembered by Ann Henderson, a temporary support secretary who worked at Chartwell at the time. 'On departing twenty miles distant, on a mission to arouse a sluggish House of Commons to a sense of Britain's peril, he always bade farewell to the household, as if setting forth on a lengthy pilgrimage', she later recalled to a friend.[27] She reflected fondly on one occasion when she was trying to find Churchill for a telephone call, and was assured by the cook that Mr Churchill could not have left for London already, as he had not yet come down to the kitchen to say goodbye.

As he rose to his feet in the House of Commons, Churchill mentioned his recent meeting with Coudenhove-Kalergi, saying, 'I was told by a friend who arrived from Vienna a few days ago one of the results of the Halifax Mission. One thing he said was that Lord Halifax had given his friend reason to believe that England would not object to German authority over Austria.'[28] Cries of 'Shame!' filled the debating chamber. Churchill wryly remarked that perhaps his new Austrian friend had misunderstood what he had heard, but said he had disclosed it that day because his belief in itself was a valuable piece of information. It showed the dangers that can arise from unofficial visits such as Halifax's, the risk of false understandings, and the demonstration of a belief that might well become commonplace in Austria. He then turned to the subject of his friend and colleague, Anthony Eden:

> Let us see what are the wider consequences of this resignation of the Foreign Secretary. They are grievous in the extreme. This last week has been a good week for dictators – one of the best they ever had. The German dictator has laid his heavy hand upon a small but historic country, and the Italian dictator has carried his vendetta to a victorious conclusion against my right hon. Friend the Member for Warwick and Leamington (Mr. Eden).[29]

The speech Churchill gave that day, including a reference to Austria having been 'laid in thrall', was far-reaching. Two days later he received a letter from George Franckenstein, the Austrian Ambassador, saying: 'I listened with great interest and much admiration to your brilliant speech in the House the other day and want to thank you very warmly for what you said about Austria.'[30] Similarly, Harcourt 'Crinks' Johnstone wrote with kind words to Churchill. 'I am writing a line to say – with great respect – how much I have admired your speeches during the Eden-Austria period. They seem to me to have been a marvellous contribution to the steadiness, good judgement and courage of the nation.'[31] There were cynics, however, with one observer saying that Churchill's speech was 'yet another bid on his part to lead an Independent, perhaps Centre, party'.[32]

It was in the aftermath of his appearance in the House of Commons that Churchill contacted Coudenhove-Kalergi to arrange another meeting, and there wasn't a moment to waste. 'Mr Churchill would be delighted if you could lunch with him tomorrow Friday at Chartwell, Westerham', the telegram read. 'Kindly telephone Westerham 81 tomorrow morning after ten o'clock.' Unfortunately, that day wasn't possible, and so the plan was changed for the pair to meet for tea at Chartwell on the afternoon of Saturday 26 February.

The delay might well have been that Coudenhove-Kalergi already had plans on Friday with his wife, Ida Roland, who had accompanied him to London. A leading actress in Vienna, she had come to London in the hope of performing in the West End. She had been offered roles on the London stage in the past, but none had been good enough for her. In an interview at their hotel with the *Daily News*, she described her immersive approach to performances. 'If her part is Lady Macbeth, she adopts for the time being long medieval robes, and wears her hair combed loosely over her shoulders.'[33] She was clearly pitching for the role, telling the journalist, 'If only it could be Macbeth. I think Lady Macbeth one of the most exquisite parts.'[34] She didn't have long to lay claim to the role, however, as she was due to return to Vienna to prepare for her new play at the Burgtheater the following week.

Despite the brief delay, the opportunity to speak again with Churchill when, in Coudenhove-Kalergi's words, 'Austria was in her death throes'[35] was too good for him to miss. He was especially grateful for the chance to discuss current affairs in private. By this time he held the view that France was too weak to withstand the combined pressures of Germany, Italy and Spain. The isolationist mood which he had observed in the British Government seemed to be diminishing, and he was convinced that Churchill represented British public opinion. With Churchill having pressed for European alliances to curtail Hitler's expansionist drive, Coudenove-Kalergi felt that he was speaking to the one leading political figure who could bring this about.

The Austrian Count's first observation of Churchill, upon meeting him at Chartwell, was that he was just the genial aristocrat that he imagined he would be. On this subject, he could speak with great authority. His father, Count Heinrich Coudenhove-Kalergi, was an Austro-Hungarian diplomat, whose noble ancestral line dated back to 1259, and who called Ronsperg Castle their family home.[36] Heinrich Coudenhove-Kalergi was the head of the Austrian Legation in Tokyo when he met Mitsuko Aoyama, the daughter of a wealthy Japanese landowner and the descendant of an old samurai family.[37] The story goes that his horse slipped on ice one day and, as he was thrown from the horse, Mitsuko dashed to his rescue. The pair fell in love and she became one of the first Japanese citizens to emigrate to Europe. Richard Coudenhove-Kalergi was, therefore, raised with a global perspective and in an atmosphere of internationalism. For this reason, he found the First World War horrifying for reasons beyond its futility and the enormous loss of life. He wrote to his wife Ida in August 1914: 'What is more terrifying than anything, perhaps for centuries to come, is the awakening of the aggressive tendency of nationalism which is nothing but the apparently vanquishing religious fanaticism reappearing under a new form.'[38]

Coudenhove-Kalergi arrived at Chartwell after lunch on a freezing February day. The pair sat down to tea, which tended to include sandwiches and Churchill's favourite Dundee cake, and discussed the horrors of the Nazi regime and the prospect of German expansion in Central Europe.[39] Coudenhove-Kalergi gave his own assessment of current thinking in Britain. He told Churchill that a strong reaction was setting in against the Government's policy of appeasement and its willingness to turn a blind eye to Germany's breaches of the Treaty of Versailles, including the Nazis' remilitarisation of the Rhineland, and rearmament. He also said he was aware of a growing resistance movement in Britain, of those who feared that continuing aggression from Germany would be met by further concessions from the British Government. As a result, Coudenhove-Kalergi argued that the political attitude of Britons towards the Third Reich did not differ significantly from the programme of his Pan-European movement. Churchill agreed in the sense of appreciating the need for European understanding, but was quick to stress the need for Anglo-American cooperation also.

Alongside the seriousness of their discussions, Churchill also showed his playful side, and Coudenhove-Kalergi noted his host's capacity for enjoying life. At one point the pair wrapped up and faced the sub-zero temperatures outside, looking out across the frozen lakes as daylight began to disappear behind the hillside. Such wintry conditions made the garden something of a winter wonderland. The winter of 1927–28, for example, had been so severe that the lakes completely froze. The family took to ice-skating across them and the household staff were invited to join, including one who bravely brought a chair from the house in order to have a comfortable seat while on the ice. Some of the party had chosen to descend from the house on sledges, allowing them to speedily dash down the hillside. From that same winter a photo survives of Churchill building a snowman in the grounds beyond the lake. The three-sphered structure measured approximately 6 feet in height, and was therefore even taller than Churchill himself, who painstakingly sculpted its facial features while smoking his cigar. It had been some years, however, since skating or snowman-building had taken place at Chartwell, and on that particular freezing day Churchill and Coudenhove-Kalergi simply admired the dramatic view covered in a glistening veil of frost.

Churchill then showed his guest the brick walls and continued down the garden to his painting studio, showing Coudenhove-Kalergi the scale and breadth of his artistic output. 'My paintings are not good enough,' his new secretary Mrs Hill later recalled him saying to visitors at this time, 'they're very amateur.'[40] Despite his modesty, he was often greeted with acclaim by those who saw his paintings, including the artist Sir John Lavery who had visited Chartwell just a few months earlier. 'I know few amateur wielders of the brush with a keener sense of light and colour', Lavery wrote some years later. 'Had he chosen painting instead of statesmanship I believe he would have been a great master of the brush.'[41]

The two men were getting on so well that Churchill invited Coudenhove-Kalergi to extend his stay. Mindful that Ida was awaiting him at their hotel, Coudenhove-Kalergi said that he ought to be getting back to London, but the invitation proved too tempting to resist. Churchill showed him to one of the guest rooms, almost certainly the 'Henry VIII room'. This would previously have been a task undertaken by his butler Inches, but his departure and the scaling-down of Chartwell's staffing meant that Churchill himself had to help his guest settle in. Churchill then described his typical late-afternoon routine, of a hot bath followed by a rest in bed, and suggested that his guest might want to follow his example. Coudenhove-Kalergi then found himself in the remarkable situation of having Churchill run a bath for him, in the smaller bathroom at the top of the main stairs, while Coudenhove-Kalergi explored the rooms nearby. After their respective restorative afternoons, Churchill's guest was impressed that this routine had the effect of making Churchill look years younger. The pair sat down to dinner at 8.15pm and were waited on by the new parlourmaid. Their menu may have reflected the dietary instructions given to Churchill recently in light of his 'very active' stomach, though Churchill did not always adhere to the medical advice he was given. 'Avoid – Highly seasoned food, cooked cheese, high game, strong coffee, marmalade peel, pickles, coarse vegetables, watercress stalks, radish, cucumbers, raw apples, pineapple, rich pastries, new bread', his diet sheet from Dr Thomas Hunt read.[42] Other instructions included to smoke fewer cigars, to limit himself to one glass of port after dinner and to eat vegetable soup rather than meat soups or broth. Churchill politely replied, but immediately attempted to justify his lack of adherence. 'I do not like vegetable soups and always have chicken broth ... I hope you do not attach importance to this', he replied, along with other suggested changes to the doctor's advice.[43]

The two gentlemen settled down to dinner and continued their discussion. 'All his thoughts and activities were concentrated on preparing his country for the decisive battle against Hitler,' Coudenhove-Kalergi later reflected, 'for he now considered this quite inevitable.' He replied to Churchill saying that he felt a united Europe should be centred around a Paris–London axis, in the hope that those states threatened by Hitler would join this alliance and thereby avert war or, failing that, win it. As the pair conversed,

Coudenhove-Kalergi found himself reflecting on his host, and was reminded of a quote by the philosopher Nietzsche: 'This is how I like a man to be: honest towards himself and towards his friends; courageous in the face of the enemy; magnanimous in his treatment of the vanquished and at all times courteous.'[44] He went on to compare his host to the likes of Shakespeare, Queen Elizabeth I and even a patrician of ancient Rome.

After an evening of lively discussion and debate, Churchill's guest retired for the night while Churchill ascended to the study to continue writing. He was tirelessly working on his final volume of *Marlborough*, having finished the bulk of the work but undertaking final revisions, and weaving in the notes suggested to him by trusted friends. As always, a secretary was on hand to assist, and his literary researcher, Bill Deakin, had been working his way through the revisions for much of the day. A number of correspondences were written that evening in response to those who had kindly sent amendments to his

19. Winston Churchill, seated at his desk in the study at Chartwell, February 1939.

near-complete manuscript. 'How like the Tory party of those days our present lot is!,' Churchill wrote in reply to his friend Keith Feiling, who had recently left the History Department of Oxford University, before adding, 'I wish I had studied history at the beginning of my life, instead of at the end.'[45] Another letter composed that day was to Sir James Hawkey, the Vice-Chairman of the Conservative Association in Churchill's constituency, who had recently been at Chartwell to dine with Heinrich Brüning. Almost certainly influenced by that evening's discussion, Churchill wrote to Hawkey, 'We look forward to the building up of a system of collective security, to the prevention of violence and bloodshed through the united action of many Nations, States and Races, and to the reign of World Law.'[46] For now, at least, his view of how the menace of dictatorial regimes could be curtailed seemed very much in line with those of his guest. The next morning, as Coudenhove-Kalergi was preparing to depart from Chartwell and travel back to London, Churchill gave him a signed copy of *Great Contemporaries*, before wishing his guest a safe journey back to Austria.

In the opening weeks of 1938 the Austrian Chancellor, Kurt von Schuschnigg, found himself under increasing pressure from activists who campaigned for union with Germany. Adolf Hitler had held a secret conference with generals and key advisors on 5 November 1937, in which he outlined his strategy for military expansion, including the annexation of Austria and the destruction of Czechoslovakia.[47] Three months later, on 20 February 1938, the day of Anthony Eden's resignation, Hitler gave a speech in the Reichstag in which he spoke of the millions of Germans in Austria and Czechoslovakia whose fate, he claimed, was of significant concern to him.

> Over 10 million Germans live in two of the states adjoining our frontiers ... it is intolerable for a self-respecting world power to know that across the frontier are kinsmen who have to suffer ... To the interests of the German Reich belongs also the protection of those fellow Germans who live beyond our frontiers.[48]

Hitler had invited the Austrian Chancellor to Berchtesgaden just a few days before, where he presented him with an ultimatum, and said refusal to sign would result in a military invasion. Schuschnigg signed, but later said that it was invalid as he had not got ratification from the President. Meanwhile, in certain quarters, support for an Anschluss with Austria seemed to be gaining momentum. Unity Mitford, one of the famous Mitford sisters and a cousin of Clementine's, wrote to Churchill on 5 March, saying that she thought he was 'misinformed about Austrian affairs'.[49] She had been present at the recent Schuschnigg/Hitler meeting and said she witnessed an outpouring of jubilation as a result. 'The population went mad with joy and one could not move in the streets for people shouting "Heil Hitler! Anschluss!" & waving Swastika flags', she told Churchill. 'By night, the hills around Vienna were ablaze with bonfires in the shape of Swastikas.'[50] Churchill forwarded it to the Austrian Ambassador to help shape his reply to his wife's cousin. Meanwhile, on Wednesday 9 March, Chancellor Schuschnigg announced that there would be a plebiscite by which the Austrian people could then vote to decide their own future that Sunday.[51] He assumed that most Austrians would opt for continuing independence rather than be absorbed by Nazi Germany, and felt certain of a victory of 70–80 per cent. Hitler was furious and instructed his generals to 'Prepare Case Otto', the plans for the invasion of Austria.[52]

At 5.30am on 11 March, Schuschnigg received a telephone call from Vienna's police headquarters. 'The German frontier at Salzburg was closed an hour ago. The German customs officials have been withdrawn. Railway communications have been cut', he was told. He was then informed that the German Army Corps were mobilising in Munich and would shortly be moving towards Austria. Hitler demanded the cancellation of the referendum while his troops were massing at the border.

By this time, Count Coudenhove-Kalergi and his wife Ida had arrived back in Austria, returning to their home in Vienna on 8 March, having taken a scenic route from London through France and Switzerland. As they progressed towards their home, they became aware that the situation in Vienna was reaching a fever pitch. On their return they found the city had become overwhelmed by a 'patriotic fervour' and was 'completely transformed'.[53] He later described Vienna as having a festive air about it, in anticipation of Hitler losing in the upcoming election battle, and with patriotic songs and demonstrations filling the streets.[54] This all changed on 11 March when, early in the afternoon, silence fell across the city, and people disappeared from the streets. Rumours began to spread, and the first swastika-laden lorries were seen.

The Churchills, meanwhile, were at a lunch party at 10 Downing Street that day, hosted by Neville Chamberlain and his wife Anne. Fellow attendees included the former German Ambassador to the United Kingdom, Joachim von Ribbentrop, who had recently been made Hitler's Foreign Secretary, and his wife Annelies, as well as Britain's new Foreign Secretary, Lord Halifax, and his wife Dorothy.[55] The group was still seated at Number 10's dining table when a Foreign Office messenger arrived with an envelope which soon made its way to Chamberlain. Though its contents were not disclosed to Churchill, he immediately sensed danger. He noticed Ribbentrop's efforts to keep the Prime Minister away from his work and his telephone, but he was not close enough to hear what was being discussed. Chamberlain then announced, 'I am sorry. I have to go now to attend to urgent business.'[56] The assembled guests hastily departed and, within an hour, Churchill learnt that the envelope he had seen across the table at lunch had stated that Hitler had demanded the resignation of Austria's Chancellor, Kurt von Schuschnigg, that day. The newly appointed replacement Chancellor, the Nazi Arthur Seyss-Inquart, then invited German troops into Austria to 'restore order' that night.[57]

In Vienna, trying to remain calm and carry on as usual, the Coudenhove-Kalergis kept their plans to host a dinner party at their home that evening. The meal was interrupted by a broadcast by Schuschnigg announcing that the plebiscite was cancelled, he had resigned, and concluding with the words 'God save Austria'. Shortly after, Coudenhove-Kalergi received an anonymous phone call telling him that he was high on the Gestapo hit list, and should leave the country immediately.[58] As a Czechoslovak citizen, he called their embassy to confirm if this was the case. The dinner party quickly dispersed as the hosts frantically packed suitcases and grabbed the smaller of their two dogs, a tiny white Pekinese called Pai-Chuan. They then dashed to the Czechoslovak embassy where they hoped to spend the night before being driven over the border the next morning. But their route was blocked by cheering crowds waving swastika flags. Plan B was the Swiss embassy, who offered the couple refuge for the night, but they decided that they could not wait, as the situation could be even more dangerous in the morning. There was just one problem: neither Coudenhove-Kalergi nor his wife knew how to drive.[59]

After some complex logistics involving their housekeeper bringing their car, along with their larger Russian sheepdog, and the Swiss Ambassador offering his driver, they left Vienna at 11pm. The crowds had grown further still, singing triumphantly and shouting 'Heil Hitler!', which made things all the more difficult when the chauffeur realised he hadn't brought his passport in order to cross the border, and so they had to make a detour via his home. While the couple sat in the Swiss-registered vehicle outside, a group of young Nazis appeared with swastika armbands and brandishing steel bars. 'One of the Nazis walked up to the car and stroked the dogs', Coudenhove-Kalergi later wrote. 'Luckily he mistook us for Swiss diplomats. The minutes which followed seemed like hours; at last our chauffeur reappeared and we drove out to the open road.'[60] The couple were largely silent and Coudenhove-Kalergi clutched his automatic pistol tightly the whole way. By the time they got to the border, the guards were still at their posts and there was no sign of the Third Reich. They had got there just in time.

From Bratislava, Coudenhove-Kalergi and his wife travelled to Budapest, Zagreb, Ljubljana, Trieste, along the shores of Lake Garda and finally to their end destination, Switzerland. They then learned that their flat in Vienna had been searched and sealed by the Gestapo, with virtually all their papers seized, including the book Churchill gave him at Chartwell.

When Churchill returned to Chartwell the next day, he composed a reply to the recent letter from his wife's cousin Unity, showing it to Clementine first. With no preamble or pleasantries, it simply said: 'There can be no doubt that a fair plebiscite would have shown that a large majority of the people of Austria loathe the idea of being under Nazi rule.' He then added, 'It was because Herr Hitler feared the free expression of opinion that we are compelled to witness the present dastardly outrage.'[61]

On 14 March, three days after Germany's annexation of Austria, Churchill appeared in the House of Commons. He reflected on Nazi Germany's 'programme of aggression, nicely calculated and timed, unfolding stage by stage'. Thinking ahead to 1940, he asked the question: 'Where shall we be two years hence, for instance, when the German Army will certainly be much larger than the French Army?' He described the persecution which would ensue in Austria, and the precarious position of Czechoslovakia. He then made a campaign for collective security as a means of defence, with words reflecting much of the conversation he and Coudenhove-Kalergi had just two weeks earlier at Chartwell:

We have been urged to make common cause in self-defence with the French Republic. What is that but the beginning of collective security? I agree with that. Not so lightly will the two great liberal democracies of the West be challenged, and not so easily, if challenged, will they be subjugated. That is the beginning of collective security. But why stop there? Why be edged and pushed farther down the slope in a disorderly expostulating crowd of embarrassed States? Why not make a stand while there is still a good company of united, very powerful countries that share our dangers and aspirations?[62]

Following the speech, hundreds of letters began to arrive at Chartwell about the fate of Austria, which Clementine pored over as well as her husband.[63] One British student resident in Vienna described the despair he felt when reading the positive coverage of recent events in *The Times*. He wrote to Churchill describing lorry-loads of Nazi supporters who were driven there 'to make it a hell hot enough to hold the Führer', and how many sickening incidents were taking place in the aftermath, including a neighbouring Jewish family of six who chose to shoot themselves upon the arrival of Nazi troops rather than live under their terror.[64] Churchill immediately forwarded the letter to Geoffrey Dawson, *The Times'* editor. Dawson replied, calling the letter a 'distressing document', but said that there had been an impression of jubilation in Vienna at the time, and so that was what had been reported.[65]

Coudenhove-Kalergi and his Jewish wife Ida were undoubtedly lucky to escape Austria when they did. Their status as refugees was announced in the British press the next day, alongside reference to him having 'recently had conversations in London with prominent politicians'.[66] He and Churchill remained in touch and when he was told about his former houseguest's terrifying escape, and the Gestapo's seizure of his signed copy of *Great Contemporaries*, Churchill immediately sent another inscribed copy to him in Switzerland. What Coudenhove-Kalergi wasn't able to tell Churchill, however, because he wasn't yet aware, was that the Gestapo had in fact sent a car in pursuit when alerted to the couple trying to flee from Vienna.[67] They were followed for much of the journey away from the city, and it was only because the Nazis' car broke down en route that they were able to safely get away.

CHAPTER 8

PLANNING A COUP

Ewald von Kleist-Schmenzin, 19 August 1938

O f all those who came to Chartwell to inform Churchill about Nazi Germany, few did so at greater personal risk than Ewald von Kleist-Schmenzin. It has since been said that he 'belonged among the most resolute and uncompromising enemies of Hitler'.[1] The testimony and evidence he brought to Churchill confirmed that his belief, of a likely attack by Germany on Czechoslovakia, was correct. There was, however, a course of action that could prevent this. Kleist-Schmenzin's mission, over the course of six days in August 1938, was to plead with influential figures in British politics and seek concrete evidence that the British Government would abandon its policy of appeasing Hitler, if he did indeed invade Czechoslovakia. If he was successful, it might just be enough to convince the German generals to stage a coup, overthrow the Führer and end the Nazi regime.

In the weeks after the Anschluss, Churchill's engagement diary was filled with meetings, lunches, dinners, speeches and parliamentary business almost every day. There are only three signatures in Chartwell's visitors' book for the spring of 1938. Professor Lindemann appears twice, and Ilona Tatham, Clementine's masseuse, came for a week-long stay to administer 'professional services in massage, electricity and Swedish exercises'. Desmond Morton visited too, though it was most likely owing to his industrial intelligence work that he was disinclined to document his visits to Chartwell. These quiet months at the Churchills' country home were in part due to a resurgence in

*20. Ewald von
Kleist-Schmenzin, the
aristocratic German
lawyer and anti-Nazi
activist, undated.*

Churchill's political standing. 'The last few days have seen a revival of
the wish to see Winston in the Government', wrote Thomas Jones,
the Deputy Secretary to the Cabinet, to a friend.[2] Suddenly finding
himself much more in demand in London, it made sense to base
himself primarily out of their London residence for a number of
weeks. As his political star rose, however, his financial stability plum-
meted, with significant share losses hitting the family finances hard.
Notes written by him on 19 March outline his difficulties, and list
possible actions he could take to increase his income, including the
quick completion of his next contracted book, *A History of the English-
Speaking Peoples*, which wasn't due for another twenty months, but
would bring in a much-needed £15,000.[3] He complained to friends
that his focus on public affairs gave him less time to write articles,

which were otherwise a consistent source of income. Fortunately, a generous friend, Sir Henry Strakosch, agreed to cover all of Churchill's share losses, which temporarily brought comfort, but was not a long-term solution. With a continuing need to reduce costs, Chartwell remained largely uninhabited.

While ensconced in their London flat, Churchill met with those who, like him, believed that Germany's Anschluss with Austria would lead to further aggression elsewhere. Heinrich Brüning was among those who visited him, having just returned from the United States, and was quickly invited to tea. Here he was also introduced to Clementine, who had been away in Austria when he visited Chartwell the year before. Brüning later wrote that he found her 'very kind and charming', with a very pro-French attitude, and added that this feeling dominated all her opinions on the subject of politics. The subject of Brüning's recent private audience with President Roosevelt quickly arose. During their four-hour meeting, he told the President that there was the possibility that Hitler could be overthrown by senior members of Germany's armed forces from 'the old families', with whom he was in contact. He also confirmed that he anticipated bloody clashes between 'the old Reichswehr and Hitler'.[4]

Sharing the outcome of his meeting at the White House, Brüning told Churchill that Roosevelt had agreed to his appeal to pursue a clear foreign policy course, but noted that the President had repeatedly lapsed into 'shallow optimism' and hoped for quick solutions. There, in Churchill's flat, Brüning then turned to the subject of the British Government, which he insisted should adopt a precise programme that, when shared with 'reliable men in the German Army', might induce them to carry out a coup d'état. They would need to know what would await, both domestically and in terms of the international response, once the Nazis had been overthrown. Brüning knew which of the General Staff officers were considering undertaking resistance action against the Third Reich, having been informed by Carl Goerdeler, a close political ally of his who had remained in Germany but 'went to work with heart and soul in opposition to Hitler'.[5] He became a member of the private intelligence network of General Ludwig Beck, the Chief of the General Staff who felt profoundly uneasy about the Anschluss with Austria. He also privately opposed the Führer's strategy of a continuing south-eastward push, which he had known about since the secret conference Hitler held in November 1937, telling those in attendance that he intended to go to war sooner or later. This view was shared at that time by Admiral Wilhelm Canaris, who had been the Head of the *Abwehr*, Germany's Military Intelligence since 1935 but, over the winter of 1937–38, had, according to one biographer, a 'secret metamorphosis'.[6] He had reportedly been in favour of a union of Germany and Austria, but not on the basis of an invasion and Nazi supremacy.[7] His role also made him all too aware of the terrible conflict that awaited if Hitler continued his trajectory towards war.

Churchill seemed impressed with the intelligence Brüning revealed, but was very grave about the situation. Brüning later recalled how his host talked about 'getting rid of the gangsters and consolidating the European position'.[8] He was in complete agreement, saying how urgent it was, as the Nazis were bound to embark on the next phase following their success in Austria, and especially given the acquiescence of public opinion in Britain.

Not all of Churchill's former informants were being so helpful. Pierre-Étienne Flandin, the former Prime Minister of France, was 'behaving very badly', according to a note from Churchill to Ava Wigram, 'and doing all manner of harm'.[9] There had been a growing feeling of uncertainty in France, and Flandin's position shifted from resistance to Germany, to appeasement, arguing for a rapprochement with the Nazis. Shortly before the Anschluss, he advocated a policy of giving a free hand to Germany in Central and Eastern Europe, insisting that France could not play the role of the *gendarme*, in Europe, alone.[10] Churchill was due to meet with Flandin during his next trip to France, departing for Paris on 25 March. The day before he left, he delivered one of the greatest orations of his political career.

The method by which the speech of 24 March was crafted was rather unusual. With Mrs Pearman's ill health, and Miss Hamblin having given her notice in order to take up a new role as secretary to the Churchills' son-in-law Duncan Sandys, much pressure fell on the Churchills' resident secretary, Mrs Hill. With diminished staff, Churchill hired a dictation machine called a 'Discavox'.[11] It was advertised, seemingly to an exclusively male clientele, as 'The new dictating method that will double his output'. Unfortunately, its recording time was just a few minutes and so Churchill quickly abandoned it. Instead, Mrs Hill had to travel from Chartwell to London and back every day. She carried a portable typewriter with her which she took into the Houses of Parliament, typing up her shorthand notes and passing them to him in the debating chamber. When asked once how often she was there when he was giving speeches, she replied, 'See Hansard! . . . I always went!'[12] That day, the Churchills hosted the former Austrian Ambassador, George Franckenstein, for lunch at 1.30pm at their London flat. He brought with him Count Colloredo-Mannsfeld, whose family were originally Italian nobles, but his branch had settled in Austria in the sixteenth century. He was also the President of the Imperial-Royal Agricultural Society in Vienna, and was targeted by the Nazis after the Anschluss.[13] The Churchills and their guests discussed what he would call, just a few hours later, the 'rape of Austria before our eyes',[14] with Mrs Hill capturing any additional speech notes for Churchill in shorthand.

As Churchill took his usual place in the House of Commons, Clementine was seated in the public gallery above.[15] She watched as Chamberlain opened proceedings at precisely 3.49pm, restating the Government's policy, being 'the maintenance and preservation of peace and the establishment of a sense of confidence that peace will, in fact, be maintained'.[16] He was followed by the Labour Party Leader, Clement Attlee, and then the Liberal Party Leader, Archie Sinclair. After almost three hours of waiting, at 6.45pm, it was Churchill's turn.

With his head thrust forward, and clutching the notes Mrs Hill had typed moments before, he began reflecting on the 'torture' of Austria, and how Czechoslovakia was very likely the next target of Nazi aggression, with Yugoslavia, Bulgaria and Romania likely to follow. 'The Nazification of the whole of the Danube States is a danger of the first capital magnitude to the British Empire. Is it all to go for nothing? Is it all to be whistled down the wind? If so, we shall repent in blood and tears our imprudence and our lack of force and energy.'[17] He insisted that a Defence of the Realm Act should be passed, giving powers to divert industry to ensure that rearmament was made a priority. Lamenting the inaction of recent years by the British Government, and his own failed campaign to sound the alarm since 1933, he reflected that: 'Two years ago it was safe, three years ago it was easy and four years ago a mere despatch might have rectified the position. But where shall we be a year hence? Where shall we be in 1940?' Finally, he concluded with words so powerful it was as if he held the fate of his country in his hands:

> ... if mortal catastrophe should overtake the British Nation and the British Empire, historians a thousand years hence will still be baffled by the mystery of our affairs. They will never understand how it was that a victorious nation, with everything in hand, suffered themselves to be brought low, and to cast away all that they had gained by measureless sacrifice and absolute victory – gone with the wind!
>
> Now the victors are the vanquished, and those who threw down their arms in the field and sued for an armistice are striding on to world mastery. That is the position, that is the terrible trans-formation that has taken place bit by bit ... Now is the time at last to rouse the nation. Perhaps it is the last time it can be roused with a chance of preventing war, or with a chance of coming through to victory should our efforts to prevent war fail. We should lay aside every hindrance to endeavour by uniting the whole force and spirit of our people to raise again a great British nation standing up before all the world, for such a nation, rising in its ancient vigour, can even at this hour save civilisation.[18]

The next day, Churchill journeyed to Paris and met with Pierre-Étienne Flandin, who declared over lunch that Czechoslovakia was now impossible to defend, to which Churchill accused him of 'black pessimism'.[19] Seeing no viable alternative, Flandin had become increasingly in favour of capitulation to Hitler. The conversation was overheard by Sir Eric Phipps, the British Ambassador to France, who sent covert updates of Churchill's 'kaleidoscopic manner' in Paris to the Foreign Secretary, Lord Halifax.[20] Alongside detailed accounts of Churchill's meetings and conversations, Phipps poked fun at Churchill's French, calling it 'most strange and at times quite incomprehensible'.[21] To this section of Phipps's account, Halifax replied that he had read it aloud in Cabinet, where attendees 'were greatly amused' by it.[22]

The weakening of his former ally's resolve was a bitter pill for Churchill to swallow, but a worse revelation awaited the following week, when the press broke the news of the potential sale of Chartwell. The *Daily Express* published the headline 'Winston Puts His Mansion Up For Sale' on the front page, where the journalist recalled a visit he had made to the Churchills' country home. 'I remember his eloquence as he pointed out the views from his windows of the Kentish Weald,' the article read, adding how Churchill called it 'A home in one of England's loveliest spots.'[23] The tone of the article made Churchill's deep fondness for his home very apparent, with implications therefore that the sale was due to financial distress. Randolph wrote to his father that day, in light of the report, urging him to take his advice more in terms of handling the press. 'If there is any information which is bound to become public, the sooner you let me have it the better', he argued to his father.[24] The following day, the *Daily Telegraph* published the story, entitled 'Mr Churchill's Home – Chartwell For Sale', saying that Churchill was prepared to consider the private sale of his home, provided a satisfactory offer was made.[25] On the same day, a descriptive brochure of Chartwell was produced by their estate agent, listing the house as follows:

About 80 Acres.

Hall, Five Reception Rooms; Nineteen Bed and Dressing Rooms, Eight Bath Rooms; Usual Domestic Offices; Company's Electric Light and Water, Central Heating throughout, Modern Drainage; Stabling and Three Garages.

Heated and Filtered Open Air Swimming Pool. Two Lakes. Hard Tennis Court. Beautiful Grounds and Gardens. Park and Woodland.[26]

*21. The drawing room at Chartwell, part of the 1922–24 extension
to the building known as the 'Tilden wing', November 1937.*

The views were a key feature in the brochure, with the house
listed as being 550 feet above sea level, and describing the 'wide views
over the Kentish Weald, along the Valley to the South and also over
a considerable stretch of undulating wooded country to the Downs
in the distance'.[27] The photographs, taken in November of the
previous year, show a home of beautiful interiors and in the Churchills'
timeless taste. The gardens and landscapes looked glorious, all of
them somehow touched and shaped by Churchill's own hand, from
the brick walls to the island on the lake and other picturesque alterations to the gardens and grounds. Across just six pages, the agents
had successfully conveyed what Chartwell was, as perfectly put by a
young friend of Sarah's who visited in the 1930s, when she called it
'a place of such great romance, beauty and almost tangible peace. It
had a detached atmosphere all of its own – the creation of the great

Churchill family whose home it was and who loved the place so much.'[28] The prospect of leaving Chartwell suddenly felt very real, and Churchill soon found himself with cold feet. By 18 April, the press were writing that Churchill had changed his mind, saying 'when it came to the point, neither he nor Mrs Churchill could bear the idea of parting with the place'.[29]

All was thrown into disarray when Mrs Pearman, the Churchills' lead secretary who had been with the family for ten years, suffered a stroke in May. Churchill had been away for a series of speeches in Manchester and Bristol, accompanied by Mrs Hill. They returned to the flat in London before going back to Chartwell and the impact of Mrs Pearman's absence was apparent. Mrs Hill later remembered, 'there was a table piled up with letters and mail, and when we got to Chartwell eventually of course there was another pile. Terrible.'[30] With the diagnosis not yet known to Churchill, he sent a heartfelt handwritten letter on 18 May. 'I am so grieved at your illness – due I fear largely to your devotion to my interests & fortunes', he wrote.[31] Clementine too thought exhaustion might well have been the cause. 'I must write to you to say how very very sorry I am about your illness & how much I feel for you', she wrote to Mrs Pearman on 21 May. 'You have been working so very hard, and combined it has been too much.'[32]

As the household at Chartwell adjusted to the loss of two of its linchpins, Mrs Pearman and Miss Hamblin, events escalated further in Europe. On the evening of 20 May 1938, there were reports of German troop movements on the border with Czechoslovakia. In response to these military measures, demonstrating Nazi Germany's preparations for offensive action, the Government in Prague passed a decree to call up military reservists, provoking a crisis in Europe.[33] Altogether, almost 400,000 men, including soldiers and reservists, marched into the Sudetenland, the region of Czechoslovakia that bordered Germany and Austria, and occupied the front-line fortifications, ready to defend against a German attack.[34] The British Government, disturbed by Germany's actions, told Britain's Ambassador in Berlin to pass a first warning on to Hitler. As a result, Hitler reportedly flew into one of his terrifying rages to the point of hysteria. Legend has it that this was one of the instances when he threw himself on the floor, gnawed on the carpet and proclaimed, 'England, I will never forget this!'[35]

At the same time, a rather strange article appeared in *The Times*. While briefly back at Chartwell, Churchill had made arrangements for a 'Memorandum on Supply Organisation', that he had written two years earlier to be published with a note saying that the Minister for Defence, Sir Thomas Inskip, had authorised the publication, but with no other contextual information.[36] With more than a hint of I-told-you-so, it detailed Churchill's original proposal for the creation of a new Ministry of Supply, which would relieve the Ministry of Defence of responsibilities related to war production. While it may have shown foresight to some, it proved a frustration to others. Letters between War Office officials stated that Churchill had made 'considerable modifications' to his original proposal for the purpose of the article.[37] The MP for Mossley, Austin Hopkinson, who was once so pro-Churchill as to nominate him for candidacy in a 1924 by-election, thought this piece was unacceptable. 'What I don't like is Winston's calm assumption that he alone has any regard for the country', Hopkinson wrote on 27 May. 'He talks and talks while some of us work, – and I doubt whether his talk does anything except hinder us.'[38]

His boldness continued when, on 9 June, Churchill wrote to the Secretary of State for Air to complain about the pace of progress in the Air Defence Research Committee. 'In all my experience of public offices,' Churchill wrote, 'I have never seen anything like the slow-motion picture which the work of this Committee has presented.'[39] The backlash against him behind the scenes was considerable. Secret memos discussing his letter include one reply remarking: 'I do most strongly resent Mr Churchill's continual pin-pricking, especially as he is in a position which enables him to use large and poisonous pins quite irresponsibly.'[40]

Meanwhile, at Chartwell, and with the need to economise still at the forefront of their minds, various measures were taken by the Churchills to scale down activity at their country home. Mary, who was 15 years old, was unaware of the extent of her parents' financial difficulties, but knew that there had been a possibility of them moving away from Chartwell. 'I used to take my goats for long walks into the woods from where I could look back across the lake to the house – and where I sat down on a log and cried bitterly', she later wrote of the thought of losing Chartwell.[41] To her it had been a Garden of Eden, and a place that had captured her heart as much as her father's. She also began to follow political developments. In the aftermath of the Anschluss with Austria, she became ever more absorbed in the fate of Czechoslovakia, with her interest piqued by the visits made to Chartwell by the journalist Shiela Grant Duff, a distant relative of Clementine's. Her fiercely intelligent and beautiful cousin would soon become a regular feature of Chartwell, always keen to pass on her observations from her time in Europe.

Other guests to the Churchills' country home that summer included David Lloyd George, the former Prime Minister and close personal friend of Churchill's, and his wife Margaret, who visited on 18 June. Lloyd George had also owned the Morpeth Mansions flat before the Churchills bought it in 1930. This led to some awkwardness when Mrs Hill, who was still learning about the political goingson of recent years, asked Mrs Pearman, 'Why do we get so many letters addressed to Miss Frances Stevenson?'[42] Little did she know that the flat had in fact been the primary residence of Lloyd George's mistress of more than 20 years. Though Lloyd George and Churchill had been close friends, colleagues and rivals for decades, the rise of Nazi Germany created a schism in their relationship. Hitler had carried out a charm offensive on the ageing statesman during his visit to Germany in 1936, including placing Lloyd George's photograph on his desk and effusively expressing his admiration. In due course, it was noted that 'Lloyd George, speaking with a tear in his throat, was deeply touched by the personal tribute of the Führer and was proud to hear it paid to him by the greatest German of the age.'[43] Even when Nazi troops marched into Vienna, Lloyd George called it 'a natural sequence of events'.[44] His opinion began to shift, however, over the course of the summer of 1938, in line with the escalating hostility and persecution taking place within Germany.

Another of Chartwell's previous visitors, the former Government Minister Gottfried Treviranus, soon felt the full force of this when the *Deutscher Reichsanzeiger und Preußischer Staatsanzeiger*, a Nazi newspaper, named him as number 25 in a list of enemies of the state whose German citizenship was revoked with immediate effect.[45]

During Parliament's summer break, Churchill mostly resided at Chartwell, although a few of its residents were missing. Three black swans had disappeared, and their escape created headlines all over the world. 'Churchill Offers Reward for Swans' featured in a newspaper in Canada, revealing a reward of £1 per swan that was returned to Chartwell, or five shillings to anyone with any information as to their whereabouts.[46] The latter offer was taken up with gusto, with swan sightings made far and wide, but to no avail. The rest of Chartwell's menagerie provided dramatic distractions in their absence, including one of their cows who was about to go into labour, and Churchill was on tenterhooks awaiting the new arrival. Meanwhile, the gardens had become, as Churchill wrote to Clementine, 'a veritable explosion of colour', with more roses than he had ever seen there before.[47] The Churchills opened their gardens to the public once or twice a year to raise money for local charities, and so those who took part on the chosen days in July and August 1938 were able to support the Kent County Nursing Association, as well as marvel at the gardens in all their midsummer glory.[48]

The Churchills' own visitors flocked to Chartwell too, including politicians, intelligence informants, publishing contacts, titans of industry and diplomats. Jan Masaryk, the Czechoslovak Ambassador and son of the first President of the Czechoslovak Republic, joined Churchill for lunch at Chartwell on Monday 11 July. The next day Churchill grilled Albert Foerster, in a meeting so secret that even his engagement card for the day listed him simply as 'German'. Foerster was the district leader of the Nazi Party in Danzig, an ethnically German city north-west of Warsaw that had been part of Germany until the end of the First World War. Foerster justified German rearmament, saying it was because Russian aerodromes were being constructed in Czechoslovakia, 'from which Berlin could be assailed in half-an-hour'. He then emphasised that there was still opportunity for cooperation between Churchill's country and Hitler's, saying 'if England and Germany would only agree together they could divide the world between them'.[49] Foerster's visit was followed shortly after by George Franckenstein, the former Austrian Ambassador, who lunched there on 23 July.

Clementine missed these meetings, as she was away at a spa resort in the French Pyrenees, but she sent many letters to her husband back at Chartwell. 'I am longing to see you', she wrote to him, while offering consolation for the fact that his most recent book, *Arms and the Covenant*, was not selling as well as hoped.[50] The collection of 41 Churchill speeches from 1928 to 1938 included many which criticised the Government's foreign policy and warned of the looming dangers in Europe. 'I'm sure it's the price', she suggested as consolation. 'The sort of people who want to hear that the Government is all wrong are not the rich ones.'[51]

Clementine's absence reduced the workload for Mrs Hill, but Churchill calculated that he would need three secretaries, given the amount he intended to write that summer, especially if he was going to submit the manuscript for the fourth and final volume of *Marlborough* and get payment from his publisher at the earliest opportunity. Millicent Broomhead had started at Chartwell in May and so just one additional secretary was required. The job advert read: 'Accurate & experienced shorthand typist required ... Must be resident of Westerham or Oxted. Own car an advantage.'[52] Josephine Parr had a trial for a week in July, following a glowing reference calling her 'one of the ablest and best educated ladies of my acquaintance'.[53] The expectation was that she would work at Chartwell for three months until Mrs Pearman returned. Unfortunately, she was offered a higher salary at a medical practice on Harley Street, and so she quickly left the Churchills' employ.[54] A few days later, Mary Penman, who was working in 'a semi-governmental office in Whitehall',[55] was offered the role, and began work at Chartwell on 3 August. Then Miss Broomhead gave her notice early in September, as the frequent journeys from Chartwell to London were too much of a strain on her existing heart condition, which forced Mrs Hill to recruit for the third time in two months. Olive Harrington, who had previously worked for Lord Russell and most recently the Imperial War Graves Commission, applied. She was appointed, and the three women, Mrs Hill, Miss Penman and Miss Harrington, became an efficient and effective trio. Together, they supported Churchill in both his literary and political work at Chartwell, day and night, during this vital time.

Where possible, Churchill took advantage of the greater privacy afforded by Chartwell, and urged his London-based network to journey out to Kent. 'I shall be here all August, within easy reach of London, so perhaps if you are in the neighbourhood you will come one day to lunch or dine, when we can have a talk', he urged the new Secretary of State for Air, Sir Howard Kingsley Wood, in a letter headed 'Secret' at the end of July.[56] Not all his visits were so carefully pitched and planned, with some being the result of urgent requests for access to Churchill. One such enquiry came to him, via his son Randolph who received a letter on 15 August. 'A friend of mine will be staying at the Park Lane Hotel from the 18th to the 23rd', the letter from Ian Colvin, Berlin correspondent for *News Chronicle*, read. 'I think it essential that he should meet your father.'[57] Colvin urged absolute secrecy, the need for which would quickly become apparent.

As a journalist working in Berlin, Colvin befriended senior politicians and developed covert friendships with high-ranking generals, making him a well placed intermediary for the Foreign Office and the British Embassy in Germany.[58] He knew many of the senior figures in the German military who were beginning to consider action against the Nazis, including General Ludwig Beck and Admiral Canaris. In addition to those in the military with misgivings about the Nazi Government's plans were individuals who lacked official positions, but were nonetheless established, well-connected and influential figures. Ewald von Kleist-Schmenzin was one such man. He was a prominent figure in politically conservative circles, but one of the few who had unambiguously opposed the Nazis before Hitler even took power in 1933.[59] He was highly thought of by Admiral Canaris, but had to tread carefully, as his rare appearances in Berlin were often watched by the Gestapo Security Services.

'Foreign allies, world opinion, the governments of such powers as Great Britain and America, must come to the aid of Germany if war was to be avoided', Kleist-Schmenzin uttered to Colvin in April 1938 at the Casino Club in Berlin.[60] He felt that there was little to be gained by campaigning to those at the British Embassy, especially as their messages were sent in cipher, which he believed could be intercepted and broken. What was needed were contacts in political circles, but not in diplomacy or intelligence. A month later, they discussed the issue of Czechoslovakia. Nazi Germany was not strong enough for war at that time; the French army numerically was nearly twice as strong as Germany's in the spring of 1938. A meeting between Kleist-Schmenzin, Admiral Canaris and General Beck was arranged in May 1938. Beck declared that foreign allies were needed to overcome Hitler, to which Canaris replied, 'England must lend us a sea anchor if we are to ride out this storm.'[61] Kleist-Schmenzin then relayed the conversation to Colvin, who recorded every detail.

In July, at the time when Churchill was searching for his swans at Chartwell, Kleist-Schmenzin and Colvin discussed whether Britain would fight if Germany attacked Czechoslovakia. 'The Admiral wants someone to go to London and find out', Kleist-Schmenzin whispered. 'We have an offer to make to the British and a warning to give them', he continued, as the planning of Case Grün, the invasion of Czechoslovakia, was well under way. A plan was formulated to leak to British intelligence that the invasion was scheduled for 15 August, to test how the Chamberlain government reacted. When the day came and went, there was a sense of relief in Whitehall that no invasion had taken place, and an even greater one in Berlin that Britain didn't appear to react to the apparent threat. General Beck, however, remained concerned, noting in his diary: 'I think it is a dangerous error to believe that Britain cannot wage a long war . . . because her strength lies in the immeasurable resources of the Empire.'[62] Beck hoped to rally support among his allies, though Hitler reportedly knew that the general was considering insurrection. 'I will have to make war on Czechoslovakia with my old generals. When I fight Britain and France I will have a new set of commanders', Hitler uttered to Beck.[63]

General Beck, Admiral Canaris and Ewald von Kleist-Schmenzin met in Beck's office. 'If you can bring me back from London positive proof that the British will make war if we invade Czechoslovakia,' Beck said to Kleist-Schmenzin, 'I will make an end of this regime.' The question then arose as to what would constitute proof, to which Beck replied,

'An open pledge to assist Czechoslovakia in the event of war.'The three men then discussed how Kleist-Schmenzin could complete this mission to London, given that he was under Gestapo surveillance, and might well be mistaken for a Nazi agent once in Britain. Canaris, demonstrating what was once called his 'usual cavalier attitude to the passport system', obtained for Kleist-Schmenzin a false passport with a fresh identity, sufficient funds, and arranged for a Mercedes to deliver him straight to the foot of the aircraft steps at Berlin Tempelhof Airport, thereby bypassing any customs or passport control checks.[64] Meanwhile, on 16 August, the British Ambassador in Berlin, Sir Nevile Henderson, telegraphed London saying that 'a Herr von Kleist' would come to London as an emissary of the moderates in the General Staff. His message stipulated that 'it would be unwise for him to be received in official quarters',[65] and so it was suggested that he should not meet with serving ministers or attend any meetings on government property.

The next day, Kleist-Schmenzin, a slight man with sandy hair and a neatly trimmed moustache, and wearing a grey suit, boarded a Lufthansa Junkers Ju 52 that would take him to London.[66] Upon landing at Croydon Airport he was taken to the Park Lane Hotel where he was met by Lord Lloyd, who took him to dinner at Claridge's. Lloyd was a long-standing ally of Churchill's and was once described by Gottfried Treviranus as 'a tireless advocate for the German opponents of Hitler'.[67] With neither speaking the other's language, the evening was spent conversing in French instead, discussing Kleist-Schmenzin's need for a letter of British opposition to Nazi aggression against Czechoslovakia. 'Everything is decided', Kleist-Schmenzin confirmed in a low voice. 'The mobilisation plans are complete, zero day is fixed, the Army group commanders have their orders. All will run according to plan at the end of September, and no one can stop it unless Britain declares an opening warning to Herr Hitler.'[68] He then described how the German people feared war, the reluctance of the generals and the unpreparedness of Germany's armed forces. He then confirmed that if Britain stood firm, and singled out Hitler as solely responsible, there was a high likelihood that the commanding generals would arrest him and end the Nazi regime. Lloyd immediately told the Foreign Secretary, Lord Halifax, all about the meeting but, in accordance with Henderson's recommendation, Halifax had no intention of meeting with Kleist-Schmenzin.

His next meeting was arranged for 18 August with Sir Robert Vansittart, who had been Anthony Eden's number two in the Foreign Office, but now only held an advisory role. Years later, Vansittart told Ian Colvin, 'Of all the Germans I saw, Kleist had the stuff in him for a revolution against Hitler.'[69] Kleist-Schmenzin told Vansittart that war was no longer just a danger, and instead was now a certainty. He stressed that it was all Hitler's doing, and that he was encouraged by his Foreign Minister, Ribbentrop, the former Ambassador to Britain, 'who keeps telling him that when it comes to the showdown neither France nor England will do anything.'[70] Kleist-Schmenzin once again urged that the British Government should make a proclamation in support of Czechoslovakia in the event of an invasion by Germany. In notes made by Vansittart later that day, he observed that Kleist-Schmenzin had said that his mission to England was tantamount to a death sentence. Furthermore, he believed that if Hitler waged war, he would be among the first to be killed, and that he had 'come out of the country with a rope round his neck to stake his last chance of life on preventing the adventure.'[71]

The next morning, on Friday 19 August, Churchill arranged for Frank Jenner, a known and trusted local taxi driver, to pick up Kleist-Schmenzin from his Park Lane Hotel and bring him to Chartwell. When the three men finally met, Randolph carefully took notes while Churchill listened, and only occasionally interrupted with questions. Kleist-Schmenzin repeated what he had told Vansittart the previous day, saying that a gesture from Britain 'was needed to crystallise the wide-spread and indeed, universal anti-war sentiment in Germany'.[72] The main thing however was to convince the generals in Germany, as they were the ones with the power to stop Hitler and prevent war. Randolph's notes read:

He was convinced that in the event of the generals deciding to insist on peace, there would be a new system of government within forty-eight hours. Such a government, probably of a monarchist character, could guarantee stability and end the fear of war forever.[73]

Churchill then informed Kleist-Schmenzin that his conversation with Vansittart the day before had been reported to the Foreign Secretary and the Prime Minister. Halifax had then told Churchill that Chamberlain's declaration of support for Czechoslovakia on 24 March still stood, despite Ribbentrop's assurances to the contrary to Hitler. Churchill then agreed to write a letter stating this, as well as outlining his own position on the subject.

Churchill's letter for Kleist-Schmenzin stated British support, despite there not being a formal alliance, quoting an excerpt of Chamberlain's speech in Parliament on 24 March:

> Where peace and war are concerned, legal obligations are not alone involved, and, if war broke out, it would be unlikely to be confined to those who have assumed such obligations. It would be quite impossible to say where it would end and what Governments might become involved. . . . This is especially true in the case of two countries like Great Britain and France, with long associations of friendship, with interests closely interwoven, devoted to the same ideals of democratic liberty, and determined to uphold them.[74]

He also gave his analysis of the likely course of a future war, weaving his insights as an historian alongside his understanding of the developments in military technology, particularly the likelihood of 'air-slaughter' on civilian populations.[75] He then concluded with his own personal hope for a peaceful solution to the Czechoslovak problem, which he believed 'would pave the way for the true reunion of our countries on the basis of the greatness and the freedom of both.'[76]

As Kleist-Schmenzin departed from Chartwell in the taxi, clutching the letter, Churchill made sure additional copies of their conversation were made. Guests were due to arrive at Chartwell for lunch shortly after Kleist-Schmenzin left, arrangements for which had been made long before Ian Colvin's urgent note just three days earlier. Those making their way to Churchill's home, who might well have passed Kleist-Schmenzin's taxi, were Arthur Richards, the secretary of Focus, and George Harrap, the Managing Director of the publisher of Churchill's two most recent books. The letters written to accompany the notes of the Kleist-Schmenzin meeting were posted the next day, with copies sent to the former and present Foreign Secretaries, Eden and Halifax. A copy was also sent to Neville Chamberlain on 24 August, with a letter in which Churchill concluded, 'I do not suppose it can do much good, but every little counts.'[77] Unfortunately, Chamberlain had already made his mind up about Kleist-Schmenzin, as illustrated by a letter he wrote at the Prime Minister's official residence at Chequers to Lord Halifax on the very day that Churchill and Kleist-Schmenzin met. In it, Chamberlain wrote: 'I take it that Von Kleist is violently anti-Hitler and is extremely anxious to stir up his friends in Germany to make an attempt at its overthrow ... And I think we must discount a good deal of what he says.'[78]

Two weeks later, on Sunday 4 September, Heinrich Brüning, who had by now become one of Churchill's regular informants, was invited to lunch at Chartwell to discuss the Czechoslovakian crisis. Randolph joined the party too, where he was likely tasked with helping his father to relay the discussions held two weeks before with Kleist-Schmenzin. Other guests of the Churchills for lunch that day included Desmond Morton as well Clementine's friend Horatia Seymour who, by that time, was living in a cottage on the Chartwell estate. The group reportedly only discussed 'political generalities' at the table but, as they were leaving their seats, Brüning voiced that he now saw only one way of avoiding conflict, which was that concessions should be made to Nazi Germany regarding the Sudetenland province of Czechoslovakia. This would, in his opinion, buy time. 'I thought that if any such agreement could be made before the winter, an attack before the next spring would be very difficult', Brüning later reflected.

At this point, Churchill became animated and took Brüning out into Chartwell's gardens, leaving the rest of the group in the dining room so he would be safely out of earshot. By the time they had neared the far corner of the lawn, Churchill had become incensed. He called the former Chancellor a coward and shouted that he would never make the slightest compromise with the Nazis. Brüning snapped back at Churchill, saying that he had braved the mobs of

Nazis who had surrounded him and threatened to kill him, and so it was hardly fair for him to be called a coward. He insisted that the safety of the British Empire was at the forefront of his thinking, at which Churchill reportedly softened at once. Brüning later recalled his next utterance:

> I said that he should have no doubt that if it came to war the initial successes of the German Army would be astonishing, although I did not doubt that in a long war they would be defeated, as England would get help again, at least in supplies, from the U.S., and the Nazis had not an adequate economic basis to win a long European war.[79]

The two then continued talking over the military possibilities, with Brüning saying that he knew the elite of the generals in Germany, including those whom Kleist-Schmenzin had spoken of, and that he held them in high esteem. He told Churchill that, with only a couple of exceptions, 'the Generals just wanted a weapon in order to compel Hitler to give up his adventures. If they were able to control him, the system would break down by itself without a coup d'etat.' He continued, 'A Government that had geared the whole economic life of the country for three years to full-scale armament could not survive without tangible successes, as otherwise scepticism would weaken it, even in its own Party.'[80]

The two men had been walking up and down the garden during this discussion until Churchill paused, looking up at the house, and told Brüning that he was likely to sell Chartwell soon. He had been advised to be ready to enter the Cabinet when the international situation became critical, and so he would then base himself in London. Before rejoining the rest of the party, Churchill asked for a telephone number on which he could reach Brüning. On both of the following two evenings, Churchill telephoned Brüning for further lengthy discussions late into the night.

Unfortunately, the trust Brüning had in the confidentiality of all his conversations with Churchill immediately vanished when the *Daily Express* ran a story on 6 September about the meeting at

Chartwell. The story confirmed that the former Chancellor had visited Churchill at his country home earlier that week, said that Brüning had seemed depressed in light of information he had received from Germany, and added that he had 'begged Churchill to influence the British Government'. Brüning was furious and assumed Randolph was the culprit for the leak to the press. He then vowed to refuse any future invitations to meet Churchill.[81] Little did he know that the leak was actually from Nellie Romilly, Clementine's little sister, to whom she had confided the discussion. A frustrated Churchill then told his sister-in-law: 'Dr. B came under the strict guarantees of secrecy which I gave him personally, and the statement and the visit attributed to him may bring upon him serious consequences.'[82] She begged for his forgiveness. 'It was an absolutely thoughtless act', she replied. 'It has made me very unhappy that I could act in any way badly towards you.'[83] Her apologies, however, made little difference, as the damage was done and Churchill's relationship with Brüning was destroyed in an instant. He lost a trusted advisor and the only person who could corroborate Kleist-Schmenzin's claim with any real authority. As events in Europe spiralled dangerously, Churchill looked around to see which other informants could offer first-hand insights as to the political and military situation in Germany, and in those countries it was likely to target next.

CHAPTER 9

THE VIEW FROM PRAGUE

Shiela Grant Duff, 29 October 1938

When a well-connected young journalist wrote to Winston Churchill, declaring herself to be a distant cousin of his wife's, and a foreign correspondent in Czechoslovakia, he may have thought it too good to be true. Clementine had never met her but, from the moment of their first encounter at Chartwell, she became a trusted family member, later referenced by Mary as 'my mother's brilliant and impassioned cousin'.[1] She was a gifted writer, with an extraordinary network of politically active and influential people. In addition to this, she was a respected authority on Czechoslovak politics and cared deeply about the plight of the Czechoslovakian people. These elements combined made her one of Churchill's most valuable informants, and meant that she received regular invitations to Chartwell during the latter years of the 1930s.

At the age of 21, Shiela Grant Duff made enquiries with *The Times* about whether they might consider her for a role reporting on events in Central Europe. She was ambitious and determined, and felt especially frustrated when the newspaper's editor replied that 'the conditions of work in this Office are such as to make it awkward to accept women as foreign sub-editors'.[2] Despite the disappointment, she refused to let the rejection stop her. Less than three months later, in January 1935 she was in the Saar, writing for *The Observer*, describing the plethora of swastikas which appeared after the plebiscite vote, likening them to a 'plague of spiders'.[3] A few days later

22. Shiela Grant Duff, journalist and foreign correspondent, 1939.

she received a letter from Edgar Mowrer of the *Chicago Daily News*, who notably was the first American correspondent to be expelled from Nazi Germany in 1933. She had worked as his secretary for several months, and he later described her as 'intelligent, full of initiative and possesses a great deal of curiosity about all sorts of human beings'.[4] Adopting the tone of a mentor, he called the Nazis a 'monstrous regime' and pleaded: 'Don't get entangled in anything political there of any sort. Observe, advise, but keep out! Please. You can do much more as an "impartial observer" than in any other capacity.'[5]

Alongside her work as a journalist, she also became involved in British politics, and worked as a secretary for Hugh Dalton, a former

Labour Party spokesperson for foreign affairs, during the 1935 General Election. The following June, Dalton wrote to Edvard Beneš, the President of Czechoslovakia, telling him that Shiela would be in Prague soon and working as news correspondent. 'She is a Socialist, and an intelligent student of Central Europe', he wrote in the letter of introduction. 'I should regard it as a great personal favour to myself, if you would be so kind as to receive her.'[6] Shortly after arriving in Czechoslovakia in the summer of 1936 she met Hubert Ripka, the diplomatic correspondent of the major Czech newspaper, *Lidové Noviny*, and a close friend of the President. At their first meeting, Shiela and Ripka stood together on a hill overlooking Czechoslovakia, Austria and Hungary from a single viewpoint. Shiela later recalled that, at this first meeting, he looked at her with a quizzical smile and remarked, 'The only thing wrong with my country is that it is too small.'[7] He and his wife Noemi soon became very close friends of Shiela's and she called their flat in Prague 'an international meeting place for all that was best in literature and politics'.[8] Ripka quickly became a key source of information for Shiela, who then relayed their conversations to her old boss, Mowrer.

Another acquaintance was Otto Strasser, brother of Gregor Strasser who had previously been an early rival of Hitler's for leadership of the Nazi Party, but was killed in the Night of the Long Knives in 1934. Otto fled Germany and by 1936 was living in exile in Prague. Writing to Mowrer, describing a conversation she had over supper with Strasser on 20 October, Shiela reported that the 'Winston Churchill group' were among the few English politicians Strasser thought highly of. She also relayed some of Strasser's advice as to how best to handle the Führer. 'The worst possible way of dealing with Hitler, as with dogs, is to show you are frightened,' he remarked, adding that European politicians should instead 'make no provocation, but arm to the teeth and be ready.'[9] Mowrer replied, grateful for the information but lamenting the situation. 'European politics have become like a pea soup,' he wrote to Shiela, 'or like a crossword puzzle where all the letters keep wandering about.'[10]

By 1937 Shiela was such an unfathomable figure in Prague that she began to be treated with some suspicion, and the Czechoslovak Foreign

Office reportedly began to investigate whether she was in fact a German spy.[11] The assumption was that she must have been paid by the Nazis, otherwise how could a single young woman afford to live alone in a new country. Mowrer urged her to cease spending time with Germans while in Prague, writing to her in March: 'You must change your attitude towards Germans a little and realize that we already – as Hitler recently put it – are in a virtual state of war.'[12] Rumours then began to circulate that she was in a relationship with a German Nazi, which then led to a torrent of 'advice' from those around her. Her fellow journalist Elizabeth Wiskemann remarked, 'If you could deal with us all a bit more gently it would put everything right.'[13] This sentiment was mirrored by Mowrer, who said: 'You ought to behave in a more feminine way . . . and you ought to learn to keep your mouth shut more and listen better,' before concluding, 'Remember that you have a fine mind which needs only to be trained and to have its corners polished.'[14]

It was around this time that her opposition to the approach of the British Government towards Central Europe solidified and, having retained her political contacts in England from the 1935 election, she began to contact them. Her former employer, Hugh Dalton, had been appointed Chairman of the Labour Party and she wrote to him describing the disastrous effect that England and France's hesitations were having on Central Europe. On one occasion she rather bluntly wrote to him saying that, 'English diplomacy is still sufficiently respected for people to believe that England may be playing a double game rather than just being stupid, but in neither case is much confidence aroused.'[15]

By the early summer of 1937, relations between Czechoslovakia and Germany took a sharp turn for the worse, with Nazi propaganda alleging poor treatment of German nationals who had been arrested by the Czechs as spies, which Shiela believed was meant to alienate Czechoslovakia and garner the sympathy of England. With this escalation, Shiela decided to take decisive action and contacted Winston Churchill for the first time on 19 June:

The tension has never been so great as it is at the present moment and this is saying much when it is remembered that in March and in November war councils were held in Berlin as to whether Germany should or should not attack Czechoslovakia ... The only protection left is the support of England ... Information has reached this country that our foreign office is hesitating. I am writing to you to ask you to do everything in your power to make our attitude firm and unfaltering. Czechoslovakia is, for the moment, entirely dependent on us.[16]

Churchill read the letter at Chartwell, and replied that he had done so with great interest. He then invited Shiela to visit them there for lunch one day. Fortunately for everyone, Shiela was back in England in mid-July and staying with her grandmother just 20 minutes from Chartwell, and so arrangements were made for her to visit the Churchills on 17 July. She knew that Churchill was primarily interested in the information and insights she could bring, but she also hoped that the two would forge an alliance, and she was not to be disappointed. On a beautiful summer's day, she drove to Chartwell and instantly became a part of family life. She was close in age to Sarah, and so quickly developed a relationship akin to a friendly cousin with Mary. Clementine, who had grown closer to her youngest daughter in recent years, appreciated the connection, which at one point included Mary giving Shiela one of her goats as a gift.[17] Mary herself later recalled, 'Shiela had excellent talks with my father, and my mother and I took to her immediately.'[18] Churchill sat beside Shiela at lunch, while she offered her observations and recalled conversations that she had over the last year in Prague. He viewed August as a dangerous month that year, believing that war might well break out, otherwise it would probably be delayed until 1938 or 1939. He told Shiela that delay would be especially dangerous because of the rapid growth of the German army and their air force. 'The Czechs are in a very, very dangerous situation', he added. 'Heaven knows whether in a year's time the country will still be there.'[19]

Once the group had finished at the table, they all went for a walk across the lawn in the sunshine. The conversation from the lunch table continued as Churchill fed the swans. 'An explosion of some sort is inevitable in Germany', he told Shiela. 'If Germany is sufficiently tightly encased by a strong alliance system, the explosion will be inside Germany and get rid of this gang.' As Shiela left Chartwell that afternoon, Churchill firmly shook her hand and told her to keep in touch, while Clementine and Mary said they hoped she would be back at Chartwell again soon.[20] As she drove back through Kent that afternoon, Shiela tried to memorise everything that had been said over lunch, and quickly made extensive notes as soon as she returned to her grandmother's house. She also had to reframe her opinion of Churchill, given her existing political inclinations. Before meeting him, she had expected 'an ugly old man, small & bent'.[21] She had been braced for prejudice and snobbery, basing much of this on what she had read of his attitude to India, which she regarded as 'archaic and impossible'. Upon meeting him, however, she found that 'all this fell away'. Instead, she had met 'a strong and curiously noble man, totally without spite or rancour or pettiness of any sort.'[22]

Shiela returned to Prague and visited Berlin that autumn, reporting her observations to Churchill. She was in Germany just after Lord Halifax's meeting with Hitler and quickly wrote to Churchill outlining what she was told by British diplomats. 'The purpose of our foreign policy was now to "get right on our side". This they said we could do by giving way as much as possible, primarily in Central Europe', she told him. She then added that the Germans were convinced that Britain 'would be neutral if they attacked Czechoslovakia'.[23] She also forwarded interesting newspaper articles to Churchill, while finding that her own were increasingly considered unpalatable to the British press. 'I am sorry not to be able to use this article. It is interesting, but I feel it rather important at this juncture to present the delicate international situation as accurately as possible,' Wilson Harris, the editor of *The Spectator*, wrote to Shiela in December 1937, 'and your picture did not in fact quite tally in certain rather important respects with the impression I got from Lord Halifax, with whom I had a talk a few days ago.'[24]

The first of the letters that Shiela wrote to Churchill in 1938 was four pages long, reporting generally on Germany's efforts to turn the tables in Central Europe. She painstakingly shared her understanding of the political and diplomatic situations in Poland, Romania, Yugoslavia,

Hungary, Austria, Germany and Czechoslovakia. Churchill read and reread the letter several times, adding his own notes in the margins. 'Pretty Bleak!', he wrote back to her from Chartwell, along with his appreciation of her continuing information.[25] Meanwhile, her friend Hubert Ripka, the diplomatic correspondent and advisor to President Beneš, asked her to undertake fact-finding missions on his behalf. 'Make an effort to find out as much as possible, make notes about everything, so you can tell me everything exactly, and in particular all the details', he instructed her at the end of January.[26] He was particularly keen for her to find out about any Anglo-Russian understanding in relation to China and, if there was any kind of agreement, what the French reaction had been.

By March 1938 Shiela was back in Prague and, realising that German armies were about to invade Austria, she caught the night train to Vienna so she could witness it first-hand. She described those intoxicated with excitement on the streets waving swastika banners, teenage boys carrying rifles, and the blaring of police sirens. She then saw the German troops, whom she described as 'rolling steadily forward like a grey wave . . . These grim, helmeted men excited anger and dread.'[27] She was horrified by what she saw and returned immediately to Prague, suspecting that she had seen a premonition of what the people of Czechoslovakia might face. On 18 March she wrote to Churchill, saying 'the Czechs are bitterly afraid of disturbances in the German districts which would give the Germans an excuse to march in.'[28] Three weeks later, she was in London, trying to schedule yet more meetings with influential figures in Westminster, including Clement Attlee, the Leader of the Labour Party, who declared himself too busy. A letter from his Private Secretary to Shiela said that he had heard from others what she had said in similar meetings and so 'it would not now be worth your while to come and see him personally'.[29] A number of Churchill's current and former allies did choose to meet with her, including Harold Macmillan, the MP for Stockton-on-Tees, and Henry Wickham Steed, the former editor of *The Times* and a fellow member of Churchill's Focus group, with full reports of the conversations then sent back to Ripka. 'I have lunch with Churchill on Sunday,' she added to one such report, 'and would very much like a letter from you on Saturday which will inform me of all your latest news, inside and outside, the advice of your statesmen and the help we can give you.'[30] He duly replied with a message for her to relay to Churchill that weekend at Chartwell, including his thoughts on the Sudetendeutsche Partei (SDP), a pro-Nazi political party in the Sudetenland region of Czechoslovakia:

Tell Churchill that the government will negotiate with the SDP and is willing to make the utmost concessions in order to reach a *modus vivendi* with Germany. There can be no talk of autonomy or that we will break our alliance with France and Russia. Draw his attention to the fact that French and English defeatism, which wants to create disinterest in Central Europe, also encourages our defeatists and thus makes our struggle with Germany very difficult.[31]

In addition, Ripka asked Shiela to tell Churchill that Czechoslovakia believed in Russia's help, and 'more importantly, that we believe that that help will be very effective. Our general staff has a very good sense of the quality and readiness of the Russian army.'[32] The second meeting between Shiela and Churchill took place on Sunday 10 April and this time Churchill dominated the conversation, seeming optimistic about France, and saying, 'France was never so unified with regard to the defence of Czechoslovakia', though he had concerns about their air force. He also thought Russian military strength might well grow, saying, 'The material is there, everything depends on the spirit.' He then turned to the situation in British politics, at which point his pessimism appeared. His continuing opposition to the Chamberlain Government meant he thought he would very likely never be offered a role in the Cabinet, and he was increasingly frustrated by the lack of energy shown in air defence and rearmament. But, Churchill concluded, 'the English are a very proud people and although we may sleep for a long time, once awake, we never give in, and the Germans know it.'[33]

There was no doubt that the information Shiela brought to Chartwell, which was arguably a direct line from the Czechoslovak President, was hugely beneficial to Churchill. A month later, Churchill

213

hosted a meeting at his flat in Morpeth Mansions over lunch. Archie Sinclair, Professor Lindemann and Konrad Henlein, the leader of the Nazi Party of the Sudetenland region of Czechoslovakia, were in attendance, with Lindemann acting as interpreter.[34] Henlein's intention for his time in London was to convince British politicians that his followers were being wronged by the Czechs. The solution he proposed, as recalled in Churchill's memoirs, was that the Sudeten German regions should enjoy local autonomy, with their own local government, but with a central parliament continuing in Prague. He also suggested that the drawing of a boundary could be undertaken by an impartial tribunal. Churchill then relayed this proposal to Jan Masaryk, the Czechoslovak Ambassador in London, who seemed content with a settlement on these lines.[35] Churchill appeared hopeful, and confident enough to announce in a speech to his constituents that 'I have good reason to believe that the kind of plans which Herr Henlein described when he was over here, would not be unacceptable to the Government of Czechoslovakia.'[36] Unfortunately for Churchill, it proved to be one of the occasions when his political judgement failed him. Henlein had promised Hitler that he would make demands that couldn't possibly be satisfied and, within two weeks of the Morpeth Mansions meeting, Hitler gave the order for the invasion of Czechoslovakia to begin by 1 October at the latest.[37]

In what was becoming a regular occurrence, Shiela met with the Churchills again on 23 June, but this time she brought Hubert Ripka with her.[38] Both Winston and Clementine took to Ripka instantly; he was charming, well-mannered and relaxed in his hosts' company. Shiela later recalled how the beautiful setting, exquisite food and excellent wine all created the perfect atmosphere.[39] The conversation was amusing and friendly, with Churchill particularly appreciative of Ripka's assessment of France's reliability as an ally. There was one moment of awkwardness, however, when Churchill reflected on the good impression Henlein had made, saying he had shown himself to be very moderate in his conversation. Ripka diplomatically responded by suggesting that Churchill should perhaps read the contents of some of the interviews that Henlein had given with journalists in recent weeks.

That evening, Churchill wrote an article for the *Daily Telegraph*, with a direct warning to Germany that, if Czechoslovakia was attacked, France, Russia and eventually Britain would all be drawn to help her. His hope for a peaceful resolution remained, and he spent much of July penning articles encouraging a settlement and reconciliation between Czechoslovakia and Germany. In the eighth of a series of articles on international affairs, Churchill declared that the Czechoslovak Government owed it to Western powers to make concessions to Germany, so long as they were in line with the sovereignty and integrity of the Czechoslovakian state. 'Having myself heard at first hand the case for both sides in Czechoslovakia,' he wrote, 'I am sure that all the essential elements of a good and lasting settlement are present, unless it is wrecked by obstinacy on the one hand, or mischievous fomentations upon the other.'[40] Churchill was unaware of the damage his words would do when quotations from the article were featured in the *Prager Tagblatt* newspaper in Czechoslovakia. It created great delight among Henlein's supporters who, according to Ripka, 'interpret it in such a way that they can increase their radicalism still further when people like Churchill hold the view he just expressed in this article'.[41]

Not quite believing what she was reading, Shiela wrote to Churchill straight away, telling him how disturbed she was by the way his article was being interpreted by Nazi supporters in Czechoslovakia. She wanted him to know how misled he had been by Henlein. 'He is apt to tell a different story in different places', she wrote to Churchill, before pleading with him to be more aware of the impact of his words. 'You are the one British statesman of whom the Germans are afraid. If you are conciliated, they consider that they can expect much greater support from the British Government whom they think are afraid.'[42] She concluded with a metaphor that Churchill might well have approved of, saying, 'I am told the only thing to do if one meets a grizzly bear and has no gun is to wave at him with an umbrella. Yours is the biggest umbrella in the country.'[43] As she became increasingly frustrated, those around her began to doubt the likely success of her efforts. David Scott Fox, the British Ambassador to Czechoslovakia, wrote to her, attempting a sort of consolation, saying 'you were born for more whimsical & higher things than the defence of lost causes'.[44]

The situation in Czechoslovakia began to darken as the summer drew to a close. Ripka wrote to Shiela on 27 August, saying: 'We live here in constant tension, but our nerves are in perfect order. If England says a decisive word now, the gangsters will hide out.'[45] It appeared that the Czechs were putting extraordinary faith in an intervention from Britain as their hope for peace and security. Meanwhile, on the same date, Churchill was at Chartwell, writing a letter to his old friend Bob Boothby, saying how he hoped the Government would do their utmost to avoid war, adding 'which I personally think is very near to us at the present time'.[46] The world watched Germany nervously, as the annual Nuremberg rally approached, with Hitler due to speak on 12 September. Days before the Führer would make his intentions clear to Germany and the world, Churchill lobbied the Foreign Secretary with a proposal that he hoped Halifax might also show the Prime Minister. On the evening of 31 August, after having had dinner with Randolph, Churchill climbed the stairs to his study and dictated the letter to his secretary. In it, he suggested to Halifax that a 'joint note' between Britain, France and Russia should be created. Such a letter should state their desire for peace, their anxiety at Germany's military preparations, their shared interest in a peaceful solution to the Czechoslovak situation and concluding that a German invasion would 'raise capital issues for all three powers'. He then suggested such a note be shown to President Roosevelt, and 'induce him to do his utmost upon it'. Perhaps then Roosevelt might address Hitler directly, and tell him that a world war would inevitably follow an invasion of Czechoslovakia. Churchill admitted in the note to Halifax that he could not know for certain that Roosevelt would do this, but the most important thing of all was the creation of a joint note.[47]

As international tensions grew, and with the thought of Britain's relations with other world powers possibly providing the key to the situation in Czechoslovakia, Ivan Maisky, the Soviet Ambassador, contacted Churchill at Chartwell on Sunday 4 September, asking for an urgent meeting that evening. Churchill agreed, and Maisky dashed to his car and motored alone to Churchill's country home.[48] The thought at the forefront of Maisky's mind, and mirroring Churchill's plea to Lord Halifax, can be seen in his diary entry of the previous night: 'A joint declaration made by Great Britain, France and the USSR, with the guaranteed moral support of Roosevelt, could do more than anything else to prevent violent acts on the part of Hitler.'[49]

Upon arriving at the Churchills' home, Maisky was struck by the beauty of Chartwell, and wrote lengthy paragraphs in his diary describing the house, the views, the landscape, the gardens and even the ponds with palpable enthusiasm. 'Churchill is fascinated by his big and small fish,' Maisky reflected that evening, 'he happily holds forth on their every detail and obviously considers them to be one of England's most characteristic attractions.'[50] Maisky also wrote about Chartwell's fruit trees which were filled with plums and peaches. Mary's collection of budgerigars also got a mention. She bred the birds, having been inspired to do so by her nanny, Moppet. They were 'azure blue and brilliant green', numbered around a hundred, and became an established part of the afternoon Chartwell gardens tour.[51] Clearly surprised by the scale of Chartwell, Maisky thought to himself that the life of a leader of the British bourgeoisie clearly wasn't a bad one. Churchill, seemingly reading Maisky's mind, gestured across the estate and said, 'You can observe all this with an untroubled soul! My estate is not a product of man's exploitation of man: It was bought entirely on my literary royalties.'[52]

Churchill also showed Maisky the cottage he was constructing, proudly slapping the brickwork and boasting of the 500 bricks a day he was laying at that point. 'I'm a bricklayer, you know', Churchill said to him proudly. 'Today I worked half the day and, look, I've put up a wall.'[53] The two gentlemen then returned to the house and, joined by Clementine, went to the dining room for tea. There was an array of alcoholic options, including an Edwardian-era bottle of vodka, which Churchill proffered to Maisky. 'That's far from being all! In my cellar I have a bottle of wine from 1793!', Churchill added. Maisky enquired as to what occasion could be special enough to toast with that bottle, to which Churchill reportedly grinned at his guest and remarked, 'We'll drink this bottle together when Great Britain and Russia beat Hitler's Germany!'[54]

In his memoirs, Churchill wrote that it was not long after Maisky's arrival that he realised the Soviet Government must have made a strategic decision to speak to him rather than the British Foreign Office. No request for secrecy was made, and so the assumption was that Churchill would tell members of the Government, but that this route would be more likely to yield the intended result.[55] Churchill listened carefully as Maisky told him that the French Government, via its embassy in Moscow, had asked what aid Russia would give Czechoslovakia against a German attack. According to the notes Churchill dictated to his secretary immediately after the meeting, Maisky 'also advocated consultation among the peaceful Powers about the best method of preserving peace, with a view, perhaps, to a joint declaration including France, Russia, and Great Britain', believing too that 'the United States would give moral support to such a declaration'.[56] Churchill replied to Maisky saying that the Government would be unlikely to take any steps unless there was a breakdown in the negotiations between Henlein of the Sudeten Nazis and President Beneš.

After the meeting, he made thorough notes of all that had been said and sent a copy to Lord Halifax. It was at this point, on the eve of the Nazis' annual Nuremberg rally, that Shiela decided to go to Berlin and contacted influential figures to gain the best insights possible. She wrote to Karl Silex, the editor of the *Deutsche Allgemeine Zeitung* newspaper, saying that she would be in attendance and suggesting they meet, to which Silex replied that he was very much looking forward to seeing her.[57] Her old friend and mentor, Edgar Mowrer, also offered to help with introductions, writing to her, 'When you are in Berlin go and see the American Ambassador, Hugh Wilson, in my name.'[58] Before making her way to Germany, she and Churchill arranged another meeting at Chartwell, on Friday 9 September, just three days before Hitler's speech.

Arriving this time by train, Shiela was collected by Cale from nearby Oxted station at 12.55pm, arriving at Chartwell by 1.15pm for lunch. She had been briefed over the phone the day before by Ripka, President Beneš's confidant, and was ready to provide an update to Churchill over the meal, at which he was joined by Clementine and her friend Horatia Seymour. Churchill quickly shared his positive impression of Russia, and added optimistically that America would very likely support Britain morally and militarily within a few weeks of any joint statement with France and Russia. He then told Shiela that he was due to see Neville Chamberlain at Downing Street the following day, where he intended to stress the urgency of a strong statement with France and Russia. 'It is very confidential,' she wrote to Ripka a few days later, 'and please don't even tell B[eneš] where it came from.'[59] Unfortunately, she soon began to question Churchill's plan. After meeting the American Ambassador in Berlin, she thought him 'very weak' and wrote at the time that he 'does not understand the situation in America'. The United States' Ambassador to Great Britain was equally unreliable, though Churchill was unaware of this at the time. Joseph P. Kennedy, who had visited Chartwell in 1935 with his wife, had been given the prestigious diplomatic post in December 1937, and the following year, while the Ambassador dined alongside Clementine Churchill, she had remarked how much Churchill liked him and would happily see him anytime.[60] This, however, was not to be, and Kennedy instead aligned himself with Neville Chamberlain. He relished his new role as close confidant of the British Prime Minister, as a result of which he could relay a constant stream of reports to Washington, DC.[61]

Churchill, too, was keen to remain on the best possible terms with Chamberlain, as demonstrated by the Prime Minister being one of the first recipients of the fourth and final volume of Churchill's biography of the Duke of Marlborough. After ten years, the concluding volume's release drew a close to a monumental chapter of Churchill's literary career. He had a copy sent to 10 Downing Street, which Chamberlain graciously accepted, telling Churchill he would read it 'whenever I can see a prospect of undisturbed tranquillity'.[62]

Meanwhile, the deluge of letters to Churchill at Chartwell continued. One gentleman wrote from nearby Croydon General Hospital while in pain and recovering from an operation, but he felt he had to write to Churchill. 'Herr Hitler is now a mad dog and as such must be dealt with', John Holman wrote from the chair by his hospital bed, adding that the danger of war was becoming more acute with each day and 'threatens to involve the whole world in another ghastly war'.[63] His and opinions like his were shared by many in politics and diplomacy, especially after the Nuremberg rally of

23. Winston Churchill, at the standing desk in the study at Chartwell, February 1939. The windows look out onto the driveway at the front of the house, and the doorway beyond him leads to his bedroom. Churchill had moved his bed from the study into a separate room, which was previously part of the nursery wing, several years earlier.

12 September. Ivan Maisky wrote in his diary the next day that, as a result of Hitler's speech, 'Disturbances and provocations have begun in the Sudetenland. The tension grows with every passing hour . . . I have the impression that the world is sliding uncontrollably towards a new world war.'[64]

Even Churchill's writing at Chartwell was affected by the situation in Europe. H. A. Pollock, editor at George Newnes Ltd, wrote to him on 16 September declaring that: 'The uneasy state of the international situation over the past two weeks has made it necessary for me to consider war publications', with plans being made for a looming national emergency, and a likely need for two new publications in the event of the outbreak of war.[65] By this time Chamberlain had flown to Hitler's holiday home in Berchtesgaden to negotiate terms and attempt to reach a diplomatic solution and so avoid war. Shiela telephoned Churchill, having heard that Chamberlain had a plan deemed acceptable to Hitler that would be forced on Czechoslovakia, and sought reassurance. Churchill said he did not have a full understanding, but believed there were 'pretty miserable' plans being made. He was, however, confident that if such a plan was created, there would be a campaign against Chamberlain and British public opinion would be split.[66]

Elsewhere, plans were being made to settle the crisis through arbitration. On 18 September, British and French Ministers met to discuss the 'Anglo-French' plan, whereby, if it was agreed, they would demand that Czechoslovakia cede to Germany all territories in which the German population represented more than 50 per cent of the inhabitants with a 'general guarantee against unprovoked aggression' for what was then left of Czechoslovakia.[67] The proposal was said to have left the Czechoslovak Ambassador to France in tears and Jan Masaryk, the Ambassador in London, cursing obscenely after having received the wording of the plan from the Foreign Secretary.[68] Churchill then composed a press statement in the study at Chartwell on 21 September, criticising what he called 'Anglo-French pressures' which he said amounted to 'a complete surrender by the Western democracies to the Nazi threat of force'. He then declared that 'the idea that safety can be purchased by throwing a small State to the wolves is a fatal delusion', before concluding that peace could only be achieved 'by a combination of all the Powers whose convictions and whose vital interests are opposed to Nazi domination'.[69]

The next day, on the morning of Thursday 22 September, Churchill telephoned a group of his closest allies asking if they could meet at his London flat at 4.30pm. They convened in the drawing room, with representatives from both the House of Lords and the House of Commons, including Chartwell regulars Archie Sinclair and Brendan Bracken. Churchill had just left Downing Street, where the Cabinet had agreed to take a firm stand. Chamberlain, who was meeting Hitler again that day, was going to demand from Hitler swift demobilisation, agreement that the transfer of the Sudeten territories must be done gradually by international commission, the insistence that any Polish or Hungarian claims must cease, and the security of the rest of Czechoslovakia beyond the Sudetenland must be guaranteed. Almost in unison, those gathered in Churchill's flat responded with 'But Hitler will never accept such terms.' Churchill replied, waving his whisky and soda, saying that, if that were the case, 'Chamberlain will return tonight and we shall have WAR.'[70] While they were together, Jan Masaryk called Churchill telling him that the Czechs were withdrawing from the Sudeten areas. Just a few days later, Masaryk wrote to Churchill of the negotiations over the fate of his country, calling them the 'Hitler–Chamberlain auction sale'.[71]

In the dying days of September 1938, Churchill still believed that a joint declaration by England, France and Russia could save peace and do so with honour.[72] On 26 September he issued a statement saying that the British Government should warn Hitler that an agreement by the three countries would mean that the invasion of Czechoslovakia would be taken as an act of war against them all. His hope remained that this would then deter Hitler from taking any further action, and thereby avoid war. He added a plea to the Government of the United States of America, and its people, to declare their support at that moment or it would be too late, concluding: 'It will indeed be a tragedy if this last effort is not made in the only way in which it may be effective to save mankind from martyrdom.'[73]

Churchill then called for another meeting at his Morpeth Mansions home at 4pm that day. Described by Leo Amery as 'a queer collection' of people, it resembled the previous gathering but this time with Professor Lindemann, Harold Macmillan, Bob Boothby and General Edward Spears also in attendance.[74] Churchill told the group that General Beck, the Chief of the Army General Staff, was opposed to war, just as he had been informed by Ewald von Kleist-Schmenzin a few weeks before at Chartwell. 'If only there were a chance of German soldiers stopping this madman', Amery wrote in his diary that evening.[75] The group also discussed whether the country should start readying for war, including whether national service should be proclaimed at once and whether a coalition government should be formed with immediate effect. Churchill also told the group that he had urged Chamberlain to mobilise the fleet and call up all reserves.[76] One of the main points of agreement among all those who gathered in Churchill's flat was that it had been a failure by the Prime Minister not to take Russia into his confidence, a view which it was strongly felt Churchill should convey to Lord Halifax as soon as possible.[77] One of the meeting's attendees, the MP Harold Nicolson, recalled his first hint of war on the Strand in London that evening after leaving Churchill's flat, where a new poster read 'City of Westminster: Air Raid Precautions: Gas Masks Notice.'[78]

On 28 September, at 2.54pm, Chamberlain began a speech in Parliament. The Russian Ambassador watched from the galleries overhead, and wrote in his diary that 'the chamber was black with MP's', with all the benches taken and thick crowds filling the gangways.[79] With the addition of a microphone, the Prime Minister's words were about to form the first speech to be recorded in the House of Commons, a fact which one onlooker confessed 'filled us with mingled horror and pride in the occasion'.[80] Churchill watched, seated in his usual place at the end of the row. Chamberlain gave a methodical synopsis of the events of recent weeks, describing negotiations with the Czechoslovaks and his visits to Herr Hitler, which he said had convinced him that the Führer was prepared 'to risk a world war'.[81] As he spoke, a piece of Foreign Office paper was quickly passed along the Government bench. When it reached Chamberlain he read it out loud. It stated that Hitler was willing to postpone mobilisation for 24 hours in order to meet with Chamberlain, Italy's Prime Minister Benito Mussolini and France's Prime Minister Édouard Daladier. The House burst into applause and cheering, as if peace had been newly declared and agreed by all. Churchill found Chamberlain after the speech and remarked to the Prime Minister, 'I congratulate you on your good fortune. You were very lucky.'[82] Shiela Grant Duff was one Churchill acquaintance who was not sanguine about the prospect of peace. She wrote to the Government's Director of Military Operations and Intelligence on the same day as Chamberlain's speech, offering her services in the event of a national emergency, suspecting by that time that war was a matter of days away.[83]

The next day Churchill met with Maisky at midday, and expressed what the Russian Ambassador called 'almost total confidence that this time Chamberlain would not be able to make any serious concessions to Hitler'.[84] Churchill then returned to Morpeth Mansions and drafted a telegram, addressed to the Prime Minister in Munich, urging him in the strongest terms not to betray the Czechoslovaks. He then gathered members of the Focus group at the Savoy, seeking signatures from as many influential individuals as he could, as well as voicing the desire that Anthony Eden and Clement Attlee sign too. Both men, however, refused. Eden was reluctant to appear in any way hostile to the Prime Minister, while Attlee did not believe he could get Labour Party approval through quickly enough. One attendee, Violet Bonham Carter, later recalled their shared sense of helplessness, and that 'when we parted there were tears in Winston Churchill's eyes'.[85]

At 2.45am on 30 September it was announced that an agreement had been reached in Munich and the peace of Europe had been secured. Nazi Germany was free to occupy the Sudetenland, and later that morning Jan Masaryk was found sobbing in the embassy in London. 'They've sold us into slavery to the Germans', Masaryk mumbled through tears while clinging on to his friend, the Russian Ambassador.[86] Chamberlain returned to London and was hailed as a saviour of peace, waving the piece of paper bearing both his and Hitler's signatures and declaring 'peace for our time'.

Churchill returned to Chartwell, devastated by the shameful outcome. It was at this time that he received a letter from the BBC, who were due to broadcast him giving a talk on 6 October on the situation in the Mediterranean. Their request was that Churchill submit the wording of his talk or meet with one of their producers as soon as possible. It was agreed that at 11am on 1 October, the day after Chamberlain returned from Munich, Churchill would meet a young BBC employee called Guy Burgess at Chartwell. Burgess, who would become known years later as one of the 'Cambridge spies', drove through the winding roads of North Kent in his Ford V8 and made his way to Churchill's home. Upon arriving he was escorted up to the study, where Churchill was seated at his desk on his own. Immediately sensing Churchill's downcast mood, Burgess offered consolation, and enquired as to his views in light of the Munich Agreement. Churchill reached into the breast pocket of his blue boiler suit and took out a letter from President Beneš, which had may well have been given to him by Shiela Grant Duff. According to Burgess's later recollections, it read: 'My dear Mr Churchill. We have met, though perhaps you do not remember. What can I do, and can you help me, about my unhappy country?' Watching Burgess read the letter, Churchill cried: 'Here I am, an old man without power and without party. What help shall I give? What assistance can I offer? What answer can I return?' Burgess replied, 'Offer him your eloquence ... make speeches, awaken people', but Churchill was too down-hearted. He told Burgess that the changed political situation meant he could no longer give his intended talk for the BBC. After giving a copy of *Arms and the Covenant* to Burgess, signed 'with admirable sentiments', Churchill walked him downstairs, patted the car, lamented the inevitability of another war, and sent him on his way.[87] Reflecting that evening on their encounter, Burgess wrote to Churchill, stressing the need for the French to reaffirm a Franco-Soviet pact and telling him, 'You alone have the force & the authority to galvanise the potential allies into action.'[88]

Over the course of October 1938, Churchill marshalled the energy he had remaining into action in the House of Commons. His speech on 5 October declared that there should never be friendship between the British democracy and the Nazi power, described by him as a regime 'which vaunts the spirit of aggression and conquest, which derives strength and perverted pleasure from persecution, and uses, as we have seen, with pitiless brutality the threat of murderous force'.[89]

Throughout this time, Shiela had been travelling across Europe, including a visit to Prague, which she told Churchill about in a meeting at Chartwell on Saturday 29 October. She was joined by Ian Colvin, the same Berlin-based journalist who had urged Randolph Churchill that his father should meet Ewald von Kleist-Schmenzin to discuss a potential coup d'état by the German generals. They were also joined by Edgar Mowrer, Shiela's unofficial mentor from the *Chicago Daily News*, for a meeting which the Churchills' daughter Mary, who had turned 16 six weeks before, remembered in her memoirs.[90] Mowrer later recalled that Churchill had been laying bricks in the garden and came in, wearing overalls covered in mortar, which also covered his hands, eyebrows and thinning hair.[91] The group, which was joined by Clementine and Mary, discussed the European situation over lunch for an hour. Shiela said that her time in Prague had been 'harrowing' but she was determined to continue the struggle for the people of Czechoslovakia.[92] The discussion then continued to the situation in France, which Churchill described as 'corrupt, divided' and 'floundering without a compass'.[93] This view worsened upon his being told that his former ally, Pierre-Étienne Flandin, had sent a note of congratulations to Hitler after the Munich Agreement was signed, leading Churchill to call him 'the accursed Flandin' in a letter to the French Minister of Justice, Paul Reynaud.[94] Churchill's ire then fell on Britain itself, which he said was 'prostrate with sleeping sickness', having 'almost given Europe to Hitler'.[95] Mowrer then posed the question, 'Do I understand that you would welcome an alliance with the Soviets?', to which Churchill's voice hardened as he replied, 'To save England I'd pact with the devil.'[96]

After lunch, Churchill took Shiela up to the study and gave her a signed copy of *Arms and the Covenant*. 'You have fought well', he said, shaking her hand solemnly.[97] In a rare moment of uncertainty, she asked him what she should do now. 'Join the Liberal Party and work with them', Churchill replied, offering to make an introduction to Archie Sinclair, who was due to visit Chartwell with his wife for dinner that evening, though the introduction would take place at a later date. As the two of them stood together in the ancient-raftered room looking out across the English countryside, he offered one final thought before Shiela, and her own allies and informants, departed from Chartwell:

Many people, no doubt, honestly believe they are only giving away the interests of Czechoslovakia, whereas I fear we shall find that we have compromised, and perhaps fatally endangered, the safety and even the independence of Great Britain and France. Do not suppose this is the end. This is only the beginning.[98]

CHAPTER 10

THROUGH THE LENS

Stefan Lorant, 3 February 1939

With the world delirious with relief upon Neville Chamberlain's return from Munich, declaring 'peace for our time', few wanted to hear Churchill's warnings that Britain was still at risk of war. But over the following months, while Churchill was largely entrenched at Chartwell, the tide of public opinion slowly began to turn, though much of the press remained supportive of the Government's policy of appeasement well into 1939. In a climate where many assumed that the risk posed by Nazi Germany had passed, it took a brave editorial decision to offer Churchill a platform to continue sounding the alarm against the Third Reich. Stefan Lorant, the editor of the *Picture Post*, and later known as 'the Godfather of Photojournalism', had more reason than most to give those who opposed Hitler a chance to reach millions of readers. Having been imprisoned in Germany, and only saved by his Hungarian citizenship resulting in diplomatic interventions, Lorant knew the horror and brutality of the Nazi regime. He became determined to secure an interview with Churchill at Chartwell, and ensured that Churchill's stance against Hitler would be read in homes across the country. As a result, his magazine boasted a front-page feature of 'Churchill on Foreign Policy' at the very moment Nazi Germany made its next move.

By November 1938, Mrs Pearman was still convalescing, and Miss Hamblin, who had left Chartwell earlier that year, was only able to return occasionally to help when the three serving secretaries needed extra hands. Churchill still felt responsible for Mrs Pearman's condition and, despite their continuing financial struggles, he offered to pay her salary of £3 a week for a year while she recovered at home. He also sent her a letter saying that she was welcome back whenever she felt ready. 'Please come and see us, and use this garden whenever you feel inclined', he wrote to her on 1 November.[1]

The new team in the secretaries' office were finding their feet as a trio, and each took their turns taking dictation for Churchill or manning the telephone exchange. It was Miss Harrington, the newest of the Churchills' secretaries, who took an astonishing telephone message at 4.30pm on 6 November 1938, which she then passed to Churchill. It was from the Press Association, which had called him at Chartwell to advise that Hitler had referred to him in a speech that day. 'He thinks he can set on one side the Germany of to-day', Hitler had announced; 'it would be better if Mr Churchill would associate less with people who are paid by Foreign States and more with German people.' Hitler then reportedly went on to offer assurance that he had no desire for another world war. 'I can assure Mr Churchill and his friends that that only happened once and will never happen again.'[2] Consequently, the Press Association was keen to know if Churchill had anything to say in response. The statement he composed that evening at Chartwell highlighted his lowly position in Parliament, and his surprise that the leader of the German people should attack him in such a way. He added that he was no warmonger, but felt that he was right that Britain should be properly defended, 'so that we can be safe and free, and also help others to whom we are bound'. Churchill then added that Hitler was 'unduly sensitive about suggestions that there may be other opinions in Germany besides his own' and added, 'It would be much wiser to relax a little.'[3]

The note passed to Churchill by Miss Harrington was far more polite in its wording than Hitler's actual utterances. He had called Churchill's opposition to the German government 'idiocy and stupidity',[4] and his targeting of Churchill did not end there. Following Germany's mass expulsion of 20,000 Jews on 28 October, a 17-year-old Jewish refugee, Herschel Grynszpan, shot a German diplomat, Ernst von Rath, in Paris on 7 November. Grynszpan stated that he acted in revenge for the thousands of Jewish refugees, including members of his own family, who had been expelled from Germany and were trapped in squalid conditions at the Polish border. Two days later, *Der Angriff*, a German newspaper, accused Churchill of being linked to the murder, with a headline reading 'The work of the instigator-international: A straight line from Churchill to Grynszpan.'[5]

On the same day that the Nazi press machine claimed Churchill had incited a Jewish boy to kill a Nazi diplomat in Paris, a coordinated rampage of anti-Semitic violence took place across Germany, supposedly in response to the murder and the purported threat posed by Jews to German citizens. On 9 November a night of brutal violence ensued, with Jewish homes, businesses and shops ransacked and destroyed. A thousand synagogues were burned, with countless holy objects desecrated and destroyed. The human cost of the night, which later became known as 'Kristallnacht', was the murder of about a hundred Jews. An estimated 30,000 Jewish men between the ages of 16 and 60, a quarter of all Jewish men still in Germany, were sent to concentration camps.[6] It was in the aftermath of this unspeakable violence that Stefan Lorant first wrote to Churchill at Chartwell, asking if he could arrange an interview.

Lorant's innovative new publication primarily featured photographs and images. 'A long experience with papers has shown me that the most powerful way to state a case is not in long political articles,' Lorant wrote, 'but in pictures with captions underneath.'[7] While there had been other pictorial news publications available beforehand, such as *The Tatler* or *The Bystander*, they tended to be read by the upper classes. With content and images that would appeal to the masses, *Picture Post* was an instant success. Having only released the first issue a month before Lorant wrote to Churchill, it was already selling a million copies on average, with an estimated five readers per magazine sold. With Lorant at the helm, it was perhaps little surprise that the publication did so well. The Hungarian photographer had become one of the most revered and successful editors in Europe.[8] On the eve of Hitler's ascendancy, Lorant was Chief Editor of the *Münchner Illustrierte Presse*, the first modern picture magazine in the world, with a weekly circulation of 750,000.

In March 1933, just a few weeks after Hitler's appointment as Chancellor, Lorant was arrested.[9] He was among the first editors to be put in political prison under the new Nazi regime, and no reason was given for his imprisonment. Instead, his incarceration was defined as *Schutzhaft*, a new form of 'protective custody' invented by the Nazis to imprison those considered enemies of the regime.[10]

While in prison, and risking his life in doing so, Lorant kept a diary. At first he used the little paper he had with him, but soon had to look for creative alternatives. 'After a while I had no paper so I wrote on lavatory paper and I was hiding my manuscript in my shoes', he later recalled.[11] He would then stuff the pages in his wife's bag when she visited. His release, six months after his arrest, was entirely thanks to his Hungarian citizenship, and negotiated between the Hungarian Ambassador and Heinrich Himmler, who was chief of police in Munich at the time. He was released to the Hungarian Consul, spent a single afternoon in a beer garden with around 20 friends, and then returned to Budapest at 9pm.[12] From that moment on, Lorant made every effort possible to warn of the horrors of the Nazi regime. His book *I Was Hitler's Prisoner* was published in 1935, sold almost a million copies, and was widely reviewed in the British press. *Country Life* called it 'one of the most devastating documents that has escaped from the New Germany'.[13] Upon the establishment of *Picture Post* in October 1938, it immediately became a vehicle for telling the British public the truth about the Nazi regime, and he saw an interview with Churchill as an effective way of supporting his wider campaign. In his proposal to Churchill, written while the buildings torched during Kristallnacht still smouldered, he wrote:

> I want to run your life story, not as a stunt, but because in the past years you have been consistently right in matters of foreign policy. Above all, in recognising the danger to this country which Nazi Germany constitutes . . . The series of pictures I have in mind will constitute a complete defence and statement of your political views, only it will be in a form which ordinary people can at once take in.[14]

Lorant added that the article should be written as soon as possible and, knowing that Churchill was mostly at Chartwell, he would be happy to come down to see him the following week. He concluded with a note about his time in prison after Hitler came to power in Germany, which he disclosed 'as a proof of my personal sympathy'.[15] Churchill considered Lorant's offer, but had been disgruntled with *Picture Post* in recent weeks, owing to an advertisement shown on the London Underground. It was described as featuring a 'composite picture' including Churchill and 'a certain lady', but sadly no record survives as to who the woman in question was.[16] Though Churchill never saw it, he was alerted to it by numerous acquaintances, including his publisher, who told him they thought it 'derogatory'.[17] Lorant was shocked by Churchill's report, saying that 'it never occurred to me that this poster could possibly give offence; otherwise, I should never have put it out.'[18] Lorant immediately ordered any still displayed to be pasted over, and he reassured Churchill that they would all be gone within three days. He then repeated his request to visit Chartwell that Friday. A handwritten note reading 'Yes can come down' was added to this letter, and a meeting was arranged for 21 November 1938 but, just a few hours before, at 12.50am, a telegram simply reading 'Please cancel your visit Chartwell Monday – Churchill' was sent to Lorant.[19]

The matter of Churchill's feature in *Picture Post* was far from the only thing on Churchill's mind. Painstaking preparations were made for a speech on 17 November in Parliament, intended to be a blistering attack on the Government, after which he planned to vote with the Labour Party on the issue of a Ministry of Supply.[20] He had urged 50 fellow Conservative MPs to do the same, but only Harold Macmillan and Bob Boothby did. He also found himself faced with serious opposition within his constituency association, and was confronted by threats of being ousted as their Conservative candidate. His criticism of the Government irritated those who thought Chamberlain's policy of appeasement had successfully averted war. Sir James Hawkey, the local Conservative Association's Vice-Chair, who had been at Chartwell for the meeting with Heinrich Brüning and Gottfried Treviranus, was convinced that Conservative Central

Office had manufactured a plot to undermine Churchill, believing that Hitler had stressed to Chamberlain the importance of silencing Churchill and his anti-German speeches.[21]

At the end of November, Ian Colvin, who had most recently visited Chartwell with Shiela Grant Duff, wrote to Churchill with information he had obtained from a German source that he could not name. It described Hitler's response to a report from London that Soviet Russia was not able to take military action in a European war, to which Hitler reportedly said that if he had known this, he would never have signed the Munich Agreement. 'It was necessary, he said, to devote attention to internal policy first. He wanted to eliminate from German life the Jews, the Churches, and suppress private industry', Colvin reported. 'After that, he would turn to foreign policy again.'[22] Hitler also apparently revelled in the confusion he had brought to political life in France, delighting in the support of Pierre-Étienne Flandin, Churchill's former ally. As for Britain, Hitler's plan was to wait for Chamberlain himself to cease being Prime Minister, at which point he could claim to no longer be bound by the Munich Agreement, and so he simply had to disrupt Chamberlain's premiership and wait for him to fall. Churchill sent a copy of Colvin's note to Lord Halifax, disguising the original sender. He then filed his own copy in the wooden box that he kept in the study which housed top-secret information and intelligence, so it would be close at hand at all times.[23]

Meanwhile, Churchill continued to meet with his most loyal friends, confidants and advisors. The Focus group gathered for lunch at the Savoy on Churchill's 64th birthday on 30 November and Churchill was delighted to be surrounded by those who had been campaigning with him for three years. Each was determined to continue, which prompted Churchill to remark 'the icy blast of Government disapproval will serve not to quench the fire which is in us, but to spread it into crackling flames.'[24]

As the festive season drew near, Churchill was still largely at Chartwell, with occasional appearances in his constituency to counter the effects of those who wanted to unseat him. Clementine, meanwhile, accompanied her husband on official engagements, and met with friends and family ahead of another voyage, this time to the Caribbean following an invitation from her former cruise companion, Lord Moyne. Unlike other holidays, it is evident from the letters she wrote to Churchill on this trip that she longed to be with him from the outset, with more than a hint of homesickness in her words. He too found himself utterly distracted by her absence. 'I feel so deeply interwoven with you that I follow your movements in my mind at every hour & in all circumstances I wonder what you are doing now', he wrote to her a week before Christmas.[25] He was at Chartwell every night, working until the early hours of the morning on his *A History of the English-Speaking Peoples*, which he hoped to finish by June the following year. At that point in December he was immersed in the Wars of the Roses, having just finished writing about Joan of Arc, whom he called 'the winner in the whole of French history', before adding, 'The leading women of these days were more remarkable and forceful than the men.'[26]

The house, however, was bitterly cold, with snow covering the landscape, and the temperature dropping to 10°F (-12°C).[27] 'I envelop myself in sweaters & thick clothes & gloves: They say it will be worse: A White Christmas!', he wrote ahead of travelling to Blenheim Palace on Christmas Eve.[28] A hastily written letter the next day gave Clementine the sad news that Sidney Peel, a suitor of hers before Churchill, had passed away. The pair had been engaged, but Clementine realised that he didn't quite spark her intellectual curiosity. She thought that life with him would be likely to be pleasant but not overly interesting, and so she had called off the engagement. 'Many are dying now that I knew when we were young', Churchill wrote to Clementine, as he contemplated his own mortality in the cold and wintry gloom of Chartwell.[29] Fortunately, he had company to stave off too many pangs of loneliness without her. Clementine's sister Nellie and her husband Bertram decided to visit. Mary, whom Churchill described as 'growing into her beauty' at this time,[30] was also largely at Chartwell, under the ever-present care of her nanny Moppet.

As always, Churchill kept his eye on events in Westminster, with a Cabinet reshuffle rumoured for January; even so, Churchill thought it unlikely that he would be invited back into Government. 'Everything goes to show that our interests are declining throughout Europe,' he told Clementine, 'and that Hitler will be on the move again in February or March, probably against Poland.'[31] As the year drew to a close, there were moments of joy for the Churchills. Diana, their eldest daughter, had another baby, this time a girl called Edwina, who arrived a month earlier than expected, weighing less than 5lb, and was described by her proud grandfather as 'tiny but perfect'.[32] The menagerie at Chartwell also provided suitable entertainment, from the poorly behaved parrot whose antisocial behaviour was attributed to the cold, to Mary's pregnant goat, and the sad tale of a heron who waited so long for the fish in the middle pond to surface that he was thought to have died from a combination of cold and starvation. 'I would gladly have sent him food if I had known of his plight', Churchill said with regret.[33] Otherwise, his daily schedule became even more ingrained without the interruptions of parliamentary business, which he described as 'reading the papers and letters, eating, building, correspondence, sleeping, dining and finally dictating until three o'clock in the morning'.[34]

With Clementine's travels in early January taking her to Antigua, Montserrat and Dominica, Churchill too made plans to holiday abroad, arranging to visit Maxine Elliot at her villa in the south of France for most of January, accompanied by his secretary Miss Penman and Professor Lindemann. 'As usual I did not leave Chartwell without a pang,' he wrote to Clementine, 'but now I am here I am sure I shall enjoy it.'[35] He replaced his Chartwell routine of building and dictating with a Riviera routine of dictating and gambling in the casinos, though his mind frequently wandered back to Chartwell. Even while relaxing in the Mediterranean sun, he decided he would build another cottage on the Chartwell estate to keep him amused in the summer, as well as helping to maintain his health. Although Churchill was pondering leisurely pursuits, the international situation was also playing on his mind, as became apparent one evening over dinner at the residence of the Duke and Duchess of Windsor. The former monarch found himself in firm disagreement with Churchill over a recent article in which the latter had argued the case for an alliance with

Soviet Russia. Curtly rebutting the Duke, Churchill declared, 'When our kings are in conflict with our constitution we change our kings.'[36] The Duke, who was sitting on the edge of the sofa by the fireplace, had been interrupting whenever he could and contesting every point Churchill made. He was finally beaten into conversational submission, when Churchill declared for all to hear that Britain was now in the gravest danger of its long history.[37]

On the way home, Churchill stopped in Paris, staying at the Ritz before boarding the Golden Arrow train and ferry on the night of 24 January. Their journey was marred by delays, firstly due to Churchill misplacing his gold dental plate. He implored Miss Penman to help him search, which she did, eventually finding it under his pillow. By now terribly late, the pair then jumped into a taxi, sped across Paris to the Gare du Nord, grabbed a porter to assist them with their luggage and sprinted to the departure platform. In their haste, Miss Penman hadn't realised that the fastenings of one of her cases were becoming loose and soon the opening tilted downwards, revealing some underwear. Her swift action prevented the contents spilling across the station floor, but not before Churchill had noticed the stray garments. He turned to her and wryly remarked, 'We must not wash our dirty linen in public', as the pair ran the last stretch towards the barrier.[38]

The mishaps did not stop in Paris, and when they reached Victoria Station in London, Churchill gave Miss Penman particular instructions around which cases should and shouldn't be opened by the customs officials. Unfortunately, she misremembered his instruction and confidently opened a case which was full of bottles of liquor. Churchill, who had just announced that they had 'nothing to declare', suddenly looked rather sheepish, apologised profusely, and duly paid the required amount.[39] It was then with some relief that the pair saw Cale, the Churchills' chauffeur, who greeted them, loaded their bags into the car and drove them back to Chartwell.

While Churchill was away in France, Stefan Lorant once again wrote to him at Chartwell, repeating his previous request for an interview. 'An article setting out your views over the past few years and the way in which they have been entirely justified by events, would be of real value at the present time', Lorant wrote persuasively to Churchill.[40] He added that the *Picture Post*'s sales were now typically in excess of 1.25 million per issue, with five people reading each copy printed. It was an opportunity that was too good to miss, and Lorant was invited to lunch at Chartwell on Friday 3 February. Lorant decided to bring along the half-Jewish and German-born photographer Kurt Hübschmann, who had emigrated to Britain in 1934 and had called himself Kurt Hutton since 1937.[41] The thinking was that Hutton could then take the photographs, leaving Lorant free to discuss the nature and tone of the articles. The two men, both of whom could be considered as refugees from Nazi Germany, then made arrangements for their journey to the Churchills' country home in Kent.

Having driven the two of them down the icy roads to Chartwell, which were often treacherous in the depths of winter, Lorant and his photographer were met at the front door and shown to the study, where Churchill was reviewing books and papers at his standing desk against the far wall, between two windows that looked out onto the driveway. To the left were typed notes with Churchill's handwritten corrections in red ink. The image of Churchill at work was a captivating one, and the photojournalist in Lorant requested that his photographer be allowed to capture the scene, taking numerous photos of Churchill standing in deep contemplation in the study.

After the initial introductions, the three men walked down the heavy oak stairs to the dining room. Once seated at the table, Churchill asked Lorant about his time in Germany. 'He listened to my description [of] what I had experienced in Munich', Lorant later recalled.[42] His six months in prison were painstakingly outlined, and he described what life was really like as a political prisoner of the Nazi regime. When lunch was served, it tellingly resembled the menus the Churchill family had previously had when no guests were expected. This was most likely owing to continuing tightening of expenditure, which was further reflected in the dining room having its curtains drawn halfway across the room, leaving only the smaller of the two tables available for use. This was a device used to

24. *Winston Churchill with Stefan Lorant in the dining room at*
Chartwell, February 1939.

shorten the space, thereby removing the furthest part of the room which afforded the beautiful views across the gardens, but it also meant only the nearest half of the room to the kitchen had to be heated and lit.

A member of the kitchen staff, probably the cook or the kitchen-maid, described rather unkindly by Lorant simply as 'a fat lady',[43] brought in their meals. The three men were served steak and kidney pie, a dish which they were told was a favourite of Churchill's, and Lorant later reflected how Churchill 'took the bowl up to his mouth and took a spoon and shovelled the steak and kidney pie', while sipping brandy and smoking his cigar.[44] Little was said while the gentlemen ate, which Lorant took as an indication that his mind was elsewhere. The same lady returned with a bowl of chocolates which Churchill then consumed while reading the series of questions about Germany and Hitler that Lorant had jotted down. 'All right, these are good. We will do it', Churchill said, much to Lorant's relief.[45] While they were still at the table, Churchill revealed that his wife was away travelling, but that he was constructing a brick building as a surprise for her on her return. Churchill threw an old army coat over his boiler suit, put on a rather worn-looking hat, and invited his guests to join him on a bitterly cold walk down the garden path towards the complex of cottages attached to Churchill's painting studio. Upon reaching what appeared to be a building site, and without explanation or introduction, Churchill knelt down and started laying bricks. He was assisted by Jackson, the new Chartwell handyman, and two supporting contractors. Initially, Jackson was handing Churchill the bricks to lay, but Lorant found himself so absorbed in the process that he soon took over. 'There was not a word, no conversation, not a word spoken', Lorant later recalled, having witnessed Churchill's complete immersion in the pastime.[46] This was typical not only of his bricklaying, but also his painting, when his complete focus was on the task in hand. Meanwhile, Hutton captured the remarkable sight, taking several photographs of a former Government minister laying bricks and tiles at the bottom of the hill in his garden.

After about half an hour of bricklaying, Churchill and Lorant walked across the lawn, with Churchill puffing on his cigar as they went. More photographs were taken, including one when he was walking back towards the house. With the most recognisable of the building's facades behind him, Lorant momentarily dashed out of the shot, asking Churchill to turn around to face the camera. With his cigar in his left hand and leaning on a walking stick with his right, Lorant's photojournalistic eye saw in that moment the vital role that the building in the background played in Churchill's life during the years of his political wilderness. 'It was very interesting to observe him, the real Churchill in his quiet moments', Lorant remembered years later.[47] They continued their discussion about the international situation, and Churchill suggested that perhaps Lorant should speak to Ambassador Kennedy about doing an issue of *Picture Post* about the United States. Over the course of their meeting, Lorant had become an even more ardent Churchill supporter. 'Churchill was a very colourful, wonderful, human being', he said years later. 'Larger than life, he was incredible to believe.'[48]

25. Winston Churchill, on the orchard path in the garden at Chartwell, February 1939.

He returned to his *Picture Post* office that afternoon and wrote to Churchill straight away, thanking him for the charming reception and the interesting talk they had had. The following week, Churchill sent the answers to Lorant's questions, which would then form an interview to be published in a March issue. The plan remained to do a two-part article about Churchill's life so far, before the interview piece. These articles would be written by Wickham Steed, and accompanied by photographs taken that day at Chartwell alongside historic ones of Churchill over the course of his life. The eight-page first half of the article featured in the issue published on 25 February 1939. It opened with a full-page image of Churchill taken on the day of the meeting three weeks earlier. The image showed him standing in front of the wall he was building, with ladders and equipment in the background. His gaze was to the side of the camera lens, and he was wearing his tattered double-breasted coat and well-worn hat. It was shown alongside the following caption:

WINSTON CHURCHILL AS THE PUBLIC DOES NOT SEE HIM: In the Garden of his Country Home ... He is at work, but this work is his recreation. He is building in the garden of his country home at Chartwell, 26 miles from London. While he builds, his constant preoccupation is with Britain, the British Empire and its position in the world. Churchill foresaw, long before any other politician, the speed and extent of German rearmament. We owe it to him that our country is not far worse prepared than it is to resist threats from abroad. In the following pages we tell the life-story of the most discussed politician of our time.[49]

Steed then opened with an astonishingly prophetic remark in describing a man ten years into his political exile, and with no obvious signs of being brought back into the Government in the near future, when he wrote 'at 64 the greatest moment of his life has still to come'.[50] Unfortunately, Churchill fell ill just as the first of the three *Picture Post* issues with articles profiling him, was about to hit the shelves. Newspapers reported he was confined to his bed at Chartwell with influenza and a raging fever, which prevented him from speaking at a scheduled meeting in his constituency.[51] Rumours began to circulate abroad that he had suffered a stroke. Churchill was alerted to this by a letter written on 27 February to his secretary Mrs Hill from Peter Peirson, a contact of his who lived in Brno, a western region of Czechoslovakia that bordered Germany. Rather handily, he had been sending Churchill written updates on the situation there since 22 January.[52] The letter continued describing how lorry-loads of Reich workmen were being brought in to work on a new motorway from Germany, and outlined a recent experience in a local restaurant. 'Every table had little swastika banners ... Each face was fanatically pro-Hitler, and every arm willing to rise at the slightest provocation ... It left a nasty impression on my mind.'[53]

Churchill's illness continued well into March, with all meetings on his engagement cards struck through until an appointment with his doctor on 9 March gave him the all-clear. His first public appearance was the very next day, speaking at another event in his constituency. In his speech he praised the Prime Minister's recent declaration affirming the solidarity between Britain and France, but he still feared that war was looming. His daughter Mary recalled in her memoirs that Churchill took to reciting a poem at this time that he had learnt as a schoolboy, inspired by a railway accident that happened when the driver fell asleep:

Who is in charge of the clattering train?
For the carriages sway and the couplings strain,
And the pace is fast, and the points are near,
And sleep had deadened the driver's ear.
And the signals flash through the night in vain
For DEATH is in charge of the clattering train.[54]

The third of the three *Picture Post* issues to feature Churchill, and this time with his extended interview on foreign policy, hit the news stands on 11 March 1939. Entitled 'What Britain's Policy Should Be', the article followed a piece called 'Life in Shanghai', which focused on the Japanese threat and declared: 'Firmness may have its dangers, but it is nothing like so dangerous as weakness.'[55] The page with Churchill's interview included a large photograph of him at the dining room table at Chartwell, cigar in hand and looking straight down the lens of the camera, with an expression that was improbably both stern and contemplative. The 13 questions were carefully chosen to cover a range of issues, including the prospect of an alliance with Russia, what policy Britain should pursue in relation to the war between China and Japan, and civilian defence on the home front. When asked what he thought Britain's foreign policy should have been since 1933, Churchill replied that it should have focused on uniting those peaceful nations who knew that no good could come from attacking one's neighbours, 'and prevent the countries which took a contrary view from putting themselves in a position to destroy civilisation by pursuing a mad-dog policy'.[56] A follow-up question asked Churchill what Britain's guiding principle should be going forward:

We can only endeavour, though in much more difficult circumstances, to maintain the same foreign policy to-day. We should try to recapture the confidence – sadly shaken by the events of last September – of the smaller nations who have everything to lose by war, and to form a group, headed by the United States, France and ourselves, which would be so formidable that to attack it would be to court disaster...If Russia were prepared to co-operate with such a group as I have outlined, I would welcome her assistance in maintaining the peace of the world.[57]

Being mindful of *Picture Post*'s readership, Lorant closed with a question about the defence of civilians on the home front, and asked Churchill whether the measures taken to date were enough to prevent demoralisation of the British people. Churchill had to carefully balance his reply. He wanted to sustain the morale of the millions who would carefully read his words and might well discuss them over the dinner table. At the same time, he intended to remain critical of the pace of progress in the readying of necessary infrastructure, especially for those Britons living in urban areas, to protect them from attacks from the air.

I am confident that our people are less liable to demoralisation than any other in the event of war. Anyone who saw our battalions under fire, or the reactions to air raiders in London in the Great War, must share this confidence. But this is no reason or excuse for neglecting any conceivable precaution to diminish the suffering which might be inflicted in gross disregard of all the laws of war by brutal air attacks upon civilian targets. The present state of our arrangements is a scandal and a danger of the gravest kind.[58]

Churchill's chosen wording was music to Lorant's ears, perfectly reflecting his own personal sentiments, while avoiding a direct attack on the Prime Minister's appeasement policy. *Picture Post* had to remain neutral in that regard since the publication's proprietor, Edward Hulton, was a staunch Conservative, urging Lorant at a meeting the year before to 'Kindly remember that I am not only a Conservative, I am a loyal supporter of Mr Neville Chamberlain.'[59] Despite the strong steer from *Picture Post*'s owner, Churchill's logical but critical assessment of the Government's chosen path allowed him to speak directly to an otherwise hard-to-reach demographic. As it turned out, the article had a reach far beyond Britain's shores, and the same Peter Peirson who was updating Churchill on news in Czechoslovakia wrote to Mrs Hill on 12 March saying that he was 'looking forward to receiving the next copy with his commentary on world affairs,' before adding, 'That is the kind of guidance that we require nowadays.'[60] The articles also allowed Lorant to continue his campaign of alerting the British public to the need to awaken to the threat posed by Nazi Germany, a threat which proved to be even more imminent than either of them could have realised when they discussed the matter over lunch at Chartwell a month earlier.

The following week, Churchill was due to speak in the House of Commons on Tuesday afternoon. By that time, Germans had begun to riot in Prague and other cities across Czechoslovakia. Radio stations in Germany announced that peace had broken down and that German citizens were experiencing a 'reign of terror', which provided the perfect excuse for Nazi military action. Long columns of German army vehicles began to move into position, and on the same day as Churchill's next scheduled speech, President Emil Hácha of Czechoslovakia, who had succeeded Edvard Beneš, was summoned to Berlin by Hitler.

At the same time as Hácha travelled from Prague to Berlin, Clementine watched from the viewing gallery of the House of Commons debating chamber, as her husband bombarded the Government for half an hour with technical questions. The subjects of his enquiries included the allocation of weapons for the Territorial

Army, the nature of reserve battalions, the improvements in army recruitment, and finally the necessary conversion of factories to the production of supplies of artillery and munitions, machine guns, anti-tank rifles and grenades.[61] Upon leaving the House of Commons he then travelled to the town of Waltham Abbey in his constituency, where he knew there would be people in attendance who had questioned whether he should continue as their Member of Parliament owing to his lack of faith in the Munich Agreement. There was, however, no conciliatory tone to his speech and he launched a blistering attack that evening on those who had naively believed that events in Munich six months earlier had secured peace in Europe.

I pointed out that Munich sealed the ruin of Czechoslovakia … I held the view that these guarantees were not worth the paper they were written on, or the breath that uttered them. What is the position now? The Czechoslovak Republic is being broken up before our eyes. Their gold is to be stolen by the Nazis. The Nazi system is to blot out every form of internal freedom. Their army is about to be reduced to negligible proportions, or incorporated in the Nazi power … They are being completely absorbed, and not until the Nazi power has passed away from Europe will they emerge again in Freedom. Why should I have said all these things? It was the truth. It was my duty to say them.[62]

Hácha arrived in Berlin at 10.40pm but was forced to wait a torturous few hours before being summoned to the Reich Chancellery to meet Hitler at 1.00am on 15 March. He was warned that the German Army was ready to march but, if he chose, a 'peaceful occupation' could take place which would guarantee the Czechs 'autonomy and a certain measure of national freedom'.[63] If he were to resist, total destruction would be inflicted on the Czech people. Hácha chose the former and ceded his country to Hitler's demands in the hope of avoiding bloodshed. At 4.30am a radio announcement was made to the people of Czechoslovakia, telling them that German occupation would commence from 6.00am, with the capital city due to be occupied at 6.30am. 'Their advance must nowhere be resisted. The slightest resistance will cause the most unforeseen consequences and lead to the intervention becoming utterly brutal', the message continued, and instructed all commanders to obey the orders of the occupying army.[64]

One of the first accounts of the occupation that made its way to Chartwell was from Peter Peirson, who had been waiting for Churchill's *Picture Post* interview with such anticipation. 'We feel very cut off now, as news is scarce,' he opened in his letter to Mrs Hill, 'and the British Vice-Consul here has committed suicide.'[65] He described the response from the people around him in Brno in Moravia, which had already morphed into being called by the Germanicised name of Brünn after just two days, as being 'extremely and amazingly quiet'. Their terror was that of stunned silence, and fear of what might await, as swastikas began to drape every building.

On the Sunday of that momentous week, Churchill invited Shiela Grant Duff and Hubert Ripka to lunch at Chartwell. Churchill asked Ripka what he thought might happen next. Ripka replied that the German Army was now nearer the Soviet frontier, which meant Russia had two options. One was to conclude a military pact not only with France but also with Britain: the other was to come to an agreement with Germany.[66] Churchill agreed and pressed the need for Britain to enter into military talks with Russia. Ripka also confirmed that the former President Edvard Beneš, who was living in exile in Putney in London, had despatched telegrams to the President of the United States, the Prime Ministers of Britain and France, the Foreign Minister of the Soviet Union and the President of the League of Nations on 15 March, saying that the German occupation of Prague wiped out the validity of the Munich Agreement. Shiela shared her intention to support Czech refugees, while Churchill remarked that Hitler would very likely continue his assault on democratic countries until the threat of a general war, or actual hostilities, halted his ambitions.

Support for Churchill's return to Government became louder as March wore on, and the extraordinary timing of the *Picture Post* article enabled him to share his views on foreign policy with millions of people, who responded to the publication's new and innovative approach to current affairs. The articles, born from the meeting at Chartwell, positioned him as a voice of authority for the masses on the subject of Britain's response to international aggression. Churchill acknowledged the role Lorant played in boosting his popularity among the general public, telling friends years later that he had been a great help in his becoming Prime Minister.[67] In the spring of 1939, however, there was no invitation to return to Government, and so Churchill remained at Chartwell, trying with all his might to remain focused on writing his *History of the English-Speaking Peoples*. He had just a few months to finish it, but noted to his former research assistant, Maurice Ashley, that: 'It is very hard to transport oneself into the past, when the future opens its jaws upon us.'[68]

CHAPTER 11

THE FUTURE PRIME MINISTER

Harold Macmillan, 7 April 1939

T he nature and purpose of visits to Chartwell shifted once again after the Nazi invasion of Czechoslovakia. Every moment mattered, and social visits made way for crisis talks. The time for information gathering had now passed. During the spring of 1939, Churchill's army of informants made way for those who held power and influence in political and military affairs. With Chamberlain's government still keeping Churchill at arm's length, his allies were often fellow backbench MPs who shared his views on appeasement and were willing to join him as outspoken critics of Neville Chamberlain. One such individual was the 44-year-old MP for Stockton-on-Tees, and future Prime Minister, Harold Macmillan. He had also become disillusioned with the Conservative leadership and, despite having only been a distant acquaintance to Churchill for much of his 14 years in Parliament, their shared opposition to Nazi Germany, and willingness to vote against the Government, rapidly brought the two men closer. He was one of a handful of young MPs who were willing to risk political suicide by opposing the Government. By March 1939 Macmillan had become one of Churchill's trusted inner circle, joining him in demanding that a national, cross-party government must be established to face the looming crisis, and even calling for the Prime Minister's resignation. The following week he was invited to Chartwell for the Easter weekend, when events took place that saw both men abandon any hope they had held for a peaceful

26. Harold Macmillan, Member of Parliament for Stockton and future Prime Minister, circa 1939.

solution to the international crisis, as war with Germany seemed increasingly unavoidable.

The earliest reference to Churchill in Macmillan's letters dates from the First World War. Lieutenant Colonel Churchill, as he then was, had recently returned from fighting on the Western Front and took his seat once again in the House of Commons. In a speech given on 23 May 1916, he reflected on his time in the trenches to give a soldier's perspective of the conflict. 'The trench population lives almost continuously under the fire of the enemy,' he declared to those MPs present at the debate, before adding that they were subject to 'the hardest of tests that men have ever been called upon to bear.'[1] The

22-year-old Captain Macmillan had only just returned to the front after a gunshot wound to his right hand. Back in active service, he wrote to his mother three days after the speech remarking that 'Colonel Winston Churchill's speech the other day has met with a good deal of favourable comment out here. I think he makes some very good points.'[2] Less than four months later, he was shot while in no-man's-land during the Battle of the Somme, with the bullet fragmenting and lodging in his pelvis. After rolling into a shell hole, he waited for hours. Remembering that he had a copy of Aeschylus' *Prometheus Bound* in his pocket, he read the Greek text while waiting to be rescued.[3] In excruciating pain, he was also forced to play dead whenever German soldiers ran along the lip of the shell hole. He remained there until darkness fell and a search party retrieved him.[4] Over the course of the war, he earned a reputation for his bravery, though he became deeply affected by survivor's guilt and was determined to play a part in solving the problems that arose in its aftermath.[5]

When Macmillan was first elected to the House of Commons in 1924, Churchill was Chancellor of the Exchequer, overseeing economic matters and public finance. The nature of Macmillan's constituency in the north-east of England, which suffered severe unemployment and deprivation, meant that he frequently lobbied the Chancellor, writing to him of 'the appalling conditions in this area & the state of the industries on which these people depend'.[6] In sharp contrast to the plight of his constituents in Stockton, the man at the helm of Britain's finances seemed 'unique, wayward, exciting, a man with a peculiar glamour of his own, that brought a sense of colour into our rather drab political life'.[7] Macmillan was drawn into Churchill's orbit by his close political friend Bob Boothby, who was Churchill's Parliamentary Private Secretary from 1926 to 1929. Recalling how he and fellow Churchill acolytes spent their evenings, Macmillan later wrote:

[We] would sit round, sometimes late into the night, smoking, drinking and arguing, and of course listening. The flow of Churchill's rhetoric once it got under way was irresistible. Nevertheless, he quite happily allowed rival themes to be put forward in different parts of the room and took little notice of interruption. It was the first time that I had come across this kind of method of conducting political talk, and it was the beginning of a very long association which later ripened into close friendship with this man, the greatest figure and greatest inspiration in my life.[8]

Despite their apparent rapport, Churchill didn't initially bring Macmillan into his inner circle. While Boothby became a regular guest at Chartwell, Macmillan was sidelined. When new names were being considered for Churchill's exclusive cross-party dining group, the Other Club, in July 1927, Macmillan was on a list of suggested individuals alongside Bob Boothby. Macmillan's was the only name to be struck through with the word 'no' written by Churchill in the margin. There is no explanation given on the note, but Macmillan's serious, introverted and somewhat awkward personality was the most likely reason for his omission. Boothby, on the other hand, was much more like Churchill, sharing his traits of exuberance, the desire to entertain, and love of the limelight. Churchill might have appreciated Macmillan's intellect, and admired the bravery of a fellow veteran of the Great War, but he was never going to be the life and soul of the party.

The two men drifted further apart in the early 1930s over the subject of Indian independence. This was followed by a difference of opinion over the abdication crisis, which effectively sealed their separation. 'I didn't want to quarrel with him so I rather dropped out of his circle', Macmillan later recalled.[9] Beyond political disagreements, there were personal reasons for Macmillan to distance himself from certain members of Churchill's inner circle, too. His wife Dorothy had been having an affair with Boothby since the summer of 1929, and for the next five years the pair attended society events, to all intents and purposes as a couple. They were very much in love but Macmillan refused to grant Dorothy a divorce and the affair became more painful for all involved as time passed. Boothby wrote to a confidant in September 1932: 'it has become unendurable. No basis & no meaning for me. Just an interminable series of agonising "goodbyes" with nothing to go back to. Living always for the "next time".'[10] Dorothy's determination to keep Boothby led her to derail his efforts to form romantic attachments with anyone else, including one instance when he proposed to another woman in Venice, after which she travelled all the way to Italy to break the engagement. 'She was relentless, there was a streak of cruelty in her,' Boothby later recalled, 'but we were absolutely fixed upon each other.'[11] For Macmillan, the pain of Dorothy's adultery endured for the rest of his life, and so it is perhaps little wonder that Macmillan had little desire to attach himself to the political ally of his wife's lover.

Despite the distance created by his own heartbreak, Macmillan's political compass bore a remarkable resemblance to Churchill's own. In his 1935 election manifesto, alongside what he called his 'war on poverty', his campaign focused on the need for collective security between nations. He also argued that rearmament was essential 'to maintain the efficiency of our defence services'.[12] A year later, in the aftermath of Nazi Germany's reoccupation of the Rhineland, Macmillan wrote a bulletin for his constituents reiterating his stance on foreign affairs, and so justifying his opposition to the Government:

I regard the Government policy as disastrous. The banding together of the peaceful nations of the world in a League to uphold the rule of law is the only way to restrain or defeat the aggressor. The common-sense practical realist does not make war. It is the misty dreamers; the half-mad Dictators ... These are the madmen who nearly destroyed the world in 1914 and who, if we are to encourage their insane nationalism, may finally destroy it in 1940.[13]

However, as the situation in Europe darkened, the two men found common ground through their shared opposition to the Prime Minister's foreign policy. Macmillan, like Churchill, was shocked by the sudden and unexpected resignation of the Foreign Secretary, Anthony Eden, in February 1938. In the debate that followed Churchill's only sleepless night at Chartwell, Macmillan was one of 21 MPs who joined him in abstaining. This group evolved into an anti-appeasement collective, but with subdivisions. At this point Macmillan found himself drawn into Eden's orbit, joining a group known as 'the Glamour Boys', as opposed to Churchill's contingent, which included Boothby, who were labelled 'the Old Guard'.[14] The strength of his conviction, however, mirrored Churchill's. After Germany's annexation of Austria in March, Macmillan was transfixed as he listened to Churchill speak in the House of Commons. 'He spoke with gravity and authority, but without bitterness or recrimination,' Macmillan later recalled, before adding: 'He displayed full command of his subject, based on his profound study of history and the art of war.'[15]

Churchill's biography of his ancestor, the Duke of Marlborough, had been devoured by Macmillan in recent months. He had finished the first three volumes and was eagerly awaiting the fourth. It was at this point that Macmillan realised that Churchill's understanding of the past seemed particularly pertinent in 1938. The need to curtail the ambition of an aggressor in Europe, just as Marlborough had fought against the armies of Louis XIV, seemed to be playing out once again. In that moment, something shifted in Macmillan. In Churchill he saw a man who spoke as if he held no political allegiance and cared only for the safety and security of his country. Three days later, on 17 March 1938, at a meeting of the women's branch of his local Conservative Association, Macmillan gave a speech which seemed imbued with Churchill's influence:

We are in a situation not dissimilar to that of 1914. Many people have felt and many historians have felt that if Sir Edward Grey and the Liberal Government of 1914 had made it perfectly clear in the July of that year that this country would support Belgium if attacked, there might never have been a war. If we mean to make the invasion of Czechoslovakia a reason for going to war . . . we had better say so now, that is if we mean to join with Russia and France; and not when it has happened.[16]

His speech was printed in full the next day in the *Northern Echo*, the most widely read newspaper in his constituency. It included his calls to bring about a national government, and his declaration: 'I should also like to see the inclusion of a great outside figure like Mr. Winston Churchill, to demonstrate to the world that the party divisions which properly divide us in our internal affairs are subservient to the unity which we display when we are faced with threats from the outside.'[17] By the end of 1938, his loyalty to Churchill was beyond question. Like Churchill he despaired after the Munich Agreement. By that time the number of Conservative dissenters was around 30, and Macmillan's role evolved into that of a link between the Eden and Churchill factions. He corralled their support towards a shared anti-appeasement stance with members of the Labour Party, and aided the creation of a new 'Middle Way' coalition group.

As a critical post-Munich debate neared, regarding a Labour Party motion to establish a Ministry of Supply, the divisions among the anti-appeasement Conservatives became apparent. Many of those who had voiced support began to lose their nerve. Anthony Eden was one of those who decided not to oppose the Government, fearing a split in the Conservative Party would only serve to strengthen Labour's hand. As a result, Macmillan began to question whether he had chosen the right ally after all. As support for open opposition evaporated, there were only three Conservative MPs who voted in favour of the establishment of a Ministry of Supply, and therefore voted against the Government, and their party, that night: Winston Churchill, Brendan Bracken and Harold Macmillan.[18] From that point on, there was no question in Macmillan's mind as to where his political allegiance should lie.

In the early months of 1939, Churchill was once again firmly rooted at Chartwell, writing to friends, 'it is absolutely necessary for me to be in the country every possible night this year, in order to complete the history I am writing.' This meant that, in terms of evening invitations, he was 'accordingly refusing practically everything'.[19] Lunch meetings in London, however, could still be squeezed into his diary, including one in February with Leo Amery and Count Coudenhove-Kalergi at Amery's house. Amery's son later recalled the gathering, and in particular the moment Coudenhove-Kalergi said: 'You do realise, Mr Churchill, that Hitler and Stalin are just about to conclude an agreement.' Churchill appeared shocked, replying: 'Not possible. I see the Soviet Ambassador Mr Maisky quite often. I don't think this can happen.' Coudenhove-Kalergi then confirmed that his sources were from the Vatican, which tended to be well informed on such matters. This reportedly was one of the few instances when Churchill fell completely silent.[20] Another lunch took place with the American Ambassador, Joe Kennedy, on 2 March. Among other things, the pair discussed whether Kennedy would consider joining an upcoming Focus group meeting. Churchill was so keen that he attend, that he left the date up to the Ambassador, who gave the impression of being delighted at the prospect of receiving the invitation.[21]

Macmillan, like Churchill, found himself busy writing at this time. He had published *The Price of Peace*, outlining his opposition to Chamberlain's policy of appeasement, in October 1938, and called for an alliance between Britain, France and Soviet Russia.[22] He followed this with *Economic Aspects of Defence* in February 1939, which was highly critical of the Government and highlighted the futility of rearmament unless accompanied by an adequate foreign policy.[23] He did so at the risk of incurring similar ire from his constituents to that which Churchill had experienced, and he was forced to confront his local Conservative Association at its Annual General Meeting on 10 March. Standing on the stage of a local dance hall, Macmillan announced that he did not regret any action he had taken and his only regret was that they had not taken a hard line earlier.[24]

At Chartwell, Churchill's mood sank following the invasion of Czechoslovakia in mid-March. 'The crisis seems to be becoming more serious', his 16-year-old daughter Mary wrote in her diary on 18 March. She added that her father had said, 'Before God Almighty I swear I do not wish for war', noting that she had witnessed him saying it, and underlining it in her diary.[25] Her reflections from Chartwell in the latter weeks of March fluctuate between hope and despair, writing excitedly of her father's reports of Britain's positive relations with France on 24 March, only to follow it the next day with 'News is pretty bad!!'[26] Churchill continued to advocate for the formation of a national government, this time supported by Anthony

Eden, Harold Macmillan and Duff Cooper, who had resigned from Government after the Munich Agreement.

Throughout this time, family life continued in parallel with Churchill's political life. The closing weeks of March included the christening of the Churchills' new granddaughter Edwina and visits to Chartwell from their two eldest daughters and their husbands. Other Chartwell visitors included regulars such as Professor Lindemann and Desmond Morton, but there were also a few less familiar faces who frequented their country home. Air Marshal Sir Hugh Dowding, the commanding officer of the newly created RAF Fighter Command, joined the Churchills for Sunday lunch on 26 March. They discussed a letter Churchill had recently received from Group Captain Lachlan MacLean containing notes on aircraft speeds, petrol consumption and interception. Describing how best to defend against attacking German squadrons, the letter said that opposition should take place hundreds of miles from British shores, 'in order to force the enemy to full speed flight and then maximum consumption of fuel for as long as possible'. This would reportedly 'provide a reasonable period to allow for an adequate and repeated series of attacks to be developed'.[27] The hope had been that both MacLean and Wing Commander Charles Anderson, the former Director of Training at the Air Ministry, who had been providing Churchill with RAF intelligence and analysis since 1937, could join them at Chartwell that day. Sadly, neither was available. Dowding and Churchill, meanwhile, discussed the letter over lunch amid clouds of smoke from Churchill's cigars and Dowding's pipe. They were joined by Clementine and her old friends Horatia Seymour and Venetia Stanley, alongside Professor Lindemann, Randolph and Mary. It was in this moment that Chartwell ceased to be a place for theoretical discussions regarding the conduct of war. Instead, it became the site for planning strategy and tactics in the likely event of German attacks on Britain.

The day after Dowding's afternoon at Chartwell, a group of parliamentarians met in London, including Duff Cooper, Leo Amery, Anthony Eden, Harold Macmillan, Harold Nicolson and Lord Woolmer. They debated which was the more urgent priority: the formation of a coalition government or conscription.[28] Unable to decide, the group made an appeal to the Prime Minister for both, via a motion in Parliament. Duff Cooper was due to see Churchill that evening and promised that he would get him to join them. The next day, on Tuesday 28 March, a group of 34 Members of Parliament, including Churchill and Macmillan, made a bold and challenging appeal to the Prime Minister:

> In view of the grave dangers by which Great Britain and the Empire are now threatened, following upon the successive acts of aggression in Europe and increasing pressure on smaller States, this House is of the opinion that these menaces can only success-fully be met by the vigorous prosecution of the foreign policy outlined by the Foreign Secretary. It is further of opinion that for this task, a National Government should be formed on the widest possible basis, and that such a Government should be entrusted with full powers over the nation's industry, wealth and manpower to enable this country to put forward its maximum military effort in the shortest time.[29]

With the resulting debate scheduled for the following Monday, 3 April, Churchill returned to Chartwell. He began to work on a speech for a meeting of the New Commonwealth Society for the Promotion of International Law and Order, due to be given on 30 March. In it his stark warnings gave way to bleak realities, as he spoke in terms relating to 'when the war is over'.[30] Events continued to escalate with the British Government's guarantee to Poland on 31 March. It was agreed that, if Poland were attacked, Britain and France would come to its aid. A number of MPs, including Churchill's old friend, the former Prime Minister David Lloyd George, said that, without Russia, it was an impossible guarantee. He called it 'the most reckless commitment that any country has ever entered into'.[31] They would not find the Prime Minister easily persuaded on the subject, as just a few days earlier he had written privately, 'I must confess to the most profound distrust of Russia.'[32]

When the day of the debate came, it was the last day Parliament would meet before Easter. Clementine joined her husband in the

House of Commons debating chamber, watching overhead from the viewers' gallery as Churchill urged the acceleration of air defence measures. He pleaded for those in attendance not to underestimate the ordeal to which Britons would be subjected if air terror on civilian populations was to become a weapon of war.[33] He also argued the importance of forming an alliance with the Russians, who he said were 'profoundly affected by the German Nazi ambitions', before adding that 'the aggression of Japan upon China has brought Japan at this moment into close grips with the Eastern Russian Power'.[34]

Immediately after the debate, Churchill was seen speaking in what one onlooker described as 'a triumphant huddle' with the Russian Ambassador, Ivan Maisky, alongside David Lloyd George, Bob Boothby and Randolph.[35] 'Now look here, Mr Ambassador, if we are to make a success of this new policy, we require the help of Russia', Churchill declared. The subject then shifted to Italy, at which point Maisky said that Russia would not enter any alliance which included Italy, and that they would have no confidence in France or Britain if they started 'flirting with Italy and opening negotiations with Mussolini'. Churchill tried to keep the focus on Germany, stating that it was the main enemy, but added that even a lesser and unreliable ally to Germany could still be dangerous. Lloyd George was more concerned, saying that Italian action in the Mediterranean would be extremely damaging and would weaken Britain considerably.[36]

As Parliament broke for Easter, Churchill returned to Kent, with an announcement on 5 April in the *Daily Telegraph*'s 'Court Circular' that 'Mr and Mrs Winston Churchill will spend Easter at Chartwell, Westerham'.[37] His mood was improved at the outset of the long weekend, by the recent announcement that he had been made an Honorary Air Commodore of 615 (County of Surrey) Squadron of the Auxiliary Air Force. Soon after, he received a letter from the Air Chief Marshal Sir Cyril Newall welcoming him to the Royal Air Force.[38] It was but a brief moment of joy, in sharp contrast with discussions he had with friends about where his grandchildren might be safe in the event of war. He reflected that the countryside, and therefore Chartwell itself, was where his infant grandson and grand-daughter would be safest if hostilities broke out.[39] In the midst of the rolling beauty of the countryside, Churchill would have doubtless considered how the landscape he loved so much might be permanently changed, or at the very least scarred, by German forces. Situated directly on the flight path from mainland Europe to London, and just a few miles from the Royal Air Force Station at Biggin Hill, Chartwell seemed a natural target for enemy bombers.

At a time when every spare moment counted in terms of readying for war, Churchill invited Harold Macmillan to join him at Chartwell that weekend. Macmillan in turn requested that his political secretary tell any enquirers that he was unavailable, saying he 'has to be away from London for a few days'.[40] It was a decade since Macmillan's last signature in Chartwell's visitors' book, but he had earned his place in Churchill's inner circle at that critical time. Before their meeting, however, Churchill had one last gathering in London, with politicians and newspaper proprietors at the home of Lord Beaverbrook, owner of the *Daily Express*.

The paper's editor, Arthur Christiansen later recalled the evening, saying he had spoken with Churchill at length as the pair stood by the fire while Brendan Bracken played backgammon with Beaverbrook. Remembering their conversation, and Churchill's distinct manner of speaking, Christiansen described it as follows:

'Where is the – ah – the British Fleet to-night?' He asked me, rolling the words around his palate and licking them before they are uttered. 'It ish lolling in the Bay of Naples. No doubt, the – ah – the Commander of the British ships at Naples is – ah – being entertained ashore, entertained no doubt on the orders of – ah – Mussholini himself at the Naples Yacht Club ... And where should the British Fleet be to-night? On the other side of that long heel of a country called Italy. In the Adriatic Sea, to make the rape of Albania impossible ... That is why, my boy, Mussholini is entertaining the British Fleet ashore at Naples tonight.'[41]

As the sun rose on Good Friday, the household prepared for the day's visitors. Mary attended a three-hour-long church service in nearby Oxted that morning, after which she spent most of the afternoon picnicking with friends, missing lunch with Macmillan.[42] It was while her father and his guest were enjoying their meal, discussing the international situation, that one of the secretaries brought a telephone message to the table that filled Churchill's face with dread. Benito Mussolini, the Italian dictator, had invaded Albania. Churchill rose from the table and dashed to the secretaries' office, with Macmillan following close behind. 'Where is the British fleet?', Churchill asked with fear and frustration as he stood over the table in the middle of the room, knowing it had been stationed on the wrong side of the Italian Peninsula the night before. All the energy of Chartwell was instantly channelled into that one room as maps were brought out, and the telephone switchboard lit up with call after call to Churchill. Macmillan was instantly impressed by the efficiency of the operation at Chartwell, which had become a well-oiled machine. 'That considerable staff which, even as a private individual, Churchill always maintained to support his tremendous outflow of literary and political effort was brought into play', Macmillan later recalled.[43] The power of Churchill in that moment, even though he held no public office, was an image that Macmillan would always remember. 'He alone seemed to be in command,' he reflected years later, 'when everyone else was dazed and hesitating.'[44] The meeting came to an abrupt halt. All plans for the afternoon were instantly derailed, and the springtime amble around the garden that would otherwise have followed would have to wait. There was no time for discussion and not a moment to lose. Chartwell instantly shifted into its mode as an unofficial government department, and Churchill needed to get to work. Though there is no record of the details of Macmillan's departure, it would seem likely that he made a rather swift exit.

When Mary returned from her sunny day of church and picnics and 'carefree joy', Churchill told her what had happened that morning at dawn in the Adriatic Sea. She confided to her diary on that Good Friday, writing 'we hear Italy has attacked Albania. Is all the world as I know it breaking up? Must the world go mad again? Must Christ hang in vain? O God lighten our darkness!'[45]

Before the Easter weekend was finished, Chamberlain wrote to his sister saying that he was being 'badgered' for a meeting of Parliament and that Churchill was 'the worst of the lot, telephoning almost every hour of the day'. He added, 'I suppose he has prepared a terrific oration which he wants to let off.'[46] A speech would indeed follow, but first Churchill steeled his nerve and, striding up and down the study at Chartwell, dictated a press statement to his secretary, Mrs Hill. The wording was informed by a telephone call Churchill received from Randolph, who had spoken to the Conservative MP, Sir Roger Keyes. Keyes had previously served as Admiral of the Fleet and he still had contacts in the Admiralty, who confirmed that the four battleships in the Mediterranean Command were spread far and wide, with the

27. Winston Churchill's study at Chartwell, located in the oldest (sixteenth-century) part of the house, late 1930s.

destroyers divided between the ports of Corsica, Tunisia and Gibraltar and the bulk of cruisers at Malta. Churchill questioned why, in light of the common knowledge that the Italian fleet had been concentrating in the Adriatic, and a general belief that a descent upon Albania was imminent, was the British fleet in the Mediterranean so widely dispersed? Churchill despaired, declaring: 'Not only was a grave risk run but an opportunity of making sea power count was squandered.'[47] Churchill's draft statement was never released, and instead he used it to inform a speech he would give in the House of Commons once Parliament had returned from the Easter break. Meanwhile, calls for Churchill's return to government reached fever pitch. On Chartwell headed paper, he wrote to Chamberlain on Easter Sunday insisting that Parliament should be recalled:

It seems to me that hours now count ... What is now at stake is nothing less than the whole of the Balkan Peninsula. If these States remain exposed to German and Italian pressure while we appear, as they may deem it, incapable of action, they will be forced to make the best terms possible with Berlin and Rome. How forlorn will our position become! We shall be committed to Poland and thus involved in the East of Europe while at the same time cutting off from ourselves all hope of the large alliance which once effected might spell salvation.[48]

Harold Macmillan, meanwhile, had returned to his home in Haywards Heath in West Sussex where he was due to welcome Father Ronald Knox, a former tutor of his from his time at Oxford University with whom he had remained on friendly terms.[49] The reunion was overshadowed by the international crisis, and Macmillan's fury that Chamberlain remained in power. The scene he had observed at Chartwell also put the actions of Anthony Eden into harsh perspective. Just a few days after his meeting with Churchill, Macmillan said that Eden and his followers were 'too soft and gentlemanlike' in their attitude to Chamberlain. The following Tuesday, Macmillan said of the Prime Minister that 'no man in history has made such persistent and bone-headed mistakes'.[50] He also wrote to Alan 'Tommy'

Lascelles, the Assistant Private Secretary to King George VI, regarding the need to postpone a diplomatic visit, concluding: 'The world gets more horrible every day.'[51]

On 11 April Churchill telephoned Leslie Hore-Belisha, the Secretary of State for War, urgently requesting his presence at Chartwell, as he had injured his foot and there was no way he could travel to London. Such was Churchill's newly elevated standing that he could seemingly command Cabinet Ministers to travel to rural Kent at a moment's notice. Hore-Belisha arrived at 10pm and was greeted at the door by Churchill, whose injured foot was encased in a special felt slipper. The pair had a late dinner alone and discussed the matter of conscription, a policy which Hore-Belisha was advocating for in government, but doing so meant that he was taking a serious political risk. 'I saw something of him in this ordeal,' Churchill later recalled, 'and he was never sure that each day in office would not be his last.'[52] Hore-Belisha wrote of their lengthy meeting in his diary once he got home, noting Churchill's account of similar difficulties he had faced proposing unpopular actions in the First World War. 'He had advocated measures in the Cabinet,' Hore-Belisha noted, 'which had been turned down by his colleagues, and then had suffered violent opposition because these measures had not been carried out.'[53] A few days later, Churchill expressed his admiration for Hore-Belisha, who he knew was among the few pushing for powerful measures which might see Britain's latent strength mobilised in time, calling him 'one of the most active of Ministers'.[54]

Early the next morning, Clementine and Mary left for a few days in Brighton. They were accompanied by Horatia Seymour, Clementine's old friend, whose cottage was just a hundred metres from Chartwell, and so she was readily available for such excursions. Churchill, meanwhile, had an engagement in his constituency, but otherwise had the day and night at Chartwell to finalise the speech he would give in the House of Commons on 13 April. It was the first opportunity to speak to the House since the attack on Albania. He concluded his address with a dire warning to all parliamentarians who were present, and made a rallying cry for a national government to be formed once and for all:

The danger is now very near. A great part of Europe is to a very large extent mobilised. Millions of men are being prepared for war. Everywhere the frontier defences are manned. Everywhere it is felt that some new stroke is impending ... We are no longer where we were two or three months ago ... What we should not have dreamt of doing a year ago, when all was so much more hopeful, what we should not have dreamt of doing even a month ago, we are doing now ... We must keep nothing back. How can we bear to continue to lead our comfortable and easy life here at home ... How can we continue – let me say it with particular frankness and sincerity – with less than the full force of the nation incorporated in the governing instrument? These very methods ... may rescue our people and the people of many lands from the dark, bitter waters which are rising fast on every side'.[55]

Among the first to praise Churchill's speech was Bob Boothby, who called it 'the best speech I have ever heard in the House of Commons'.[56] In the speech's aftermath, there was a strong feeling that Churchill should be appointed to a new Ministry of Supply, which Churchill himself began to believe might come to fruition. But Chamberlain still refused to invite him to join the Government. In a letter to his sister, Chamberlain referred to the calls Churchill made to him from Chartwell, saying 'he was at the telephone all day urging that Parliament should be summoned for Sunday & that the Fleet should go & seize Corfu that night! Would he wear me out resisting rash suggestions of this kind?'[57]

For the time being, no offer to join the Government was forthcoming, although events at Chartwell had cemented Macmillan's belief that Churchill was the only political figure who had the knowledge to command, the courage to act and the ability to lead. 'So the days and weeks dragged on. It was a period of waiting', Macmillan later recalled.[58] His invitation to Chartwell had been an indication that Churchill was willing to embrace colleagues who had differed or drifted from him in the past, if they were of a like mind about the urgent need to prepare for war and showed due loyalty and belief in Churchill himself.

By mid-April, the dominoes of peace were falling at a quickening rate. There was a strong likelihood that Czechoslovakia would become a base for aggression against Poland and northern Europe. Albania had now become embroiled and would very likely become a springboard for aggression in southern Europe. President Roosevelt sent Hitler and Mussolini a 'Peace Appeal' on 14 April asking for assurances that their armed forces would not invade a total list of 25 countries, including Britain, Russia and Poland. The appeal made headlines around the world, with the *China Mail*, the country's oldest newspaper, under a derisive front-page headline of 'Axis Telephone Line Busy', reporting that Hitler was too busy with his birthday celebrations to reply.[59] Two weeks later, Hitler mocked Roosevelt's appeal in a speech in the Reichstag, reading out the list in a mocking way which was intended to garner laughter from those in attendance. Churchill tried to offer reassurance to the President via a broadcast to American listeners, in which he said the President's endeavour had rendered a service to the cause of peace and had 'earned the gratitude of almost the whole world'.[60] He also voiced hope that America's role had already helped curtail aggression in the Far East, saying: 'The more prudent attitude adopted by Japan in refusing to join in an anti-democracy movement, which fact cannot have been absent from Herr Hitler's mind, is of course directly attributable to the movement of the United States fleet to the Pacific Ocean.'[61]

As Europe hurtled towards war, it was as if a morbid countdown to oblivion had begun. There appeared to be no possible way to avoid a second global conflict in just a quarter of a century. 'The vessel of peace was springing a leak from every seam',[62] Churchill wrote, accepting that all that could be done now was to strengthen Britain's resources, and relations with those nations who intended to fight – or who indeed were already fighting – against tyranny.

CHAPTER 12

A FINAL PLEA

Quo Tai-chi, 11 August 1939

As the world moved unknowingly into its final months of peace, Churchill was entrenched at Chartwell, working day and night to complete as many chapters as possible of his *History of the English-Speaking Peoples*. Those who received invitations to Chartwell in the last summer before war were almost all close family, old friends or trusted allies who had supported him steadfastly over the last six years. To this rule there was one distinct exception. On the same day that Churchill's article 'A Word to Japan!' was published in the *Daily Mirror*, His Excellency the Chinese Ambassador Quo Tai-chi was invited to Chartwell.[1] Accompanied by his close friend, the academic and philosopher Peng-chun 'P.C.' Chang, the Ambassador made his way from London to rural Kent to join the Churchills at their country home. Over tea and cake, the group discussed events in China and the apparent inevitability of a global war. The result for Churchill was a direct line, through the Ambassador, to Chiang Kai-shek, Head of the Chinese Nationalist Government. His political wilderness was almost at an end, and world leaders began to manoeuvre for the ear of Winston Churchill.

Throughout the summer of 1939, there was a growing demand among the general public for Churchill's inclusion in the Government. Letters and telegrams in support of Churchill's political stance were sent to Chartwell from all over the world, including from as far afield as Australia and Canada. The deluge was more than could possibly be answered by Churchill's three secretaries. 'Never mind, put them all in a sack and you answer them in three or six months' time', Churchill told Mrs Hill. 'They'll be pleased to hear from you then.'[2] He simply did not have time to answer everything, as he usually tried to do. He was writing more than ever before in the hope of paying off his debts before the end of the year but all of the family at Chartwell knew that time was running out.

Despite the looming horrors of war, the Churchills had a remarkably happy final few months at Chartwell. Clementine, whose health and energy had suffered earlier in the year, was fit and well once again. 'She spent a lot of time at Chartwell with me', Mary later recalled of those months. 'I was basking in the glow of parental praise and approval at the time, having, to everyone's astonishment, passed my School Certificate with considerable success.'[3] As a result, Mary was given a horse of her own, which she proudly rode at Chartwell, often accompanied by her parents. It was perhaps their sense that the years of peace were coming to an end that brought a greater appreciation of the joy that summer at Chartwell could bring. The family swam, played tennis and enjoyed the riot of colour across their gardens in full bloom. Outings to London included a trip to the zoo on 5 May for what Mary later called a 'private audience with Ming, the baby giant panda, who has stolen the limelight from Greta Garbo and sent Chamberlain & the dictators onto the second page!'[4] Churchill enjoyed the afternoon of respite too, remarking to his daughter, 'The baby giant panda satisfies the much felt sense of world cuddlability!'[5]

The moments of fun beyond the grounds of Chartwell, however, were few and far between, and Churchill was acutely aware that matters of international diplomacy were evolving day by day. While Churchill continued to campaign for overt cooperation with Russia, such an alliance was also at the forefront of thinking in embassies across the world. On the same day as the Churchills' zoo outing, officials at the Foreign Office received a telegram from Sir Archibald Clark Kerr, the British Ambassador to China. It relayed a conversation he had during a long walk with Chiang Kai-shek, China's Head of State, about the ongoing campaign of resistance to Japan, who had launched a full-scale invasion of China in 1937. According to Kerr, Chiang had 'urged that H.M. Government, in the present negotiations with the Soviet Union, should not let slip the opportunity to spread the scope of any understanding to the Far East'.[6] His argument was that, if war broke out in Europe, the 1936 Anti-Comintern Pact between Nazi Germany and Japan would, by definition, see the latter brought into such a conflict. The telegram also pointed out the apparent frustrations of the Chinese Ambassador in London, Quo Tai-chi. He too had been lobbying Britain to include China as they considered international alliances, but had reportedly been given 'a somewhat discouraging reply'.[7]

A few days later, Churchill received a number of letters, forwarded to him by Lord Cecil, President of the League of Nations. They

28. *Quo Tai-chi (Guo Taiqi), the Chinese Ambassador, seen visiting the Foreign Office in London, August 1937.*

included correspondence between Cecil and Anthony Eden, in which Cecil said he had seen the Chinese Ambassador, known in Westminster as 'Mr Quo', who intended to urge that fresh efforts should be made to help China, mainly by depriving Japan of war material. 'I do feel very strongly that we ought to do this if we possibly can,' Cecil wrote to Eden, 'both out of regard for China and also because a defeat of Japan would have most valuable repercussions in Europe.'[8] Eden, however, had written back advising against such interventions. Instead, Cecil turned to Churchill, writing: 'If Japan triumphs it will be a tremendous encouragement to totalitarian forces everywhere.'[9] He proposed that Britain buy all of Canada's nickel, or place a ban on imports of these strategic resources to Japan. Churchill, however, wrote back somewhat confused, saying, 'I do not see what I can do at this present time', but added, 'I suppose the Government will be very anxious not to provoke Japan unduly at a moment when everything hangs in the balance over here.'[10]

Churchill's views on Japan had seen a remarkable shift over the years. Japan first became an ally of Britain's when the Anglo-Japanese Treaty was signed in 1902. It was as a result of this alliance that Japan, in support of Britain, declared war on Germany, at the outset of the First World War in 1914. Though the alliance came to an end in 1921, many Conservatives expressed regret at the concluding of the agreement.[11] It was in this climate that, in 1924, Churchill wrote to the Prime Minister saying: 'A war with Japan! But why should there be a war with Japan? I do not believe there is the slightest chance of it in our lifetime.'[12]

Seven years later, in 1931, the Japanese army invaded the Chinese province of Manchuria. 'The Manchurian issue is no longer a Sino-Japanese issue', Quo announced a year later, in December 1932. 'It is an issue in which the whole civilised world stands confronted by Japan.'[13] It was in response to this outburst and the League's subsequent condemnation that Japan withdrew from the international organisation, an act of defiance which was followed not long afterward by both Italy and Germany.[14] Churchill's response, shaped by his belief in the evils of communism, was initially one of sympathy for Japan:

I hope we should try in England to understand a little the position of Japan, an ancient state with the highest sense of national honour and patriotism, and with a teeming population and a remarkable energy. On the one side they see the dark menace of Soviet Russia. On the other the chaos of China, four or five provinces of which are actually now being tortured under Communist rule.[15]

His view however had drastically changed by the middle of the decade, not only because of Japan's pact with Nazi Germany in 1936, but also because of his growing concerns about Japan becoming a totalitarian state. 'Let us gaze for a moment at Japan . . . where every voice of moderation is silenced by death; where the murder of political opponents has been for some years accepted practice: where even trusted commanders may be slaughtered by their supporters for suspected luke-warmness.'[16] He immediately saw that the two countries' intentions were tied, and argued: 'should Germany at any time make war in Europe, we may be sure that Japan will immediately light a second conflagration in the Far East.'[17]

Throughout this time, Quo was China's representative in Britain, initially as Minister before being elevated to Ambassador. He had previously studied political science at the University of Pennsylvania before becoming one of China's most outstanding diplomats.[18] In a Foreign Office report at the time, he was described as one of a clique of Chinese diplomats whose policy was 'to be on friendly terms with Europe and America in order to check Japanese aggression'.[19] He was also one of those who were alarmed by a report in *The Times* referencing 'Japan's "special position" in regard to China' in May 1937.[20] The article was sent to Chiang Kai-shek, who was said to be 'disturbed' by it, and alarmed that the Japanese appeared to be succeeding in their efforts to effect a rapprochement with the Government of Great Britain.[21] Reassurance was quickly offered with *China Press* reporting that 'the cardinal point in the British position would be the strict preservation of Chinese rights and interests'.[22] Less than two months later, Japanese and Chinese troops clashed, resulting in the escalation to a full, though undeclared, war between China and Japan. 'The Far East is on fire', Ivan Maisky, the

Russian Ambassador, wrote in his diary on 1 August. 'The consequences are hard to foresee, but they may be immense.'[23]

One of the witnesses to the impact of Japan's attacks was P.C. Chang, an academic and philosopher who had studied in the United States, having gained admittance to Columbia University thanks to the Boxer Scholarship, a Congressionally approved fund to support Chinese students studying at American universities.[24] He completed his PhD at Columbia and then returned to China, spending much of the 1920s and 1930s teaching at Nankai University, until Japan's military assault in 1937. Chang later said, 'I left China in September after personally witnessing the destruction of my own university by bombing, bombarding and burning.'[25] He initially travelled to Nanking where he witnessed devastating air raids. He then left China, agreeing to act as an official representative of the Department of Foreign Affairs to inform influential international leaders of the nature of Japan's brutality in China.[26] He travelled extensively around the world between 1937 and 1939, including numerous visits to London. One such visit, in October 1937, saw him speak at the Royal Albert Hall, at a meeting entitled 'Japan's Attack against Civilians'. The 8,000 people in attendance were shown a film called 'Bombs on China', and listened to Chang give his own personal account of the destruction of his university.[27] The hope of its organisers was to awaken the British public to Japan's brutality towards China's civilian population. By 1939 his mission had evolved. From that point on he sought funding to finance China's war against Japan as well as urging the implementation of economic sanctions against Japan.

Having rapidly developed concerns about Japan even before its full-scale attack on China, Churchill published a number of articles on the subject in the years that followed. In May 1938 he published a piece in the *Evening Express* entitled 'Merely an "Incident" in China, But Then', a reference to the fact that, although war had not yet formally been declared, one was clearly under way. As well as explaining the conduct of the conflict to date, Churchill voiced:

General Chiang Kai-shek is a national hero amongst the most numerous race of mankind. He may well become a world hero, as a patriot and leader, who amid a thousand difficulties and wants, does not despair of saving China from a base and merciless exploitation ... It may well be that from the opposite side of the earth will come that exemplary discomfiture of a brutal aggression which will cheer the democracies of the Western world and teach them to stand up for themselves while time remains.[28]

Churchill also shone a spotlight on the plight of China through his speeches. On Sunday 16 October 1938 he gave one such address in a broadcast to the United States, entitled 'The Lights Are Going Out'. Though its main focus was the recent Munich Agreement, he also made reference to conflicts beyond Europe, declaring: 'China is being torn to pieces by a military clique in Japan; the poor, tormented Chinese people there are making a brave and stubborn defence.'[29] The reference did not go unnoticed, and Quo Tai-chi wrote to Churchill two days later from the Chinese Embassy. 'Thank you for your effective allusion to China in your speech', Quo wrote. 'Your reference on Sunday night was a real service in setting forth the inter-actions of aggression that do not even leave the Americas out of their calculations.'[30] The Ambassador's view of the British Government, however, was often far less favourable. By the end of 1938 he was writing to the Foreign Secretary, Lord Halifax, to tell him that confusing statements made by Ministers in Parliament had 'given rise to apprehension among the Chinese people' regarding the stance and policies of His Majesty's Government towards China.[31]

The Churchills had known Quo for some time as they had attended a number of functions at the Chinese Embassy. As the conflict with Japan wore on, contacts in Hong Kong also alerted the couple to their own observations. Sir Robert Ho Tung wrote to Clementine with Christmas greetings as well as two boxes of tea, but felt compelled to add his own account of events in China. He told her that, despite living in a British colony, 'we are still daily in contact with all the evidence of the cruelties of modern warfare. Refugees, wounded soldiers, wounded civilians and pauperised merchants have been pouring in to this little island refuge from all parts of China.'[32] In her telegram reply she replied, 'All good wishes to you and China.'[33]

The outset of 1939 marked a shift in the nature of the conflict, as reflected in a newspaper article by Chang entitled 'New Phase of War in China – Offensive as Well as Defensive Action.'[34] Calls for Britain to intervene grew louder and Chiang Kai-shek was advised that the British Government 'have the proposals for assistance to China under their most careful consideration'.[35] Quo continued to campaign from the Embassy while Chang appealed directly to the Foreign Office where he detailed the nature of China's military measures countering Japanese aggression. When he was asked about the Chinese view of the political situation in Japan, Chang reportedly said that 'the position of Japan after a year and a half of fighting in China was like that of a man who plunges his fist into a pot of warm glue, which, while apparently yielding to pressure, closes in on him when he tries to withdraw.'[36] At one meeting with the Foreign Secretary in February 1939, Chang gave a full account of the Chinese Government's preparations to shift from defensive operations to the offensive. There were just two things China needed to ensure success. The first was material aid from foreign powers to help China accomplish her plan. The second, a much harder ask for Halifax to guarantee, was that there must be 'no state of great war or tension in Europe during the next year or so'.[37]

Meanwhile, as the weather warmed at Chartwell, Churchill continued to pour the bulk of his energy into writing and hardly left his country home. A one-sentence reply was used to decline invitations to London: 'Alas am toiling in the country.'[38] Despite his increasingly reclusive nature, which became a necessity in order to write as much as possible, the press were shouting loudly for his return to high political office. One article at the end of April in the *Sunday Pictorial* pleaded with the Prime Minister to bring Churchill back into the Cabinet, calling his omission 'The Great Churchill Scandal'.[39]

As the year progressed, there was an increased appetite among the general public for insights into Churchill's life away from politics. To satisfy their interest, one journalist was granted access in May and Mary gave him a guided tour. She showed him the ancient well that gave the property its name, and the adjoining ponds, the waterfall and the swimming pool. They walked together through the rose garden and the orchard which was filled with trees covered in apples, pears and peaches. Her route continued towards the cottage Churchill had just finished building and the Marycot he had built for his youngest daughters a decade earlier. The pair then entered the house, tiptoed up the main stairs to the study and marvelled at the range of books on history, war, politics and strategy that adorned the wall. 'Miss Mary,' the journalist added, 'is a Minister of Supply to the family pets, a parrot, dogs, goats with a small family, and two tiny fox cubs ... She walks and rides in all this wild commonland, and we both agreed how beautiful it all was.'[40]

A flurry of visitors travelled to Kent to see the Churchills at that time, including Léon Blum, the former French Prime Minister, who had been keeping Churchill updated on the state of French aviation for several years. The assembled group who gathered on 10 May included Blum and the artist Paul Maze, both of whom had been met by Randolph in London, who then drove them to Chartwell. They were joined by the anti-appeasement Conservative MP Richard Law, who was the son of Andrew Bonar Law who had been Prime Minister in 1922–23. His wife Mary, the daughter of a New York silk manufacturer, also joined the party, each of whom was welcomed at the door by Churchill. Being greeted by their host on the driveway had become the norm for Chartwell's guests in recent years, in part because a butler remained an unaffordable extravagance.

'Conversation rendered difficult by Clemmie's constant interference in the conversation & her desire to translate to show up her French (which was very good)', Maze noted in his diary when describing their lunch.[41] Photographs were taken of Clementine, Law, Blum and Churchill sitting on the wall at the edge of the terrace lawn. Within hours, the photographs had been shared with the press, and the story featured in both regional and national newspapers the next day. The images had a somewhat staged feel, showing Clementine stroking one of the tame foxes, and everyone displaying jovial expressions. Unfortunately, the meeting was not a leisurely one and had to be concluded promptly as Blum had to be back in London for a meeting with Lord Halifax at 3.45pm, no doubt with messages to relay from Churchill.

Other guests included Ian Colvin, the foreign correspondent in Berlin who had introduced the Churchills to Ewald von Kleist-Schmenzin and was invited to lunch on 12 May. He was followed that evening by Victor Cazalet, another anti-appeasement Conservative MP who travelled to Chartwell along with his godson Frederick Smith, the son of F. E. Smith, who had arguably been Churchill's closest friend but sadly passed away in 1930. Dame Rachel Crowdy, a social reformer who at that time was the only woman to occupy a senior administrative position in the League of Nations, visited two days later and brought her friend, the former Czech Ambassador Jan Masaryk. These more unusual guests were always interspersed with appearances from the Chartwell regulars. Desmond Morton would pop in for tea, Brendan Bracken joined for dinners, Professor Lindemann took frequent advantage of the Churchills' dine-and-sleep option and the Sinclairs were known to join for the weekend. Any respite from international events, however, was short-lived. On 22 May, Hitler and Mussolini signed their 'Pact of Steel'. Churchill later called it 'the challenging answer to the flimsy British network of guarantees in Eastern Europe'.[42] The next day, Hitler held a meeting with his Chiefs of Staff, the minutes of which indicated that Russia remained an uncertainty in his strategic thinking, but Japan was seen as a key ally in the event of a global war:

If there were an alliance of France, England and Russia, against Germany, Italy and Japan, I should be constrained to attack England and France with a few annihilating blows. I doubt the possibility of a peaceful settlement with England. We must prepare ourselves for the conflict.[43]

The Soviet Union had been in negotiations with the British and French governments since April, but found itself in what Churchill called 'an unbreakable deadlock'.[44] Germany, on the other hand, had been gradually softening its approach to Russia. Since the speech of 28 April in which Hitler mocked President Roosevelt's 'Peace Appeal' and denounced the Anglo-German Naval Agreement of 1935, the Führer had omitted his usual hostile references to Soviet Russia. By the end of May, the German Ambassador in Moscow had been told, 'contrary to the policy previously planned, we have now decided to undertake definite negotiations with the Soviet Union'.[45] Meanwhile, Hitler had issued directives for the attack on Poland and, until any pact was made with Russia, was working on the assumption that Russia would oppose a German offensive. 'Should Russia take steps to oppose us,' Hitler declared, 'our relations with Japan may become closer.'[46]

A week later, in the House of Lords, the Foreign Secretary found himself subject to enquiries regarding the situation in the Far East. 'I should like to ask the noble Viscount if he can give us any information about the state of our present relations with China', Lord Snell, the Labour Party's leader in the House of Lords enquired. Snell stated that Dr Wellington Koo, the Chinese Ambassador in Paris, had recently spoken at a League of Nations meeting, arguing that since Japan was guilty of aggression, it should be subject to strict economic sanctions. Lord Halifax, who was in attendance, reportedly gave a 'disturbingly unsympathetic' reply.[47] Koo, a close ally of Quo's, hoped his plea might win public sympathy from the West, as did Snell as he pressed Halifax for an official Government response. Halifax's reply, however, focused on British interests in Asia, and he vehemently denied that he had offered Koo anything other than his deepest sympathies. In the same debate, Halifax addressed the subject of Germany, implying that Britain might still reach some sort of arrangement with Hitler.

While hosting his daughter Diana and her young family at Chartwell the following weekend, Churchill took a moment away from the family fun and the pressures of his writing deadlines to compose a note to Halifax about his recent speech. 'Naturally I was a little disturbed by your speech in the Lords', Churchill wrote. He then relayed the reports he had received, describing the oppression and terrorism the people already conquered by the Nazi regime were having to endure. 'It is even said that many executions by the Gestapo have already taken place.'[48] He requested that Halifax join him for lunch at his Morpeth Mansions flat on 14 or 15 June to discuss the speech and its implications. 'I stay as much as I can in the country during this beautiful weather, but I shall be in London on both these days.'[49] His time spent at Chartwell had not been in vain and he had reached 450,000 words towards the half-million-word manuscript he owed his publishers for *A History of the English-Speaking Peoples*.[50] It was agreed that Halifax and Churchill would meet on Wednesday 14 June. Churchill was determined to eke out as many meetings as he could while in London; his engagement diary listed five separate appointments for that day, the last of which was dinner with friends. In attendance with Churchill were the Labour Member of Parliament Harold Nicolson, the Director of the National Gallery Kenneth Clark, the biologist Julian Huxley and the American political commentator Walter Lippmann and his wife. Lippmann informed the group that the American Ambassador, Joseph P. Kennedy, had told him that war was inevitable and that Britain would get 'licked' by Germany. Churchill was horrified and appalled. With his whisky and soda in one hand, and stubbing his cigar with the other, he erupted into one of the most magnificent impromptu orations he ever uttered:

It may well be true, it may well be true that this country will at the outset of this coming and to my mind almost inevitable war be exposed to dire peril and fierce ordeals. It may be true that steel and fire will rain down upon us day and night scattering death and destruction far and wide. It may be true that our sea-communications will be imperilled and our food-supplies placed in jeopardy. Yet these trials and disasters, I ask you to believe me, Mr Lippmann, will but serve to steel the resolution of the British people and to enhance our will for victory. No, the Ambassador should not have spoken so, Mr Lippmann; he should not have said that dreadful word. Yet supposing – as I do not for one moment suppose – that Mr Kennedy were correct in his tragic utterance, then I for one would willingly lay down my life in combat, rather than, in fear of defeat, surrender to the menaces of these most sinister men ... Nor should I die happy in the great struggle which I see before me, were I not convinced that if we in this dear dear island succumb to the ferocity and might of our enemies, over there in your distant and immune continent the

276

torch of liberty will burn untarnished and – I trust and hope – undismayed.[51]

He returned to Chartwell the next day, where letters continued to arrive offering thoughts on wartime strategy. Sir Kingsley Wood, the Secretary of State for Air, wrote to Churchill regarding possible steps to guard against the landing of enemy troops by aircraft.[52] General Sir Edmund Ironside, the newly appointed Inspector General of Overseas Forces, wrote regarding a belief that Britain couldn't afford to commence military operations in Eastern Asia, and that British troops might need to be stripped from the region if the crisis developed.[53] A number of these letters were burned in the study's fireplace by Churchill to ensure secrecy.

He began to consider the security of both of his homes and their likely roles in the event of war. He wrote to the manager of the building which housed his London flat asking what provisions had been taken to ensure its basement could provide shelter, advising that any intended measures would need to be in place by the end of July.[54] Chartwell's fate had yet to be decided. 'I am afraid I continue to take a sombre view of our affairs', he wrote on 24 June 1939. He called that time 'the last chance to avert the ordeals of war' in a *News of the World* article three weeks earlier. By the end of the month, any such hopes had evaporated.

Hostility towards Britain, meanwhile, had begun to escalate in Japan. There was reportedly a growing view that Britain, despite its official neutrality, sympathised with China and Chiang Kai-shek. As a result, Japan started to think of Britain as its enemy, and so began to oppress British interests in China. At 6am on 14 June, the day of Churchill's impromptu speech against Joe Kennedy, Japanese forces blockaded the British trading concession at Tientsin. The Foreign Office issued a statement in response saying:

What is demanded [by Japan] is that the British authorities co-operate with the Japanese in the construction of a 'New Order' in the East by abandoning their 'pro-Chiang Kai-Shek' policies ... If, unhappily, the new demands foreshadowed from official

Japanese sources in North China should be persisted in, then it must be said at once that an extremely serious situation will arise, and that the British Government will have to consider what immediate and active steps it can take for the protection of British interests in China.[55]

The reply issued by the Japanese News Agency declared that, if the British Government chose to take such steps, 'Japan would be constrained to take the necessary measures to meet the new situation.'[56] A top secret memorandum from the day of the blockade noted that Kijiro Miyake, of the Japanese Foreign Office, had said to the British Ambassador in Tokyo: 'If Britain ceased to support Chiang Kai-shek, the Japanese would discuss the question of "protecting" Britain's interests.' When the Ambassador insisted that Britain wanted to be friends with a strong and prosperous Japan, Miyake replied, 'Then stop helping Chiang Kai-shek.'[57] Many saw Tientsin as another opportunity for the British Government to either stand up to aggression or yield to the aggressors. The *Hong Kong Telegraph* reported on 8 July, 'We have already permitted Japan liberties of far-reaching significance. To permit further encroachment on our rights is merely to invite new and more expensive demands,' before concluding, 'Tientsin must now be the Munich of the Far East.'[58]

Professor Chang was in the United States at the time of the blockade, on what one Foreign Office report called 'a propaganda tour'.[59] On 5 July he gave a radio address in New York saying that the aggression witnessed in recent years across the world began with the Japanese invasion of Manchuria in 1931. 'After Manchuria followed Abyssinia, Austria, Spain, Czecho-Slovakia, Memel, Albania', he declared. 'So far the aggressive powers have been able to win wherever and whenever they wish to make a move. Where is Abyssinia now? And where are Austria, Czechoslovakia, Memel, and Albania?'[60] The Chinese Ambassador in London, meanwhile, was lobbying the Foreign Office at every opportunity, including meetings with Lord Halifax to discuss British financial and economic assistance for China. The campaign soon reached Churchill, including letters and telegrams from the Federation of China Relief Funds in Southern

Asia, saying it was men like Churchill in whom they had 'great confidence', and adding that the interests of Britain and China were identical. 'China to-day, though apparently fighting aggression on her own behalf, is in fact fighting on behalf of Great Britain and the whole world.'[61]

It was perhaps little wonder that such organisations had begun to turn to Churchill for influence and support. Throughout the summer of 1939 the public demand for Churchill's inclusion in the Government became deafening. Cartoons making fun of the Prime Minister began to appear, including 'Calling Mr Churchill' in the *Daily Express* on 6 July, which featured Chamberlain sitting in an armchair surrounded by various press lords demanding that Churchill be summoned to join the Government.[62] Winston's supporters had begun to actively campaign for his inclusion in the Cabinet, arguing that such an appointment would be an effective way of warning Hitler that Britain 'means business'.[63] His omission, therefore, was thought to indicate that Chamberlain had not abandoned his policy of appeasement, thereby undermining any gestures of resistance towards the dictators. Chamberlain described 'the drive to put Winston into the government' as a 'conspiracy' which was being aided by the Russian Ambassador and Randolph Churchill.[64]

Despite the increasing noise in favour of Churchill's return, there was still a considerable group within the Conservative Party who were opposed to Churchill holding any office. 'Anything that Winston attempts is always overdone', Samuel Hoare, the former Foreign Secretary, wrote to a colleague. 'I believe that if there was a ballot of Conservative Back Bench Members on the subject, four out of five would be against him.'[65]

A tried and tested way of boosting public support then presented itself. On 5 July 1939 Stefan Lorant wrote to Churchill at Chartwell about contributing to an upcoming issue of *Picture Post* which would appear on 5 August. He proposed a pictorial story entitled 'How the War Began', and asked if Churchill could write the article of around 1,200 words to go with the pictures. The deadline was 17 July and, despite his other demands and obligations, Churchill enthusiastically obliged. 'This is exactly what we hoped you would write for us',

Tom Hopkinson, the assistant editor, wrote to Churchill on receiving the text.[66] 'I feel certain it will make a great impression', Lorant added.[67]

Lorant, always an innovator, wanted to follow the 5 August piece with another Churchill article called 'The Answer to Encirclement' saying that Britain was not trying to encircle Germany and that there was no hostility in England towards the German people. Lorant's imaginative plan was that *Picture Post* would include the article in English on one side of a page, and have it translated into German on the other. Wanting to beat Goebbels's propaganda machine, Lorant would ask readers to 'buy the paper, cut out the page, put it in an envelope and send it to their German friends before Goebbels woke up'.[68] Churchill loved the idea, duly wrote the piece and it was published on 19 August. Lorant later learnt that Goebbels 'went absolutely frantic' when he found out, and it proved to be a resounding success for Churchill and Lorant.

Before Parliament's break for the summer, Churchill and Archie Sinclair, the Leader of the Liberal Party, agreed that it should only take place if a means could be devised for maintaining contact between Ministers and Members of Parliament across all political parties.[69] The fear was that a complete break would make it harder for the Government to rapidly respond to any escalation in world events. Unfortunately, they found little appetite for such measures and so Churchill filled his diary with meetings in the narrow window of time before much of his network dispersed for the summer.

Those who visited him in late July found a man obsessed with the international situation. 'Winston talked about nothing but the prospect of war over dinner,' one visitor to Chartwell recalled, 'and went on about it over the brandy until Clemmie ordered us out.'[70] The following week a visit from General Ironside saw discussions between the two continue from the early evening until dawn. By this time, the two men knew that it was only a matter of time before Britain would be at war. 'You are destined to play a great part, you will be Commander in Chief. You must be clear on what is going to happen', Churchill said standing in front of a large map and gesturing towards it.[71] First would be the annihilation of Poland. Italy would then be tasked with creating diversions before capturing Egypt. There would then be pressure towards the Black Sea via Romania and finally an alliance with Russia. Churchill walked back and forth suggesting military responses, focusing on the Royal Navy, including sending a squadron of battleships in the Baltic to paralyse the Germans. 'What a man. Whisky and cigars all the time', Ironside wrote in his diary. He made particular note of Churchill having remarked 'that he would have to pull in his horns considerably if he ever took office, because he would have to cease making money by writing'.[72] Ironside came out of the meeting convinced that Churchill would have been made First Lord of the Admiralty if war had broken out in September 1938. Instead, if war came soon, he felt certain that he had just spent the evening with a future Prime Minister.

There was a growing number among the general public who carefully watched Churchill's questions and answers in the House of Commons on the subject of foreign affairs. To some, he became their sole trusted source, and his silence on the subject of the conflict between China and Japan in late July caused concern. Jean MacDougall of Sevenoaks, near Chartwell, wrote to him: 'You haven't said a word or asked a question about it . . . You, who are the greatest custodian of our honour that we have at the present time, [have] said nothing. I don't know whether to take it as a good sign or bad.'[73] She received one of the standard 'ack and thank' letters, typed by one of the Churchills' secretaries in the office at Chartwell.[74] Hundreds of these letters were sent over the summer of 1939, such was the volume of enquiries either seeking Churchill's reassurance about world events or voicing their opinions to someone who they believed would soon be elevated to a high position in British politics. Not all the letters sent to Chartwell during these weeks were so effusive, however. One particularly alarming communication from the British Consulate in Salonica, Greece, sent directly to Chartwell, wrote of a possible assassination attempt on Churchill, predicted to take place on 3 September 1939. Speaking of the source of this intelligence, the Consul General noted that 'the American Consul tells me that he has a certain standing in his office since last May when he predicted that an attempt on President Roosevelt would take place, but fail, and the attack actually did take place.'[75]

A debate was scheduled on 2 August to discuss whether the House of Commons should adjourn for the summer. The day before, Churchill had lunched at Chartwell with General Spears, the Conservative MP who had known him since the First World War and had joined Heinrich Brüning at a previous meeting. Spears observed that Churchill was 'determined to speak with great violence and to vote against' the adjournment motion. Upon hearing Spears's account that evening, Anthony Eden telephoned Churchill and begged him not to be too forceful in his argument, but Churchill wouldn't be persuaded. Eden then asked Macmillan to telephone Churchill, believing he would be a moderating influence and have a better chance of persuading him. Macmillan's efforts must have succeeded. Accounts of the speech included those critics of Churchill's who called it 'funny but sad' when Churchill 'gave many reasons including his theme song that the dictators help themselves to a country whilst we are on holiday!'[76] Churchill argued that, had Parliament returned earlier the year before, the additional time would have allowed Britain to mobilise the fleet, make an agreement with Russia and save the independence of Czechoslovakia. The same mistake should therefore not be made twice. When Chamberlain vehemently rebutted the allegations about the year before, he was given what he called 'an extraordinary ovation', with cheering lasting for a full two minutes.[77] Churchill, meanwhile, was described as being 'in a state of red fury' as a result.[78] Chamberlain wrote about Churchill shortly after, saying 'his are summer storms, violent but of a short duration and often followed by sunshine. But they make him uncommonly difficult to deal with.'[79]

The next day, Friday 4 August, was the last day that Parliament sat that summer. The subject of the conflict between China and Japan was raised at the adjournment debate, at which both Churchill and Chamberlain were present. The Labour MP Philip Noel-Baker opened the debate, arguing for an immediate halt to Britain's purchasing of the Japanese exports that helped fund their military campaigns. 'It may well be that the next world war will begin with a clash in the Far East,' he announced, 'but if we take this action it might be that, by courage instead of surrender, we should avert a

European war.'[80] Chamberlain responded saying that, though it made his blood boil to hear of the atrocities happening in China, 'there may be even graver and nearer problems to be considered in the course of the next few months,' and so, 'We must conserve our forces to meet any emergency that might arise.'[81]

The debate finished just before 3pm, after which Churchill's chauffeur Cale drove him back to Chartwell where he remained for the next two weeks. An early August bank holiday gave the Churchills a few hours' respite when they attended a horse show in nearby Edenbridge. Otherwise, Churchill and his literary assistant, Bill Deakin, worked round the clock on finishing the manuscript.

One remarkable exception came on 9 August when, at 12.45am, Churchill broadcast a speech to America. The time difference meant it aired to the intended audience in the United States on the evening of 8 August. Mary had gone to bed early so she could be awoken at

29. *Winston Churchill delivering a speech, broadcast live to the United States, from the study at Chartwell, August 1939.*

12.30am in order to watch her father, who was seated at his desk, with his notes in front of him, a cigar in his right hand and leaning towards the NBC microphone. He opened his speech to America with reference to the arrival of the summer holiday season for many, but then swiftly turned to the situation in China.[82]

There is a hush over all Europe, nay, over all the world, broken only by the dull thud of Japanese bombs falling on Chinese cities, on Chinese Universities or near British and American ships. But then, China is a long way off, so why worry? The Chinese are fighting for what the founders of the American Constitution in their stately language called: 'Life, liberty and the pursuit of happiness.' And they seem to be fighting very well. Many good judges think they are going to win. Anyhow, let's wish them luck! Let's give them a wave of encouragement – as your President did last week, when he gave notice about ending the commercial treaty. After all, the suffering Chinese are fighting our battle – the battle of democracy. They are defending the soil, the good earth, that has been theirs since the dawn of time against cruel and unprovoked aggression. Give them a cheer across the ocean – no one knows whose turn it may be next.[83]

The 15-minute broadcast was intended to make Americans aware of the risk of letting dictators have a free hand, and arouse them to support the coming battle. He told his American audience that while China fought Japanese forces, Europe was in 'a hush of suspense' awaiting the next steps to be taken by Germany and Italy.[84] He warned of the rise of tyrants at the head of governments and declared that it was entirely in Hitler's hands whether the continent descended into war. 'Britain and France are determined to shed no blood except in self-defence or in defence of their allies', he declared, before concluding that they prayed for peace, an end to the prolonged uncertainty, and a future which would 'no longer leave the whole life of mankind dependent upon the virtues, the caprice, or the wickedness of a single man'.[85]

The speech, which was made with his family silently listening just outside the study door, was met with a wave of praise and admiration from its listeners. 'Your broadcast thrilled my family,' wrote one man from New Jersey, 'and I expect many thousands of other families, who are eagerly seeking courageous and fresh leadership in this new crisis.'[86] Another remarkable message arrived from a gentleman who had lived in Germany under Nazi rule. He told Churchill, 'there seems to be no-one in English public life at the present time who understands so well as you do the psychology of Germany's present rulers.'[87] Meanwhile, a British nurse living in Detroit pleaded: 'Please help Britain now, Mr Churchill, and the lives already sacrificed through the years will not have been in vain.'[88]

The speech gained significant coverage in the British papers on 9 and 10 August, several of which published lengthy passages, starting from the mention of Japan's attacks on China.[89] It was almost certainly in response to this coverage that a meeting was arranged for the appreciative Quo Tai-chi and P.C. Chang at Chartwell the next day, on 11 August. Time was of the essence as Churchill only had a few more days at home before he was due to depart for France on the morning of Monday 14 August.

As the letters in response to his America broadcast continued to make their way to Chartwell, Churchill attended a number of engagements, but only those close to his country home. On 10 August he visited Biggin Hill airfield, just north of Chartwell, which had been established as a key fighter station for the potential defence of London. It had been brought to 'immediate readiness for war' following the Munich Agreement in September 1938, with the aerodrome disguised by camouflage and 601 (County of London) Auxiliary Squadron partly mobilised at the beginning of 1939.[90] The visit, scheduled for 4.15pm, was also attended by the Air Secretary and was framed in the press as an 'inspection'.[91] The two men examined the planes, talked to pilots and watched fighter exercises. Churchill also used the encounter to lobby for the compulsory purchase of nearby land in Croydon for his 615 (County of Surrey) Auxiliary Squadron. The Air Secretary confirmed that he was in talks with the Treasury on whether or not this would be possible.[92]

At the same time that Churchill was inspecting the airfield nearest to Chartwell, Quo was attending meetings with the Foreign Secretary.

285

The pair met on Thursday afternoon and then again on Friday morning for half an hour, to discuss economic and financial matters.[93] It was in an issue of the *Daily Mirror* that same morning that an article of Churchill's entitled 'A Word to Japan!' appeared. It had originally been called 'Japanese Aggression',[94] but Churchill had decided to reposition it as a warning rather than an observation. The article praised the 'great national leader and commander Chiang Kai-shek'.[95] He also included complex details about the location of Japanese armies across China, and described the success of their uninterrupted local governance in much of the country despite the conflict. It compared the outcomes of a Japanese victory, which would result in the end of European and American interests in East Asia, whereas a Chinese victory, if China were aided by 'the great democracies', would result in a century of continuing trade in the region. A similar article of his entitled 'We Won't Give Way to Bullying by the Japs' had featured in the *Belfast Telegraph* the day before, which also analysed the political and military situation in East Asia and how it related to Europe.[96] What would not have been apparent to readers was that much of the detail that Churchill used to enrich both of these articles was provided to Churchill by Quo, who had already begun to brief Churchill on the conduct of the war in China.

The meeting between Churchill, Clementine, Quo Tai-chi and P.C. Chang was arranged for 5pm on 11 August. Quo and Chang were driven to Chartwell in an embassy car, through the rolling English countryside on that hot summer's day. As the two men journeyed through the winding roads, speeding past fields and woods, Churchill was at his home continuing to work on his *English-Speaking Peoples* with Bill Deakin. For the first two weeks of August, Deakin was 'in almost constant attendance' with Churchill at Chartwell.[97] His morning was spent working on his manuscript, while the household staff prepared for Churchill's upcoming trip to France. The break for tea, however, provided a thought-provoking distraction. Chang, who was invited because of his friendship with the Ambassador, has since been described as 'a Chinese Renaissance man', who was a playwright, literary critic, musician, educator and philosopher.[98] His mission that day was to convey to Churchill the nature of what he had witnessed in China. He described the massacres that had taken place, including the 'Rape of Nanking', in which Chinese civilians were indiscriminately raped and massacred by Japanese soldiers; historians estimate over 350,000 innocents were slaughtered in just a few weeks.[99] The Ambassador and his friend vehemently made their case for British support, just as Quo had done to Lord Halifax a few hours earlier. Churchill in turn offered his views on the current situation in terms of international relations, including his thoughts on the conduct of the conflict itself. He also thanked Quo for the information he had provided to enhance the *Daily Mirror* article that hit newsstands that very day, and asked if both guests might read it and let him know their thoughts. As their meeting concluded, Churchill asked if Quo could pass on his best wishes to China's Premier and Generalissimo, Chiang Kai-shek. Upon Quo's return to the Embassy that evening, he made two requests of his staff there. First, he asked them to source a copy of Churchill's article so he could let his host know his thoughts before he departed for France. Second, he sent a telegram to Chiang Kai-shek, conveying Churchill's personal regards and good wishes.

On the eve of Churchill's departure for France, Quo wrote thanking him for the invitation, and saying how much they had enjoyed the visit to Chartwell. 'My friend Prof P. C. Chang was grateful for the opportunity of meeting you and learning at first hand something of your views on the international, especially the Far Eastern, situation.'[100] He also offered his praise for Churchill's 'A Word to Japan!' article, saying he regarded it as very helpful, both in Britain and in the Far East. 'I am sure it will be much appreciated in China,' he added; 'I have sent a copy by air-mail to Madame Kai-shek.'[101] The President's wife, Soong Mei-ling, known to many as 'Madame Chiang' or 'Madame Kai-shek', had recently been called 'the most powerful woman in the world' by *Life* magazine.[102] *Liberty* magazine had also declared, 'The greatest man in Asia is a woman', before adding that she was 'the real brains and boss of the Chinese government'.[103] Quo's decision to send Churchill's article to her was therefore highly significant, as it included Churchill's very public declaration of confidence: 'High military opinion in France and England inclines to the view that in another two years China will have defeated Japan.'[104]

On 17 August, Quo wrote again to Churchill, having heard back from Chiang Kai-shek. The Generalissimo had asked that his sincere thanks be passed on to Churchill for his kind message, and that his own regards and good wishes be sent in return. With these messages, the Chinese Ambassador positioned himself as an intermediary between Chiang Kai-shek and Churchill, who was still without a Government role, and could only act as a private individual. However, by this time, few thought he would remain so for much longer. After a decade in political exile, the tide had now turned to the extent that those world leaders, of countries already at war, were keen to count Churchill among their allies.

One of the last letters that reached Churchill at Chartwell before he departed for France was from A. H. Richards, the secretary of the Focus group. It was he who had organised and coordinated the activities of those individuals who had gathered so often over the previous four years in the name of the defence of freedom and peace. 'Dread days loom before us and darken the skies,' he wrote, 'and if we are to face with courage and confidence, the spectre of war stalking across Europe menacing our beloved land, I am persuaded that in the hour of dire need our people, with one voice, will turn to you to deliver us and to lead us into the "Paths of Peace".'[105] Similar letters were opened as Churchill's staff readied his luggage for the journey to Paris.

Clementine and Mary decided to visit Diana and her family in London for the day while Churchill undertook final pre-holiday preparations, including a quick haircut. Churchill's barber, Mr Reed, whom he normally saw in London, had to travel especially out to Chartwell, and was collected from nearby Oxted station by Cale the chauffeur. The household staff generally was somewhat depleted that weekend, as a number had been invited to be guests at the wedding of Miss Penman, one of the Churchills' trio of secretaries, who was married in St Mary's Church in Westerham on Saturday 12 August. Her dress, which was likely the subject of much discussion in the secretaries' office beforehand, was white broderie anglaise over ice blue, and her long tulle veil was held in place by a coronet of white heather. The local press reported that Churchill had given two wedding gifts to the happy couple: a cheque and an autographed photo of himself.[106]

Deakin, meanwhile, continued to work on Churchill's manuscript, combing through the notes kindly sent to Chartwell from those friends who had been asked to help review the text. Despite their diminished staffing, Randolph visited, as did Clementine's old friend Sylvia Henley, and a pleasant summer weekend passed before the family parted ways. Churchill and a temporary secretary, brought in to replace Miss Penman, were driven to Croydon Airport on the morning of Monday 14 August. As he boarded the plane, in his pinstripe three-piece suit and clutching that morning's newspapers, he did so knowing that it might well be his last holiday before war.

The first day of his trip was spent at the Ritz in Paris, where he wrote to Clementine asking that any urgent messages be sent to him there, even though he was due to be away until Thursday afternoon, as he would ring the hotel each evening to check.[107] From Paris he travelled to Strasbourg to see the Maginot Line, the chain of defensive fortresses along the French border with Germany. Churchill was shown sections never before revealed to any foreigner, including those where German troops could be seen beyond the Rhine. 'The trip tore to shreds any illusion that it was not Germany's intention to wage war and to wage it soon', General Spears, who accompanied Churchill, later recalled.[108]

On 17 August, Clementine and Mary made their way to Paris to join Churchill. Mary delighted in all that she saw, and described it in her diary as the 'city of my dreams!'[109] She spoke with her father about the French soldiers he had met in recent days, whom he called 'wonderful', as the pair visited Napoleon's tomb. The three Churchills then travelled to Saint-Georges-Motel for a handful of 'sunshine days', as Churchill later recalled. He spent much of his time there painting with his old friend, the artist Paul Maze. 'This is the last picture we shall paint together for a very long time', Churchill said to Maze on Sunday 20 August.[110] Two days later he decided to go home. He had found himself unable to relax, and became frustrated with being out of touch. 'War seems so horribly near, so inevitable', Mary wrote in her diary from France, where she and her mother decided to continue their holiday.[111] That night, Churchill was back at Chartwell, and so began his final week at his country home before the final awful tumbling towards war.

30. Winston Churchill painting the Moulin de Montreuil, the mill of the Château Saint-Georges-Motel, in northern France, August 1939.

On 23 August 1939 the Soviet Union signed a non-aggression pact with Nazi Germany. In doing so, the Russians had opted, via a rapprochement with Germany, to remain distant from any European war and to manoeuvre independently in their own interests.[112] Upon hearing of the agreement, Neville Chamberlain was reportedly 'very depressed but resolute'.[113] Churchill left Chartwell for London that morning and reassured friends that the French were half-mobilising and preparing to support Poland. Meanwhile, the staff at Chartwell were overseeing another of the 'Garden Open' days to raise money for local causes, which had been scheduled when it was envisaged that the family would still be in France. Those who wandered around the gardens that day had no idea that they would be among the last to do so before war. From that point, in the dying days of August, Churchill conducted his political machinations from his Morpeth Mansions flat. 'He had these meetings,' Mrs Hill later recalled of that week, 'where there was Lord Lloyd, Mr Sandys, Archie Sinclair ...'[114] Other visitors included Anthony Eden and Leslie Hore-Belisha. Events moved too quickly for Churchill to be away from London for any length of time, and so any thought of returning to Chartwell would have to wait.

Meanwhile, the House of Commons had returned early on 24 August to deal with the looming crisis. Throughout proceedings, Churchill reportedly held his face in his hands, occasionally nodding in agreement with the Prime Minister.[115] Parliament approved the Emergency Powers Bill, which gave the Government special powers to take almost any action necessary to carry out war successfully. Clementine and Mary hastily made arrangements to travel back to England. Clementine's engagement diary for that day had only three words, 'Crisis go home', while Mary described Paris as 'calm but prepared & very busy'.[116] Their journey, via Dunkirk, was delayed by fog, which meant their ferry was almost two hours late. Diana met them on their return to England and told them that her children had been sent to Chartwell where they would hopefully be safer than staying in London. Amidst all of the upheaval and urgent preparations, Churchill found time to reply to the Chinese Ambassador, whose second letter had been awaiting him at Chartwell on his return. 'Thank you very much for your kind letter', Churchill wrote to Quo, keen to keep the communications with Chiang Kai-shek open. 'I am most glad to receive the message from your Generalissimo.'[117] Their meeting at Chartwell was the last that Churchill had with representatives of any foreign power before the outbreak of war.

On Friday 25 August the Anglo-Polish treaty of mutual assistance was signed in London, meaning that the United Kingdom would come to the defence of Poland if attacked by a foreign power. The Churchills returned to Chartwell for the last weekend of peace. The extraordinary guest list included Churchill's brother Jack and his wife Goonie. General Ironside brought favourable reports of the Polish

Army, having just returned from Poland. Other guests included Churchill's long-time advisors and confidants Professor Lindemann and Desmond Morton. Horatia Seymour, Clementine's friend since childhood, and Emerald Cunard, the American-born society hostess, were also in attendance. Bill Deakin, Churchill's faithful literary assistant, was invited to join too along with his wife Margaret. The Churchills' daughters Sarah and Diana came back home for the weekend as well, along with Diana's husband Duncan and Bob Boothby. Noel Coward joined them on Sunday evening, and sang and played many of his songs, including 'Stately Homes of England', 'Mad Dogs and Englishmen' and 'Bitter Sweet Waltz'.[118] The atmosphere was a poignant one. So many of those in attendance had visited Chartwell in recent months and years to aid Churchill's campaign to prevent war through collective security and a rearmament programme intended to act as a deterrent. With war possibly just days away, it is easy to imagine the scene of stoic resilience as Coward sang his melancholic lyrics: 'I'll see you again, whenever Spring breaks through again. Time may lie heavy between, but what has been is past forgetting.'

As the guests departed from Chartwell, Churchill's mind turned to what war with Germany might look like. Having witnessed Nazi tactics elsewhere, he assumed that the outbreak of war could be followed by a strategy of sabotage and murder. Knowing that there were 20,000 German Nazis residing in England, and understanding that Hitler already saw him as an implacable foe, Churchill asked his former Scotland Yard detective, Walter Thompson, to come to Chartwell. 'I told him to come along and bring his pistol with him', Churchill later recalled. 'I got out my own weapons, which were good. While one slept the other watched.'[119] It was during these final hours of peace, during his nocturnal thoughts, that Churchill felt certain that the arrival of war would see a major burden fall upon his shoulders, a belief which would soon be proved correct.[120]

On 31 August, the Churchills told the authorities to add Chartwell to the list of places of refuge available for women and children being evacuated from London. The next day, Mary awoke early and, aided by the household staff, began moving furniture and making everything ready for the arriving families. By 9am the rumour that

292

Germany had marched on Poland and that bombings were under way had been confirmed to Churchill by the Polish Ambassador. War in Europe had begun, though the British Government had not yet made any declaration. Churchill telephoned General Ironside telling him: 'They've started. Warsaw and Krakow are being bombed now.'[121] Ironside in turn rang the War Office and spoke to Lord Gort, the Military Secretary to the War Minister. According to Ironside's diary, Gort had heard nothing of an invasion of Poland and didn't believe it. Ironside insisted it was fact and that the War Minister needed to be told immediately. Ironside was astonished that the War Office was ignorant of the German attack, when Churchill had been informed in the comfort of his own country home.

Just before lunch, Churchill received a telephone call from the Prime Minister requesting his presence in London. Cale was summoned from his cottage and drove the car from the garages around to the front driveway.[122] Churchill bid farewell to Clementine and Mary, and the staff at Chartwell, not knowing when he would next be there with them. Mrs Hill grabbed her coat and hat and her portable typewriter and climbed into the front passenger seat as Churchill took his usual seat in the back of the car with his newly appointed security guard, Walter Thompson. The panoramic view from Chartwell across the Kent countryside, which had captured his heart and never left it, quickly faded into the distance as the car sped towards London. Upon arriving at the flat in London just under an hour later, all Churchill could do was wait for word from the Prime Minister, staring at the telephone, willing it to ring.

THE DAWN OF WAR

Neville Chamberlain, London, 1 September 1939

When reports spread that Germany had attacked Poland on 1 September, the mood in Parliament's corridors was described by one onlooker as 'nervous and panicky'.[1] The session that evening was due to start at 6pm and the dignitaries gathered in the diplomatic gallery overhead included those who had visited Chartwell in recent years. Ivan Maisky greeted Quo Tai-chi in a friendly fashion, and they took seats beside one another. They were joined by Joe Kennedy, who initially went to sit on Maisky's other side but, upon recognising the Russian Ambassador, reportedly leapt out of his seat, made a clumsy gesture and instead moved to the second row. The assembled diplomats looked down at the chamber of the House of Commons, which was as crowded as the press, guest and Lords' galleries overhead.

Churchill had visited Chamberlain at Downing Street that afternoon. The Prime Minister said he saw no hope of averting war and proposed to form a small War Cabinet.[2] Nothing was formally agreed then, as Britain had not yet made any declarations of war. Churchill made a case for the inclusion of Liberal MPs, which would naturally include their party leader, Archie Sinclair, who had been such a frequent visitor to Chartwell in recent years, and was a co-creator of the 'Chartwell Plan' at the height of the abdication crisis. At that time it was thought that Labour would refuse to join a coalition government, as they would not be willing to serve under Neville Chamberlain as Prime Minister, and so the priorities were thought to be the unification of the Conservative Party, and successfully bringing in the Liberals.

When Neville Chamberlain rose to his feet in the debating chamber that evening, a hush descended. 'I do not propose to say many words tonight', he began, acknowledging that the time had come for actions. With German troops having crossed the Polish border that morning, the British Ambassador in Berlin had handed a document to the German Government, saying that unless assurances were given that all aggressive action against Poland had been suspended, and their forces withdrawn, the Government of the United Kingdom would fulfil its full obligations to Poland. Chamberlain outlined steps being taken for defensive preparation, including the immediate mobilisation of the Royal Navy, the Army, and the Royal Air Force. To ensure sufficient manpower for all three forces, the Military Training Act would be expanded, which meant all fit men between 18 and 41 would be called upon for military service. 'We have no quarrel with the German people,' Chamberlain then exclaimed, 'except that they allow themselves to be governed by a Nazi Government.'[3] Describing the Nazis' 'sickening technique' of attack, which had by now become familiar to all in attendance, he concluded by banging his fist on the famous box on the Speaker's table and declared: 'We are now resolved that these methods must come to an end.'[4]

There were a number in attendance who criticised Chamberlain's wording and delivery given how pivotal a moment in Britain's history his speech was likely to be. Quo Tai-chi was among those who were unimpressed not just with the speech, but also with the policy of appeasement that had led to it. He remarked afterwards, implying that the British Government's actions in recent years had led to that outcome: 'The sky is black with chickens coming home to roost.'[5]

The next day, by which time Poland had been under heavy attack for 30 hours, Churchill waited anxiously at Morpeth Mansions. 'I was surprised to hear nothing from Mr Chamberlain during the whole of September 2', he later wrote.[6]

Back in rural Kent, evacuees began to arrive at Chartwell, including one mother with five children, and another with three children, all from Elephant and Castle in South London. The children were aged between two months and seven years. The babies were something of a surprise to Mary, who had been informed they would only be housing children of school age.[7] They were greeted at the front door by Moppet, Mary's nanny, who made arrangements for their comfort and showed them around the country manor house that was to be their new home.[8]

Meanwhile, Churchill had spent much of the day in Morpeth Mansions, to ensure he did not miss any calls. As he waited, he instructed Mrs Hill, in anticipation of likely blackouts, to go out and buy '1 Torch for Mrs Churchill; Dark material for door; Adhesive tape, gum and black paper'.[9] That evening, parliamentarians gathered in the House of Commons at 7.30pm, where Neville Chamberlain seemed to waver in his resolve, announcing that the withdrawal of German forces from Poland would allow Britain to resume negotiations. Many were appalled, including the Conservative MP Leo Amery, who wrote in his memoirs: 'For two whole days the wretched Poles had been bombed and massacred, and we were still considering within what time-limit Hitler should be invited to tell us whether he felt like relinquishing his prey!'[10] Another Munich suddenly seemed to be a possibility at a time when, as Churchill later recalled, 'the temper of the House was for war'.[11]

By evening, Churchill had become infuriated by the Government's inaction and irritated that he had not yet been brought into the Cabinet. He invited Anthony Eden, who by then was Dominions Secretary, Bob Boothby, Brendan Bracken, Duncan Sandys and Alfred 'Duff' Cooper to meet him at his Morpeth Mansions flat at 10.30pm. Churchill immediately declared that he had been very ill treated, having been asked by the Prime Minister to join a new War Cabinet when it was officially created, but had not heard a word from him since.[12] All in attendance were enraged, with Boothby especially irate and insisting that Churchill should go to the House of Commons the next day and somehow take Chamberlain's place as Prime Minister, though he admitted that doing so risked splitting the country. Churchill reportedly declared that he had no wish to be Prime Minister.[13] The offer the day before was merely a place in the War Cabinet as a Minister without portfolio.[14] Those in attendance argued that he should refuse to serve unless Eden was included in the War Cabinet also. Bracken added to the noise, saying that those who had resigned because of their consciences at the time of the Munich Agreement should also be included.

Churchill withdrew from the group to write a letter to the Prime Minister saying that events that day had created a new situation, and that he hoped an announcement of his inclusion in the War Cabinet was imminent. A flurry of telephone calls followed, and Churchill alluded to the group that 'a friend' would shortly tell him what had taken place at Cabinet that day. His attempts to be covert were quickly ruined by Mrs Hill, who politely entered the room and announced 'Mr Hore-Belisha is on the telephone'. Churchill took the call, in which Hore-Belisha described that day's stormy Cabinet meeting, and confirmed that they had decided to deliver the ultimatum to Germany the next morning. Churchill disclosed to those gathered in his flat that he would still send his letter to the Prime Minister if he had heard nothing by the following morning.

True to his word, when he had not yet been summoned, Churchill gave his letter to Mrs Hill to deliver to Downing Street on the morning of 3 September. 'I remember delivering a letter to Number 10,' she later recalled of her walk on that blue-skied Sunday morning; 'that was my first sight of Number 10, delivering a letter from Mr Churchill to Chamberlain saying "You said when war was declared that I would be invited to join the Cabinet."'[15] The letter, which Mrs Hill had typed for Churchill the night before, read as follows:

I have not heard anything from you since our talks on Friday, when I understood that I was to serve as your colleague, and when you told me that this would be announced speedily. I really do not know what has happened during the course of this agitated day; though it seems to me that entirely different ideas have ruled from those which you expressed to me when you said 'the die was cast'. I quite realise that in contact with this tremendous European situation changes of method may become necessary, but I feel entitled to ask you to let me know how we stand, both publicly and privately, before the debate opens at noon.[16]

This was followed by the announcement at 10am of Britain's ultimatum to Germany, which would expire in one hour. People gathered and watched the minute hand on their clocks creeping towards 11am. At 11.15am the Prime Minister broadcast to the British people, and announced to the world that Britain was now at war with Germany. Churchill listened to it on the radio in his flat with Clementine by his side. The eerie stillness that followed was interrupted by what Churchill described as 'a strange, prolonged, wailing noise'. It was assumed by many to be an air-raid siren, to which the cool Clementine simply remarked that she was impressed by how prompt Germany was.[17] Churchill grabbed a bottle of brandy, placed it under his arm and calmly made his way out of the flat, accompanied by Clementine, Thompson and Mrs Hill.[18] They made their way to their designated shelter, an open basement which, much to Churchill's frustration, had no telephone or portable wireless.[19] The Churchills and their staff were joined by the tenants of several flats. 'Everyone was cheerful and jocular, as is the English manner when about to encounter the unknown', Churchill remembered years later.[20] He, however, could not get the image of London in ruins out of his mind and pictured the horrors of explosions and collapsing buildings. After ten minutes they heard the cry of 'All Clear' and Churchill hurried towards Westminster.

At the same time, a group of MPs had been making their way towards the Houses of Parliament when the sirens began. 'We had better make for the House', Anthony Eden instructed those who were with him, which included Bob Boothby and Churchill's son-in-law Duncan Sandys.[21] Upon arriving, the group was told to go down to the air-raid refuge. A stifling ten minutes followed with everyone from Cabinet ministers to cooks crowded in corridors. Some asserted that they had heard gunfire and bombs, but it was later confirmed that the raid warning had been activated in error, and all present were told they were free to go.

At noon, the House of Commons debating chamber filled with MPs. Chamberlain looked pale and unwell, but proclaimed: 'You can imagine what a bitter blow it is to me that all my long struggle to win peace has failed.' He gave his version of events of recent days, describing the course of Germany's aggression against Poland and Britain's determination, together with France, to implement their guarantees by declaring war. He concluded as if in a state of heart-broken disbelief, saying: 'Everything that I have believed in during my public life has crashed into ruins.'[22] Unfortunately, neither his words nor his tone inspired the much-needed courage and fortitude for the gathered parliamentarians. 'His was not the speech of a man who intended to lead us through the struggle', Boothby wrote to Churchill later that day.[23] Harold Macmillan later reflected: 'It would have been better if, at this moment of failure and disappointment, he had passed the burden into other and stronger hands.'[24] Churchill then followed with his own speech, in which he reflected on Britain's ill-starred efforts for peace, and the resilience, strength and energy that would be needed for the path that lay ahead.

Outside, the storms of war may blow and the lands may be lashed with the fury of its gales, but in our own hearts this Sunday morning there is peace. Our hands may be active, but our consciences are at rest ... We are fighting to save the whole world from the pestilence of Nazi tyranny and in defence of all that is most sacred to man. This is no war of domination or imperial aggrandisement or material gain; no war to shut any country out of its sunlight and means of progress. It is a war, viewed in its inherent quality, to establish, on impregnable rocks, the rights of the individual, and it is a war to establish and revive the stature of man.[25]

What Churchill refrained from disclosing in his speech, though it was already being speculated in the press, was that he had received a note from Chamberlain asking him to meet him after the House had adjourned for the day. '10 Downing Street, Thompson', he told his bodyguard after the speeches had finished. When Churchill returned to his car after leaving the Prime Minister's office, he opened the door and sat next to Clementine, who had been waiting anxiously for him. 'It's the Admiralty,' he told his wife; 'That's a lot better than I thought.'[26]

*31. Winston Churchill leaving his London residence
at Morpeth Mansions, 3 September 1939.
His secretary, Kathleen Hill, can just be seen on
the stairs behind him.*

Having been at the helm of a navy at war 25 years earlier, Churchill knew the opening hours of war were vital. He sent word to the Admiralty that he would arrive at 6pm, and did so with his secretary, Mrs Hill, who later recalled the moment of their arrival:

There were lots of photographers and I shrank into the background, and he ran up the stairs. He knew where this First Lord's room was from his first time in office as First Lord in 1911, and he went straight to the panelling and flung open the doors. There it was, a map flagged with the position of the German naval fleet as it had been the day he left.[27]

Churchill couldn't believe his old chart, which he had ordered to be constructed in 1911, was still there. It showed the position of every German battleship on the day he left office in 1915, and it appeared that no one had looked at it in almost a quarter of a century. The new First Lord of the Admiralty was unique, being the only top-ranking Cabinet minister from either side during the last war who held high political office at the outbreak of this one. That evening, Mary wrote a letter to her father saying how proud she was and how glad she was that he was in the Cabinet. 'Don't get too tired,' she added, 'and remember that you always have your very loving daughter.'[28]

Britain's declaration of war on Germany had a transformative effect on Churchill, taking him from political wilderness to one of the most senior roles in Government. The rapid changes were equally felt by those who had visited him at Chartwell between 1933 and 1939, including those German visitors to his country home. Hundreds of enemy aliens were immediately detained in the Olympia Internment Camp in London, including Eugen Spier, the financial backer behind Churchill's Focus group. Shortly after arriving, he met 'Internee No. 12',[29] Ernst Hanfstaengl, the man who had hoped to introduce Churchill to Hitler in 1932 and had been living in West Kensington in London since 1937. Hanfstaengl was arrested on 2 September and quickly expressed a desire to serve British interests through the publication of his memoirs. When discussions turned to Hanfstaengl supporting anti-Hitler messaging, he emphasised that, if any propaganda were to succeed, it would have to be conveyed as 'blonde Englishman to blonde German'.[30] In June 1940 Hanfstaengl was among a group of more than 2,000 internees who were shipped to Canada. He remained there until the summer of 1942 when the Roosevelt Administration decided that he might be useful in the war effort. He was taken to the USA on 30 June 1942 and spent much of the war supporting a government project focused on psychological warfare against the Nazis, known as the 'S-Project'.[31]

Another German national whose departure was exceptionally timed was Gottfried Treviranus, who had visited Chartwell with the former Chancellor Heinrich Brüning, and hastily left Britain for

Canada on 2 September 1939.³² Brüning, who had not seen Churchill since his visit to Chartwell had been featured in the press, still split his time between the United States and Great Britain. In the same month that he cut ties with Churchill, he was appointed as the Lucius N. Littauer Professor of Government at Harvard.³³ He tended to return to England during the semester breaks, including one idyllic visit to the north of England during Easter 1939, which included visits to York Minster and Durham Cathedral.³⁴ By the summer, however, he knew that he needed to be in the United States if war erupted in Europe. The signing of the Nazi–Soviet pact was his cue to conclude his summer trip and he boarded a ship from Southampton on 26 August. He described his last day in Britain to a friend as 'a golden one, resembling a sunset before a long dark night'.³⁵ He was still crossing the Atlantic when Germany invaded Poland, and for the rest of the crossing all telegrams ceased and the portholes had to remain closed until the ship docked in America.

There were those among Churchill's guests at Chartwell whose treatment had begun to resemble that of enemy aliens, even though they weren't German nationals. Stefan Lorant, the editor of *Picture Post* who had retained his Hungarian citizenship, left England because of the humiliation of being forced to report to Bow Street police station every Thursday after war broke out, lining up with other 'enemy aliens' in its basement, solely because of Hungary's close alignment with Germany at the outset of the war. Some Nazi newspapers were reportedly calling him 'Germany's Number One Enemy', owing to the success of his anti-Nazi campaigns. Despite his fierce and active opposition to Hitler, he felt that he was being treated like a criminal. He also had the very real concern that a German invasion of England would equate to a death sentence for him. 'When Hitler and the Nazis might move in like one expected, I would be the first', he disclosed in an interview years later. 'I was on the top of their list and no one would defend me.'³⁶ As a result, he too crossed the Atlantic for his own safety in July 1940.

A fellow Chartwell visitor who had long since given up the hope of returning to Europe following his departure in 1933 was Albert Einstein. By the summer of 1939 he was firmly rooted in the United

States. He and a group of physicists, including several who had fled Nazi Germany, had begun to discuss their fears that Germany was developing a uranium-based weapon. The group decided to alert President Roosevelt of their concerns. A letter was drafted on 2 August 1939 urging the US government to beat Germany in the race to develop nuclear weapons, though the outbreak of war meant it wasn't delivered to Roosevelt until 11 October. 'This new phenomenon would also lead to the construction of bombs,' the letter read, 'and it is conceivable – though much less certain – that extremely powerful bombs of a new type may thus be constructed.'[37] After reading the letter, the President told his military advisor General Edwin Watson, 'This requires action.' The action President Roosevelt requested eventually evolved into the Manhattan Project.

Of those US citizens who were in Britain when war was declared, there were few more influential than Joseph P. Kennedy, who continued to regularly meet with the Prime Minister, Neville Chamberlain. He despatched his family back to the United States two days after the declaration of war. In the months that followed, he professed ill-informed views and showed a complete lack of understanding of events. At one point, when talking about British resistance to Germany, he said, 'I still don't know what they are fighting for that is possible of accomplishment.'[38] His pessimistic opinions were becoming a liability to the Roosevelt Administration, and so the President began to liaise with British political figures directly, including Winston Churchill. Kennedy complained in his diary in October 1939 that Roosevelt 'calls Churchill up and never contacts me' and added that it was a 'rotten way to win men's loyalty'.[39] Kennedy was removed from the Ambassadorship in October 1940 and he returned to the United States. The following February, Kennedy was overheard on a plane speaking with the President's son, Franklin D. Roosevelt Junior. The language was so rude that a fellow traveller, who was accompanied by his 14-year-old daughter, asked Kennedy to clean up his language so she wouldn't hear his obscenities. 'Who is that man?', Kennedy asked. 'I don't know but he looks like an Englishman', the President's son replied. 'I thought so', Kennedy gruffly retorted. 'I hate all those goddamned Englishmen from Churchill down.'[40] The gentleman who had heard these remarks told John Jacob Astor, the chief proprietor of *The Times*. Astor recorded Kennedy's words in a letter, with a note saying, 'At first I was rather taken in by "Jo" and stuck up for him perhaps longer than most, but he is a bad man',[41] and sent it to Brendan Bracken who immediately showed it to Churchill. The man whom he had entertained in his home at Chartwell, and with whom Churchill once held out hope of Anglo-American naval cooperation, was now apparently openly disparaging him in public. By that time, however, Kennedy's opinion hardly mattered and Churchill simply forwarded the note to the Foreign Office.[42]

Fortunately for Churchill, there was another member of the Kennedy family who had a much higher opinion of the new First Lord of the Admiralty, and whose legacy would prove far more enduring. The young John Fitzgerald Kennedy, who had been in a hospital bed in London during his father's visit to Chartwell, was an avid student of Churchill's writing, having become absorbed in his books during his numerous instances of being bedridden during his adolescence. Kay Halle, a family friend who by coincidence could also count Randolph Churchill among her admirers, recalled that the first time she saw the young Kennedy, aged just 13, he was in his hospital bed reading Winston Churchill's history of the First World War.[43] His fascination with Churchill's books continued and he counted the multi-volume history of the Duke of Marlborough as one of his favourite books of all time. When studying at Harvard, John F. Kennedy wrote his thesis on the Munich Crisis, which singled out Churchill as an heroic figure. He titled his work *Why England Slept*, echoing Churchill's *While England Slept*, the American title of his book of speeches made during the 1930s.[44] The thesis was published in 1940 and, while acknowledging that Churchill was a contentious political figure through much of his career, strongly supported the stances he had taken in the 1930s:

Even though Churchill vigorously pointed out the dangers, the people were much more ready to put their confidence in those who favored a strong peace policy. The result of this attitude is that a democracy will always be behind a dictatorship ... in a democracy the cry of 'war-monger' will discourage any politician who advocates a vigorous arms policy.[45]

His admiration for Churchill as a writer and leader never waned. As President of the United States, he conferred upon Churchill honorary citizenship of the United States, just seven months before Kennedy's untimely death. Churchill became the first person to ever be given the honour during their lifetime, and to this day is one of only two such recipients.

Meanwhile, in Europe, after the declaration of war in September 1939, many influential voices predicted defeat, including Pierre-Étienne Flandin, Churchill's informant up until the time of the Munich Agreement. Since 1938 he had, in Churchill's words, been 'completely convinced that there was no hope for France except in an arrangement with Germany'.[46] During the early months of war, Flandin blamed the 'war party' in London, who he said were in cahoots with Jews and Freemasons, for prosecuting a war that France was wholly unprepared for and couldn't possibly win.[47] Upon the establishment of the Vichy Government, which was collaborationist in its approach to Nazi Germany, Flandin was appointed Foreign Minister. Churchill later wrote to Flandin saying that when he learnt of the appointment, 'I thought to myself "here is a friend of England in high position in the Vichy Government, and I am sure that will lessen the danger of that Government declaring formal war on us".'[48] Churchill, however, suspected that the Germans would most likely oust him relatively quickly, which they did the following year. At the end of the war, Flandin was tried for treason because of his support of the Vichy Government. Churchill wrote a letter vouching for Flandin, despite his collaborationist stance while war raged. His support proved highly effective and, combined with other evidence in defence, very likely saved Flandin's life as the charges were dropped the following year.

Unfortunately, one visitor to Chartwell kept a letter from Churchill that had the opposite effect. When Ewald von Kleist-Schmenzin returned to Germany, he did so clutching the letter Churchill had written at Chartwell. 'I am sure that the crossing of the frontier of

Czechoslovakia will bring about a renewal of the world war', Churchill's letter read on Chartwell headed paper. Kleist-Schmenzin gave a copy to Admiral Canaris, the Head of Germany's Military Intelligence, and kept the original in his desk drawer. In July 1944 an assassination attempt was made on Hitler, code-named 'Operation Valkyrie'. A briefcase bomb was to be taken to the site of an underground meeting with Hitler in attendance.[49] The plot had several leaders, including General Ludwig Beck, the former Chief of the General Staff with whom Kleist-Schmenzin had liaised ahead of his visit to Chartwell. As the meeting began, a staff officer absent-mindedly moved the briefcase behind a heavy oak table leg, which shielded Hitler from the worst of the blast. Hitler survived and, after the failed attempt, orders were given to arrest all enemies of the regime. Kleist-Schmenzin was among the first to be rounded up, as the SS had found his name listed as a future political officer in the conspirators' planning documents. The Gestapo went through his writing desk at dawn and seized the letter.[50] Churchill's letter was used as evidence against him, and became part of the case that condemned him to death.

Another of Chartwell's former visitors who was at great personal risk was Count Richard Coudenhove-Kalergi. After his escape from Vienna, he established a new home in Switzerland, although he returned to London numerous times and often met with Churchill on those visits. When Czechoslovakia fell to the Nazis, Coudenhove-Kalergi and his family applied for French citizenship.[51] They received their new passports from the French Embassy on 30 August 1939 and soon made their way to Paris. When German forces attacked France on 10 May 1940, he had returned to Switzerland, though feared that country might be the next to fall to the Nazis. According to Foreign Office reports, he then secured a Japanese visa thanks to his mother's nationality. Given Japan's increasingly close relationship with Germany, he then had second thoughts and instead sought a visa for the United States. That attempt misfired as well and he complained that 'the Americans are making great difficulties'.[52] Lisbon was his next destination, where he successfully obtained a visa for the United Kingdom, while continuing to seek Canadian visas for him and his family. 'Count Kalergi would be as much in danger as the other Austrians in Lisbon if he fell into German hands', another Government report confirmed on 31 July 1940.[53] He frantically tried to outrun the Nazis, trying to predict which countries would and wouldn't be safe in the weeks ahead, and still fearing for his life, just as he had when he and his wife fled from Austria. It was only when Secretary of State Cordell Hull intervened that American visas were finally granted to them.[54] On 3 August they left war-torn Europe behind them, and flew to a new life in New York.

For those in diplomatic roles at the outbreak of war, many continued in their posts. Quo Tai-chi remained at the Chinese Embassy in London until April 1941, when he returned to China following his appointment as Foreign Secretary. A reception was held at the Embassy on the eve of his departure and was attended by notable figures from London's diplomatic and political circles, including Winston Churchill, Anthony Eden and David Lloyd George.[55] In a farewell message, the outgoing Ambassador expressed his country's close and friendly relationship with Britain.

After nearly nine years of happy residency in this island, I feel really sad to leave its shores and friendly people, but I am only going from one front to another of the same struggle for freedom and the ways of a democratic life that we Chinese, and you British, both believe in.[56]

It was Quo Tai-chi, in his role as Foreign Minister, who made China's declaration of war against Germany and Italy, as well as Japan. He did so on 8 December 1941, the day after the attacks by Japan on the United States naval base at Pearl Harbor. It was at a press conference, delivered by candlelight, that Quo announced that Japan 'has now treacherously launched an attack against China's friends, the United States and Britain, thus extending the theatre of her aggressive activities'.[57] He argued that all nations who had been attacked must present a united front against aggressor powers. Upon the conclusion of the press conference, it was noted that those in attendance 'applauded wildly' at China's declaration of war in support of Britain and the United States.[58]

Concerns for the safety of British citizens, meanwhile, led to the evacuation of many women and children out of London. Clementine's cousin, Shiela Grant Duff, was 'placed' in Oxford, where she had studied Politics, Philosophy and Economics in the early 1930s. 'It feels like a total nightmare to find myself back like I was when I was young,' she wrote a week after Britain declared war on Germany, 'forced to work and be together with people I don't like ... and my job is stupid and has nothing to do with victory or with the relief of sorrow and evil.'[59] Despite her initial frustrations, she found other ways to contribute to the war effort using the same skills that had helped her inform Churchill of conditions in Europe during the late 1930s. She stayed in touch with her extraordinary network of contacts across Europe, who sent intelligence from those countries under Nazi occupation, with accompanying notes urging her to show the information to Churchill.[60] Her persistence and determination paid off and by 1942 she had published *A German Protectorate: The Czechs under Nazi Rule* and had been appointed as the first editor of the Czech section of the BBC's new European Service.

Those parliamentarians who had made their way to Chartwell, in support of Churchill, played their part also. Many, however, found they were doing so in a climate where the expectations of war didn't meet the reality, especially in the early months of what has since been called the 'phoney war'. Given the vehemence of Stanley Baldwin's warnings that 'the bomber will always get through', Britons were braced for devastating bombardments from the air, which did not happen until the Blitz the following year. In the interim, Harold Macmillan was among those who felt that the false sense of security was hampering the pace of mobilisation, and that the Government was badly mismanaging the mobilisation of both manpower and weapons production as a result.[61] On 18 October 1939 he reminded the House of Commons of the total nature of the war in which they were now embroiled:

It means that the total energy of the nation has to be organised and directed to secure the maximum results and, therefore, that every error of policy or administration, even on the remote fringes of economic activity, will be paid for by a prolongation of the struggle and the consequent sacrifices of additional lives.[62]

He also continued to adamantly support Churchill, saying in the House of Commons that he should 'be given major credit for having fought this battle alone for ten years' and as a result was 'holding a position greater than that of any other Member of this House'.[63] Three months later, Churchill was appointed Prime Minister, and he made Macmillan Parliamentary Secretary at the Ministry of Supply, the department which he and Churchill had campaigned to create. 'Thus came to an end for me, after some sixteen years, the carefree although sometimes frustrating irresponsibility of the back-benches', he later wrote.[64] Meanwhile, those around Macmillan noted with amusement his obvious enjoyment of his new role. He remained a government minister for the rest of the war, but the height of his political career was a decade away. Following the resignation of his friend and colleague Anthony Eden, Macmillan served as Britain's Prime Minister from January 1957 until October 1963.

The vital task of defending Britain from attacks from the enemy bombers fell to Archie Sinclair, whom Churchill made Secretary of State for Air. He had previously been offered a position by Chamberlain in September 1939 but declined the offer, in part because of his lack of faith in the Prime Minister.[65] It was in a critical debate in the House of Commons on 7–8 May 1940 that Sinclair joined with other parliamentarians, in telling Chamberlain he had to go. When Churchill invited him to lead the Air Ministry, Sinclair wrote to him that he considered it 'a mark of your confidence which I do most gratefully appreciate'. He continued: 'It would be a colossal task, but my personal inclination urges me to attempt it under the inspiration of your leadership.'[66] The man who had served as Churchill's second in command on the Western Front now accepted the invitation to serve under him again in war. He remained in the post from that moment until victory was declared in May 1945.

There was one ally of Churchill's, a hero of the Great War, who had served in the ranks of the Royal Air Force, and whose absence he felt long after their last meeting at Chartwell: T. E. Lawrence. Years after his tragic death, a mutual acquaintance sent Churchill a letter Lawrence had written years earlier, on Armistice Day in 1922. In it, Lawrence praised Churchill, calling him 'a great man, and for whom I have not merely admiration, but a very real liking'. He added, 'several times I've seen him chuck the Statesmanlike course and do the honest thing instead.'[67] Churchill was touched, and profusely thanked the sender for their kindness and for the 'most valuable and interesting letter'.[68] In a speech Churchill gave at the unveiling of a memorial to Lawrence, he said: 'Those who knew him best miss him most; but our country misses him most of all; and misses him most of all now. For this is a time when the great problems upon which his thought and work had so long centred, problems of aerial defence ... fill an ever larger space in our affairs', but, as Churchill said that day, 'It was not to be.'[69]

As the Churchills relocated almost completely to London, Chartwell was effectively closed by late September, a process that Miss Hamblin, the Churchills' secretary there from 1932 to 1938, called 'putting it to sleep'.[70] The families from London stayed for just two days before returning home. The risk of staying in London proved to be much lower than anticipated in the early months of war, though the evacuations acted as a well-executed dress rehearsal when it became necessary during the Blitz the following summer. For the Churchills, it was decided that a three-bedroom cottage in the grounds could be used if ever needed. With Churchill's new appointment including accommodation in the top two floors of Admiralty House, there was little need to keep paying the running costs of their country home and they soon considered selling their London flat. Their new home in Admiralty Arch was big enough to accommodate their secretaries also. Mrs Hill remained on Churchill's staff, and later said 'it was a strain because he didn't want anybody but me, so I had to wait about a long time, you know, to be on hand.'[71] Miss Hamblin, who had left Chartwell the year before, returned at Clementine's request in September 1939 and so also joined them at Admiralty House. 'I was pleased and quite excited, particularly with the war looming. It was a great challenge because I was still quite a country girl, and to go and work at Admiralty House was quite something', she later recalled.[72]

In the Churchills' absence, Moppet would effectively run Chartwell. She stayed in the house alongside a number of the Churchills' staff, including May the housemaid, Margaret the cook, Kathleen the kitchen maid and George the parlourman.[73] A new resident, Miriam Buckles, joined this established group at the outset of the war, as a nanny to look after Diana's young children when they were there.[74] Albert Hill, the head gardener, continued to live in his cottage on the estate with his family.[75] He ran the gardens and wider estate, though did so entirely alone once all the young men who worked under him had been called up. As a result, he removed the planting from some parts of the garden to let them go fallow, including Clementine's rose garden, and instead prioritised the productive garden, from which fresh fruit, vegetables, flowers and honey were sent to Downing Street throughout the war. Patrick Jackson, the handyman, remained in his cottage with his wife Mary and young son, Patrick junior.[76] Among his first tasks upon the declaration of war was to create a means by which all the house's windows could be covered at night to ensure that no light escaped and so make any possible targeting of Chartwell by German bombers more difficult. Cale and his wife Gladys also continued to live in their cottage next door to the Jacksons, though his role as the Churchills' chauffeur meant he was frequently called to London.[77]

Mary, the Churchills' youngest daughter and only member of the family to remain at Chartwell after the outbreak of the war, celebrated her seventeenth birthday there on 15 September 1939. In her diary the night before, she wrote: 'I shall always have the memory of my first 17 years – a golden, glowing memory of pleasures, loves, friendships and heavenly rapture of living at peace in the beautiful place that is my home.'[78]

The house itself, however, was far from safe during the war, a fact that was quickly recognised when a friend of Churchill's remarked the day after his appointment to the Admiralty that 'some ambitious enemy bomber may let fly a shot at Chartwell'.[79] Its location on high ground, the two rather conspicuous lakes and the house's distinct T-shape from above made it a highly visible target for enemy bombers, a fact which became increasingly likely upon Churchill's appointment as Prime Minister in May 1940. The following month, the Nazis created a list of British residents to be arrested upon Germany's successful invasion and occupation of Britain. The list, which later became known as 'The Black Book', included the entry 'Churchill, Winston Spencer, Ministerpräsident, Westerham/Kent, Chartwell Manor.'[80] The place that had been his very own citadel during the 1930s had now become an easy and recognisable target, on a path that German bombers were flying through night after night. As measures were taken to increase Churchill's safety at Chequers, the official residence of the Prime Minister, so too were interventions considered for the defence of Chartwell. 'I think some experienced person should go down to Chartwell and let us know what local arrangements are necessary', a Downing Street official wrote to the Air Ministry.[81] Aerial reconnaissance was arranged 'to see if Chartwell is particularly conspicuous from the air and, if so, whether any camouflage is advisable'.[82] In the meantime, it was felt that Churchill would be in 'a precarious position' for three reasons if he were to return to Chartwell:

(1) Chartwell is within the radius of enemy penetration by day as well as by night.
(2) Its position is easily found ... Immediately above Chartwell lie Biggin Hill, Kenley and Croydon, and between them is a ridge which is a good landmark.
(3) Determined pilots would very likely reach Chartwell by day, in face of opposition.[83]

It was for these reasons that an air-raid shelter was constructed on the ground floor of the south-facing wing of Chartwell by the Ministry of Works and Buildings in the spring of 1941, though it was of a modest scale and could only shelter a handful of people at a time.[84] Then, on 25 March 1941, the RAF's reconnaissance aircraft flew over Chartwell, taking photographs of the house, the ancillary buildings, the gardens and the grounds. Some photographs showed the walls that Churchill had painstakingly built, including the miniature cottage he had constructed for his youngest daughters. They

32a&b. Aerial photographs of Chartwell, showing the view of the gardens and grounds looking south-east (above) and towards the house looking west (below), March 1941.

showed several interventions that had already been made at Chartwell to try to disguise it. The upper lake had been completely camouflaged and the nearby swimming pool, where Churchill had spent countless hours of fun with friends and family, was drained and obscured with dirt and leaves. Some features were still untouched, including the lake with the island that Churchill had planned and created. Parts of the garden appeared ordered but barren, like Clementine's rose garden, which was, by then, totally bare. Despite the changes, it was still unmistakably Chartwell, the place that Churchill had loved so dearly for 20 years. When the photos arrived at the Air Ministry, it was decided that copies should be sent to Churchill for his own personal enjoyment, and so he could see his home from a new perspective. 'There's nothing like Chartwell',[85] he would often say upon driving through the house's mighty oak gates, and so he very likely thought upon seeing the remarkable photos of his home, in the depths of war, from the sky.

The interventions made to conceal Chartwell from enemy aircraft proved effective, and the Luftwaffe never found it. By sheer chance, a bomb was dropped on the edge of the estate, but the German pilot had probably jettisoned his ordnance without ever knowing how close he came to hitting Churchill's home. As a result, Churchill's citadel withstood the storms of war. All the family, and almost all the Churchills' staff, safely negotiated the war years. The exceptions included Violet Pearman, the chief secretary who Churchill called 'Dearest Mrs P', and who had served him at Chartwell from 1928 to 1938 when she fell ill. Even then, she continued to do some tasks for Churchill from her home until she died of a stroke in 1941. Another exception was Albert Hill, the Churchills' head gardener since 1927, who died from leukemia on the morning 6 June 1944,[86] the very same day that thousands of allied troops were landing on the beaches of Normandy. Three days later, Mary Churchill wrote from Downing Street to his widow, saying 'Chartwell will not be the same - he was so much part of it, and added so much to its beauty.'[87]

When arrangements were made in the winter of 1946–47 for Chartwell to one day be opened by the National Trust, the Churchills asked that their home be shown in its 1930s decor and configuration.

These were the years that Clementine called 'the golden age of Chartwell', in which Churchill worked day and night, in his political exile, hosting gatherings of informants, allies and advisors at his country home. These meetings armed Churchill with the weapons needed to fight the battle to alert Britain to its impending danger. It is no exaggeration to say that these meetings and the events that took place at Chartwell during these crucial years changed the course of history. They gave him the knowledge and authority to return to political power upon the outbreak of war. Without them, Churchill may not have been called to lead the British Government in May 1940, and the world could easily have been denied the courage, determination and era-defining leadership that inspired the people of Britain, and led them from the brink of defeat to victory.

ACKNOWLEDGEMENTS

I recently curated an exhibition at Chartwell called 'A History of Winston Churchill in 50 Objects' and wanted to weave in a quote about Churchill's career as a writer. There were, naturally, many to choose from, but one leapt out at me as being especially indicative of how he found the process of writing a book.

'Writing a book is an adventure', he said. 'To begin with it is a toy, then an amusement. Then it becomes a mistress, and then it becomes a master, and then it becomes a tyrant and, in the last stage, just as you are about to be reconciled to your servitude, you kill the monster and fling him to the public.' I could never have known just how true those words were until I began the process of researching and writing *Churchill's Citadel*, but I could not have fought that monster alone. I am indebted to the many kind, encouraging and wise individuals who I was fortunate to know or encounter along the way, and the many supportive organisations, without whom my book may well not have got beyond the master-and-tyrant phases of its creation.

My first thanks must go to Joanna Godfrey of Yale University Press. From our first meeting, to my putting the finishing touches on my manuscript, she has been truly inspiring and an absolute pleasure to work with. I am so grateful to her for championing me as an author, and for everything she has done to help me take this book from an idea to a reality.

I was also fortunate enough to benefit from the wise counsel of Allen Packwood, Director of the Churchill Archives Centre, as well as Lord Roberts and Lord Dobbs, who together offered invaluable advice early on in terms of structure, tone and how to create a page-turner of a story as well as a deeply researched work of history. Their words of wisdom often rang in my ears over the course of my research and writing, and I have no doubt that this book is all the better for their wisdom at the outset.

I am also truly grateful to the Churchill family for their support over the course of the creation of this book. I was particularly touched when I was awarded the Jennie Churchill Fund, which was invaluable in enabling me to undertake onsite archival research. Similarly, I am grateful to Garry Rayant and Kathy Fields, whose generosity upon hearing about my book enabled me to commission remote researchers to access international archives that I was unable to visit in person.

To the many archivists and experts with whom I liaised over the course of my research, I am so thankful for the time you spent poring through records and answering my many questions. A handful of those who were especially wonderful include Martin Dunton of the National Archives, Oliver House of the Bodleian Libraries, Emma Quinlan of the archives of Nuffield College, Lucy Smith of the Wilson Archives at Magdalen College, Harriet Coates and Martin Gething of the T. E. Lawrence Society, Abigail Malangone of the John F. Kennedy Presidential Library and Antonia Keaney, Kate Ballenger and Carmen Alvarez of Blenheim Palace. My particular thanks go to the phenomenal team at the Churchill Archives Centre, including Katharine Thomson, Sophie Bridges, Hannah James, Chris Knowles and Nicole Allen. I should add further thanks once again to Allen Packwood, who not only leads this wonderful team but has patiently answered more questions of mine than I could begin to count. I truly can't thank him enough for all his kindness and guidance over the course of my research for this book.

I am also indebted to those whose efforts in the past have captured, in the form of oral histories, some of the most wonderful recollections to feature in this book. Mike Hallett's numerous interviews with Stefan Lorant provided a wealth of material beyond what I could ever have hoped for, and Patricia Ackerman's interviews with former secretaries of the Churchills offered extraordinary insights. It has been a particular pleasure to weave their memories into this history of Chartwell, and ensure that their stories get a much-deserved spotlight. Similarly, I am grateful to the National Trust for allowing my use of excerpts from a wonderful interview undertaken in situ at Chartwell in 1980 with Grace Hamblin, which offered similarly enlightening and entertaining recollections.

For those who so kindly opened up their photo archives for me to excitedly explore, unearthing the most wonderful gems as I went, I am truly indebted. To Matt Butson of Getty Images/Hulton Archive, I can't thank you enough for the time you spent helping me go through many boxes of wonderful photographs. I am also incredibly grateful to Flora Smith of TopFoto, whose phenomenal archive has been a source of inspiration to me for many years, and which provided so many of the wonderful images of those individuals who made their way to Chartwell during those fateful years. My particular and heartfelt appreciation goes to those who so kindly allowed me to see the personal family albums of members of the Churchill family, and who were then generous enough to allow me to share these private moments, to illustrate what life was like at the Churchills' home between the wars.

There have also been those beyond the archives who have played their part in the creation of this book. To Cédric Bunel, who provided countless translations of letters originally written in French and to Andrew Sergeef, who combed through online archive listings to help steer my research for my final chapter, I am very grateful.

Much like Winston Churchill himself, over time I formed a group of 'trusted advisors', who painstakingly combed through my entire draft manuscript and were more generous with their time in doing so than I could ever have asked for. This group included Robert Courts KC MP, Michael F. Bishop and Kevin Weddle, and to each of them I am more thankful than I can begin to put into words.

Then there are my cheerleaders, my wonderful and joy-inducing family and friends, whose encouragement helped spur me on every step of the way, and who kept me going right up to the finish line.

ACKNOWLEDGEMENTS

I would like to conclude with thanks to three gentlemen, without whom this book would never have been possible.

Firstly, to Winston Churchill himself. I don't know how usual it is for an author to thank their subject, especially when that individual has long since passed, but it was the character and courage of Churchill that compelled me to write this history, and to shine a new light on the vital role that his country home played in the 1930s, not only in terms of his life, but in changing the course of history. I feel honoured that my first book has been about one of the most iconic figures of modern history, and am grateful for each moment of humour, wisdom and determination that he showed in those years, that made this book too good not to write.

Secondly, to my Dad, who lit the flame of historical interest in my heart when I really was far too young to be a history geek, but thanks to him it was a childhood badge I wore proudly. He ensured that road trips and days out went via medieval cathedrals, archaeological sites or military fortifications, while providing commentary on the history of whichever musical artist was playing in the car as we went. He recorded virtually every history documentary that aired onto VHS tapes just so we could have them to watch again and again whenever we liked. His decision that my and my siblings' childhoods should be spent in York meant that virtually every outing involved navigating streets, and seeing sights, with stories going back hundreds if not thousands of years. It is thanks to him that there could never have been a path for me other than history. Thank you, Pa, for always letting me follow my heart, for which I will be forever grateful.

Last but not least, my unending thanks go to my wonderful husband Iain. It's hard to put into words what I owe to him for his support, encouragement and belief in me and this book of mine. He has lived and breathed Churchill-and-Chartwell with me in each moment of this 'adventure', as Churchill called the process of writing a book. I can't think of anyone I would want to accompany me on this adventure, and all my adventures, more than him. Thank you for everything, my love.

TIMELINE

Churchill and Chartwell	General
1932	

30 AUGUST:
The Near Miss: Winston Churchill and his family in Munich, Germany, and due to meet Adolf Hitler for dinner, but he never appears

14 SEPTEMBER:
Winston Churchill falls ill, writing that he is 'laid up with paratyphoid' in a hospital in Salzburg. His illness continues into early October

17 OCTOBER:
Winston Churchill's article 'Let Us Have Peace' is published in the *Daily Mail*

8 NOVEMBER:
Franklin D. Roosevelt elected as President of the United States

10 NOVEMBER:
Winston Churchill's book *Thoughts and Adventures* is published (titled *Amidst These Storms* in the United States and published there two weeks later)

10 NOVEMBER:
Speech by Stanley Baldwin, Leader of the Conservative Party and former Prime Minister, advocating international disarmament as a means of preventing war

23 NOVEMBER:
Winston Churchill gives a speech in the House of Commons saying there will be another conflict with Germany, which he says has a 'war mentality', if steps are not taken immediately

29 NOVEMBER:
Franco-Soviet Pact of Non-Aggression signed

8 DECEMBER:
China's Ambassador to Britain, Quo Tai-chi, declares that 'the whole civilised world stands confronted by Japan'. Japan had invaded the Chinese province of Manchuria the year before

12 DECEMBER:
Diana Churchill marries John Milner Bailey at St Margaret's, Westminster

1933

30 JANUARY:
Adolf Hitler becomes Chancellor of Germany

9 FEBRUARY:
King and Country debate at the Oxford Union entitled 'This House will in no circumstances fight for its King and Country'

27 FEBRUARY:
Fire engulfs the German parliament building, the Reichstag

Albert Einstein writes, 'I dare not enter Germany because of Hitler'

4 MARCH:
Inauguration of Franklin D. Roosevelt as the 32nd President of the United States

5 MARCH 1933:
German election sees the Nazi Party win 43.9% of the vote and become the largest party

10 MARCH:
In the House of Commons, Winston Churchill opposes the Government's proposals to reduce spending on the air force for the second year in a row

14 MARCH:
Winston Churchill's first speech in the House of Commons warning of the need to rebuild Britain's air defences

16 MARCH:
MacDonald Plan of disarmament proposals submitted by Britain's Prime Minister, Ramsay MacDonald, to the Disarmament Conference in Geneva

19 MARCH:
Benito Mussolini, Prime Minister of Italy, calls for the creation of the Four-Power Pact between Italy, the United Kingdom, France and Germany

22 MARCH:
Dachau concentration camp opens in southern Germany, initially as a camp for political prisoners

23 MARCH:
Enabling Act passed, giving Adolf Hitler absolute power in Germany

27 MARCH:
Japan leaves the League of Nations

1 APRIL:
Nazi Party organises a nationwide boycott of Jewish-owned shops and businesses in Germany

7 APRIL:
Law is passed banning Jews from holding civil service, university and state positions in Nazi Germany

26 APRIL:
Gestapo, the official secret police of Nazi Germany, is established

10 MAY:
Public burning of books not approved by the German state, including those by Jews and political dissidents

16 MAY:
Pamphlet entitled 'Elimination of Weapons of Offensive Warfare' by President Roosevelt is published

17 MAY:
Adolf Hitler gives a speech in the Reichstag, intended to offer reassurance of his peaceful intentions. He proclaims that the sacrifice resulting from any military action in Europe, even if completely successful, 'would be out of all proportion to any possible gains'

28 JUNE:
Winston Churchill speaks on India at a meeting of the Conservative Central Council but fails to change policy

14 JULY:
Nazi Party is proclaimed as the only authorised political party, leading to a one-party dictatorship in Germany

22 JULY:
Sounding the Alarm: Albert Einstein's visit to Chartwell with Frederick Lindemann and Oliver Locker-Lampson

12 AUGUST:
Winston Churchill gives a speech in his constituency urging that the Government keep Britain's armed forces 'in a proper state of efficiency' so they could be 'strong enough if war should come in Europe'

6 OCTOBER:
Winston Churchill's biography of his ancestor, *Marlborough, Volume 1*, is published

8 OCTOBER:
Winston Churchill tells James Roosevelt, son of the President, 'I wish to be Prime Minister and in close and daily communication by telephone with the President of the United States'

14 OCTOBER:
Germany withdraws from the World Disarmament Conference and the League of Nations

7 NOVEMBER:
Winston Churchill gives speech in the House of Commons warning that Germany has already begun to rearm

1934

3 JANUARY:
Winston Churchill writes to the Leader of the Conservative Party, Stanley Baldwin, predicting 'it is the European quarrel that will shape our lives'

26 JANUARY:
Germany and Poland sign a 10-year non-aggression pact

7 FEBRUARY:
Winston Churchill argues in the House of Commons for maintenance of fleet strength and creation of 'shadow factories' which can be quickly converted to war production

25–26 FEBRUARY:
Defence against the Sky: T. E. Lawrence visits Chartwell, alongside Archibald Sinclair, Marigold Sinclair, Sylvia Henley, Ridley Pakenham-Walsh and Diana Churchill

28 FEBRUARY:
British Government, at a secret cabinet meeting, decides to sell 118 aeroplane engines to Germany

8 MARCH:

In 'Air Estimates' debate in the House of Commons, Winston Churchill urges an increase in spending on the Royal Air Force and campaigns for stronger air defences. He declares 'Germany is arming fast'

30 JUNE–2 JULY:

Night of the Long Knives – a murderous purge of political opponents and rivals of Adolf Hitler, both within and outside the Nazi Party

2 AUGUST:

Death of President Hindenburg. With the support of Germany's armed forces, Adolf Hitler becomes President of Germany

19 AUGUST:

German citizens are asked to vote on whether they approve of the merging of the offices of Chancellor and President. 95% vote in favour. As a result, Adolf Hitler abolishes the office of President and declares himself Führer

22 OCTOBER:

Winston Churchill's biography of his ancestor, *Marlborough, Volume 2*, is published

16 NOVEMBER:

Winston Churchill gives a speech, broadcast on the BBC, describing the 'group of ruthless men preaching a gospel of intolerance and racial pride' in Germany, and adding, 'We are no longer safe in our island home'

28 NOVEMBER:

Winston Churchill, in a speech in the House of Commons, warns that Germany will reach parity in air strength with Britain in 1935. He adds that Britain's air defences are no longer adequate to secure peace and the safety of Britons

18 DECEMBER:
Clementine Churchill departs on her 4-month voyage on the *Rosaura* with Lord Moyne to the Dutch East Indies (present-day Indonesia) to bring back Komodo dragons for London Zoo

29 DECEMBER:
Winston Churchill's article 'While the World Watches' is published in *Collier's Weekly*. He writes that President Roosevelt comes from 'a narrow view of American self-interest' but praises 'the courage, the power and the scale of his effort'

1935

13 JANUARY:
The Saar plebiscite, a referendum on territorial status, sees 90% of voters opt for reunification with Germany

30 JANUARY:
Radio broadcast by Winston Churchill entitled 'The Great Betrayal' on the subject of Indian independence

8 MARCH:
Winston Churchill writes to Clementine that 'the German situation is increasingly sombre'

14 MARCH:
Randolph Churchill backs an independent candidate in the Norwood by-election, who performs so poorly that he loses his deposit. The successful candidate was the Conservative, Duncan Sandys

16 MARCH:
Adolf Hitler announces the expansion of the German Army and the reintroduction of conscription in Germany

7 APRIL:
First recorded visit by Ralph Wigram, Winston Churchill's Foreign Office informant, to Chartwell

TIMELINE

2 MAY:
Clementine Churchill returns to from her voyage on the *Rosaura* and journeys back to Chartwell

19 MAY:
Death of T. E. Lawrence six days after being injured in a motorcycle accident

31 MAY:
Winston Churchill gives a speech in the House of Commons saying that Britain is 'entering a corridor of deepening and darkening danger'

9 JULY:
Winston Churchill joins the Committee of Imperial Defence on Air Defence Research

16 JULY:
Randolph Churchill runs as the Conservative candidate in the West Toxteth by-election and is defeated

2 MAY:
Franco-Soviet Treaty of Mutual Assistance signed

22 MAY:
Stanley Baldwin admits that he had been incorrect in his response to Winston Churchill the year before about Luftwaffe estimates, saying, 'There I was completely wrong'

7 JUNE:
Resignation of Ramsay MacDonald as Britain's Prime Minister, leading the National (coalition) Government. Succeeded by Stanley Baldwin of the Conservative Party

18 JUNE:
Anglo-German Naval Agreement is signed, allowing Germany up to 35% of the aggregate naval strength of Britain and the British Commonwealth combined

TIMELINE

24 JULY:
Winston Churchill gives speech in Harlow declaring: 'Both in the air and in the Navy we will have to make substantial preparations to put ourselves in a state of security'

2 AUGUST:
The Government of India Act becomes law

11 SEPTEMBER:
Winston Churchill declares 'Germany arming at breakneck speed, England lost in a pacifist dream, France corrupt and torn by dissension' and 'America remote and indifferent'

15 SEPTEMBER:
The Nuremberg Laws are introduced. As a result, Jews are no longer considered German citizens

16 SEPTEMBER:
Diana Churchill marries Duncan Sandys at St Ethelburga's, Bishopsgate, in the City of London

3 OCTOBER:
Italian army under Mussolini invades Abyssinia (present-day Ethiopia)

5 OCTOBER:
The Anglo-American Disagreement: Joseph P. Kennedy and Rose Kennedy visit Chartwell

29 OCTOBER:
Germany makes a diplomatic protest to Britain over an article written by Winston Churchill entitled 'The Truth about Hitler', published in *The Strand*

14 NOVEMBER:
Winston Churchill is re-elected as a Member of Parliament for Epping for the Conservatives but is not invited to join the new government

14 NOVEMBER:
UK general election resulting in a large, though reduced, majority for the National Government. The largest party, as before, are the Conservatives and the Government continues to be led by Stanley Baldwin

9 DECEMBER:
The Hoare-Laval Plan, a secret agreement between Britain, France and Italy, leaks to the press. The plan is to partition Abyssinia and give considerable land to Italy. Widespread condemnation of the plan follows

30 DECEMBER:
Winston Churchill writes to Clementine saying that France will expect Britain's 'service' when the 'peril of Hitler becomes active'

1936

20 JANUARY:
King George V dies and he is succeeded by his son King Edward VIII

2 FEBRUARY:
Winston Churchill writes to King Edward VIII predicting that he would be 'the bravest and best beloved of all the sovereigns who have worn the island Crown'

10 FEBRUARY:
Randolph Churchill contests and loses the by-election at Ross and Cromarty

20 FEBRUARY:
Meeting takes place between Winston Churchill and Vic Oliver, who is courting Sarah Churchill. Churchill calls Oliver 'common as dirt'

25 FEBRUARY:
Meeting of the British Government takes place, in which a report is approved that calls for the expansion of the Royal Navy and re-equipping of the British Army

7 MARCH:
German troops march into the Rhineland, an area of land which had been demilitarised as part of the the Treaty of Versailles

TIMELINE

10 MARCH:
Winston Churchill speaks in the House of Commons urging that a Ministry of Supply should be established

21 MAY:
Winston Churchill speaks in the House of Commons saying that German rearmament is 'proceeding upon a colossal scale, and at a desperate break-neck speed'

12 JUNE:
Winston Churchill's article 'How to Stop War' is published in the *Evening Standard*

17 JULY:
The Spanish Civil War begins

28 JULY:
Winston Churchill meets with Stanley Baldwin and tells him 'We are facing the greatest danger and emergency of our history'

1–16 AUGUST:
Summer Olympics are held in Berlin

22 AUGUST:
Winston Churchill's doctor tells him he needs to adopt a stricter diet, smoke fewer cigars and limit his alcohol intake

15 SEPTEMBER:
Sarah Churchill runs away to New York to be with Vic Oliver

3 OCTOBER:
Winston Churchill attends the unveiling of a memorial to T. E. Lawrence

21 OCTOBER:
Nazi Germany's Foreign Office attacks Winston Churchill in the *Diplomatische Korrespondenz*, saying he was unfairly accusing them of preparing for 'unfriendly acts' against other countries

22 OCTOBER:
Winston Churchill's biography of his ancestor, *Marlborough, Volume 3*, is published

25 OCTOBER:
Adolf Hitler and Benito Mussolini form the Rome–Berlin Axis

12 NOVEMBER:
Winston Churchill, speaks in the 'Defence' debate in the House of Commons. He declares that the Government is 'decided only to be undecided, resolved to be irresolute, adamant for drift, solid for fluidity, all-powerful to be impotent'

21–22 NOVEMBER:
The Case for France: Pierre-Étienne Flandin visits Chartwell alongside Jack Churchill, Goonie Churchill, Eddie Marsh and Frederick Lindemann

23 NOVEMBER:
'Mr Churchill's deputation', a group of parliamentarians led by Winston Churchill, including representatives from the House of Commons and House of Lords, meets with Stanley Baldwin to discuss the state of Britain's defences

25 NOVEMBER:
Winston Churchill gives a speech at the New Commonwealth Society Luncheon warning that 'Europe, and it might well be the world, is now approaching the most dangerous moment in history'

25 NOVEMBER:
Germany and Japan sign the Anti-Comintern Pact

27 NOVEMBER:
Concerns about the Churchill family's finances escalate. Winston Churchill writes to Clementine that 'We must get Chartwell down to a smaller scale if we are to keep it'

3 DECEMBER:
The Focus Group/Anti-Nazi Council holds a public meeting at the Royal Albert Hall

5–7 DECEMBER:
An Abdication Formula: Archibald Sinclair visits Chartwell with Marigold Sinclair, alongside Harcourt Johnstone, Christine Churchill, Christopher Hassall and Bob Boothby

7 DECEMBER:
Winston Churchill is shouted down in the House of Commons while speaking in support of King Edward VIII, and has to abandon his speech

10 DECEMBER:
King Edward VIII formally abdicates the throne, which is given legal effect the next day. His younger brother becomes King George VI

24 DECEMBER:
Sarah Churchill marries Vic Oliver in New York

31 DECEMBER:
Ralph Wigram dies aged 46

1937

2 FEBRUARY:
Winston Churchill writes to Clementine reflecting that 'my life is probably in its closing decade'

12 MAY:
Coronation of King George VI and Queen Elizabeth at Westminster Abbey

28 MAY:
Winston Churchill meets the German Ambassador von Ribbentrop and warns him 'Do not underrate England'

28 MAY:
Prime Minister Stanley Baldwin retires and is succeeded by Neville Chamberlain

7 JULY:
A skirmish between Japanese and Chinese troops, known as the Marco Polo Bridge incident, escalates and sparks a full-scale invasion of China by Japan. Within days the conflict has become a full, but undeclared, war between the two countries

4 AUGUST:
Hitler's Predecessor: Heinrich Brüning visits Chartwell with Gottfried Treviranus, Edward Spears, Mary Borden, Michael Spears, Frederick Lindemann, James Hawkey, Dinah Hawkey and Roger Keyes

8 AUGUST:
Beijing falls as Japanese troops enter the city

30 AUGUST:
Winston Churchill publishes an article in *Collier's* magazine describing the 'remorseless conquest and subjugation of parts of China by Japan'

4 OCTOBER:
Winston Churchill's book *Great Contemporaries* is published

5 NOVEMBER:
A secret conference is held between Adolf Hitler and his senior advisors and generals. Hitler outlines his strategy for military expansion, including the annexation of Austria and the destruction of Czechoslovakia

6 NOVEMBER:
Rome–Berlin Axis merges with the German-Japanese Anti-Comintern pact

22 NOVEMBER:
Knight, Frank & Rutley estate agents are instructed that the Churchills are willing to consider offers for Chartwell. The first visit of a potential buyer takes place

20–25 NOVEMBER:
Lord Halifax, the Leader of the House of Lords, travels to Germany for a five-day 'unofficial visit', including private talks with Adolf Hitler and other senior political figures

TIMELINE

13 DECEMBER:
Japanese troops enter the city of Nanking with orders to 'kill all captives'. The 'Rape of Nanking' over the following six weeks results in the massacre of an estimated 350,000 civilians

1938

7 JANUARY:
Winston Churchill publishes 'Britain Rearms' article in the *Evening Standard*, praising army recruitment efforts but saying that investment is urgently needed in equipment and supplies

8 FEBRUARY:
Winston Churchill writes to a friend that Germany 'is in the hands of violent men' and 'I fear very much lest something should happen in Central Europe'

20 FEBRUARY:
Anthony Eden resigns as Foreign Secretary as a protest against Neville Chamberlain's policy of coming to friendly terms with fascist Italy

Adolf Hitler gives a speech in the Reichstag stating that 10 million Germans are suffering in Austria and Czechoslovakia, and his ambition to 'protect' them

26–27 FEBRUARY:
The Pan-European Count: Richard Coudenhove-Kalergi visits Chartwell

9 MARCH:
Austrian Chancellor Kurt von Schuschnigg announces a referendum to decide the future of the country's relationship with Germany

10 MARCH:
Adolf Hitler instructs his generals to 'Prepare Case Otto', his plans for the invasion of Austria

11 MARCH:
Adolf Hitler demands the cancellation of the Austrian vote as German troops mass on the border. Schuschnigg cancels the referendum

12 MARCH:
German troops cross the border into Austria

13 MARCH:
Adolf Hitler proclaims the Anschluss, resulting in the union of Germany and Austria

14 MARCH:
Winston Churchill speaks on the German annexation of Austria in the House of Commons. He references Nazi Germany's 'programme of aggression, nicely calculated and timed, unfolding stage by stage'

24 MARCH:
Winston Churchill speaks of the 'rape of Austria before our eyes' in a speech as part of the 'Foreign Affairs and Rearmament' debate in the House of Commons

2 APRIL:
Stories appear in several newspapers saying that Chartwell is for sale

19 MAY:
German troops temporarily mass on the border with Czechoslovakia. Czechoslovakia mobilises the next day in response, but no military activity takes place, and the crisis soon passes

24 JUNE:
Winston Churchill's book *Arms and the Covenant* (*While England Slept* in the US), a collection of his speeches during the years of appeasement, is published

19 AUGUST:
Planning a Coup: Ewald von Kleist-Schmenzin visits Chartwell

2 SEPTEMBER:
Winston Churchill's biography of his ancestor, *Marlborough, Volume 4*, is published

12 SEPTEMBER:
Adolf Hitler speaks at the Nazi Party's annual Nuremberg rally, announcing that the oppression of Sudeten Germans in Czechoslovakia must end

23 SEPTEMBER:
German troops mass on the border with Czechoslovakia

26 SEPTEMBER:
Winston Churchill issues a statement advising the British Government to warn Adolf Hitler that an agreement between England, France and Russia would mean an invasion of Czechoslovakia would be taken as an act of war against them all. He adds that the United States should intervene also

30 SEPTEMBER:
Munich Agreement signed by representatives of Britain, France, Italy and Germany. The agreement forces Czechoslovakia to surrender the Sudeten region (western Czechoslovakia) to Germany

5 OCTOBER:
Winston Churchill denounces the Munich Agreement, in a speech in the House of Commons, as 'a defeat without war'

16 OCTOBER:
Winston Churchill broadcasts a speech to the United States. The speech is primarily about the Munich Agreement, but Churchill adds how 'China is being torn to pieces by a military clique in Japan'

29 OCTOBER:
The View from Prague: Shiela Grant Duff visits Chartwell with Ian Colvin and Edgar Mowrer

6 NOVEMBER:
Adolf Hitler references Winston
Churchill in a speech, saying 'it would
be better if Mr Churchill would
associate less with people who are paid
by Foreign States and more with the
German people'. Churchill replies with
a press statement calling Hitler 'unduly
sensitive' and advising 'It would be
much wiser to relax a little'

9–10 NOVEMBER:
Kristallnacht (Night of Broken Glass),
an anti-Jewish pogrom, results in mass
destruction of Jewish businesses and
synagogues. An estimated 30,000 Jews
are sent to concentration camps

22 DECEMBER:
Winston Churchill predicts in a letter
to his wife Clementine that 'Hitler will
be on the move again in February or
March'

1939

30 JANUARY:
Adolf Hitler gives a speech in the
Reichstag announcing 'if war erupts it
will mean the extermination of
European Jews'

3 FEBRUARY:
Through the Lens: Stefan Lorant visits
Chartwell with Kurt Hutton

14 FEBRUARY:
Winston Churchill writes to a friend: 'it
is absolutely necessary for me to be in
the country every night this year, in order
to complete the history I am writing'

14 MARCH:
Winston Churchill gives a speech in his
constituency on the 'ruin of
Czechoslovakia' and says that 'not until
the Nazi power has passed away from
Europe will they emerge again in
Freedom'

15 MARCH:

Adolf Hitler meets with the Czechoslovak President Emil Hácha and threatens to inflict bombing raids on Prague unless German troops are allowed to enter Czechoslovakia. Fearing the bloodshed if he refuses, Hácha agrees

Adolf Hitler proclaims a new German Protectorate of Bohemia and Moravia, and the end of Czechoslovakia

25 MARCH:

Eight-page *Picture Post* article about Winston Churchill is published. It includes the comment 'at 64 the greatest moment of his life has still to come'

28 MARCH:

Appeal by 34 Members of Parliament, including Winston Churchill, to the Prime Minister, Neville Chamberlain, saying that a National Government should be formed as a result of the 'grave dangers' facing Britain and the British Empire

31 MARCH:

Britain and France offer a guarantee of Polish sovereignty against any act of aggression

3 APRIL:

Winston Churchill gives a speech in the House of Commons pleading that those present should not underestimate the terror of attacks from the air on civilian populations

6 APRIL:

First records of plans for Chartwell should war break out, including the Churchills' grandchildren being evacuated from London to live in one of the cottages

TIMELINE

7 APRIL:
The Future Prime Minister: Harold Macmillan visits Chartwell

7 APRIL:
Italy invades Albania

9 APRIL:
Winston Churchill writes to Neville Chamberlain from Chartwell saying, 'it seems to me that hours now count'

11 APRIL:
Churchill contacts Leslie Hore-Belisha, Secretary of State for War, asking him to visit Chartwell urgently. Hore-Belisha is at Chartwell within hours and the pair discuss national conscription

13 APRIL:
Winston Churchill speaks in the House of Commons and says 'The danger is now very near'

14 APRIL:
President Roosevelt sends his ill-fated 'Peace Appeal' to Adolf Hitler and Benito Mussolini

23 APRIL:
The *Sunday Pictorial* publishes an article entitled 'The Great Churchill Scandal', pleading with the Prime Minister to bring Winston Churchill into the Cabinet

10 MAY:
Former French Prime Minister Léon Blum visits Chartwell with Richard Law

22 MAY:
Adolf Hitler and Benito Mussolini sign the Pact of Steel and agree to a formal political and military alliance, cementing the relationship that had existed between Germany and Italy as the Rome–Berlin Axis since 1936

23 MAY:
Adolf Hitler tells his Chiefs of Staff, 'If there were an alliance of France, England and Russia, against Germany, Italy and Japan, I should be constrained to attack England and France with a few annihilating blows'

27 JUNE:
Winston Churchill's *Step by Step*, a collection of articles on foreign affairs between March 1936 and May 1938, is published

8 JULY:
Neville Chamberlain writes to his sister that the drive to put Winston Churchill into the Government is a 'conspiracy'

18 JULY:
Visitor to Chartwell later recalls 'Winston talked about nothing but the prospect of war over dinner'

8/9 AUGUST:
Winston Churchill broadcasts a speech to the United States from his study at Chartwell, saying Britain and France are in 'a hush of suspense' as they wait for Germany to make its next move. He added that the hush is 'broken only by the dull thud of Japanese bombs falling on Chinese cities'

11 AUGUST:
A Final Plea: Quo Tai-chi visits Chartwell with Peng-chun Chang

Winston Churchill's article 'A Word to Japan!' published in the *Daily Mirror* saying that military opinion in France and England is that 'in another two years China will have defeated Japan'

340

TIMELINE

15–22 AUGUST:
Winston Churchill travels to France, including a three-day tour of the French defences known as the Maginot Line and several days painting. He returns to Chartwell earlier than scheduled as the international situation reaches crisis point

23 AUGUST:
Nazi Germany and the Soviet Union sign a Non-Aggression Pact

24 AUGUST:
British Parliament approves the Emergency Powers (Defence) Bill, giving the Government special powers to take almost any action necessary for the successful conduct of war

25 AUGUST:
Anglo-Polish treaty of mutual assistance is signed in London

31 AUGUST:
The Churchills tell the local authorities to add Chartwell to the list of places of refuge available for those being evacuated from London

1 SEPTEMBER:
The Dawn of War: Winston Churchill departs from Chartwell for London in anticipation of being summoned to Downing Street and invited to join the Government

1 SEPTEMBER:
Germany invades Poland

2 SEPTEMBER:
France mobilises

3 SEPTEMBER:
Winston Churchill is appointed First Lord of the Admiralty and becomes a member of Britain's War Cabinet

3 SEPTEMBER:
Britain and France declare war on Germany

ENDNOTES

Introduction: The Near Miss

1. Winston S. Churchill, speaking in the House of Commons. 23 November 1932. Hansard, 5th Series, Vol. 272, c86.
2. Grace Hamblin, 'Chartwell Memories', speech given at The Adolphus, Dallas, Texas, 30 October 1987. Churchill Archives Centre (hereafter CAC), The Papers of Grace Hamblin, HAMB 1/2.
3. Winston S. Churchill to Stanley Baldwin, 24 September 1930. CAC, The Papers of Sir Winston Churchill, CHAR 2/572/84.
4. Ibid.
5. Stanley Baldwin to Winston S. Churchill, 14 October 1930. Ibid., CHAR 2/572/75.
6. Leo Amery, Diary, 26 May 1930. In J. Barnes and D. Nicholson (eds), *The Empire at Bay: The Leo Amery Diaries, Volume 2: 1929–45* (Hutchinson: London: 1988), p. 72.
7. Winston S. Churchill, *The Second World War, Volume 1: The Gathering Storm* (Cassell & Co.: London: 1950), p. 45.
8. Winston S. Churchill to Stanley Baldwin, 27 January 1931. CAC, The Papers of Sir Winston Churchill, CHAR 2/572/76.
9. Harold Nicolson Diary, 28 January 1931. Nigel Nicolson (ed.), *Harold Nicolson: Diaries and Letters, 1930–1939* (Collins: London: 1966) p. 67.
10. Nancy Astor to Winston S. Churchill, 13 March 1931. CAC, The Papers of Sir Winston Churchill, CHAR 2/572/29.
11. Winston S. Churchill to Nancy Astor, 14 March 1931. Ibid., CHAR 2/572/26.
12. 'Mr Churchill's Position', *The Times*, 4 April 1931, p. 10.
13. Stanley Baldwin to Winston S. Churchill, 6 April 1931. CAC, The Papers of Sir Winston Churchill, CHAR 2/572/246.
14. Churchill, *The Second World War, Volume 1*, p. 47.
15. Interview with Grace Hamblin (Secretary to Winston S. Churchill 1932–38, Secretary to Clementine Churchill 1939–65, First Administrator of Chartwell 1965–72). CAC, Churchill Oral History Collection, CHOH 1 HMBL – Tape 1, Side 1.

16. Winston S. Churchill, 'My New York Misadventure', *Daily Mail*, 4–5 January 1932.
17. Winston S. Churchill to Maurice Ashley, 1 June 1932. CAC, The Papers of Sir Winston Churchill, CHAR 8/307/35.
18. Churchill, *The Second World War: Volume 1*, p. 82.
19. Winston S. Churchill to Keith Feiling, 19 September 1932. CAC, The Papers of Sir Winston Churchill, CHAR 8/207/122.
20. Sarah Churchill to Eleanor Sotheron-Estcourt, September 1932. CAC, Miscellaneous Holdings, MISC 108/3.
21. Ibid.
22. Churchill, *The Second World War, Volume 1*, p. 65.
23. Randolph S. Churchill, writing for the *Sunday Graphic*, 31 July 1932. In Randolph S. Churchill, *Twenty-One Years* (Riverside Press: Cambridge: 1965), p. 124.
24. Winston S. Churchill recalls in *The Gathering Storm* that they stayed at the Regina Hotel during their time in Munich. Letters written by members of Churchill's party on Grand Hotel Continental headed paper indicate that Hanfstaengl's recollection is correct. See letters from Sarah Churchill to Eleanor Sotheron-Estcourt in CAC, Miscellaneous Holdings, MISC 108/3.
25. Foreign Office Memorandum entitled 'Unity Mitford', undated. The National Archives (hereafter TNA), KV 2/882, p. 37a.
26. Ernst Hanfstaengl, *Zwischen Weißem und Braunem Haus* (R. Piper & Co.: Munich: 1970), p. 274.
27. Blaine Taylor, *Hitler's Headquarters: From Beer Hall to Bunker, 1920–1945* (Potomac Books: Washington, DC: 2007), p. 4.
28. Hanfstaengl, *Zwischen Weißem und Braunem Haus*, p. 274.
29. Ibid., p. 275.
30. 'Germany before the Elections: I. Hitler – Pen-Portrait of a Demagogue', *Sunday Express*, 22 July 1932, p. 9.
31. Hanfstaengl, *Zwischen Weißem und Braunem Haus*, p. 275.
32. Ibid., p. 276.
33. Churchill, *The Second World War: Volume 1*, p. 83.
34. Ernst Hanfstaengl, *Hitler: The Memoir of a Nazi Insider Who Turned against the Führer* (Arcade Publishing: New York: 2011), p. 185.
35. Hanfstaengl, *Zwischen Weißem und Braunem Haus*, p. 276.
36. Hanfstaengl, *Hitler: The Memoir of a Nazi Insider*, p. 186.
37. 'Women around Hitler', Intelligence Report. 25 February 1946. Cabinet Office – Enemy Documents Section: Folder 1 – Adolf Hitler: 1922–1936. TNA, WO 208/4475, p. 5.
38. Ibid., p. 7.
39. Hanfstaengl, *Hitler: The Memoir of a Nazi Insider*, p. 186.
40. Hanfstaengl, *Zwischen Weißem und Braunem Haus*, pp. 276–77.
41. Ibid.
42. Mary Soames, *A Daughter's Tale: The Memoir of Winston Churchill's Youngest Child* (Doubleday: London: 2011), p. 79.
43. Mary Soames, 'Rough notes of speech made at Chartwell press conference', June 1966. CAC, The Papers of Lady Soames, MCHL 7/1.
44. Hamblin, 'Chartwell Memories'.
45. Winston S. Churchill to Charles Scribner, 14 September 1932. CAC, The Papers of Sir Winston Churchill, CHAR 8/314/28.

46. Violet Pearman to Sir Alfred Knox, 28 September 1932. Ibid., CHAR 2/189/105.
47. 'Personalities of the Week: People in the Public Eye', *Illustrated London News* (Saturday 15 October 1932), p. 582.
48. Winston S. Churchill to Violet Bonham Carter, 7 October 1932. Bodleian Archives & Manuscripts, Papers of Lady Violet Bonham Carter, MS. Bonham Carter 165.
49. Grace Hamblin interview conducted by Robin Bryer, March 1980. National Trust.
50. Winston S. Churchill, speaking in 'King's Speech: Debate on the Address', 23 November 1932. Hansard, 5th Series, Vol. 272, cc74–92.
51. Ibid.
52. Ibid.

Chapter 1: Sounding the Alarm

1. Sarah Churchill to Eleanor Sotheron-Estcourt, September 1932. CAC, Miscellaneous Holdings, MISC 108/3.
2. Ibid., MISC 108/4.
3. Clementine Churchill to Winston S. Churchill, 20 or 27 July 1921. In Mary Soames (ed.), *Speaking for Themselves: The Personal Letters of Winston and Clementine Churchill* (Black Swan: London: 1999), p. 239.
4. Philip Tilden, *True Remembrances: The Memoirs of an Architect* (Country Life: London: 1954), p. 116.
5. Grace Hamblin interview conducted by Pat Ackerman. CAC, Churchill Oral History Collection, CHOH 1 HMBL – Tape 1, Side 2.
6. Clementine Churchill to Winston S. Churchill, 29 January 1923. CAC, The Papers of Clementine Ogilvy Spencer-Churchill, Baroness Spencer-Churchill of Chartwell, CSCT 1/12/1–3.
7. Winston S. Churchill to Clementine Churchill, 2 September 1923. In Mary Soames, *Clementine Churchill* (Doubleday: London: 2003), p. 252.
8. Winston S. Churchill to Philip Tilden, 5 April 1925. CAC, The Papers of Sir Winston Churchill, CHAR 1/395/77–78.
9. Note of telephone conversation between Winston S. Churchill's secretary (unnamed) and Philip Tilden's secretary (unnamed), 24 October 1927. Ibid., CHAR 1/395/120–121.
10. Sarah Churchill to Eleanor Sotheron-Estcourt, 6 July 1932. CAC, Miscellaneous Holdings, MISC 108/3.
11. Jack Fishman, *My Darling Clementine: The Story of Lady Churchill* (David McKay Company: New York: 1963), p. 306.
12. Sarah Churchill, *A Thread in the Tapestry* (Andre Deutsch: London: 1977), p. 38.
13. Soames, *Clementine Churchill*, p. 254.
14. Sarah Churchill to Eleanor Sotheron-Estcourt. CAC, Miscellaneous Holdings, MISC 108/4.
15. Winston S. Churchill to Louis Alber, 20 November 1932. Alber Papers. In Martin Gilbert (ed.), *The Churchill Documents, Volume 12: The Wilderness Years, 1929–1935* (Hillsdale College Press: Hillsdale, MI: 2012), p. 495.
16. Grace Hamblin interview conducted by Pat Ackerman. CAC, Churchill Oral History Collection, CHOH 1 HMBL – Tape 1, Side 1.

17. Samuel Howes, 'Samuel M. Howes: Recollections', letter to Martin Gilbert. In Gilbert (ed.), *The Churchill Documents, Volume 12*, p. 503.
18. Winston S. Churchill, 'Let Us Have Peace', *Daily Mail*, 17 October 1932.
19. Winston S. Churchill, Daily Mail Article Draft Notes, 17 October 1932. CAC, The Papers of Sir Winston Churchill, CHAR 8/317/101.
20. Stanley Baldwin, 'A Fear for the Future', Speech before the House of Commons, 10 November 1932. Hansard, 5th Series, Vol. 270, c632.
21. Martin Ceadel, 'The King and Country Debate, 1933: Student Politics, Pacifism and the Dictators', *Historical Journal*, Vol. 22, No. 2 (1979), pp. 397–422.
22. Martin Gilbert, *Prophet of Truth: Winston S. Churchill, 1922–1939* (Minerva: London: 1990), p. 456.
23. Albert Einstein to Frederick Lindemann, 1 May 1933. Nuffield College Archives, The Papers of F. A. Lindemann, Viscount Cherwell of Oxford, CHERWELL+D.57.11.
24. Frederick Lindemann to Albert Einstein, 4 May 1933. Ibid.
25. Albert Einstein. Interview with *New York Times*, 12 December 1930. In David E. Rowe and Robert Schulmann (eds), *Einstein on Politics: His Private Thoughts and Public Stands on Nationalism, Zionism, War, Peace and the Bomb* (Princeton University Press: Princeton, NJ: 2013), p. 238.
26. Albert Einstein to Margarete Lenbach, 27 February 1933. In Otto Nathan and Heinz Norden (eds), *Einstein on Peace* (Simon and Schuster: New York: 1960), p. 210.
27. Albert Einstein interview conducted by Evelyn Seeley, *New York Times*, 10 March 1933. In Ronald W. Clark, *Einstein: The Life and Times* (Hodder and Stoughton: London: 1973), p. 436.
28. Oliver Locker-Lampson to Albert Einstein, 25 March 1933. In Andrew Robinson, *Einstein on the Run: How Britain Saved the World's Greatest Scientist* (Yale University Press: New Haven and London: 2019), p. 209.
29. Albert Einstein to Max Born, 30 May 1933. In Max Born, *The Born–Einstein Letters: Correspondence between Albert Einstein and Max and Hedwig Born from 1916 to 1955 with Commentaries by Max Born* (Macmillan: London: 1971), p. 112.
30. Conversation between Adolf Hitler and Carl Bosch, May 1933. In Richard Willstätter, *Aus meinem Leben: von Arbeit, Muße und Freunden* (Verlag Chemie: Weinheim: 1949), p. 273.
31. Albert Einstein to Professor Frederick Lindemann, 1 May 1933. Nuffield College Archives, The Papers of F. A. Lindemann, Viscount Cherwell of Oxford, CHERWELL+D.57.1.
32. Churchill, *The Second World War, Volume 1*, p. 80.
33. Maurice Ashley, speaking to the International Churchill Society, 19 August 1989. *Proceedings of the International Churchill Societies 1988–89* (International Churchill Society: 1990).
34. 'Within Sight of St Paul's', *Winnipeg Tribune*, 16 March 1933, p. 17.
35. Maurice Ashley, speaking to the International Churchill Society, 19 August 1989. *Proceedings of the International Churchill Societies 1988–89* (International Churchill Society: 1990).
36. Hugh Martin, *Battle: The Life Story of the Rt Hon. Winston S. Churchill* (Sampson Low, Marston & Co: London: 1932), p. 138.

37. Winston S. Churchill to W. R. D. Perkins, 10 April 1933. CAC, The Papers of Sir Winston Churchill, CHAR 2/193/32.
38. Lord Linlithgow to Winston S. Churchill, 1 May 1933. Ibid., CHAR 2/193/67–68.
39. Violet Pearman to Winston S. Churchill. Notes of Telephone Message from Lord Lloyd. 20 April 1933. CAC, Churchill Papers, 2/197/28.
40. C. H. Arnold. In Jean Medawar and David Pyke, *Hitler's Gift: The True Story of the Scientists Expelled by the Nazi Regime* (Arcade Publishing: New York: 2012), p. 43.
41. Winston S. Churchill, Parliamentary Debates, *Hansard*, 13 April 1933. In Martin Gilbert, *Churchill and the Jews* (Henry Holt & Co: New York: 2007), p. 100.
42. Grace Hamblin interview conducted by Pat Ackerman. CAC, Churchill Oral History Collection, CHOH 1 HMBL – Tape 1, Side 2.
43. Ibid.
44. Robinson, *Einstein on the Run*, p. 235.
45. Albert Einstein writing to Lionel Ettinger, 20 July 1933. Shapell Manuscript Foundation, SMC 794.
46. Albert Einstein in conversation with students at Oxford University, which was later disclosed to the author. In R. F. Harrod, *A Personal Memoir of Lord Cherwell* (Macmillan & Co.: London: 1959), p. 48.
47. Ibid., p. 49.
48. S. Churchill, *A Thread in the Tapestry*, p. 38.
49. Ibid., p. 37.
50. Oliver Locker-Lampson to Frederick Lindemann, 20 July 1933. Nuffield College Archives, The Papers of F. A. Lindemann, Viscount Cherwell of Oxford, CHERWELL+D.57.22.
51. Albert Einstein to Mileva Einstein, 19 July 1933. Private Collection.
52. Albert Einstein to Lionel Ettlinger, 20 July 1933. Shapell Manuscript Foundation, SMC 794.
53. Adolf Hitler, Speech to the German Reichstag, 17 May 1933, Concerning the German Government's Desire for Peace. In *Völkischer Beobachter*, Berlin, 18 May 1933.
54. Ibid.
55. Albert Einstein to Professor Frederick Lindemann, 7 May 1933. Nuffield College Archives, The Papers of F. A. Lindemann, Viscount Cherwell of Oxford, CHERWELL+D.57.12.
56. Clementine Churchill to Margery Street, 9 June 1933. CAC, The Papers of Lady Soames, MCHL 5/1/78.
57. Winston S. Churchill to Charles Spencer Churchill, 18 July 1933. CAC, The Papers of Sir Winston Churchill, CHAR 8/323/52.
58. R. Churchill, *Twenty-One Years*, p. 108.
59. Thornton Butterworth to Winston S. Churchill, 19 September 1932. CAC, The Papers of Sir Winston Churchill, CHAR 8/312/109.
60. S. Churchill, *A Thread in the Tapestry*, p. 22.
61. Michael Hardwick and Mollie Hardwick, *Writers' Houses: A Literary Journey in England* (Phoenix House: London: 1968), p. 29.
62. J. Glasspool and W. L. Andrew, 'The Exceptional Summer of 1933', *Quarterly Journal of the Royal Meteorological Society* (Jan. 1934), p. 29.

63. Sarah Churchill to Eleanor Sotheron-Estcourt, 6 August 1932. CAC, Miscellaneous Holdings, MISC 108/3.
64. Clementine Churchill to Margery Street, 7 September 1933. CAC, The Papers of Lady Soames, MCHL 5/1/78.
65. Maurice Hankey to Henry Hankey, 22 October 1933. CAC, The Papers of Adeline, Lady Hankey, AHKY 1/1/45.
66. Clementine Churchill to Margery Street, 7 September 1933. CAC. The Papers of Lady Soames, MCHL 5/1/78.
67. Soames, *A Daughter's Tale*, p. 51.
68. Author interview with Annie Gray, author of *Victory in the Kitchen: The Life of Churchill's Cook* (Profile Books: London: 2020), 30 June 2023.
69. Grace Hamblin interview conducted by Robin Bryer, March 1980. National Trust.
70. Fishman, *My Darling Clementine*, p. 532.
71. Maria Floris, *Bakery: Cakes and Simple Confectionery* (Wine and Food Society: London: 1968), p. 67.
72. Clementine Churchill to Margery Street, 7 September 1933. CAC, The Papers of Lady Soames, MCHL 5/1/78.
73. Winston S. Churchill to Clementine Churchill, 8 March 1935. CAC, The Papers of Clementine Ogilvy Spencer-Churchill, Baroness Spencer-Churchill of Chartwell, CSCT 2/25/58–61.
74. Soames, *A Daughter's Tale*, p. 27.
75. William Manchester, *The Caged Lion: Winston Spencer Churchill, 1932–1940* (Pan Macmillan: London: 1988), p. 7.
76. Martin Gilbert, *Winston S. Churchill. Companion Volume V. Part 3: The Coming of War, 1936–1939* (Houghton Mifflin Company: Boston, MA: 1983), p. 338.
77. Soames, *Clementine Churchill*, p. 342.
78. *Daily Mirror*, 25 July 1933, p. 3.
79. Grace Hamblin interview conducted by Pat Ackerman. CAC, Churchill Oral History Collection, CHOH 1 HMBL – Tape 1, Side 1.
80. Grace Hamblin interview conducted by Robin Bryer, March 1980. National Trust.
81. Account told by Lady Soames to Chartwell staff.
82. Albert Einstein to Alfred Nahon, 20 July 1933. In Clark, *Einstein: The Life and Times*, p. 459.
83. Dr Ernst Neyman, correspondence with the Prussian Academy of Sciences. In Albert Einstein (trans. A. Harris), *The World As I See It* (Covici Friede: New York: 1934), pp. 85–6.
84. Reference to Albert Einstein's anxieties about his deficiencies in English in the late 1920s, and letters declining invitations due to his limited English around this time: see Robert Fox, 'Einstein in Oxford', *Notes and Records: The Royal Society Journal of the History of Science*, Vol. 72, No. 3 (May 2018), pp. 293–318.
85. Albert Einstein to Elsa Einstein, 22 July 1933. In Albrecht Fölsing, *Albert Einstein: A Biography* (Viking: London: 1997), p. 677.
86. Ibid.
87. John Spencer Churchill, 'Painting for Uncle Winston', *The Atlantic* (January 1962).
88. Fishman, *My Darling Clementine*, p. 306.
89. Clementine Churchill to Margery Street, 7 September 1933. CAC, The Papers of Lady Soames, MCHL 5/1/78.

90. Soames, *A Daughter's Tale*, p. 62.
91. Albert Einstein to Elsa Einstein, 22 July 1933. In Fölsing, *Albert Einstein: A Biography*, p. 677.
92. Oliver Locker-Lampson, 'Nationality of Jews', 26 July 1933. Hansard, 5th Series, Vol. 280, c2604.
93. 'London Day by Day: Dr Einstein's Departure', *Daily Telegraph*, 28 July 1933, p. 12.
94. Albert Einstein to Professor Frederick Lindemann, 22 January 1935. Nuffield College Archives, The Papers of F. A. Lindemann, Viscount Cherwell of Oxford, CHERWELL+D.57.27.
95. Winston S. Churchill speaking at Theydon Bois Fete, 12 August 1933. CAC, The Papers of Sir Winston Churchill, CHAR 9/106/21–25.
96. Ibid.
97. Albert Einstein to Elsa Einstein, 10 September 1933. The Albert Einstein Archives at the Hebrew University of Jerusalem: 143–260.
98. 'Professor Einstein's Meeting', *The Times*, 28 September 1933, p. 12.
99. 'An Unwise Agitation', *Daily Mail*, 26 September 1933, p. 10.
100. 'Stop this Fooling', *Evening News*, 3 October 1933, p. 8.
101. 'Science and Civilisation', speech given at the Royal Albert Hall on 3 October 1933. Special Collections at Bodleian Library, Oxford University Library Services.

Chapter 2: Defence Against the Sky

1. Mary Soames, 'Rough notes of speech made at Chartwell press conference', June 1966. CAC, The Papers of Lady Soames, MCHL 7/1.
2. Kathleen Hill interview conducted by Pat Ackerman. CAC, Churchill Oral History Collection, CHOH 1 KHLL – Tape 1, Side 1.
3. Clementine Churchill to Margery Street, 7 September 1933. CAC, The Papers of Lady Soames, MCHL 5/1/78.
4. Footage shown on *Britain in Color. Episode 3: Churchill*. Smithsonian Channel. Aired 12 November 2019.
5. S. Churchill, *A Thread in the Tapestry*, pp. 48–9.
6. Clementine Churchill to Margery Street, 30 November 1933. CAC, The Papers of Lady Soames, MCHL 5/1/78.
7. Grace Hamblin interview conducted by Robin Bryer, March 1980. National Trust.
8. John Pearson, *The Private Lives of Winston Churchill* (Simon & Schuster: New York: 1991), p. 247.
9. Clement Attlee, 6 February 1934, speaking in 'Disarmament' debate. Hansard, 5th Series, Vol, 285, cc1003–1004.
10. Referenced in '1935 Defence Policy Review'. TNA, Records of the Air Ministry, AIR 20/32.
11. Lord Londonderry, Cabinet Minutes, 28 February 1934. TNA, Cabinet Papers, 23/78/7.
12. T. E. Lawrence to Ralph D. Blumenfeld, 11 November 1922. Bodleian Archives & Manuscripts, Lawrence Papers, CV4/3, p. 2122.
13. Winston S. Churchill, *Proceedings at the Unveiling of the Memorial to Lawrence of Arabia, 3 October 1936* (J. Thornton & Son: Oxford: 1937), p. 9.

14. T. E Lawrence to Robert Graves, December 1920. In David Garnett (ed.), *The Letters of T. E. Lawrence* (Jonathan Cape: London: 1938), p. 324.
15. B. H. Liddell Hart, *T. E. Lawrence: In Arabia and After* (Jonathan Cape: London: 1936), p. 409.
16. Winston S. Churchill to Clementine Churchill, 16 February 1921. In Andrew R. B. Simpson, *Another Life: Lawrence after Arabia* (Spellmount: Stroud: 2008), p. 50.
17. Clementine Churchill to Winston S. Churchill, 18 February 1921. In Soames (ed.), *Speaking for Themselves*, p. 231.
18. A. W. Lawrence (ed.), *T. E. Lawrence by his Friends* (Jonathan Cape: London: 1935), p. 302.
19. T. E. Lawrence to Sir John Shuckburgh, 4 July 1922. In Garnett (ed.), *The Letters of T. E. Lawrence*, p. 344.
20. Liddell Hart, *T. E. Lawrence*, p. 415.
21. A. W. Lawrence (ed.), *T. E. Lawrence by his Friends*, p. 19.
22. Recollections of 'N.W.D.', Bovington Camp Archive Library, deposited in 1982.
23. Garnett (ed.), *The Letters of T. E. Lawrence*, p. 324.
24. T. E. Lawrence to John Buchan, 21 March 1930. In ibid., p. 686.
25. T. E. Lawrence to Charlotte Shaw, 1 November 1926. In Jeremy Wilson and Nicole Wilson (eds), *T. E. Lawrence: Correspondence with Bernard and Charlotte Shaw* (Castle Hill Press: Fordingbridge: 2000), p. 207.
26. Ibid., p. 163.
27. Winston S. Churchill, *Great Contemporaries* (Thornton Butterworth: London: 1939), p. 161.
28. T. E. Shaw to H. S. Ede, 5 April 1935. In Ronald Blyth, *The Age of Illusion: England in the Twenties and Thirties: 1919–1940* (Hamish Hamilton: London: 1963), p. 77.
29. T. E. Shaw to Winston S. Churchill, 12 December 1933. In Garnett (ed.), *The Letters of T. E. Lawrence*, p. 781.
30. T. E. Shaw to Winston S. Churchill, 12 December 1933. Magdalen College Oxford, Papers of Jeremy Wilson, P450/R/REM/3/95 – Nov 1933 – Dec 1933.
31. Ibid.
32. Grace Hamblin interview conducted by Robin Bryer, March 1980. National Trust.
33. Grace Hamblin interview conducted by Pat Ackerman. CAC, Churchill Oral History Collection, CHOH 1 HMBL – Tape 1, Side 2.
34. 'Secretaries of Famous Men', *Sunday Express*, 25 March 1934. In Martin Gilbert (ed.), *The Churchill Documents, Volume 13: The Coming of War, 1936–1939* (Hillsdale College Press: Hillsdale, MI: 2012), pp. 77–78.
35. Winston S. Churchill to T. E. Shaw, 15 December 1933. Magdalen College Oxford, Papers of Jeremy Wilson, P450/R/REM/3/95 – Nov 1933 – Dec 1933.
36. Grace Hamblin interview conducted by Pat Ackerman. CAC, Churchill Oral History Collection, CHOH 1 HMBL – Tape 1, Side 2.
37. Soames, *Clementine Churchill*, p. 263.
38. Hibbert, 'My War Years', via https://www.bbc.co.uk/history/ww2peopleswar/ stories/55/a2759655.shtml. Permission for use kindly given by Mrs Gwen Hibbert.

39. Janet Wallach, *Desert Queen: The Extraordinary Life of Gertrude Bell, Adventurer, Adviser to Kings, Ally of Lawrence of Arabia* (Anchor Books: New York: 2005), p. 300.
40. Fishman, *My Darling Clementine*, p. 67.
41. T. E. Shaw to Clementine Churchill, 17 December 1933. In Soames, *A Daughter's Tale*, p. 82.
42. Winston S. Churchill to Stanley Baldwin, 3 January 1934. Baldwin Papers. In Gilbert (ed.), *The Churchill Documents, Volume 12*, p. 695.
43. T. E. Shaw to Clementine Churchill, 17 January 1934. CAC, The Papers of Clementine Ogilvy Spencer-Churchill, Baroness Spencer-Churchill of Chartwell, CSCT 3/27.
44. Ibid.
45. T. E. Shaw to Clementine Churchill, 10 February 1934. Ibid.
46. Translated quotations from Adolf Hitler, *Mein Kampf* (Verlag Franz Eher Nachfolger: Munich: 1925). CAC, The Papers of Sir Winston Churchill, CHAR 2/293/26.
47. Reginald Clarry, speaking in 'Inadequate defences of Great Britain and the Empire from Foreign Attacks' debate, 7 February 1934. Hansard, 5th Series, Vol. 285, cc1145–1148.
48. Winston S. Churchill, speaking in 'Inadequate defences of Great Britain and the Empire from Foreign Attacks' debate, 7 February 1934. Hansard, 5th Series, Vol. 285, cc1197–1209.
49. Austen Chamberlain to Hilda Chamberlain, 15 February 1934. In Charles Petrie (ed.), *The Life and Letters of the Right Hon. Sir Austen Chamberlain* (Cassell: London: 1939), p. 408.
50. Spencer Churchill, 'Painting for Uncle Winston'.
51. Ibid.
52. 'Oxford University Conservative Association: Questions to Mr Winston Churchill', Richard Storry papers. In Gilbert (ed.), *The Churchill Documents, Volume 12*, p. 727.
53. Ibid.
54. T. E. Lawrence to R. A. Guy, 18 February 1934. Magdalen College Oxford, Papers of Jeremy Wilson, P450/R/REM/3/96 – Jan 1934 – Apr 1934.
55. T. E. Lawrence to Lady Astor, 21 February 1934. Ibid.
56. Clare Sydney Smith, *The Golden Reign: The Story of my Friendship with 'Lawrence of Arabia'* (Cassell & Co.: London: 1949), p. 8.
57. T. E. Shaw to B. E. Leeson, 21 December 1933. Magdalen College Oxford, Papers of Jeremy Wilson, P450/R/REM/3/95 – Nov 1933 – Dec 1933.
58. Archibald Sinclair to Winston S. Churchill, 22 January 1928. CAC, The Papers of Sir Winston Churchill, CHAR 1/199/10.
59. Grace Hamblin interview conducted by Pat Ackerman. CAC, Churchill Oral History Collection, CHOH 1 HMBL – Tape 2, Side 4.
60. Celia Sandys, *Churchill's Little Redhead* (Fonthill: London: 2021), p. 28.
61. Clementine Churchill to Winston S. Churchill, 27 December 1937. CAC, The Papers of Sir Winston Churchill, CHAR 1/322/12–15.
62. Soames, *A Daughter's Tale*, p. 80.
63. Ibid.
64. Eleanor Morris-Keating, article sent to *Tatler* magazine about Sarah Churchill, April 1983. CAC, Miscellaneous Holdings, MISC 108/7.

65. Simpson, *Another Life*, p. 192.
66. R. Meinertzhagen, *Middle East Diary: 1917–1956* (Cresset Press: London: 1959), p. 33.
67. Smith, *The Golden Reign*, p. 35.
68. Major Francis Charles Claypon Yeats-Brown to T. E. Lawrence, 7 February 1934. Magdalen College Oxford, Papers of Jeremy Wilson, P450/R/REM/3/96 – Jan 1934 – Apr 1934.
69. T. E. Lawrence to Lionel Curtis, 19 March 1934. Ibid.
70. Martin Gilbert, *Winston S. Churchill: 1922–1939* (Houghton Mifflin: London: 1966), p. 707.
71. Based on a letter sent from T. E. Lawrence to Clementine Churchill, with note 'Probably after Feb '34 visit'. CAC, The Papers of Clementine Ogilvy Spencer-Churchill, Baroness Spencer-Churchill of Chartwell, CSCT 3/27.
72. Diana Cooper to Conrad Russell, 14 September 1934. CAC, The Papers of Lady Diana Cooper, DIAC 1/1/3.
73. Diana Cooper, *The Light of Common Day: Autobiography* (Century Publishing: London: 1984), p. 153.
74. Eleanor Morris-Keating, article sent to *Tatler* magazine about Sarah Churchill, April 1983. CAC, Miscellaneous Holdings, MISC 108/7.
75. Ibid.
76. David Garnett, 'Notes from David Garnett Lecture – Given in 1964 at Texas University and Davis College, Sacramento, California'. Magdalen College Oxford, Papers of Jeremy Wilson, P450.
77. T. E. Lawrence to Clementine Churchill, date unknown, 'Probably after Feb '34 visit'. CAC, The Papers of Clementine Ogilvy Spencer-Churchill, Baroness Spencer-Churchill of Chartwell, CSCT 3/27.
78. T. E. Lawrence to Lionel Curtis, 19 March 1934. Magdalen College Oxford, Papers of Jeremy Wilson, P450/R/REM/3/96 – Jan 1934 – Apr 1934.
79. Ibid.
80. T. E. Lawrence to Ernest Haik Riddall Altounyan, 16 January 1934. Ibid.
81. Grace Hamblin interview conducted by Robin Bryer, March 1980. National Trust.
82. Maurice Ashley, speaking to the International Churchill Society, 19 August 1989. *Proceedings of the International Churchill Societies 1988–89* (International Churchill Society: 1990).
83. Soames, *A Daughter's Tale*, p. 80.
84. Eleanor Morris-Keating, article sent to *Tatler* magazine about Sarah Churchill, April 1983. CAC, Miscellaneous Holdings, MISC 108/7.
85. Grace Hamblin interview conducted by Robin Bryer, March 1980. National Trust.
86. Smith, *The Golden Reign*, p. 38.
87. T. E. Shaw to Clementine Churchill, 17 December 1933. In Soames, *A Daughter's Tale*, p. 81.
88. T. E. Lawrence to Nancy Astor, 31 December 1933. Magdalen College Oxford, Papers of Jeremy Wilson, P450/R/REM/3/95 – Nov 1933 – Dec 1933.
89. Grace Hamblin interview conducted by Robin Bryer, March 1980. National Trust.
90. Spencer Churchill, 'Painting for Uncle Winston'.

91. T. E. Lawrence to Clementine Churchill, date unknown, 'Probably after Feb '34 visit'. CAC, The Papers of Clementine Ogilvy Spencer-Churchill, Baroness Spencer-Churchill of Chartwell, CSCT 3/27.
92. Ibid.
93. Otto C. Pickhardt, prescription for Winston S. Churchill, 26 January 1932. In Max Arthur, *Churchill: The Life – An Authorised Pictorial Biography* (Octopus Publishing Group: London: 2015), p. 153.
94. T. E. Lawrence to Lionel Curtis, 19 March 1934. Magdalen College Oxford, Papers of Jeremy Wilson, P450/R/REM/3/96 – Jan 1934 – Apr 1934.
95. Winston S. Churchill, speaking in 'Air Estimates' debate, 8 March 1934. Hansard, 5th Series, Vol. 286, cc2027–89.
96. Ibid.
97. Winston S. Churchill to Sir Samuel Hoare, 11 March 1934. In Martin Gilbert, *Churchill: A Life* (Minerva: London: 1992), p. 527.
98. T. E. Lawrence to Philip Sassoon, 20 November 1934. TNA, Records of the Air Ministry, AIR 1/2703.
99. T. E. Lawrence to Philip Sassoon, 7 December 1934. Ibid.
100. T. E. Lawrence to Winston S. Churchill, 22 March 1935. CAC, The Papers of Sir Winston Churchill, CHAR 1/270/104.
101. T. E. Shaw to Nancy Astor, 8 May 1935. In Andrew Norman, *T. E. Lawrence: Unravelling the Enigma* (Halsgrove: Tiverton: 2003), p. 123.
102. H. Montgomery Hyde, *Solitary in the Ranks: Lawrence of Arabia as Airman and Private Soldier* (Atheneum: New York: 1978), p. 253.
103. Winston S. Churchill, eulogy notice in *The Times*, 20 May 1935, p. 16.
104. 'Books at Clouds Hill'. In A. W. Lawrence (ed.), *T. E. Lawrence by his Friends*, p. 482.

Chapter 3: The Anglo-American Disagreement

1. Winston S. Churchill, 11 September 1935. In Vincent Sheean, *Between the Thunder and the Sun* (Macmillan & Co.: London: 1944), p. 44.
2. Rose Kennedy, 'Visit to Churchills at Westerham, Kent', 1935 [misdated 1933, 1936 and 1937], John F. Kennedy Presidential Library, Rose Fitzgerald Kennedy Personal Papers, p. 2.
3. In the early 1930s, the BBC excluded Members of Parliament from broadcasting speeches unless they were nominated by either the leaders of political parties or the party whips. Because Churchill was out of political favour, and often held opposing views to the leaders of the Conservative Party, this effectively blocked his access to a rapidly growing number of radio listeners in Britain. In a letter in 1933, Churchill called it 'an entirely new principle of discrimination in British public life'. As a result, between June 1929 and September 1939, Churchill only spoke 11 times on the BBC, which included two appeals for charitable causes. After January 1935, he spoke more on international radio stations than the BBC.
4. Winston S. Churchill, 'We lie within a few minutes' striking distance' speech, 16 November 1934. In Winston S. Churchill (Jnr) (ed.), *Never Give In!: The Best of Winston Churchill's Speeches* (Pimlico: London: 2004), p. 109.
5. Harold Balfour to Winston S. Churchill, 17 November 1934. CAC, The Papers of Sir Winston Churchill, CHAR 2/210/38.

6. Violet Pearman to Hilda Neal, 2 April 1934. CAC, Other Deposited Collections, WCHL 1/23.
7. Ibid.
8. 'Memories of Winston Churchill in the 1930s'. Recollections by Joyce Morgan (née Cutting), shared by her daughters. CAC, Other Deposited Collections, WCHL 1/23.
9. Grace Hamblin, 'Chartwell Memories', speaking at The Adolphus, Dallas, Texas, 30 October 1987. CAC, The Papers of Grace Hamblin, HAMB 1/2.
10. Grace Hamblin, speaking at the Inner Wheel Club, 1974. CAC, The Papers of Grace Hamblin, HAMB 1/1.
11. Grace Hamblin interview conducted by Pat Ackerman. CAC, Churchill Oral History Collection, CHOH 1 HMBL – Tape 1, Side 1.
12. Winston S. Churchill, 'Debate On The Address', 28 November 1934. Hansard, 5th Series, Vol. 295, cc857–983.
13. Harold A. Albert, 'The Diary of a Modern Young Man', Sunday Mercury, 9 December 1934, p. 4.
14. Ibid.
15. Both Winston and Clementine Churchill had been invited by their friend Lord Moyne to join him on an expedition to capture and deliver a number of Komodo dragon lizards for London Zoo. As the journey was expected to take four months, Churchill declined as he could not afford so long a period away from his political and literary obligations. For Clementine it became the adventure of a lifetime and lasted from 18 December 1934 until 2 May 1935.
16. Clementine Churchill to Winston S. Churchill, 18 December 1934. In Soames (ed.), Speaking for Themselves, p. 363.
17. Clementine Churchill to Violet Pearman, 29 December 1934. CAC, The Papers of Sir Winston Churchill, CHAR 1/256/132.
18. Winston S. Churchill to Clementine Churchill, 31 December 1934. Ibid., CHAR 1/273/62.
19. Winston S. Churchill to Lord Londonderry, 1 January 1935. Ibid., CHAR 2/243/1.
20. 'Mr Churchill Again to Rescue of Mary Smith', Evening Standard, 16 October 1934, p. 5.
21. Winston S. Churchill to Clementine Churchill, 'Chartwell Bulletin No. 3', 21 January 1935. CAC, The Papers of Clementine Ogilvy Spencer-Churchill, Baroness Spencer-Churchill of Chartwell, CSCT 2/25/18–19.
22. C. J. Hill, 'Great Britain and the Saar Plebiscite of 13 January 1935', Journal of Contemporary History, Vol. 9, No. 2 (April 1974), p. 121.
23. 'The Saar Votes to Go Back to Germany', China Weekly Review, Vol. 71, No. 8 (19 January 1935), p. 1.
24. Shiela Grant Duff, 'Saar Minority's Plight', The Observer, 20 January 1935. Bodleian Archives & Manuscripts, Archive of Shiela Grant Duff, MS. 9663/66.
25. Ibid.
26. Albert Einstein to Frederick Lindemann, 22 January 1935. Nuffield College Archives, The Papers of F. A. Lindemann, Viscount Cherwell of Oxford, CHERWELL+D.63.4.
27. Winston S. Churchill to Charles Colebaugh, 23 February 1932. CAC, The Papers of Sir Winston Churchill, CHAR 8/310/1–3.
28. Ibid.

29. Winston S. Churchill, 'While the World Watches', *Collier's Weekly*, 29 December 1934, p. 24.
30. Ibid.
31. Kay Halle, *Irrepressible Churchill* (World Publishing Company: Cleveland, OH: 1966), pp. 7–8.
32. Churchill, *The Second World War, Volume 1*, pp. 79–80.
33. S. Churchill, *A Thread in the Tapestry*, p. 32.
34. Winston S. Churchill, 'Chartwell Bulletin No. 8', 8 March 1935. CAC, The Papers of Clementine Ogilvy Spencer-Churchill, Baroness Spencer-Churchill of Chartwell, CSCT 2/25/60.
35. Winston S. Churchill, 'India "The Great Betrayal": A Broadcast Address', 30 January 1935. CAC, Other Deposited Collections, WCHL 4/15, 4/22, 4-26–28.
36. Sarah Churchill, *Keep on Dancing* (Coward, McCann & Geoghegan: New York: 1981), p. 43.
37. Winston S. Churchill, 'Chartwell Bulletin No. 10', 5 April 1935. CAC, The Papers of Clementine Ogilvy Spencer-Churchill, Baroness Spencer-Churchill of Chartwell, CSCT 2/25/70–76.
38. Martin Gilbert, *The Wilderness Years* (Houghton Mifflin Company: Boston, MA: 1982), p. 118.
39. Churchill, *The Second World War, Volume 1*, p. 81.
40. Gilbert, *The Wilderness Years*, p. 118.
41. 'Notes of Anglo-German conversations, held at the Chancellor's Palace, Berlin, on March 25 and 26, 1935', *Printed for the Cabinet*. TNA: Cabinet Papers, CAB/24/254, p. 4.
42. Ibid., p. 6.
43. Sir Herbert Samuel, speaking in 'Foreign Office' debate, 31 May 1935. Hansard, 5th Series, Vol. 302, c1428.
44. Winston S. Churchill to Clementine Churchill, 13 April 1935. CAC, The Papers of Clementine Ogilvy Spencer-Churchill, Baroness Spencer-Churchill of Chartwell, CSCT 2/25/80–88.
45. Adolf Hitler to Lord Rothermere, 3 May 1935. CAC, The Papers of Sir Winston Churchill, CHAR 2/235/71–78(English)/79–86(German).
46. Ibid.
47. Winston S. Churchill to Lord Rothermere, 12 May 1935. CAC, The Papers of Sir Winston Churchill, CHAR 2/235/90.
48. Stanley Baldwin, 'Defence Policy', 22 May 1935. Hansard, 5th Series, Vol. 302, cc359–486.
49. Winston S. Churchill, speaking in 'Foreign Office' debate, 31 May 1935. Hansard, 5th Series, Vol. 302, cc1423–1510.
50. Ibid.
51. Klaus Hildebrand, *The Foreign Policy of the Third Reich* (University of California Press: Berkeley, CA: 1973), p. 39.
52. Ralph Wigram to Winston S. Churchill, 18 June 1935. CAC, The Papers of Sir Winston Churchill, CHAR 2/236/64.
53. Winston S. Churchill, speaking at Harlow, 24 July 1935. In Churchill (Jnr) (ed.), *Never Give In!*, p. 119.
54. Winston S. Churchill to Ava Wigram, 2 July 1935. CAC, The Papers of Sir Winston Churchill, CHAR 1/271/85.

55. Richard Davenport-Hines, *Ettie: The Intimate Life and Dauntless Spirit of Lady Desborough* (Weidenfeld & Nicolson: London: 2008), p. 58.
56. Cecil Beaton, *The Glass of Fashion: A Personal History of Fifty Years of Changing Tastes and the People Who Have Inspired Them* (Weidenfeld & Nicolson: London: 1954), p. 351.
57. 'Frederick Peake Led Arab Legion', *New York Times*, 2 April 1970.
58. Grace Hamblin interview conducted by Pat Ackerman. CAC, Churchill Oral History Collection, CHOH 1 HMBL – Tape 1, Side 1.
59. Soames, *A Daughter's Tale*, p. 64.
60. G. D. Birla to M. K. Gandhi, 25 August 1935. Birla Papers. In Gilbert (ed.), *The Churchill Documents, Volume 12*, p. 1243.
61. Ibid.
62. Ibid.
63. Ibid., p. 1245.
64. Ibid.
65. Soames, *A Daughter's Tale*, p. 79.
66. Grace Hamblin interview conducted by Pat Ackerman. CAC, Churchill Oral History Collection, CHOH 1 HMBL – Tape 1, Side 2.
67. Clementine Churchill to Margery Street, 21 August 1935. In Soames, *Clementine Churchill*, p. 275.
68. Winston S. Churchill to Clementine Churchill, 1 September 1935. CAC, The Papers of Clementine Ogilvy Spencer-Churchill, Baroness Spencer-Churchill of Chartwell, CSCT 2/25/90.
69. Winston S. Churchill to Lord Winterton, 30 September 1935. In Gilbert, *Winston S. Churchill: 1922–1939*, p. 672.
70. Bernard Baruch to Winston S. Churchill, 25 September 1935. CAC, The Papers of Sir Winston Churchill, CHAR 2/237/59.
71. Winston S. Churchill to Joseph P. Kennedy, 27 September 1935. CAC, The Papers of Sir Winston Churchill, CHAR 2/237/58.
72. Memorandum of Arthur Krock, 2 July 1935. In Amanda Smith (ed.), *Hostage to Fortune: The Letters of Joseph P. Kennedy* (Viking: New York: 2001), pp. 155–6.
73. Joseph P. Kennedy to Cissy Patterson, 23 September 1935. Ibid., p. 160.
74. Joseph P. Kennedy to Franklin Roosevelt, 2 October 1935. Ibid., p. 161.
75. 'Note from Violet Pearman [Private Secretary to WSC] on 1st Lord Lloyd [of Dolobran]'s telephone call to arrange WSC's amendment to Sir Edward Grigg's resolution [at the Conservative Party Conference], on the Government's duty to provide adequate Armed Forces for defence' – 1 October 1935. CAC, The Papers of Sir Winston Churchill, CHAR 2/237/89.
76. Churchill, *The Second World War, Volume 1*, p. 155.
77. Ibid., p. 156.
78. Samuel Howes, 'Samuel M. Howes: Recollections', letter to Martin Gilbert. In Gilbert (ed.), *The Churchill Documents, Volume 12*, p. 503.
79. Grace Hamblin interview conducted by Pat Ackerman. CAC, Churchill Oral History Collection, CHOH 1 HMBL – Tape 1, Side 1.
80. 'Mr Baldwin's Speech', *The Times*, 5 October 1935, p. 13.
81. 'American Foreign Policy', ibid.
82. Grace Hamblin interview conducted by Pat Ackerman. CAC, Churchill Oral History Collection, CHOH 1 HMBL – Tape 1, Side 1.

83. Winston S. Churchill to Bernard Baruch, 5 October 1935. CAC, The Papers of Sir Winston Churchill, CHAR 1/272/19.
84. Rose Kennedy, 'Visit to Churchills at Westerham, Kent,' 1935 [misdated 1933, 1936 and 1937], John F. Kennedy Presidential Library, Rose Fitzgerald Kennedy Personal Papers, p. 1.
85. Clementine Churchill to Margery Street, 21 August 1935. CAC, The Papers of Lady Soames, MCHL 5/1/78. (Note: 8 stone 9lb is equal to 121lb or 55kg.)
86. Winston S. Churchill, 'Dissertation on Dining Room Chairs', 1922. CAC, The Papers of Sir Winston Churchill, CHAR 1/157/83-84.
87. Rose Kennedy, 'Visit to Churchills at Westerham, Kent,' 1935 [misdated 1933, 1936 and 1937], John F. Kennedy Presidential Library, Rose Fitzgerald Kennedy Personal Papers, p. 2.
88. Laurence Leamer, *The Kennedy Men: 1901–1963: The Laws of the Father* (Harper Perennial: New York: 2002), pp. 4–5.
89. Rose Kennedy, 'Visit to Churchills at Westerham, Kent', 1935 [misdated 1933, 1936 and 1937], John F. Kennedy Presidential Library, Rose Fitzgerald Kennedy Personal Papers, p. 2.
90. Ibid.
91. Ibid.
92. Winston S. Churchill, 'Painting as a Pastime', *Strand Magazine* (Jan. 1922) pp. 535–8. In CAC, The Papers of Sir Winston Churchill, CHAR 8/201/8–9.
93. Joseph P. Kennedy to Bernard Baruch, 9 October 1935. The Personal Papers of Joseph P. Kennedy, John F. Kennedy Presidential Library.
94. Winston S. Churchill to Joseph P. Kennedy, 12 October 1935. Ibid.
95. David Nasaw, *The Patriarch* (Penguin Press: New York: 2012), pp. 238–9.
96. Winston S. Churchill to Joseph P. Kennedy, 12 October 1935. The Personal Papers of Joseph P. Kennedy, John F. Kennedy Presidential Library.
97. Joseph P. Kennedy to Winston S. Churchill, 19 October 1935. Ibid.
98. Winston S. Churchill, 'To the Electors of the Epping Division of Essex', 28 October 1935, p. 2.
99. Ibid., p. 3.
100. Churchill, *The Second World War, Volume 1*, p. 66.
101. Joseph P. Kennedy. Diary entry, 5 October 1939. The Personal Papers of Joseph P. Kennedy, John F. Kennedy Presidential Library.

Chapter 4: The Case for France

1. Winston S. Churchill to Pierre-Étienne Flandin, 14 November 1945. CAC, The Papers of Sir Winston Churchill, CHUR 2/149/80–83.
2. James C. Robertson, 'The British General Election of 1935', *Journal of Contemporary History*, Vol. 9, No. 1 (Jan. 1974), p. 156.
3. Memo by Hugh Lloyd Thomas, 7 October 1935. TNA, Records of the Foreign Office, FO 371/19144. J5922/1/1.
4. Winston S. Churchill, 'The Truth about Hitler', *Strand Magazine* (Nov. 1935), pp. 10–21.
5. Ibid., p. 12.
6. Ibid., p. 15.
7. 'Mr Churchill's Article – Germany Deeply Offended', *The Argus* (Melbourne, Victoria), 1 November 1935, p. 9.

8. Harold Nicolson Diary, 21 November 1935. Nigel Nicolson (ed.), *Harold Nicolson: Diaries and Letters*, p. 228.
9. 'Mr R Churchill Fined – Motoring Offences', *Liverpool Daily Post*, 26 November 1935, p. 4.
10. Clementine Churchill to Margery Street, 30 December 1935. In Soames, *Clementine Churchill*, p. 276.
11. 'M. Flandin the Next Premier?', *Daily Telegraph*, 28 November 1933, p. 10.
12. Churchill, *The Second World War, Volume 1*, p. 77.
13. Winston S. Churchill, *While England Slept: A Survey of World Affairs, 1932–1938* (G. P. Putnam's Sons: New York: 1938), p. 63.
14. Winston and Clementine Churchill to Pierre-Étienne Flandin, 11 November 1934. CAC, The Papers of Sir Winston Churchill, CHAR 2/210/27.
15. John Gunther, *Inside Europe* (Harper & Brothers: New York: 1940), p. 196.
16. Winston S. Churchill to Pierre-Étienne Flandin, 23 July 1935. CAC, The Papers of Sir Winston Churchill, CHAR 2/236/146.
17. Ibid.
18. Winston S. Churchill to Ava Wigram, 2 July 1935. CAC, The Papers of Sir Winston Churchill, CHAR 1/271/85a.
19. Pierre-Étienne Flandin to Winston S. Churchill, 11 July 1935. Ibid., CHAR 2/236/119.
20. Pierre-Étienne Flandin to Winston S. Churchill, 18 November 1935. Ibid., CHAR 2/238/32.
21. Stanley Baldwin to Edward Winterton, 22 November 1935. Bodleian Archives & Manuscripts, Archive of Edward Turnour, 6th Earl Winterton, MS. 9663/66.
22. Winston S. Churchill to Pierre-Étienne Flandin, 26 November 1935. CAC, The Papers of Sir Winston Churchill, CHAR 2/238/65.
23. Ibid.
24. Ibid.
25. Pierre-Étienne Flandin to Winston S. Churchill, 29 November 1935. Ibid., CHAR 2/238/87.
26. Clementine Churchill to Margery Street, 7 December 1935. CAC, The Papers of Lady Soames, MCHL 5/1/78.
27. Randolph Churchill to Winston S. Churchill, 16 December 1935. CAC, The Papers of Randolph Churchill, RDCH 1/3/3.
28. Randolph Churchill to Winston S. Churchill, 17 December 1935. Ibid.
29. Winston S. Churchill to Clementine Churchill, 8 January 1936. CAC, The Papers of Clementine Ogilvy Spencer-Churchill, Baroness Spencer-Churchill of Chartwell, CSCT 2/26/1–7.
30. Winston S. Churchill to Clementine Churchill, 30 December 1935. Ibid., CSCT 2/25/101–102.
31. Ibid., CSCT 2/25/104.
32. Ibid., CSCT 2/25/104–105.
33. Clementine Churchill to Winston S. Churchill, 7 January 1936. Ibid., CSCT 1/21/3–4.
34. John Churchill, Duke of Marlborough. In Winston S. Churchill to Clementine Churchill, 8 January 1936. Ibid., CSCT 2/26/3.
35. Kathleen Hill interview conducted by Pat Ackerman. CAC, Churchill Oral History Collection, CHOH 1 KHLL – Tape 1, Side 1.

36. Winston S. Churchill to Clementine Churchill, 17 January 1936. CAC, The Papers of Clementine Ogilvy Spencer-Churchill, Baroness Spencer-Churchill of Chartwell, CSCT 2/26/10.
37. Winston S. Churchill to Sir Reginald Barnes, 26 January 1936. CAC, The Papers of Sir Winston Churchill, CHAR 1/284/11.
38. Winston S. Churchill to King Edward VIII, 2 February 1936. Ibid., CHAR 1/284/19.
39. Winston S. Churchill to Katherine, Duchess of Atholl MP, 4 February 1936. Ibid., CHAR 2/251/21.
40. Churchill, *The Second World War, Volume 1*, p. 64.
41. Henry Page Croft, *My Life of Strife* (Hutchinson: London: 1948), p. 285.
42. Henry Page Croft to Winston S. Churchill, 18 February 1936. CAC, The Papers of Sir Winston Churchill, CHAR 1/284/42.
43. Austen Chamberlain to Ida Chamberlain, 23 February 1936. In Robert C. Self (ed.), *The Austen Chamberlain Diary Letters: The Correspondence of Sir Austen Chamberlain with his Sisters Hilda and Ida, 1916–1937* (Cambridge University Press: Cambridge: 1995), p. 500.
44. Croft, *My Life of Strife*, p. 123.
45. Austen Chamberlain to Ida Chamberlain, 23 February 1936. In Self (ed.), *The Austen Chamberlain Diary Letters*, p. 500.
46. Sir Edward Grigg to Winston S. Churchill, 25 February 1936. CAC, The Papers of Sir Winston Churchill, CHAR 1/284/55.
47. Robert Boothby to Winston S. Churchill, 24 February 1936. Ibid., CHAR 1/284/54.
48. Winston S. Churchill to Clementine Churchill, 21 February 1936. CAC, The Papers of Clementine Ogilvy Spencer-Churchill, Baroness Spencer-Churchill of Chartwell, CSCT 2/26/18.
49. Austen Chamberlain to Ida Chamberlain, 23 February 1936. In Self (ed.) *The Austen Chamberlain Diary Letters*, p. 500.
50. S. Churchill, *A Thread in the Tapestry*, p. 51.
51. Ibid., p. 50.
52. Eleanor Morris-Keating, article sent to *Tatler* magazine about Sarah Churchill, April 1983. CAC, Miscellaneous Holdings, MISC 108/7.
53. S. Churchill, *A Thread in the Tapestry*, p. 51.
54. Winston S. Churchill to Clementine Churchill, 21 February 1936. CAC, The Papers of Clementine Ogilvy Spencer-Churchill, Baroness Spencer-Churchill of Chartwell, CSCT 2/26/16.
55. Ibid.
56. Ibid., CSCT 2/26/17.
57. Clementine Churchill to Winston S. Churchill, 27 February 1936. Ibid., CSCT 1/21/9.
58. Winston S. Churchill to Clementine Churchill, 21 February 1936. Ibid., CSCT 2/26/17.
59. 'Required', *Sevenoaks Chronicle*, 28 February 1936, p. 24.
60. Winston S. Churchill to Clementine Churchill, 3 March 1936. CAC, The Papers of Clementine Ogilvy Spencer-Churchill, Baroness Spencer-Churchill of Chartwell, CSCT 2/26/19.
61. Grace Hamblin interview conducted by Pat Ackerman. CAC, Churchill Oral History Collection, CHOH 1 HMBL – Tape 1, Side 1.

62. Winston S. Churchill to Clementine Churchill, 3 March 1936. CAC, The Papers of Clementine Ogilvy Spencer-Churchill, Baroness Spencer-Churchill of Chartwell, CSCT 2/26/19.
63. Ibid.
64. Adolf Hitler, speaking in the Reichstag, 7 March 1936. In Max Domarus (ed.), *Hitler: Speeches and Proclamations 1932–1945* (Bolchazy-Carducci Publishers: Würzburg: 1990), p. 774.
65. Ibid., p. 765.
66. Ibid., p. 770.
67. Ibid., p. 776.
68. Winston S. Churchill to Pierre-Étienne Flandin, 7 March 1936. CAC, The Papers of Sir Winston Churchill, CHAR 2/274/1–2.
69. Gilbert (ed.), *The Churchill Documents, Volume 13*, p. 523.
70. Winston S. Churchill, speaking in 'Establishment of a Ministry of Supply – Proposal by the Rt Hon. Winston Churchill, MP.' 10 March 1936. Hansard, 5th Series, Vol. 309, c2017. TNA: Cabinet Papers, CAB 64/31.
71. Churchill, *The Second World War, Volume 1*, p. 168.
72. Winston S. Churchill to Austen Chamberlain, 12 March 1936. CAC, The Papers of Sir Winston Churchill, CHAR 2/252/28.
73. 'The European Issue: Mr Churchill on France's Offer', *The Times*, 16 March 1936, p. 19.
74. Ibid.
75. Churchill, *The Second World War, Volume 1*, p. 170.
76. Harold Nicolson to Vita Sackville-West, 17 March 1936. In N. Nicolson (ed.), *Harold Nicolson: Diaries and Letters*, p. 250.
77. Ibid., p. 251.
78. Ibid.
79. *Documents on German Foreign Policy, 1918–1945* (Her Majesty's Stationery Office: London: 1966), p. 237.
80. A. L. Rowse, *Appeasement: A Study in Political Decline, 1933–1939* (Norton: New York: 1961), p. 40.
81. S. Churchill, *A Thread in the Tapestry*, p. 32.
82. 'House Parlourmaid', *Kent and Sussex Courier*, 20 March 1936, p. 24.
83. Winston S. Churchill to Violet Pearman, 23 March 1936. Pearman Papers. In Gilbert (ed.), *The Churchill Documents, Volume 13*, pp. 77–8.
84. Grace Hamblin interview conducted by Pat Ackerman. CAC, Churchill Oral History Collection, CHOH 1 HMBL – Tape 1, Side 2.
85. Winston S. Churchill to Sir Thomas Inskip, 3 June 1936. TNA, Cabinet Papers, CAB 64/5: Air defence research: correspondence with the Rt Hon. Winston Churchill, MP.
86. Gilbert, *The Wilderness Years*, p. 128.
87. Ralph Wigram to Winston S. Churchill, 26 March 1936. CAC, The Papers of Sir Winston Churchill, CHAR 2/273/1–2.
88. Clementine Churchill to Winston S. Churchill, 18 May 1936. CAC, The Papers of Clementine Ogilvy Spencer-Churchill, Baroness Spencer-Churchill of Chartwell, CSCT 1/21/12–13.
89. Ibid.
90. Winston S. Churchill, speaking in 'Supply' debate, 21 May 1936. Hansard, 5th Series, Vol. 312, cc1437–57.

91. Ibid.
92. Stanley Baldwin, quoted in Thomas Jones Diary, 22 May 1936. Thomas Jones Papers, Aberystwyth University Archives. In Gilbert (ed.), *The Churchill Documents, Volume 13*, p. 166.
93. J. S. Churchill, 'Painting for Uncle Winston'.
94. Winston S. Churchill, 'How to Stop War', *Evening Standard*, 12 June 1936.
95. Winston S. Churchill, speaking at Rolls Park, Chigwell, 20 June 1936. CAC, The Papers of Sir Winston Churchill, CHAR 9/120/74.
96. Winston S. Churchill, 28 July 1936. In Churchill, *The Second World War, Volume 1*, p. 195.
97. Winston S. Churchill to Clementine Churchill, 5 September 1936. CAC, The Papers of Clementine Ogilvy Spencer-Churchill, Baroness Spencer-Churchill of Chartwell, CSCT 2/26/22.
98. Lord Lloyd to his son, 6 September 1936. Lloyd Papers. In Gilbert (ed.), *The Churchill Documents, Volume 13*, pp. 338–9.
99. Winston S. Churchill to Clementine Churchill, 13 September 1936. CAC, The Papers of Clementine Ogilvy Spencer-Churchill, Baroness Spencer-Churchill of Chartwell, CSCT 2/26/25.
100. Pierre-Étienne Flandin to Winston S. Churchill, 5 September 1936. CAC, The Papers of Sir Winston Churchill, CHAR 1/285/166.
101. Pierre-Étienne Flandin to Winston S. Churchill, 10 September 1936. Ibid., CHAR 1/285/163.
102. Winston S. Churchill to Clementine Churchill, 13 September 1936. CAC, The Papers of Clementine Ogilvy Spencer-Churchill, Baroness Spencer-Churchill of Chartwell, CSCT 2/26/25.
103. Clementine Churchill to Winston S. Churchill, 8 September 1936. Ibid., CSCT 1/21/16.
104. Winston S. Churchill to Clementine Churchill, 13 September 1936. Ibid., CSCT 2/26/25.
105. Ibid.
106. Kathleen Hill interview conducted by Pat Ackerman. CAC, Churchill Oral History Collection, CHOH 1 KHLL – Tape 1, Side 2.
107. Sarah Churchill to Clementine Churchill, undated. CAC, The Papers of Sarah Churchill, SCHL 1/1/5.
108. 'Churchill's Son Chases Sister across Atlantic', *Chicago Tribune*, 17 September 1936.
109. Mary Soames, 'Father Always Came First, Second and Third', *Finest Hour: The Journal of the International Churchill Society*, Vol. 116 (Autumn 2002).
110. Winston S. Churchill, 5 November 1936. In Eugen Spier, 'Recollections', Spier Papers (November 1953). In Gilbert (ed.), *The Churchill Documents, Volume 13*, p. 388.
111. 'Mr Churchill Accused of Desiring Encirclement of Germany', *Reuters*, 21 October 1936. CAC, The Papers of Sir Winston Churchill, CHAR 2/268/87.
112. Winston S. Churchill, Press Statement, 24 October 1936. Ibid., CHAR 2/268/85.
113. Winston S. Churchill, speaking in 'Debate on the Address', 12 November 1936. Hansard, 5th Series, Vol. 317, cc1081–1155.
114. Grace Hamblin interview conducted by Robin Bryer, March 1980. National Trust.

115. Menu Book, 1936–1937. 18 and 19 November 1936. CAC, The Papers of Clementine Ogilvy Spencer-Churchill, Baroness Spencer-Churchill of Chartwell, CSCT 9/3/1.
116. Menu Book, 1936–1937. 21 and 22 November 1936. Ibid.
117. Pierre-Étienne Flandin to Winston S. Churchill, 28 November 1936. CAC, The Papers of Sir Winston Churchill, CHAR 2/260/172.
118. Eleanor Morris-Keating, article sent to *Tatler* magazine about Sarah Churchill, April 1983. CAC, Miscellaneous Holdings, MISC 108/7.
119. Soames, *A Daughter's Tale*, p. 21.
120. Note dictated to Violet Pearman by Wing Commander Anderson, 18 November 1936. CAC, The Papers of Sir Winston Churchill, CHAR 2/271/103.
121. 'Cabinet to Reveal Arms Secrets to Churchill', *Daily Mirror*, 23 November 1936, p. 5.
122. 'Record of Discussion', 23 November 1936. TNA, Records of the Prime Minister's Office, 1/193. In Gilbert (ed.), *The Churchill Documents, Volume 13*, p. 427.
123. Ibid.
124. Ibid., p. 428.
125. Winston S. Churchill to Pierre-Étienne Flandin, 17 December 1936. CAC, The Papers of Sir Winston Churchill, CHAR 2/261/69.

Chapter 5: An Abdication Formula

1. Martin Gilbert, *Winston S. Churchill, Volume V: 1922–1939: The Prophet of Truth* (Houghton Mifflin Company: Boston, MA: 1977), p. 826.
2. 'All the World Shares the Empire's Mourning for the Man Who Was their Sovereign', *Evening Despatch*, 21 January 1936, p. 3.
3. David Cannadine, 'Churchill and the British Monarchy', *Transactions of the Royal Historical Society*, Vol. 11 (2001), p. 257.
4. Winston S. Churchill, Obituary to King George V, *News of the World*, 26 January 1936. In Gilbert (ed.), *The Churchill Documents, Volume 13*, p. 20.
5. Ibid.
6. Churchill, *The Second World War, Volume 1*, p. 186.
7. Winston S. Churchill to King Edward VIII, 2 February 1936. CAC, The Papers of Sir Winston Churchill, CHAR 1/284/19.
8. Philip Ziegler, *King Edward VIII* (HarperCollins: London: 1991), p. 94.
9. Prince Edward to Freda Dudley Ward, 19 January 1931. Dudley Ward papers. In Ziegler, *King Edward VIII*, p. 193.
10. Winston S Churchill, 'The Abdication of King Edward VIII'. CAC, The Papers of Sir Winston Churchill, CHAR 2/264/6.
11. Blenheim Palace Visitors' Book, 27–28 June 1936. Blenheim Palace Archives.
12. King Edward VIII, 16 July 1936. Royal Archives. In Gilbert (ed.), *The Churchill Documents, Volume 13*, p. 230.
13. King Edward VIII to Winston S. Churchill, 17 July 1936. CAC, The Papers of Sir Winston Churchill, CHAR 2/264/114.
14. A. G. Clark, 'Report on Visit to Germany, Switzerland and France', 16 April 1936. Ibid., CHAR 2/280/9–13.

15. Gill Bennett, *Churchill's Man of Mystery: Desmond Morton and the World of Intelligence* (Routledge: London: 2007), p. 135.
16. Cecil Roberts, *Sunshine and Shadow: Being the Fourth Book of an Autobiography 1930–1946* (Hodder & Stoughton: London: 1972), p. 134.
17. Viscount Swinton to Winston S. Churchill, 15 June 1936. TNA, Cabinet Papers, CAB 64/5: Air defence research: correspondence with the Rt Hon. Winston Churchill, MP.
18. Winston S. Churchill to Viscount Swinton, 22 June 1936. Ibid.
19. Harold Nicolson to Vita Sackville-West, 23 June 1936. In N. Nicolson (ed.), *Harold Nicolson: Diaries and Letters*, p. 266.
20. Ibid.
21. Winston S. Churchill, 'Notes: The Abdication of King Edward VIII, December 1936'. CAC, The Papers of Sir Winston Churchill, CHAR 2/264/9.
22. Ibid.
23. 'King Edward to Wed Mrs Simpson in June', *New York American*, 26 October 1936, p. 1. Ibid., CHAR 2/300/3.
24. Eugen Spier, *FOCUS: A Footnote to the History of the Thirties* (Oswald Wolff: London: 1963), p. 21.
25. Ibid.
26. 'Famous Mansion Sold – Residence of Kings', *Daily Telegraph*, 18 October 1928, p. 18.
27. Spier, *FOCUS*, p. 33.
28. Ibid., p. 43.
29. Grace Hamblin interview conducted by Pat Ackerman. CAC, Churchill Oral History Collection, CHOH 1 HMBL – Tape 1, Side 2.
30. Ibid.
31. Violet Pearman to Sir James Hawkey, 27 November 1936. Pearman Papers. In Gilbert (ed.), *The Churchill Documents, Volume 13*, p. 443.
32. Ibid., p. 444.
33. Harcourt Johnstone to Viscount Swinton, 27 July 1936. TNA, Cabinet Papers, CAB 64/5: Air defence research: correspondence with the Rt Hon. Winston Churchill, MP.
34. Sarah Churchill to Winston S. Churchill, 1 November 1936. CAC, The Papers of Sir Winston Spencer Churchill, CHAR 1/288/72.
35. Henry Channon, Diary, 12 November 1936. In Robert Rhodes James (ed.), *Chips: The Diaries of Sir Henry Channon* (Weidenfeld & Nicolson: London: 1967), p. 79.
36. Walter Monckton to Stanley Baldwin, 20 November 1936. TNA, Records of the Prime Minister's Office, PREM 1/448.
37. Lord Citrine, *Men and Work* (Hutchinson: London: 1964), p. 328.
38. Ibid.
39. Cosmo Gordon Lang to Stanley Baldwin, 25 November 1936. TNA, Records of the Prime Minister's Office, PREM 1/448.
40. Frank William Iklé, *German–Japanese Relations, 1936–1940: A Study in Totalitarian Diplomacy* (Bookman Associates: New York: 1956), p. 16.
41. Tom Clarke, 'Why Ribbentrop', *Reynolds's Newspaper*, 29 November 1936, p. 6.
42. Winston S. Churchill, New Commonwealth Society Luncheon, Dorchester Hotel, 25 November 1936. In Churchill (Jnr) (ed.), *Never Give In!*, p. 154.

43. Winston S. Churchill to Clementine Churchill, 27 November 1936. CAC, The Papers of Clementine Ogilvy Spencer-Churchill, Baroness Spencer-Churchill of Chartwell, CSCT 2/26/27–28.
44. Lord Zetland to Lord Linlithgow, 27 November 1936. India Office Records. In Gilbert (ed.), *The Churchill Documents, Volume 13*, p. 439.
45. Rhodes James (ed.), *Chips: The Diaries of Sir Henry Channon*, p. 90.
46. Churchill, *The Second World War, Volume 1*, p. 195.
47. Spier, *FOCUS*, pp. 66–9.
48. Winston S. Churchill, 3 December 1936. In Spier, *FOCUS*, p. 71.
49. Harold Macmillan, *Winds of Change, 1914–1939* (Macmillan: London: 1966), p. 441.
50. Winston S. Churchill, 'Notes: The Abdication of King Edward VIII, December 1936'. CAC, The Papers of Sir Winston Churchill, CHAR 2/264/12.
51. Ibid., CHAR 2/264/12–13.
52. Edward, Duke of Windsor, *A King's Story: The Memoirs of HRH the Duke of Windsor* (Cassell and Company: London: 1951), p. 382.
53. Ibid., p. 383.
54. Winston S. Churchill to Stanley Baldwin, 5 December 1936. TNA, Records of the Prime Minister's Office, PREM 1/448.
55. Winston S. Churchill, Press Statement, 5 December 1936. CAC, The Papers of Sir Winston Churchill, CHAR 2/264/105–109.
56. Ibid.
57. Grace Hamblin interview conducted by Robin Bryer, March 1980. National Trust.
58. Winston S. Churchill to King Edward VIII, 5 December 1936. CAC, The Papers of Sir Winston Churchill, CHAR 2/264/101.
59. Menu Book, 1936–1937. 5 December 1936. CAC, The Papers of Clementine Ogilvy Spencer-Churchill, Baroness Spencer-Churchill of Chartwell, CSCT 9/3/1.
60. Samuel Howes, 'Samuel M. Howes: Recollections', letter to Martin Gilbert. In Gilbert (ed.), *The Churchill Documents, Volume 12*, p. 511.
61. Duke of Windsor, *A King's Story*, p. 391.
62. Ibid., pp. 386–7.
63. Desmond Morton to Winston S. Churchill, 6 December 1936. CAC, The Papers of Sir Winston Churchill, CHAR 2/264/96.
64. Walter Newbold to Winston S. Churchill, 6 December 1936. Ibid., CHAR 2/264/98.
65. Violet Pearman to Clementine Churchill, 19 December 1936. Ibid., CHAR 2/597A/1.
66. Dorothy Abram to Winston S. Churchill, 6 December 1936. Ibid., CHAR 2/597A/13.
67. Marjorie Deans to Winston S. Churchill, 6 December 1936. Ibid., CHAR 2/597A/104.
68. Ethel Scarborough to Winston S. Churchill, 7 December 1936. Ibid., CHAR 2/599/67.
69. Gray, *Victory in the Kitchen*, p. 152.
70. Gerard J. De Groot, *Liberal Crusader: The Life of Sir Archibald Sinclair* (C. Hurst & Co.: London: 1993), p. 123.
71. Robert Boothby to Winston S. Churchill, 11 December 1936. CAC, The Papers of Sir Winston Churchill, CHAR 2/264/71–72.

72. Ibid.
73. Winston S. Churchill to King Edward VIII, 7 December 1936. Ibid., CHAR 2/264/89.
74. Winston S. Churchill to Robert Boothby, 12 December 1936. Boothby Papers. In Gilbert (ed.), *The Churchill Documents, Volume 13*, pp. 77–8.
75. Robert Boothby to Winston S. Churchill, 11 December 1936. CAC, The Papers of Sir Winston Churchill, CHAR 2/264/71–72.
76. Harold Nicolson Diary, 8 December 1936. Nicolson Papers. In Gilbert (ed.), *The Churchill Documents, Volume 13*, p. 465.
77. Leo Amery Diary, 7 December 1936. Amery Papers. In ibid., p. 464.
78. Harold Nicolson to Vita Sackville-West, 7 December 1936. N. Nicolson (ed.), *Harold Nicolson: Diaries and Letters*, p. 282.
79. Henry Channon Diary, 7 November 1936. In Rhodes James (ed.), *Chips: The Diaries of Sir Henry Channon*, pp. 94–5.
80. Robert Boothby to Winston S. Churchill, 7 December 1936. CAC, The Papers of Sir Winston Churchill, CHAR 2/264/93.
81. Ibid.
82. Duke of Windsor, *A King's Story*, p. 394.
83. Harold Nicolson Diary, 8 December 1936. Nicolson Papers. In Gilbert (ed.), *The Churchill Documents, Volume 13*, p. 465.
84. Duke of Windsor, *A King's Story*, p. 394.
85. Edward VIII signed his declaration of abdication on 10 December 1936 but he remained King until giving royal assent to His Majesty's Abdication Act, which he did on 11 December. His abdication speech to the nation was given that day.
86. Winston S. Churchill to Whom It May Concern, 20 December 1936. Howes Papers. In Gilbert (ed.), *The Churchill Documents, Volume 13*, p. 502.
87. Ibid.
88. 'Churchill Bride Home To-Morrow', *Sunday Dispatch*, 27 December 1936, p. 16.
89. Grace Hamblin interview conducted by Pat Ackerman. CAC, Churchill Oral History Collection, CHOH 1 HMBL – Tape 1, Side 2.

Chapter 6: Hitler's Predecessor

1. Prince Bismarck: Memorandum, 20 October 1930. German Foreign Office Documents: K567878/A2386. In Gilbert (ed.), *The Churchill Documents, Volume 13*, p. 196.
2. Herbert Hömig, *Brüning – Politiker ohne Auftrag: Zwischen Weimarer und Bonner Republik* (Ferdinand Schöningh: Paderborn: 2005), p. 148.
3. William Evans Scott, *Alliance Against Hitler* (Duke University Press: Durham, NC: 1962), p. 48.
4. William L. Patch, Jr, *Heinrich Brüning and the Dissolution of the Weimar Republic* (Cambridge University Press: Cambridge: 1998), p. 304.
5. N. Nicolson (ed.), *Harold Nicolson: Diaries and Letters*, p. 174.
6. Gunther, *Inside Europe*, p. 56.
7. Gottfried R. Treviranus, *Für Deutschland im Exil* (Econ Verlag: Düsseldorf: 1973), pp. 17–18.
8. Ibid., p. 21.

9. Heinrich Brüning, 'Accounts of Conversations with Notable People'. Harvard University Archives, Heinrich Brüning Papers. Unspecified Accession 14078 Box 1; Unspecified Folder 2.

10. Ibid.

11. Ibid.

12. Hömig, *Brüning*, p. 165.

13. Brüning, 'Accounts of Conversations with Notable People'.

14. Ibid.

15. Soames, *Clementine Churchill*, p. 306.

16. Winston S. Churchill to Ava Wigram, undated. In Martin Gilbert, *In Search of Churchill* (HarperCollins: London: 1994), p. 134.

17. Ava Wigram to Winston S. Churchill, 2 January 1937. CAC, The Papers of Sir Winston Churchill, CHAR 1/300/77.

18. Winston S. Churchill to Anne, Lady Islington, 17 January 1937. Grigg Papers. In Gilbert (ed.), *The Churchill Documents, Volume 13*, p. 542.

19. Winston S. Churchill to Clementine Churchill, 25 January 1937. CAC, The Papers of Clementine Ogilvy Spencer-Churchill, Baroness Spencer-Churchill of Chartwell, CSCT 2/27/10–12.

20. Winston S. Churchill to Clementine Churchill, 7 January 1937. Ibid., CSCT 2/27/6–9.

21. Grace Hamblin interview conducted by Pat Ackerman. CAC, Churchill Oral History Collection, CHOH 1 HMBL – Tape 1, Side 2.

22. Mr Cale's first name has been an enigma to historians, as no documentation is recorded as having survived with his full name. The publication of the 1939 census in 2015 provided the answer, and has allowed for a full understanding of those staff living onsite at Chartwell at the outbreak of war. 'Charles A Cale' (Chauffeur, b. 7 June 1911), Census return for 'The Garage (2) Chartwell', Sevenoaks, Kent. The 1939 Register, via www.ancestry.co.uk.

23. Winston S. Churchill to Clementine Churchill, 20 January 1937. CAC, The Papers of Sir Winston Churchill, CHAR 1/298/20–23.

24. Account from Mrs Massey's Agency for Servants, London, 12s 6d, fee for engaging Head Parlourmaid, M. Jackson, 30 September 1937. Paid by Mrs Winston Churchill on 6 October 1937. CAC, The Papers of Sir Winston Churchill, CHAR 1/314/139.

25. Soames, *A Daughter's Tale*, p. 114.

26. Winston S. Churchill to Clementine Churchill, 2 February 1937. CAC, The Papers of Clementine Ogilvy Spencer-Churchill, Baroness Spencer-Churchill of Chartwell, CSCT 2/27/13–19.

27. Ibid.

28. 'June 30 Fugitive', *Daily Telegraph*, 14 January 1937. Press Cutting. TNA, Records of the Security Service, KV 2/344.

29. Baron Kurt von Tippelskirch to the German Embassy, Washington, DC, 10 April 1937. Ibid., KV 2/344.

30. 'Hitlerites Turn Ire on Bruening for Talks Here', *Boston Evening Transcript*, 15 April 1936. Press Cutting. TNA, Captured Records of the German, Italian and Japanese Governments, GFM 33/501.

31. Report: Ernst Hanfstaengl, PF.42252/B.2b., 27 July 1938. TNA, Records of the Security Service, KV 2/469.

32. Peter Conradi, *Hitler's Piano Player: The Rise and Fall of Ernst Hanfstaengl, Confidant of Hitler, Ally of FDR* (Carroll & Graf: New York: 2006), pp. 195–96.
33. Hermann Göring to Ernst Hanfstaengl, 19 March 1937. In Ernst Hanfstaengl, *Hitler: The Missing Years* (Arcade Publishing: New York: 1994), p. 18.
34. Pierre Cot to Winston S. Churchill, May 1937. CAC, The Papers of Sir Winston Churchill, CHAR 2/307/17.
35. Desmond Morton to Winston S. Churchill, 2 June 1938. Ibid., CHAR 2/307/19.
36. Sir Henry Channon, Diary, 4 May 1937. In Rhodes James (ed.), *Chips: The Diaries of Sir Henry Channon*, p. 122.
37. Soames, *Clementine Churchill*, p. 306.
38. Ibid.
39. Winston S. Churchill to the Duke of Windsor, 17 May 1937. CAC, The Papers of Sir Winston Churchill, CHAR 2/300/39–41.
40. Winston S. Churchill to Percy Cudlipp, 10 July 1937. Private Collection.
41. John Weitz, *Hitler's Diplomat: The Life and Times of Joachim von Ribbentrop* (Ticknor & Fields: New York: 1992), p. 130.
42. Winston S. Churchill, *The Second World War, Volume 1*, p. 190.
43. Ibid.
44. Ibid.
45. Neville Chamberlain, speech on becoming Leader of the Conservative Party, 31 May 1937. Bodleian Archives & Manuscripts, Conservative Party Archive, PUB 207/3.
46. C. Roberts, *Sunshine and Shadow*, p. 233.
47. 'Bruning, ex-chancelier d'Allemagne n'est plus que le Docteur Anderson professeur à l'Université de Harvard', *Paris-Soir*, 3 June 1937. Press Cutting. TNA, Captured Records of the German, Italian and Japanese Governments, GFM 33/501.
48. Kathleen Hill interview conducted by Pat Ackerman. CAC, Churchill Oral History Collection, CHOH 1 KHLL – Tape 1, Side 1.
49. Ibid.
50. Soames, *Clementine Churchill*, accompanying text for illustration 52.
51. Gwen Hibbert, 'My War Years: Childhood Memories of Chartwell: Part 1', via https://www.bbc.co.uk/history/ww2peopleswar/stories/55/a2759655.shtml. Permission for use kindly given by Mrs Gwen Hibbert, daughter of Mr Hill, Chartwell's head gardener from 1927 to 1944.
52. Spier, *FOCUS*, p. 104.
53. Nicolae Titulescu to Winston S. Churchill, 15 June 1937. CAC, The Papers of Sir Winston Churchill, CHAR 1/299/53.
54. Edward M. Bennett, *Separated by Common Language: Franklin Delano Roosevelt and Anglo-American Relations 1933–1939* (iUniverse: Bloomington, IN: 2002), p. 123.
55. Winston S. Churchill to *Collier's* magazine, 30 August 1937. CAC, The Papers of Sir Winston Churchill, CHAR 8/576/214.
56. Winston S. Churchill, speaking in 'Supply' debate, 19 July 1937. Hansard, 5th Series, Vol. 326, cc1799–1927.
57. Edward Spears to Winston S. Churchill, 19 July 1937. CAC, The Papers of Sir Winston Churchill, CHAR 1/299/98.
58. Violet Pearman to Winston S. Churchill, 28 July 1937. Ibid., CHAR 1/299/97.

59. Edward Spears to Winston S. Churchill, 29 July 1937. Ibid., CHAR 1/299/96.
60. Winston S. Churchill to Edward Spears, 31 July 1937. Ibid.
61. Winston S. Churchill to Clementine Churchill, 3 August 1937. CAC, The Papers of Clementine Ogilvy Spencer-Churchill, Baroness Spencer-Churchill of Chartwell, CSCT 2/27/1.
62. Treviranus, *Für Deutschland im Exil*, p. 59.
63. Ibid., p. 52.
64. Winston S. Churchill, *The Story of the Malakand Field Force* (Longmans: London: 1901), p. 172.
65. Brüning, 'Accounts of Conversations with Notable People'.
66. Ibid.
67. Heinrich Brüning to Hans Bernd Gisevius, 20 August 1946. Harvard University Archives, Heinrich Brüning Papers, HUG FP 93.10 Box 11.
68. Treviranus, *Für Deutschland im Exil*, p. 56.
69. Ibid.
70. Ibid., p. 57.
71. Winston S. Churchill to Clementine Churchill, 3 August 1937. CAC, The Papers of Clementine Ogilvy Spencer-Churchill, Baroness Spencer-Churchill of Chartwell, CSCT 2/27/1–4.
72. Winston S. Churchill to Heinrich Brüning, 4 August 1937. CAC, The Papers of Sir Winston Churchill, CHAR 8/548/83.
73. Heinrich Brüning to Winston S. Churchill, 5 August 1937. In Heinrich Brüning, *Briefe und Gespräche 1934–1945* (Deutsche Verlags-Anstalt: Stuttgart: 1974), p. 143.
74. Heinrich Brüning to Winston S. Churchill, 9 August 1937. CAC, The Papers of Sir Winston Churchill, CHAR 2/307/58.
75. Kathleen Hill interview conducted by Pat Ackerman. CAC, Churchill Oral History Collection, CHOH 1 KHLL – Tape 1, Side 1.
76. Leslie Hore-Belisha to Clementine Churchill, 28 August 1937. CAC, The Papers of Sir Winston Churchill, CHAR 1/299/137.
77. Heinrich Brüning to Winston S. Churchill, 9 August 1937. Ibid., CHAR 2/307/59.
78. Heinrich Brüning to Winston S. Churchill, 9 August 1937. Ibid., CHAR 2/307/61–62.
79. Gottfried Treviranus to the Under-Secretary of State, Aliens' Department, Home Office, 16 August 1937. TNA, Records of the Home Office, HO 382/694.
80. Clementine Churchill to Winston S. Churchill, 30 November 1937. CAC, The Papers of Lady Soames, MCHL 6/2/17.

Chapter 7: The Pan-European Count

1. Lord Rothermere to Winston S. Churchill, 9 December 1937. CAC, The Papers of Sir Winston Churchill, CHAR 1/300/67.
2. Winston S. Churchill, 'Britain Rearms', *Evening Standard*, 7 January 1938. In Gilbert (ed.), *The Churchill Documents, Volume 13*, p. 857.
3. Brigadier Pakenham-Walsh, Diary, 15 December 1937. Pakenham-Walsh papers. In ibid., p. 860.

4. Winston S. Churchill to Clementine Churchill, 10 January 1938. CAC, The Papers of Clementine Ogilvy Spencer-Churchill, Baroness Spencer-Churchill of Chartwell, CSCT 2/28/6.
5. N. Nicolson (ed.), *Harold Nicolson: Diaries and Letters*, p. 312.
6. Winston S. Churchill to Clementine Churchill, 10 January 1938. CAC, The Papers of Clementine Ogilvy Spencer-Churchill, Baroness Spencer-Churchill of Chartwell, CSCT 2/28/6.
7. Winston S. Churchill to Maxine Elliot, 30 December 1937. CAC, The Papers of Sir Winston Churchill, CHAR 1/300/86.
8. Winston S. Churchill to Clementine Churchill, 18 January 1938. CAC, The Papers of Clementine Ogilvy Spencer-Churchill, Baroness Spencer-Churchill of Chartwell, CSCT 2/28/9.
9. Frank McDonough, *Neville Chamberlain, Appeasement, and the British Road to War* (Manchester University Press: Manchester: 1998), p. 52.
10. 'Report on Visit to Berlin. Conversation with Sir Nevile Henderson', 13 June 1938. CAC, The Papers of Sir Winston Churchill, CHAR 2/340B/114.
11. Winston S. Churchill to Maxine Elliot, 8 February 1938. Ibid., CHAR 1/323/12–13.
12. Count Richard Coudenhove-Kalergi to Winston S. Churchill, 2 February 1938. Ibid., CHAR 2/328/30.
13. Ibid.
14. Count Richard Coudenhove-Kalergi to Winston S. Churchill, 4 February 1938. Ibid., CHAR 2/328/38.
15. William T. Stone, 'The Briand Project for European Union', *Foreign Policy Associations*, Vol. 6, No. 13 (17 Sept. 1930).
16. Violet Pearman to Clementine Churchill, 11 February 1938. CAC, The Papers of Sir Winston Churchill, CHAR 2/328/37.
17. L. S. Amery to Winston S. Churchill, 11 February 1938. Ibid., CHAR 2/328/46.
18. L. S. Amery, Diary, April 1936. In Martyn Bond, *Hitler's Cosmopolitan Bastard: Count Richard Coudenhove-Kalergi and his Vision of Europe* (McGill-Queen's University Press: Montreal: 2021), p. 183.
19. L. S. Amery, Diary, February 1938. In Bond, *Hitler's Cosmopolitan Bastard*, p. 185.
20. By the autumn of 1937, Churchill had moved his bed from the north-east corner of the study to an adjoining room in the former self-contained 'nursery wing' (which housed his younger daughters' bedrooms) to the south of the house, as evidenced by the photographs taken for Chartwell's potential sale in winter 1937–38. Though the date of this move has not been recorded, it may have been prompted by Sarah Churchill leaving Chartwell to marry Vic Oliver in 1936, and a resulting repurposing of the configuration and use of rooms within that wing.
21. Winston S. Churchill, *The Second World War, Volume 1*, p. 217.
22. Ibid.
23. Ibid.
24. Papers of General Beck. In Ian Goodhope Colvin, *Master Spy: The Incredible Story of Admiral Wilhelm Canaris, Who, While Hitler's Chief of Intelligence, Was a Secret Ally of the British* (McGraw-Hill: New York: 1952), p. 45.
25. Lois G. Schwoerer, 'Lord Halifax's Visit to Germany: November 1937', *The Historian*, Vol. 32, No. 3 (May 1970), pp. 358–9.

26. Anthony Eden, *Facing the Dictators: The Memoirs of Anthony Eden* (Cassell: London: 1962), p. 577.
27. C. Roberts, *Sunshine and Shadow*, p. 287.
28. Winston S. Churchill, speaking in 'Foreign Affairs' debate, 22 February 1938. Hansard, 5th Series, Vol. 332, cc244–45.
29. Ibid., cc242–43.
30. George Franckenstein to Winston S. Churchill, 24 February 1938. CAC, The Papers of Sir Winston Churchill, CHAR 2/328/58.
31. Harcourt Johnstone to Winston S. Churchill, 24 February 1938. In Gilbert (ed.), *The Churchill Documents, Volume 13*, p. 916.
32. Sir Henry Channon, Diary, 22 February 1938. In Rhodes James (ed.), *Chips: The Diaries of Sir Henry Channon*, p. 146.
33. 'Accent Foils Actress', *Daily News (London)*, 22 February 1938, p. 3.
34. Ibid.
35. Richard N. Coudenhove-Kalergi, *An Idea Conquers the World* (Roy Publishers: New York: 1953), p. 212.
36. Dietmar Grieser, *Wien: Wahlheimat der Genies* (Heyne: Munich: 1996), p. 241.
37. Ibid., p. 242.
38. Count Coudenhove-Kalergi to Ida Roland, August 1914. In Richard N. Coudenhove-Kalergi, *Pan-Europe* (Alfred Knopf: New York: 1926), p. 11.
39. Bond, *Hitler's Cosmopolitan Bastard*, p. 185.
40. Kathleen Hill interview conducted by Pat Ackerman. CAC, Churchill Oral History Collection, CHOH 1 KHLL – Tape 1, Side 1.
41. John Lavery, *The Life of a Painter* (Cassell: London: 1940), p. 177.
42. Dr Thomas Hunt to Winston S. Churchill, Diet Sheet, 22 August 1936. CAC, The Papers of Sir Winston Churchill, CHAR 1/351/149.
43. Winston S. Churchill to Thomas Hunt, 23 August 1936. CAC, The Papers of Sir Winston Churchill, CHAR 1/351/150–151.
44. Coudenhove-Kalergi, *An Idea Conquers the World*, p. 212.
45. Winston S. Churchill to Keith Feiling, 26 February 1938. CAC, The Papers of Sir Winston Churchill, CHAR 8/595/76.
46. Winston S. Churchill to Sir James Hawkey, 26 February 1938. In Gilbert (ed.), *The Churchill Documents, Volume 13*, pp. 918–19.
47. Gerhard L. Weinberg, *Hitler's Foreign Policy, 1933–1939* (Enigma Books: New York: 2010), p. 439.
48. Adolf Hitler, 20 February 1938. In Thomas L. Jarman, *The Rise and Fall of Nazi Germany* (New York University Press: New York: 1977), p. 226.
49. Unity Mitford to Winston S. Churchill, 5 March 1938. CAC, The Papers of Sir Winston Churchill, CHAR 2/328/75.
50. Ibid.
51. R. H. Haigh, D. S. Morris and A. R. Peters, *The Years of Triumph? German Diplomatic and Military Policy 1933–41* (Barnes & Noble Books: Totowa, NJ: 1986), p. 83.
52. Alfred Jodl, Diary, 10 March 1938. In William L. Shirer, *The Rise and Fall of the Third Reich: A History of Nazi Germany* (Simon & Schuster: New York: 2011), p. 335.
53. Coudenhove-Kalergi, *An Idea Conquers the World*, p. 208.
54. Ibid.

55. Rhodes James (ed.), *Chips: The Diaries of Sir Henry Channon*, p. 150.
56. Manchester, *The Caged Lion*, p. 279.
57. Donald E. Shepardson, *Conflict & Diplomacy from the Great War to the Cold War* (P. Lang: New York: 1999), pp. 75–6.
58. Bond, *Hitler's Cosmopolitan Bastard*, p. 187.
59. Coudenhove-Kalergi, *An Idea Conquers the World*, p. 209.
60. Ibid., p. 210.
61. Winston S. Churchill to Unity Mitford, 5 March 1938. CAC, The Papers of Sir Winston Churchill, CHAR 2/328/107.
62. Winston S. Churchill, speaking in 'Foreign Affairs (Austria)' debate, 14 March 1938. Hansard, 5th Series, Vol. 333, cc99–100.
63. Fishman, *My Darling Clementine*, p. 99.
64. David Hindley-Smith to Winston S. Churchill, 18 March 1938. CAC, The Papers of Sir Winston Churchill, CHAR 2/328/139.
65. Geoffrey Dawson to Winston S. Churchill, 23 March 1938. Ibid., CHAR 2/328/140.
66. 'Prague "Panicky"', *Liverpool Echo*, 12 March 1938, p. 16.
67. Bond, *Hitler's Cosmopolitan Bastard*, p. 188.

Chapter 8: Planning a Coup

1. Lawrence D. Stokes, 'Conservative Opposition to Nazism in Eutin, Schleswig-Holstein, 1932–1933'. In Francis R. Nicosia and Lawrence D. Stokes (eds), *Germans against Nazism: Nonconformity, Opposition and Resistance in the Third Reich* (Berg Publishers: New York: 1990), p. 37.
2. Thomas Jones, letter to an American friend, 20 March 1938. Jones Papers. In Gilbert (ed.), *The Churchill Documents, Volume 13*, p. 954.
3. Winston S. Churchill, 'Against the foregoing the following assets can, if desired, be immediately produced', 19 March 1938. CAC, The Papers of Sir Winston Churchill, CHAR 1/328/3.
4. Hömig, *Brüning – Politiker ohne Auftrag*, pp. 214–16.
5. Shirer, *The Rise and Fall of the Third Reich*, p. 372.
6. Colvin, *Master Spy*, p. 45.
7. Ibid., p. 50.
8. Brüning, 'Accounts of Conversations with Notable People'.
9. Winston S. Churchill to Ava Wigram, 22 March 1938. CAC, The Papers of Sir Winston Churchill, CHAR 1/323/29.
10. Alexander Werth, *France and Munich before and after the Surrender* (Harper and Brothers Publishers: New York: 1939), p. 58.
11. Invoice – Discavox: Dictating Machine Company, 18 February 1938. CAC, The Papers of Sir Winston Churchill, CHAR 8/608/2.
12. Kathleen Hill interview conducted by Pat Ackerman. CAC, Churchill Oral History Collection, CHOH 1 KHLL – Tape 1, Side 1.
13. Lothar Höbelt, 'Nostalgic Agnostics: Austrian Aristocrats and Politics, 1918–1938'. In Karina Urbach (ed.), *European Aristocracies and the Radical Right 1918–1939* (Oxford University Press: Oxford: 2007), p. 184.
14. Winston S. Churchill, speaking in 'Foreign Affairs and Rearmament' debate, 24 March 1938. Hansard, 5th Series, Vol. 333, cc1399–1514.
15. Fishman, *My Darling Clementine*, p. 97.

16. Neville Chamberlain, speaking in 'Foreign Affairs and Rearmament' debate, 24 March 1938. Hansard, 5th Series, Vol. 333, cc1399–1514.
17. Winston S. Churchill, speaking in 'Foreign Affairs and Rearmament' debate, 24 March 1938. Ibid.
18. Ibid.
19. Sir Eric Phipps to Lord Halifax, 27 March 1938. Phipps Papers. In Gilbert (ed.), *The Churchill Documents, Volume 13*, p. 960.
20. Sir Eric Phipps to Lord Halifax, 28 March 1938. Foreign Office Papers: 800/311. In ibid., p. 960.
21. Ibid.
22. Lord Halifax to Sir Eric Phipps, 30 March 1938. Foreign Office Papers: 800/311. In ibid., p. 960.
23. 'Winston Puts His Mansion Up for Sale'/'Winston Selling Home', *Daily Express*, 1 April 1938, pp. 1–2.
24. Randolph Churchill to Winston S. Churchill, 1 April 1938. CAC, The Papers of Randolph Churchill, RDCH 1/3/3.
25. 'Mr Churchill's Home – Chartwell for Sale', *Daily Telegraph*, 2 April 1938, p. 14.
26. Chartwell: Estate Agent's Descriptive Brochure. 'Chartwell. Westerham', 2 April 1938. CAC, Mary Churchill Papers, MCHL 5/1/296.
27. Ibid.
28. Eleanor Morris-Keating, article sent to *Tatler* magazine about Sarah Churchill, April 1983. CAC, Miscellaneous Holdings, MISC 108/7.
29. 'A London Letter for Women', *Liverpool Daily Post*, 18 April 1938, p. 5.
30. Kathleen Hill interview conducted by Pat Ackerman. CAC, Churchill Oral History Collection, CHOH 1 KHLL – Tape 1, Side 1.
31. Winston S. Churchill to Violet Pearman, 18 May 1938. Pearman Papers, Private Collection. In Gilbert (ed.), *The Churchill Documents, Volume 13*, p. 1033.
32. Clementine Churchill to Violet Pearman, 21 May 1938. Pearman Papers, Private Collection. In ibid., p. 1036.
33. Igor Lukes, 'The Czechoslovak Partial Mobilization in May 1938: A Mystery (almost) Solved', *Journal of Contemporary History*, Vol. 31, No. 4 (Oct. 1996), p. 699.
34. Ibid., p. 702.
35. Pierre Galante, *Operation Valkyrie: The German Generals' Plot against Hitler* (Harper & Row Publishers: New York: 1981), p. 57.
36. 'Defence Supply: A Memorandum by Mr Churchill', *The Times*, 20 May 1938. Press Cuttings Section, Ministry of Labour. TNA, Cabinet Papers, CAB 64/31.
37. H. H. Stellar to T. A. G. Charlton, 23 May 1938. TNA, Cabinet Papers, CAB 64/31.
38. Austin Hopkinson to Lord Winterton, 27 May 1938. Bodleian Archives & Manuscripts, MS. 9663/66 – Archive of Edward Turnour, 6th Earl Winterton – Correspondence, 1930–1962.
39. Winston S. Churchill to Sir Howard Kingsley Wood, 9 June 1938. CAC, The Papers of Sir Winston Churchill, CHAR 25/17/45–46.
40. Memorandum by Sir Henry Tizard on Mr Winston Churchill's Letter of June 9th to the Secretary of State for Air, 22 June 1938. TNA, Cabinet Papers, CAB 64/5.

41. Soames, *A Daughter's Tale*, p. 114.
42. Kathleen Hill interview conducted by Pat Ackerman. CAC, Churchill Oral History Collection, CHOH 1 KHLL – Tape 1, Side 1.
43. Rowse, *Appeasement*, p. 47.
44. David Lloyd George, 13 March 1938. In A. J. Sylvester, *Life with Lloyd George* (Barnes and Noble: New York: 1975), p. 201.
45. 'Bekanntmachung', *Deutscher Reichsanzeiger und Preußischer Staatsanzeiger*, 22 June 1938. TNA, Records of the Security Service, KV 2/344.
46. 'Churchill Offers Reward for Swans', *Windsor Star* (Ontario, Canada), 4 July 1938, p. 23.
47. Winston S. Churchill to Clementine Churchill, 8 July 1938. The Papers of Clementine Ogilvy Spencer-Churchill, Baroness Spencer-Churchill of Chartwell, CSCT 2/28/12–13.
48. National Gardens Scheme. Receipt for £19 with proceeds to go to the Kent County Nursing Association, 6 July 1938. CAC, The Papers of Sir Winston Churchill, CHAR 1/339/73.
49. 'Memorandum of Mr Churchill's Interview with Herr Foerster, 14 July, 1938'. Ibid., CHAR 2/340B/135–138.
50. Clementine Churchill to Winston S. Churchill, 12 July 1938. CAC, The Papers of Clementine Ogilvy Spencer-Churchill, Baroness Spencer-Churchill of Chartwell, CSCT 1/23/1.
51. Ibid., CSCT 1/23/2.
52. Secretary job advertisement, July 1938. Chartwell Archives Centre, The Papers of Sir Winston Churchill, CHAR 8/594/145.
53. Henry Yellowlees to Winston S. Churchill, 25 June 1938. Ibid., CHAR 8/594/135.
54. Josephine Parr to Winston S. Churchill, 24 July 1938. Ibid., CHAR 8/594/129–130.
55. Mary Penman to Unnamed, 15 July 1938. Ibid., CHAR 8/594/148.
56. Winston S. Churchill to Howard Kingsley Wood, 26 July 1938. TNA, Records of the Air Ministry, AIR 2/3354.
57. Ian Colvin to Randolph Churchill, 15 August 1938. CAC, Randolph Churchill Papers. In Gilbert (ed.), *The Churchill Documents, Volume 13*, p. 1117.
58. Hömig, *Brüning – Politiker ohne Auftrag*, p. 241.
59. Shelley Baranowski, 'Convergence on the Right: Agrarian Elite Radicalism and Nazi Populism in Pomerania, 1928–33'. In Larry Eugene Jones and James N. Retallack (eds), *Between Reform, Reaction, and Resistance: Studies in the History of German Conservatism from 1789 to 1945* (Providence: Oxford: 1993), p. 408.
60. Colvin, *Master Spy*, p. 53.
61. Ibid., p. 55.
62. Heinz Höhne, *Canaris: Patriot im Zwielicht* (Bertelsmann: Munich: 1976), p. 216.
63. Allen Roberts, *Web of Intrigue (Anti-Hitler Opposition)* (Moore Pub. Co.: Durham, NC: 1979), p. 148.
64. David Faber, *Munich, 1938: Appeasement and World War II* (Simon & Schuster: New York: 2009), p. 225.
65. 'Unofficial German Approaches, August–September, 1938'. In E. L. Woodward, Rohan Butler and Margaret Lambert (eds), *Documents on British Foreign Policy, 1919–1939* (His Majesty's Stationery Office: London: 1949), p. 683.

66. Galante, *Operation Valkyrie*, p. 57.
67. Hömig, *Brüning – Politiker ohne Auftrag*, p. 240.
68. Colvin, *Master Spy*, pp. 64–5.
69. Ibid., p. 65.
70. 'Unofficial German Approaches, August–September, 1938: Note of a Conversation between Sir R. Vansittart and Herr von Kleist [C 8520/1941/18]'. In Woodward, Butler and Lambert (eds), *Documents on British Foreign Policy, 1919–1939*, p. 684.
71. Ibid., p. 685.
72. 'Note of Conversation at Chartwell between Monsieur de K and Mr Winston Churchill. August 19 1938', CAC, The Papers of Sir Winston Churchill, CHAR 2/340A-B/153.
73. Ibid.
74. Neville Chamberlain, speaking in 'Foreign Affairs and Rearmament' debate, 24 March 1938. Hansard, 5th Series, Vol. 333, cc1405–1406. Quoted in Winston S. Churchill to Ewald von Kleist-Schmenzin, 19 August 1938. CAC, The Papers of Sir Winston Churchill, CHAR 2/340/155–157.
75. Winston S. Churchill to Ewald von Kleist-Schmenzin, 19 August 1938. Ibid.
76. Ibid.
77. Winston S. Churchill to Neville Chamberlain, 24 August 1938. CAC, The Papers of Sir Winston Churchill, CHAR 2/331/130.
78. 'Unofficial German Approaches, August–September, 1938: Letter from Mr Neville Chamberlain to Viscount Halifax, August 19 1938'. In Woodward, Butler and Lambert (eds), *Documents on British Foreign Policy, 1919–1939*, p. 685.
79. Brüning, 'Accounts of Conversations with Notable People'.
80. Ibid.
81. Ibid.
82. Winston S. Churchill to Nellie Romilly, 6 September 1938. CAC, The Papers of Sir Winston Churchill, CHAR 2/331/22.
83. Nellie Romilly to Winston S. Churchill, 7 September 1938. Ibid., CHAR 2/331/24.

Chapter 9: The View from Prague

1. Soames, *A Daughter's Tale*, p. 120.
2. Geoffrey Dawson to Shiela Grant Duff, 30 October 1934. Bodleian Archives & Manuscripts, Archive of Shiela Grant Duff, MS. 9663/66.
3. Shiela Grant Duff, 'Saar Minority's Plight', *The Observer*, 20 January 1935. Ibid., MS. 9663/66.
4. Edgar Mowrer, reference for Shiela Grant Duff, 13 November 1935. Ibid., MS. 9663/66.
5. Edgar Mowrer to Shiela Grant Duff, 23 January 1935. Ibid., MS. 9663/66.
6. Hugh Dalton to Edvard Beneš, 18 June 1936. Ibid., MS. 9663/66.
7. Shiela Grant Duff, obituary for Hubert Ripka, 9 January 1957. Ibid., MS. Grant Duff 6/5.
8. Shiela Grant Duff, obituary for Noemi Ripka, undated. Ibid., MS. Grant Duff 6/5.
9. Shiela Grant Duff. Notes about Otto Strasser, 5 October 1936. Ibid., MS. 9663/66.

10. Edgar Mowrer to Shiela Grant Duff, 13 November 1936. Ibid., MS. 9663/66.
11. Shiela Grant Duff to Edgar Mowrer, January 1937. Ibid., MS. 9663/66.
12. Edgar Mowrer to Shiela Grant Duff, 4 March 1937. Ibid., MS. 9663/66.
13. Elizabeth Wiskemann to Shiela Grant Duff, 24 March 1937. Ibid., MS. 9663/66.
14. Edgar Mowrer to Shiela Grant Duff, 5 April 1937. Ibid., MS. 9663/66.
15. Shiela Grant Duff to Hugh Dalton, 17 April 1937. Ibid., MS. 9663/66.
16. Shiela Grant Duff to Winston S. Churchill, 19 June 1937. Ibid., MS. Grant Duff 3.
17. Shiela Grant Duff, *The Parting of the Ways: A Personal Account of the Thirties* (Peter Owen: London: 1982), p. 157.
18. Soames, *A Daughter's Tale*, p. 120.
19. Shiela Grant Duff, 'Notes about Winston Churchill, July 1937'. Bodleian Archives & Manuscripts, Archive of Shiela Grant Duff, MS. Grant Duff 3.
20. Grant Duff, *The Parting of the Ways*, p. 161.
21. Grant Duff, 'Notes about Winston Churchill, July 1937'.
22. Grant Duff, *The Parting of the Ways*, p. 159.
23. Ibid., p. 163.
24. Wilson Harris to Shiela Grant Duff, 9 December 1937. Bodleian Archives & Manuscripts, Archive of Shiela Grant Duff, MS. 9663/66.
25. Winston S. Churchill to Shiela Grant Duff, 8 January 1938. Ibid., MS. Grant Duff 3.
26. Hupert Ripka to Shiela Grant Duff, 31 January 1938. Ibid., MS. Grant Duff 6/1.
27. Grant Duff, *The Parting of the Ways*, p. 165.
28. Shiela Grant Duff to Winston S. Churchill, 18 March 1938. Bodleian Archives & Manuscripts, Archive of Shiela Grant Duff, MS. Grant Duff 3.
29. Clement Attlee's Private Secretary to Shiela Grant Duff, 1 April 1938. Ibid., MS. 9663/66.
30. Shiela Grant Duff to Hubert Ripka, 6 April 1938. Ibid., MS. Grant Duff 6/1.
31. Hubert Ripka to Shiela Grant Duff, 8 April 1938. Ibid., MS. Grant Duff 6/1.
32. Ibid.
33. Shiela Grant Duff to Hubert Ripka, 12 April 1938. Bodleian Archives & Manuscripts, Archive of Shiela Grant Duff, MS. Grant Duff 6/1.
34. Keith G. Robbins, 'Konrad Henlein, the Sudeten Question and British Foreign Policy', *Historical Journal*, Vol. 12, No. 4 (Dec. 1969), p. 693.
35. Churchill, *The Second World War, Volume 1*, p. 239.
36. Winston S. Churchill, speaking at Chingford, Essex, 23 May 1938. In Robert Rhodes James (ed.), *Winston S. Churchill: His Complete Speeches 1897–1963*, 8 vols (Bowker: New York: 1974), Vol. VI, p. 5965.
37. J. Noakes and G. Pridham, *Nazism 1919–1945: Foreign Policy, War, and Racial Extermination*, Vol. 3 (University of Exeter Press: Exeter: 2010), p. 102.
38. Shiela Grant Duff recalls this meeting as taking place at Chartwell, although there are correspondences indicating that it may have taken place at the Morpeth Mansions Flat. See CAC, The Papers of Sir Winston Churchill, CHAR 2/330/68.
39. Grant Duff, *The Parting of the Ways*, p. 171.
40. Winston S. Churchill, 'What Freedom Means to France – Amid Flash of Arms in Paris, the Nation's Peaceful Genius Called out to Europe', *Daily Telegraph*, 26 July 1938, p. 14.

41. Hubert Ripka to Shiela Grant Duff, 26 July 1938. Bodleian Archives & Manuscripts, Archive of Shiela Grant Duff, MS. Grant Duff 6/1.
42. Shiela Grant Duff to Winston S. Churchill, 28 July 1938. CAC, The Papers of Sir Winston Churchill, CHAR 2/330/143.
43. Ibid., CHAR 2/330/145.
44. David Scott Fox to Shiela Grant Duff, 13 July 1938. Bodleian Archives & Manuscripts, Archive of Shiela Grant Duff, MS. 9663/66.
45. Hubert Ripka to Shiela Grant Duff, 27 August 1938. Ibid., MS. Grant Duff 6/1.
46. Winston S. Churchill to Robert Boothby, 27 August 1938. CAC, The Papers of Sir Winston Churchill, CHAR 2/331/5.
47. Winston S. Churchill to Lord Halifax, 31 August 1938. Foreign Office Papers: 800/314. In Gilbert (ed.), *The Churchill Documents, Volume 13*, pp. 1130–31.
48. Churchill writes in *The Gathering Storm* that the meeting took place on 2 September but there is no reference to the meeting in his calendar cards or Clementine's engagement diaries. The diaries of Ivan Maisky, published in 2015, reveal the meeting to have taken place on 4 September, which would then have been a matter of hours after Heinrich Brüning's last meeting with Churchill.
49. Ivan Maisky, Diary, 4 September 1938. In Gabriel Gorodetsky (ed.), *The Maisky Diaries: Red Ambassador to the Court of St James's 1932–1943* (Yale University Press: New Haven and London: 2015), p. 123.
50. Ibid., p. 124.
51. Soames, *A Daughter's Tale*, p. 110.
52. Ivan Maisky, Diary, 4 September 1938. In Gorodetsky (ed.), *The Maisky Diaries*, p. 124.
53. Ibid.
54. Ibid.
55. Churchill, *The Second World War, Volume 1*, p. 245.
56. Ibid., p. 246.
57. Karl Silex to Shiela Grant Duff, 2 September 1938. Bodleian Archives & Manuscripts, Archive of Shiela Grant Duff, MS. 9663/66.
58. Edgar Mowrer to Shiela Grant Duff, 3 September 1938. Ibid., MS. 9663/66.
59. Shiela Grant Duff to Hubert Ripka, 'About September 15 1938'. Ibid., MS. Grant Duff 6/1.
60. Joseph P. Kennedy, Diary, 4 April 1938. In Smith (ed.), *Hostage to Fortune*, p. 250.
61. Ralph F. De Bedts, *Ambassador Joseph Kennedy 1938–1940: An Anatomy of Appeasement* (P. Lang: New York: 1985), p. 85.
62. Neville Chamberlain to Winston S. Churchill, 8 September 1938. CAC, The Papers of Sir Winston Churchill, CHAR 8/596/15.
63. John Holman to Winston S. Churchill, 8 September 1938. Ibid., CHAR 2/331/30–31.
64. Ivan Maisky, Diary, 13 September 1938. In Gorodetsky (ed.), *The Maisky Diaries*, p. 128.
65. H. A. Pollock to Winston S. Churchill, 16 September 1938. CAC, The Papers of Sir Winston Churchill, CHAR 8/594/164.
66. Shiela Grant Duff to Hubert Ripka, 18 September 1938. Bodleian Archives & Manuscripts, Archive of Shiela Grant Duff, MS. Grant Duff 6/1.

67. Naomi Black, 'Decision-Making and the Munich Crisis', *British Journal of International Studies*, Vol. 6, No. 3, special number on appeasement (Oct. 1980), p. 302.
68. Ivan Maisky, Diary, 19 September 1938. In Gorodetsky (ed.), *The Maisky Diaries*, p. 132.
69. Winston S. Churchill. Press Statement. 21 September 1938. CAC, The Papers of Sir Winston Churchill, CHAR 9/132/51–52.
70. Harold Nicolson. Diary, 22 September 1938. In N. Nicolson (ed.), *Harold Nicolson: Diaries and Letters*, p. 364.
71. Jan Masaryk to Winston S. Churchill, 27 September 1938. CAC, The Papers of Sir Winston Churchill, CHAR 2/331/98.
72. Anthony Crossley to Florence Crossley, 26 September 1938. Crossley Papers. In Gilbert (ed.), *The Churchill Documents, Volume 13*, p. 1178.
73. Winston S. Churchill, 26 September 1938. In Churchill (Jnr) (ed.), *Never Give In!*, p. 140.
74. Leo Amery, Diary, 26 September 1938. Amery Papers. In Gilbert (ed.), *The Churchill Documents, Volume 13*, p. 1179.
75. Ibid., p. 1180.
76. Harold Nicolson, Diary, 26 September 1938. In N. Nicolson (ed.), *Harold Nicolson: Diaries and Letters*, p. 367.
77. Ibid.
78. Ibid., pp. 367–68.
79. Ivan Maisky, Diary, 28 September 1938. In Gorodetsky (ed.) *The Maisky Diaries*, p. 141.
80. Harold Nicolson, Diary, 22 September 1938. In N. Nicolson (ed.), *Harold Nicolson: Diaries and Letters*, p. 367.
81. Neville Chamberlain, speaking in 'Prime Minister's Statement', 28 September 1938. Hansard, 5th Series, Vol. 339, cc5–28.
82. Harold Nicolson, Diary, 28 September 1938. In N. Nicolson (ed.), *Harold Nicolson: Diaries and Letters*, p. 371.
83. Director of Military Operations & Intelligence to Shiela Grant Duff, 4 October 1938. Referencing a letter written by Grant Duff on 28 September 1938. Bodleian Archives & Manuscripts, Archive of Shiela Grant Duff, MS. 9663/66.
84. Ivan Maisky, Diary, 30 September 1938 (writing of events on 29 September). In Gorodetsky (ed.), *The Maisky Diaries*, p. 142.
85. Violet Bonham Carter. In Spier, *FOCUS*, p. 11.
86. Ivan Maisky, Diary, 30 September 1938 (writing of events on 29 September). In Gorodetsky (ed.), *The Maisky Diaries*, p. 142.
87. Guy Burgess, speaking in 1951. Account of meeting with Churchill in 1938. Recording hosted on City University of London SoundCloud account: https://soundcloud.com/cityunilondon/the-guy-burgess-tape-source.
88. Guy Burgess to Winston S. Churchill, 1 October 1938. CAC, The Papers of Sir Winston Churchill, CHAR 2/350/24.
89. Winston S. Churchill, speaking in 'Policy of His Majesty's Government', 5 October 1938. Hansard, 5th Series, Vol. 339, cc337–454.
90. Soames, *A Daughter's Tale*, p. 120.
91. Edgar Ansel Mowrer, *Triumph and Turmoil: A Personal History of our Time* (Weybright and Talley: New York: 1968), p. 220. Note: Mower references this as his first meeting with Churchill, and dates it to after the Munich Agreement,

though in his memoirs he states that he was the only guest. All other records indicate he visited alongside Shiela Grant Duff and Ian Colvin on 29 October 1938, with no post-Munich Agreement visit before then.
92. Grant Duff, *The Parting of the Way*, p. 194.
93. Mowrer, *Triumph and Turmoil*, p. 220.
94. Winston S. Churchill to Paul Reynaud, 10 October 1938. CAC, The Papers of Sir Winston Churchill, CHAR 2/332/44–45.
95. Mowrer, *Triumph and Turmoil*, p. 220.
96. Ibid. Shiela Grant Duff also recalls this remark in Grant Duff, *The Parting of the Ways*, p. 194.
97. Grant Duff, *The Parting of the Ways*, p. 194.
98. Winston S. Churchill, quoted in ibid., p. 194.

Chapter 10: Through the Lens

1. Winston S. Churchill to Violet Pearman, 1 November 1938. CAC, The Papers of Sir Winston Churchill, CHAR 8/594/174.
2. Olive Harrington to Winston S. Churchill, 6 November 1938. Ibid., CHAR 9/133/14.
3. Winston S. Churchill, Press Statement, 6 November 1938. Ibid., CHAR 9/133/18–19.
4. Adolf Hitler, speech, 6 November 1938. TNA, Records of the Foreign Office, 371/21708.
5. 'The work of the instigator-international: A straight line from Churchill to Grynszpan', *Der Angriff*, 9 November 1938. In Gilbert (ed.), *The Churchill Documents, Volume 13*, p. 1258.
6. Martin Gilbert, *Kristallnacht: Prelude to Destruction* (HarperPress: London: 2006), p. 1.
7. Stefan Lorant to Winston S. Churchill, 12 November 1938. CAC, The Papers of Sir Winston Churchill, CHAR 2/333/47.
8. Michael Hallett, *The Real Story of Picture Post* (ARTicle Press: Birmingham: 1994), p. 79.
9. Thierry Gervais, *The Making of Visual News: A History of Photography in the Press* (Bloomsbury: London: 2017), p. 115.
10. Wolfgang Benz and Barbara Distel, *Terror ohne System: Die ersten Konzentrationslager im Nationalsozialismus 1933–1935* (Metropol: Berlin: 2001), p. 10.
11. Michael Hallett interview with Stefan Lorant, 10 April 1992. The Stefan Lorant Collection is part of the Michael Hallett Archive, deposited at the Library of Birmingham (LoB).
12. Ibid.
13. 'Three Jubilees', *Country Life*, Vol. 77, No. 2000 (18 May 1935), p. 529.
14. Stefan Lorant to Winston S. Churchill, 12 November 1938. CAC, The Papers of Sir Winston Churchill, CHAR 2/333/47.
15. Ibid., CHAR 2/333/48.
16. Thornton Butterworth to Winston S. Churchill, 18 November 1938. Ibid., CHAR 8/605/158.
17. Private Secretary of Winston S. Churchill to Stefan Lorant, 14 November 1938. Ibid., CHAR 2/333/51.

18. Stefan Lorant to Winston S. Churchill, 16 November 1938. Ibid., CHAR 2/333/58.
19. Winston S. Churchill to Stefan Lorant, 21 November 1938. Ibid., CHAR 2/333/71.
20. Stuart Ball, 'Churchill and the Conservative Party', *Transactions of the Royal Historical Society*, Vol. 11 (2001), p. 321.
21. David Arthur Thomas, *Churchill: The Member for Woodford* (F. Cass: Ilford: 1995), p. 98.
22. Ian Colvin Memorandum, 23 November 1938. CAC, The Papers of Sir Winston Churchill, CHAR 2/340/162–165.
23. '(Secret box)' written in the upper right corner of Colvin's letter, as well as numerous other correspondences. Other such documents included a map of Europe from 1938 entitled 'Germany in 1950'. It included reference to a 'German Empire' which would total 250 m people and consist of 'Germany, Austria-Hungary, Portion of Russia, Holland, Belgium, Denmark & Balkan Provinces'. It also included reference to France having a half-German population by that date. Over Great Britain the only thing that is written is a question mark. See CAC, The Papers of Sir Winston Churchill, CHAR 2/340/198.
24. Harold Nicolson, Diary, 30 November 1938. In Gilbert (ed.), *The Churchill Documents, Volume 13*, p. 1293.
25. Winston S. Churchill to Clementine Churchill, 19 December 1938. CAC, The Papers of Clementine Ogilvy Spencer-Churchill, Baroness Spencer-Churchill of Chartwell, CSCT 2/28/19.
26. Winston S. Churchill to Clementine Churchill, 29 December 1938. Ibid., CSCT 2/28/27.
27. Winston S. Churchill to Clementine Churchill, 22 December 1938. Ibid., CSCT 2/28/23.
28. Winston S. Churchill to Clementine Churchill, 19 December 1938. Ibid., CSCT 2/28/19.
29. Winston S. Churchill to Clementine Churchill, 29 December 1938. Ibid., CSCT 2/28/30.
30. Winston S. Churchill to Clementine Churchill, 5 January 1939. Ibid., CSCT 2/29/2.
31. Winston S. Churchill to Clementine Churchill, 22 December 1938. Ibid., CSCT 2/28/23.
32. Winston S. Churchill to Clementine Churchill, 29 December 1938. Ibid., CSCT 2/28/25.
33. Ibid., CSCT 2/28/28.
34. Ibid., CSCT 2/28/29.
35. Winston S. Churchill to Clementine Churchill, 5 January 1939. Ibid., CSCT 2/29/2.
36. Sheean, *Between the Thunder and the Sun*, p. 73.
37. Ibid.
38. Mary Penman, Journal, 24 January 1939. Penman Papers. In Gilbert (ed.), *The Churchill Documents, Volume 13*, p. 1353.
39. Mary Penman, Journal, 25 January 1939. Penman Papers. In ibid., p. 1353.
40. Stefan Lorant to Winston S. Churchill, 23 January 1939. CAC, The Papers of Sir Winston Churchill, CHAR 8/635/1.
41. Halla Beloff, *Camera Culture* (Basil Blackwell: Oxford: 1985), p. 114.

42. Notes from 'The Life and Death of Picture Post' for BBC Television, 1977. In Michael Hallett, *Conversations with Lorant* (Crabapple Publications: Worcester: 2020), p. 14.
43. Michael Hallett interview with Stefan Lorant, 29 April 1991. The Stefan Lorant Collection, LoB.
44. Michael Hallett interview with Stefan Lorant, 10 April 1992. Ibid.
45. Michael Hallett interview with Stefan Lorant, 29 April 1991. Ibid.
46. Michael Hallett interview with Stefan Lorant, 10 April 1992. Ibid.
47. Michael Hallett interview with Stefan Lorant, 29 April 1991. Ibid.
48. Michael Hallett, 'Stefan Lorant Obituary', in *Published Work on Lorant* (Crabapple Publications: Worcester: 2020), p. 21.
49. Wickham Steed, 'Churchill', *Picture Post*, Vol. 2, No. 8 (25 February 1939), p. 15.
50. Ibid., p. 16.
51. 'Mr Winston Churchill Ill', *Liverpool Daily Post*, 25 February 1939, p. 8.
52. Peter Peirson to Kathleen Hill, 27 February 1939. CAC, The Papers of Sir Winston Churchill, CHAR 2/357/214–215.
53. Ibid.
54. Poem originally featured in *Punch*, 4 October 1890. In Soames, *A Daughter's Tale*, p. 124.
55. 'Life in Shanghai', *Picture Post*, Vol. 2, No. 10 (11 March 1939), p. 19.
56. Winston S. Churchill, 'What Britain's Policy Should Be', *Picture Post*, Vol. 2, No. 10 (11 March 1939), p. 28.
57. Ibid.
58. Ibid., p. 29.
59. Mary Ann Nicholas, 'Review – Picture Post', *British Journalism Review*, Vol. 6, No. 1 (1995), p. 74.
60. Peter Peirson to Kathleen Hill, 12 March 1939. CAC, The Papers of Sir Winston Churchill, CHAR 2/358/30–31.
61. Winston S. Churchill, speaking in 'Army (Royal Ordnance Factories) Supplementary Estimate, 1938', 14 March 1939. Hansard, 5th Series, Vol. 345, cc241–332.
62. Winston S. Churchill, speaking in Waltham Abbey, 14 March 1939. In Randolph S. Churchill (ed.), *Into Battle: Speeches by the Right Hon. Winston S. Churchill, P.C., M.P.* (Cassell and Company: London: 1941), p. 76.
63. C. A. Macdonald and Jan Kaplan, *Prague in the Shadow of the Swastika: A History of the German Occupation, 1939–1945* (Quartet Books: London: 1995), p. 19.
64. Ibid.
65. Peter Peirson to Kathleen Hill, 18 March 1939. CAC, The Papers of Sir Winston Churchill, CHAR 2/358/51.
66. Hubert Ripka recollections of a meeting at Chartwell on 19 March 1939. Bodleian Archives & Manuscripts, Archive of Shiela Grant Duff, MS. Grant Duff 6/5.
67. Michael Hallett, *Stefan Lorant: Godfather of Photojournalism* (Scarecrow Press: Lanham, MD: 2005), p. 71.
68. Winston S. Churchill to Maurice Ashley, 24 March 1939. CAC, The Papers of Sir Winston Churchill, CHAR 8/626/150.

Chapter 11: The Future Prime Minister

1. Winston S. Churchill, speaking in 'Statement by the Prime Minister', 23 May 1916. Hansard, 5th Series, Vol. 82, cc2003–69.
2. Harold Macmillan to Helen Macmillan, 26 May 1916. In Alistair Horne, *Macmillan 1894–1956: Vol. 1 of the Official Biography* (Membury Press: London: 1988), p. 41.
3. Horne, *Macmillan 1894–1956*, p. 45.
4. Charles Williams, *Harold Macmillan* (Phoenix: London: 2010), pp. 44–5.
5. D. R. Thorpe, *Supermac: The Life of Harold Macmillan* (Pimlico: London: 2011), pp. 57–8.
6. Harold Macmillan to Winston S. Churchill, 10 April 1926. CAC, The Papers of Sir Winston Churchill, CHAR 2/147/73.
7. Macmillan, *Winds of Change*, p. 176.
8. Harold Macmillan, *The Past Masters: Politics and Politicians, 1906–1939* (Macmillan: London: 1975), p. 150.
9. Alistair Horne taped interviews with Harold Macmillan, 1979–1986. In Horne, *Macmillan 1894–1956*, p. 110.
10. Robert Boothby to Cynthia Mosley, 14 September 1932. In Robert Rhodes James, *Robert Boothby: A Portrait of Churchill's Ally* (Viking: New York: 1991), p. 115.
11. Alistair Horne, *Harold Macmillan: The Official Biography* (Penguin Books: New York: 1991), p. 87.
12. Harold Macmillan, 'To the Electors of Stockton and Thornaby: What I Stand For', 6 November 1935. Bodleian Archives & Manuscripts, Archive of Harold Macmillan, MS. Macmillan dep. c. 990, p. 232.
13. Harold Macmillan, 'Macmillan's Bulletin', July 1936. Vol. 1, No. 2. Bodleian Archives & Manuscripts, Archive of Harold Macmillan, MS. Macmillan dep. c. 990, pp. 272-273.
14. Williams, *Harold Macmillan*, p. 87.
15. Macmillan, *Winds of Change*, p. 542.
16. Harold Macmillan, quoted in *Northern Echo*, 18 March 1938. In Macmillan, *Winds of Change*, p. 543.
17. Ibid.
18. R. Aldous and S. Lee (eds), *Harold Macmillan: Aspects of a Political Life* (Palgrave Macmillan: London: 1999), p. 148.
19. Winston S. Churchill to Harcourt Johnstone, 14 February 1939. CAC, The Papers of Sir Winston Churchill, CHAR 1/343/52.
20. Julian Amery, speaking at the Kemper Lecture, America's National Churchill Museum, 27 March 1994.
21. Winston S. Churchill to Arthur Richards, 3 March 1939. CAC, The Papers of Sir Winston Churchill, CHAR 2/376/19.
22. Harold Macmillan, *The Price of Peace: Notes on the World Crisis* (Macmillan and Co.,: London: 1938).
23. Harold Macmillan, *Economic Aspects of Defence* (Macmillan and Co.,: London: 1939), pp. 1–19.
24. 'Minutes of the Annual General Meeting of the Organisation held in Palais de Dance, Stockton, on Friday 10 March 1939 at 7 p.m.', Bodleian Archives & Manuscripts, Archive of Harold Macmillan, MS. Macmillan dep. c. 131, fold 1–188.

25. Mary Soames, Diary, 18 March 1939. CAC, The Papers of Lady Soames, MCHL 1/1/1.
26. Mary Soames, Diary, 24 and 25 March 1939. Ibid.
27. Lachlan MacLean to Winston S. Churchill, 21 March 1939. CAC, The Papers of Sir Winston Churchill, CHAR 2/371/44–45.
28. Harold Nicolson, Diary, 27 March 1939. In Gilbert (ed.), *The Churchill Documents, Volume 13*, p. 1418.
29. 'Call for Policy of Lord Halifax', *Daily News (London)*, 29 March 1939, p. 1.
30. Harold Nicolson, Diary, 27 March 1939. In N. Nicolson (ed.), *Harold Nicolson: Diaries and Letters*, p. 393.
31. David Lloyd George, speaking in 'Military Training Bill' debate, 8 May 1939. Hansard, 5th Series, Vol. 347, cc45–167.
32. Neville Chamberlain to Ida Chamberlain, 26 March 1939. Birmingham University Library, Papers of Neville Chamberlain, NC 18/1/1091.
33. Winston S. Churchill, speaking in 'European Situation' debate, 3 April 1939. Hansard, 5th Series, Vol. 345, cc2475–2588.
34. Ibid.
35. Rhodes James (ed.), *Chips: The Diaries of Sir Henry Channon*, p. 192.
36. Harold Nicolson, Diary, 3 April 1939. In Gilbert (ed.), *The Churchill Documents, Volume 13*, pp. 1429–30.
37. 'Court Circular', *Daily Telegraph*, 5 April 1939, p. 17.
38. Cyril Newall to Winston S. Churchill, 5 April 1939. CAC, The Papers of Sir Winston Churchill, CHAR 2/358B/123.
39. Winston S. Churchill to Bernard Baruch, 6 April 1939. Ibid., CHAR 1/343/92.
40. Political Secretary of Harold Macmillan to Edward Casey, 5 April 1939. Bodleian Archives & Manuscripts, Archive of Harold Macmillan, MS. Macmillan dep. c. 131, fold 1–188.
41. Winston S. Churchill, quoted in Arthur Christiansen, *Headlines All My Life* (Harper: New York: 1961), p. 178.
42. Mary Soames, Diary, 7 April 1939. CAC, The Papers of Lady Soames, MCHL 1/1/1.
43. Macmillan, *Winds of Change*, p. 539.
44. Ibid.
45. Mary Soames, Diary, 7 April 1939. CAC, The Papers of Lady Soames, MCHL 1/1/1.
46. Neville Chamberlain to Ida Chamberlain, 9 April 1939. In Robert Self (ed.), *The Neville Chamberlain Diary Letters, Vol. 4, The Downing Street Years: 1934–1940* (Ashgate: Aldershot: 2000), p. 403.
47. Winston S. Churchill, Draft Press Statement, 8 April 1939. In Gilbert (ed.), *The Churchill Documents, Volume 13*, pp. 1435.
48. Churchill, *The Second World War, Volume 1*, p. 288.
49. Harold Macmillan to Ronald Knox, 30 March 1939. Bodleian Archives & Manuscripts, Archive of Harold Macmillan, MS. Macmillan dep. c. 131, fold 1–188, p. 230.
50. Harold Nicolson, Diary, 11 April 1939. In N. Nicolson (ed.), *Harold Nicolson: Diaries and Letters*, p. 397.
51. Harold Macmillan to Alan F. Lascelles, 11 April 1939. Bodleian Archives & Manuscripts, Archive of Harold Macmillan, MS. Macmillan dep. c. 131, fold 1–188, p. 237.

52. Churchill, *The Second World War, Volume 1*, p. 291.
53. Leslie Hore-Belisha, Diary, 11 April 1939. In Gilbert, *Winston S. Churchill, Volume V: The Prophet of Truth*, p. 1057.
54. Winston S. Churchill to Eric Long, 15 April 1939. CAC, The Papers of Sir Winston Churchill, CHAR 2/371/73.
55. Winston S. Churchill, speaking in 'European Situation' debate, 13 April 1939. Hansard, 5th Series, Vol. 346, cc5–140.
56. Robert Boothby to Winston S. Churchill, 15 April 1939. CAC, The Papers of Sir Winston Churchill, CHAR 2/358/161.
57. Neville Chamberlain to Ida Chamberlain, 15 April 1939. In Self (ed.), *The Neville Chamberlain Diary Letters, Vol. 4*, p. 407.
58. Macmillan, *Winds of Change*, p. 541.
59. 'Axis Telephone Line Busy', *China Mail*, 17 April 1939, No. 30, 654, p. 1.
60. Winston S. Churchill, Broadcast of 28 April 1939, Transcript. In Martin Gilbert, *Churchill and America* (Free Press: New York: 2005), p. 171.
61. Ibid.
62. Churchill, *The Second World War, Volume 1*, p. 288.

Chapter 12: A Final Plea

1. Quo Tai-chi, also known as Guo Taiqi. The former is used in this text as it reflects how the Ambassador was typically referenced in contemporary records and documents in the United Kingdom at the time, including press coverage, diplomatic correspondence and official Government documents on British foreign policy. It is for this reason that all Chinese names of people and places appear in this book using the Wade-Giles system of romanisation.
2. Kathleen Hill interview conducted by Pat Ackerman. CAC, Churchill Oral History Collection, CHOH 1 KHLL – Tape 1, Side 1.
3. Soames, *Clementine Churchill*, p. 313.
4. Mary Soames, Diary, 5 May 1939. CAC, The Papers of Lady Soames, MCHL 01/01/01.
5. Ibid.
6. Archibald Clark Kerr to Foreign Office, 4 May 1939. TNA, Records of the Foreign Office, FO 676/409, Anglo Chinese Relations, p. 80.
7. Ibid., p. 81.
8. Lord Cecil to Anthony Eden, 4 May 1939. CAC, The Papers of Sir Winston Churchill, CHAR 2/349/6.
9. Lord Cecil to Winston S. Churchill, 10 May 1939. Ibid., CHAR 2/349/4–5.
10. Winston S. Churchill to Lord Cecil, 13 May 1939. Ibid., CHAR 2/349/8.
11. Charles Nelson Spinks, 'The Termination of the Anglo-Japanese Alliance', *Pacific Historical Review*, Vol. 6, No. 4 (Dec. 1937), pp. 321–40.
12. Winston S. Churchill to Stanley Baldwin, 15 December 1924. In Gilbert, *Winston S. Churchill, Volume V: The Prophet of Truth*, p. 76.
13. Quo Tai-chi, 'Statement of the Chinese delegate in the League Assembly, Dec. 8, 1932'. In Westel W. Willoughby, *The Sino-Japanese Controversy and the League of Nations* (Johns Hopkins University Press: Baltimore, MD: 1935), p. 457.
14. Arnold C. Brackman, *The Last Emperor* (Scribner: New York: 1975), p. 194.
15. Winston S. Churchill, speaking at the 25th meeting of the Anti-Socialist and Anti-Communist Meeting, 17 February 1933. In Gilbert, *Winston S. Churchill, Volume V: The Prophet of Truth*, pp. 456–57.

16. Winston S. Churchill, 'Germany and Japan' speech, 27 November 1936. In Winston S. Churchill, *Step by Step: Political Writings, 1936–1939* (Bloomsbury Academic: London: 2015), p. 53.
17. Ibid.
18. 'Personalities in the News', *China Journal*, Vol. 31 (1939), p. 153.
19. 'Monthly Review of Chinese Affairs, February 1937'. TNA, Records of the Foreign Office, FO 676/263, 1937: Chinese Affairs.
20. 'Japan's Position', *The Times*, 3 May 1937, p. 15.
21. Hughe Montgomery Knatchbull-Hugessen to Foreign Office, 4 May 1937. TNA, Records of the Foreign Office, FO 676/330, Anglo Chinese Relations.
22. 'British Say China Fears Groundless', *China Press*, 16 May 1937. Ibid.
23. Ivan Maisky, Diary, 1 August 1937. In Gorodetsky (ed.), *The Maisky Diaries*, p. 85.
24. Robin I. Mordfin, 'Seeking the Past: Early Chinese Scholars at the Law Schools', University of Chicago Law School, Fall 2012, p. 15.
25. Hans Ingvar Roth, *P. C. Chang and the Universal Declaration of Human Rights* (University of Pennsylvania Press: Philadelphia, PA: 2018), p. 69.
26. P. C. Chang, 'Civilisation and Social Philosophies', *Progressive Education Booklet*, No. 9, 1938, pp. 5–6.
27. Roth, *P. C. Chang*, p. 71.
28. 'Merely an "Incident" in China, But Then', *Evening Express*, 27 May 1938. Press Cutting. CAC, The Papers of Sir Winston Churchill, CHAR 8/611/62.
29. Winston S. Churchill, 'The Lights Are Going Out', broadcast to the United States, 16 October 1938. In Churchill (Jnr) (ed.), *Never Give In!*, p. 183.
30. Quo Tai-chi to Winston S. Churchill, 18 October 1938. CAC, The Papers of Sir Winston Churchill, CHAR 2/349/9.
31. Quo Tai-chi to Lord Halifax, 7 November 1938. In E. L. Woodward and Rohan Butler (eds), *Documents on British Foreign Policy, 1919–1939* (Her Majesty's Stationery Office: London: 1955), pp. 198–9.
32. Sir Robert Ho Tung to Clementine Churchill, 23 November 1938. CAC, The Papers of Sir Winston Churchill, CHAR 1/343/2–3.
33. Clementine Churchill to Sir Robert Ho Tung, 2 January 1939. Ibid., CHAR 1/343/1.
34. 'New Phase of War in China – Offensive as Well as Defensive Action', 18 January 1939. TNA, Records of the War Office, WO 106/5795, China 189: 2. Dr P. C. Chang.
35. Notes related to Telegram to D. M. Chungking, 20 January 1939. British Embassy, Nanking. TNA, Records of the Foreign Office, FO 676/409, Anglo Chinese Relations, pp. 92–3.
36. R. G. Howe to Archibald Clark Kerr, 4 February 1939. TNA, Records of the War Office, WO 106/5795, China 189: 2. Dr P. C. Chang.
37. 'Notes on the views of Professor P.C. Chang who is visiting the D.M.O&I [Directorate of Military Operations and Intelligence] on Friday 10 February, 1939'. TNA, Records of the War Office, WO 106/5795, China 189: 2. Dr P. C. Chang.
38. Winston S. Churchill to Leo Amery, June 1939. CAC, The Papers of Sir Winston Churchill, CHAR 1/343/140.
39. 'The Great Churchill Scandal', *Sunday Pictorial*, 23 April 1939, p. 1.
40. John E. Walsh, 'Kent – The Home of Heroes', *Daily Herald*, 6 May 1939, p. 12.

41. Paul Maze, Diary, 10 May 1939. In Gilbert (ed.), *The Churchill Documents*, *Volume 13*, p. 1496.
42. Churchill, *The Second World War, Volume 1*, p. 307.
43. Adolf Hitler, speaking on 23 May 1939. 'Minutes of Fuehrer Conference, 23 May 1939, Concerning Indoctrination on the Political Situation and Future Aims', *Trials of War Criminals before the Nuernberg Military Tribunals under Control Council Law No. 10* (Government Printing Office: Washington, DC: 1951), p. 674.
44. Churchill, *The Second World War, Volume 1*, p. 309.
45. L. B. Namier, *Europe in Decay* (Macmillan & Co.: London: 1950), p. 264.
46. F. H. Hinsley, *Hitler's Strategy* (Cambridge University Press: Cambridge: 1951), p. 17.
47. 'Extract from "Parliamentary Debates", House of Lords Official Report (Unrevised), Vol. 133, No. 70, Thursday, 8 June, 1939'. TNA, Records of the Foreign Office, FO 676/409, Anglo Chinese Relations.
48. Winston S. Churchill to Lord Halifax, 11 June 1939. CAC, The Papers of Sir Winston Churchill, CHAR 2/359/106–107.
49. Ibid.
50. Winston S. Churchill to Edward Marsh, 6 June 1939. Ibid., CHAR 8/626/66.
51. Winston S. Churchill, quoted in Harold Nicolson, Diary, 14 June 1939. N. Nicolson (ed.), *Harold Nicolson: Diaries and Letters*, p. 403.
52. Kingsley Wood to Winston S. Churchill, 15 June 1939. CAC, The Papers of Sir Winston Churchill, CHAR 25/17/48.
53. Edmund Ironside to Winston S. Churchill, 17 June 1939. Ibid., CHAR 2/371/141–142.
54. Winston S. Churchill to James Gordon Bill, 22 June 1939. CAC, The Papers of Sir Winston Churchill, 1/351/25.
55. 'The Blockade at Tientsin – Statement by the British Foreign Office', 16 June 1939. In *Bulletin of International News*, Vol. 16, No. 13 (1 July 1939), pp. 10–11.
56. Ibid., p. 11.
57. 'Memorandum – British Assistance to China', R. L. Craigie, British Embassy, Tokyo, 14 June 1939. TNA, Records of the Foreign Office, FO 676/409, Anglo Chinese Relations, pp. 73–75.
58. Lawrence Impey, 'Man in Tientsin', *Hong Kong Telegraph*, 8 July 1939, p. 8.
59. Note from the Directorate of Military Operations and Intelligence, 8 February 1939. TNA, Records of the War Office, WO 106/5795, China 189: 2. Dr P. C. Chang.
60. Extracts from an address by Dr. P. C. Chang, 5 July 1939, WEVD Station. TNA, Records of the War Office. Clippings and mimeographed material: China, 1892–1943. Folder 3 (1934–1943), p. 9.
61. Tan Kah Tee to Winston S. Churchill, 1 August 1939. CAC, The Papers of Sir Winston Churchill, CHAR 2/361/2–3.
62. Martin Gilbert, *Churchill: A Photographic Portrait* (Houghton Mifflin Company: Boston, MA: 1974), p. 193.
63. Sir Henry Channon, Diary, 9 July 1939. In Rhodes James (ed.), *Chips: The Diaries of Sir Henry Channon*, p. 204.
64. Neville Chamberlain to Ida Chamberlain, 8 July 1939. Templewood Papers. In Gilbert (ed.), *The Churchill Documents, Volume 13*, p. 1556.
65. Sir Samuel Hoare to William Astor, 11 July 1939. Templewood Papers. In ibid., pp. 1561–62.

66. Tom Hopkinson to Winston S. Churchill, 13 July 1939. CAC, The Papers of Sir Winston Churchill, CHAR 8/635/35.
67. Stefan Lorant to Winston S. Churchill, 26 July 1939. Ibid., CHAR 8/635/39.
68. 'Notes from "The Life and Death of *Picture Post*" for BBC Television, 1977'. In Hallett, *Conversations with Lorant*, p. 14.
69. Archibald Sinclair to Winston S. Churchill, 10 July 1939. CAC, The Papers of Sir Winston Churchill, CHAR 2/360/8–10.
70. Julian Amery, 'Recollections' – Letter to the Author, 30 October 1981. Recalling a dinner at Chartwell on 18 July 1939. In Gilbert (ed.), *The Churchill Documents, Volume 13*, p. 1569
71. General Sir Edmund Ironside, Diary, 25 July 1939. Ironside Papers. In ibid., p. 1576.
72. Ibid., p. 1575.
73. Jean MacDougall to Winston S. Churchill, 29 July 1939. CAC, The Papers of Sir Winston Churchill, CHAR 2/360/78.
74. Private Secretary of Winston S. Churchill to Jean MacDougall, 2 August 1939. Ibid., CHAR 2/361A/20.
75. E. C. Hole to Winston S. Churchill, 28 July 1939. Ibid., CHAR 2/361A/73–74.
76. Sir Henry Channon, Diary, 2 August 1939. In Rhodes James (ed.), *Chips: The Diaries of Sir Henry Channon*, p. 207.
77. Neville Chamberlain to Ida Chamberlain, 5 August 1939. In Gilbert (ed.), *The Churchill Documents, Volume 13*, p. 1583.
78. Ibid.
79. Ibid.
80. Philip Noel-Baker, speaking in 'Adjournment Debate', 4 August 1939. Hansard, 5th Series, Vol. 350, cc2852–92.
81. Neville Chamberlain, speaking in 'Adjournment Debate', 4 August 1939. Ibid.
82. Mary Soames, Diary, 8 August 1939. CAC, The Papers of Lady Soames, MCHL 1/1/1.
83. Winston S. Churchill, 'A Hush over Europe' speech delivered from Chartwell, 8/9 August 1939. In Churchill (Jnr) (ed.), *Never Give In!*, p. 191.
84. Ibid., p. 192.
85. Ibid.
86. Laurence H. Marks to Winston S. Churchill, 8 August 1938. CAC, The Papers of Sir Winston Churchill, CHAR 2/361A-B/104.
87. J. W. Eaton to Winston S. Churchill, 12 August 1938. Ibid., CHAR 2/361A-B/135.
88. Martha Durnell to Winston S. Churchill, 13 August 1938. Ibid., CHAR 2/361A-B/168-16.
89. 'Mr Churchill on War Fears', *Daily Telegraph*, 9 August 1939, p. 12. Also 'Europe in Suspense', *The Times*, 10 August 1939, p. 14.
90. Bob Ogley, *Biggin on the Bump* (Froglets Publications: Westerham: 1990), p. 29.
91. 'Picture Gallery', *The Times*, 11 August 1939, p. 15.
92. Departmental Note to Sir Kingsley Wood, 9 August 1939. TNA, Records of the Air Ministry, 19/26.
93. 'Lord Halifax Sees Chinese Envoy', *Liverpool Daily Post*, 11 August 1939, p. 9.

94. Earlier draft of the article entitled 'Japanese Aggression'. CAC, The Papers of Sir Winston Churchill, CHAR 8/650/48.
95. Winston S. Churchill, 'A Word to Japan!', *Daily Mirror*, 11 August 1939, p. 15.
96. Winston S. Churchill, 'We Won't Give Way to Bullying by the Japs', *Belfast Telegraph*, 10 August 1939.
97. Gilbert, *The Wilderness Years*, p. 257.
98. Mary Ann Glendon, *A World Made New* (Random House: New York: 2001), p. 33.
99. Iris Chang, *The Rape of Nanking: The Forgotten Holocaust of World War II* (Basic Books: New York: 2014), pp. 1–2.
100. Quo Tai-chi to Winston S. Churchill, 13 August 1939. CAC, The Papers of Sir Winston Churchill, CHAR 2/364/31.
101. Ibid.
102. 'Mei-ling ("Beautiful Mood") Helps her Husband Rule China', *Life*, 16 August 1937, Vol. 3, No. 7, p. 17.
103. Hannah Pakula, *The Last Empress: Madame Chiang Kai-shek and the Birth of Modern China* (Simon & Schuster: New York: 2009), p. 305.
104. Winston S. Churchill, 'A Word to Japan!', *Daily Mirror*, 11 August 1939, p. 15.
105. A. H. Richards to Winston S. Churchill, 11 August 1939. In Gilbert (ed.), *The Churchill Documents, Volume 13*, p. 1586.
106. 'Secretary to Mr Winston Churchill – Married at Westerham', *Kent and Sussex Courier*, 18 August 1939, p. 8.
107. Winston S. Churchill to Clementine Churchill, 14 August 1939. CAC, The Papers of Clementine Ogilvy Spencer-Churchill, Baroness Spencer-Churchill of Chartwell, CSCT 2/29/10.
108. Gilbert, *The Wilderness Years*, p. 260.
109. Mary Soames, Diary, 17 August 1939. CAC, The Papers of Lady Soames, MCHL 1/1/1.
110. Paul Maze, Diary, 20 August 1939. In Gilbert, *The Wilderness Years*, p. 261.
111. Mary Soames, Diary, 22 August 1939. CAC, The Papers of Lady Soames, MCHL 1/1/1.
112. Geoffrey Roberts, *The Unholy Alliance: Stalin's Pact with Hitler* (Indiana University Press: Bloomington, IN: 1990), p. 162.
113. Harold Nicolson, Diary, 23 August 1939. In N. Nicolson (ed.), *Harold Nicolson: Diaries and Letters*, p. 411.
114. Kathleen Hill interview conducted by Pat Ackerman. CAC, Churchill Oral History Collection, CHOH 1 KHLL – Tape 1, Side 2.
115. Henry Channon, Diary, 24 August 1939. In Rhodes James (ed.), *Chips: The Diaries of Sir Henry Channon*, p. 209.
116. Mary Soames, Diary, 24 August 1939. CAC, The Papers of Lady Soames, MCHL 1/1/1.
117. Winston S. Churchill to Quo Tai-chi, 24 August 1939. CAC, The Papers of Sir Winston Churchill, CHAR 2/364/33.
118. Mary Soames, Diary, 25–27 August 1939. CAC, The Papers of Lady Soames, MCHL 1/1/1.
119. Churchill, *The Second World War, Volume 1*, p. 324.
120. Ibid.
121. Edmund Ironside, Diary, 1 September 1939. Ironside Papers. In Gilbert (ed.), *The Churchill Documents, Volume 13*, p. 1602.

122. 'Cash drawn by M. Jowett for Cale's expenses, which had already been paid', Expenses – September 1939. CAC, The Papers of Sir Winston Churchill, CHAR 8/639/108.

Epilogue: The Dawn of War

1. Ivan Maisky, Diary, 1 September 1939. In Gorodetsky (ed.), *The Maisky Diaries*, p. 221.
2. Churchill, *The Second World War, Volume*, p. 327.
3. Speech by the Prime Minister in the House of Commons on 1 September 1939. *Documents Concerning German–Polish Relations and the Outbreak of Hostilities between Great Britain and Germany on September 3, 1939* (His Majesty's Stationery Office: London: 1939), p. 161.
4. Ibid.
5. Quo Tai-chi, speaking on 1 September 1939. Quoted in 'More Chickens', *Victoria Daily Times*, 25 July 1941, p. 4.
6. Churchill, *The Second World War, Volume 1*, p. 328.
7. Mary Soames, Diary, 2 September 1939. CAC, The Papers of Lady Soames, MCHL 1/1/1.
8. 'The Londoner's Diary', *Evening Standard*, 18 September 1939, p. 4.
9. '2 September – Mrs H (House Goods)', Expenses – September 1939. CAC, The Papers of Sir Winston Churchill, CHAR 8/639/109.
10. Leopold Amery, *My Political Life: The Unforgiving Years, 1929–1940* (Hutchinson: London: 1955), p. 324.
11. Churchill, *The Second World War, Volume 1*, p. 328.
12. Alfred Duff Cooper, Diary, 2 September 1939. Norwich Papers. In Gilbert (ed.), *The Churchill Documents, Volume 13*, p. 1603.
13. Ibid.
14. Lord Camrose, Diary, 2 September 1939. Camrose Papers. In Gilbert (ed.), *The Churchill Documents, Volume 13*, p. 1602.
15. Kathleen Hill interview conducted by Pat Ackerman. CAC, Churchill Oral History Collection, CHOH 1 KHLL – Tape 1, Side 2.
16. Winston S. Churchill to Neville Chamberlain, written on 2 September 1939, delivered on 3 September 1939. In Churchill, *The Second World War, Volume 1*, p. 328.
17. Churchill, *The Second World War, Volume 1*, p. 329.
18. W. H. Thompson: Recollections. 'Sixty minutes with Winston Churchill'. In Gilbert (ed.), *The Churchill Documents, Volume 13*, p. 1609.
19. Fritz Günther von Tschirschky: Recollections. Martin Russell Papers. In ibid., p. 1610.
20. Churchill, *The Second World War, Volume 1*, p. 329.
21. Harold Nicolson, Diary, 3 September 1939. In N. Nicolson (ed.), *Harold Nicolson: Diaries and Letters*, p. 421.
22. Neville Chamberlain, speaking in 'Prime Minister's Announcement', 3 September 1939. Hansard, 5th Series, Vol. 351, cc291–302.
23. Robert Boothby to Winston S. Churchill, 3 September 1939. CAC, The Papers of Sir Winston Churchill, CHAR 2/363/57.
24. Harold Macmillan, *The Blast of War 1939–1945* (Macmillan: London: 1967), p. 3.

25. Winston S. Churchill, speaking in 'Prime Minister's Announcement', 3 September 1939. Hansard, 5th Series, Vol. 351, cc291–302.
26. W. H. Thompson: Recollections. 'Sixty minutes with Winston Churchill'. In Gilbert (ed.), *The Churchill Documents, Volume 13*, p. 1611.
27. Kathleen Hill interview conducted by Pat Ackerman. CAC, Churchill Oral History Collection, CHOH 1 KHLL – Tape 1, Side 2.
28. Mary Soames to Winston S. Churchill, 3 September 1939. In Soames, *A Daughter's Tale*, p. 133.
29. Home Office File containing letter from solicitors to Rt Hon. Captain David Margesson, MP re. Hanfstaengl to Sir V Kell. Report from 25 September 1939. TNA, Records of the Security Service, KV 2/469: Ernst Franz Sedgwick HANFSTAENGL, 151B.
30. Interpreter, No. 4 Internment Camp to The Commandant, No. 4 Internment Camp, 4 October 1939. Ibid., 182Y.
31. Steven Casey, 'Franklin D. Roosevelt, Ernst "Putzi" Hanfstaengl and the "S-Project", June 1942–June 1944', *Journal of Contemporary History*, Vol. 35, No. 3 (July 2000), pp. 339–59.
32. V. G. Well to Maurice Burton, 12 October 1939. TNA, Records of the Security Service, KV 2/344: Gottfried Reinhold TREVIRANUS, 152A.
33. Hömig, *Brüning – Politiker ohne Auftrag*, p. 91.
34. Ibid., p. 78
35. Heinrich Brüning to Mona Anderson, 27 August 1939. In ibid., p. 281.
36. Stefan Lorant, interview with Michael Hallett, 27 August 1992. In Hallett, *Conversations with Lorant*, p. 204.
37. Albert Einstein to Franklin Delano Roosevelt, 2 August 1939. President's Secretary's File: Safe File: Alexander Sachs, Franklin D. Roosevelt Library.
38. J. Simon Rofe, 'Joseph P. Kennedy, 1938–1940', in Alison R. Holmes and J. Simon Rofe (eds), *The Embassy in Grosvenor Square: American Ambassadors to the United Kingdom, 1938–2008* (Palgrave Macmillan: Basingstoke: 2012), p. 36.
39. Joseph P. Kennedy, Diary, 6 October 1939. John F. Kennedy Presidential Library. Box 100: Appointments and Diary 1938–1951.
40. Account of Alec Tuck, February 1941. In J. J. Astor to Brendan Bracken, 19 February 1941. TNA, Records of the Foreign Office, FO 371/2617 – 1941 United States. File 339.
41. J. J. Astor to Brendan Bracken, 19 February 1941. Ibid.
42. J. M. Martin to W. I. Mallet, 21 February 1941. Ibid.
43. Peter Collier and David Horowitz, *The Kennedys* (London: Secker & Warburg: 1984), p. 61.
44. John F. Kennedy, *Why England Slept* (Wilfred Funk: New York: 1940).
45. Ibid., p. 223.
46. Churchill, *The Second World War, Volume 1*, p. 236.
47. Douglas Porch, *Defeat and Division: France at War, 1939–1942* (Cambridge University Press: Cambridge: 2022), p. 450.
48. Winston S. Churchill to Pierre-Étienne Flandin, 14 November 1945. In Martin Gilbert, *Winston S. Churchill: Never Despair, 1945–1965* (Houghton Mifflin Company: Boston, MA: 1988), p. 169.
49. Michael Baigent and Richard Leigh, *Secret Germany: Stauffenberg and the True Story of Operation Valkyrie* (Skyhorse Publishing: New York: 2008), pp. 37–42.

50. Ian Colvin, *Chief of Intelligence* (Read Books: London: 2013), p. 202.
51. Bond, *Hitler's Cosmopolitan Bastard*, p. 197.
52. Foreign Office Memo regarding Count de Coudenhove Kalergi, 6 July 1940. TNA, Records of the Foreign Office, FO 371/24359 – Political Central France Files. C.
53. F. K. Roberts to C. W. Dixon, 31 July 1940. Ibid.
54. Bond, *Hitler's Cosmopolitan Bastard*, p. 203.
55. 'Farewell Luncheon – Mr Quo Tai-chi Entertains at his Embassy', *Tatler*, 23 April 1941, No. 2078, p. 127.
56. Quo Tai-chi, quoted in 'Mr Quo Tai Chi Says Goodbye (1941)', *British Pathé*, https://www.britishpathe.com/asset/66173/.
57. 'China Declares War – On Japan, Germany and Italy', *Civil & Military Gazette*, 11 December 1941, p. 3.
58. 'U.S. Expected to ask for Siberian Airfields', *Daily Telegraph*, 10 December 1941, p. 5.
59. Shiela Grant Duff to Hubert Ripka, 9 September 1939. Bodleian Archives & Manuscripts, Archive of Shiela Grant Duff, MS. Grant Duff 6/2.
60. Otto Strasser to Shiela Grant Duff, 13 September 1949. Ibid., MS. 9663/66.
61. Macmillan, *The Blast of War*, p. 5.
62. Harold Macmillan, speaking in 'Economic Co-ordination' debate, 18 October 1939. Hansard, 5th Series, Vol. 352, cc905–1000.
63. Harold Macmillan, speaking in 'Economic Organisation' debate, 1 February 1940. Hansard, 5th Series, Vol. 356, cc1309–1438.
64. Macmillan, *The Blast of War*, p. 78.
65. Ian Hunter (ed.), *Winston and Archie: The Collected Correspondence of Winston Churchill and Sir Archibald Sinclair* (Politico's: London: 2005), p. 217.
66. Archibald Sinclair to Winston S. Churchill, 11 May 1940. In ibid., p. 222.
67. T. E. Lawrence to R. D. Blumenfeld, 11 November 1922. CAC, The Papers of Sir Winston Churchill, CHAR 1/299/39.
68. Winston S. Churchill to R. D. Blumenfeld, 2 June 1937. Ibid., CHAR 1/299/45.
69. Winston S. Churchill, speaking at unveiling of the memorial to T. E. Lawrence at Oxford High School, 3 October 1936. In Churchill (Jnr) (ed.), *Never Give In!*, pp. 139–42.
70. Grace Hamblin interview conducted by Pat Ackerman. CAC, Churchill Oral History Collection, CHOH 1 HMBL – Tape 2, Side 3.
71. Kathleen Hill interview conducted by Pat Ackerman. Ibid., CHOH 1 KHLL – Tape 1, Side 2.
72. Grace Hamblin interview conducted by Pat Ackerman. Ibid., CHOH 1 HMBL – Tape 2, Side 3.
73. 'Maryott Whyte' (Children's Nurse, b. 10 November 1895), 'May Ward' (Housemaid, b. 29 May 1893), 'Margaret Roche' (Cook Domestic, b. 14 January 1907), 'Kathleen Goodson' (Kitchenmaid, b. 17 March 1922), 'George Collins' (Parlourman, b. 27 November 1914), Census return for 'Chartwell Manor', Sevenoaks, Kent. The 1939 Register, via www.ancestry.co.uk.
74. 'Miriam Buckles' (Children's Nurse, b. 24 December 1900), ibid.
75. 'Albert E Hill' (Head Gardener, b. 31 July 1894), Census return for 'Chartwell Gardeners Cottage', Sevenoaks, Kent. The 1939 Register, via www.ancestry.co.uk.

76. 'Patrick Jackson' (Estate Carpenter Handyman, b. 31 May 1898), 'Mary Jackson' (Unpaid Domestic Duties, b. 19 January 1900), 'Patrick V Jackson' (At School, b. 26 January 1934), Census return for 'The Garage (1) Chartwell', Sevenoaks, Kent. The 1939 Register, via www.ancestry.co.uk.
77. 'Charles A Cale' (Chauffeur, b. 7 June 1911), 'Gladys M Cale' (Unpaid Domestic Duties, b. 1 November 1911), Census return for 'The Garage (2) Chartwell', Sevenoaks, Kent. The 1939 Register, via www.ancestry.co.uk.
78. Mary Soames, Diary, 14 September 1939. CAC, The Papers of Lady Soames, MCHL 1/1/1.
79. Ian Hamilton to Winston S. Churchill, 4 September 1939. CAC, The Papers of Sir Winston Churchill, CHAR 2/365/60.
80. Sonderfahndungsliste (Special Search List) – known as 'The Black Book' – compiled by the Reich Central Security Office, p. 32.
81. C. R. Thompson to R. S. Crawford, 5 March 1941. TNA, Records of the Air Ministry, AIR 2/5240.
82. Air Ministry Minute Sheet. Most Secret. 20 March 1941. File No. S.7419. Ibid.
83. Ibid.
84. C. R. Thompson to R. S. Crawford, 24 March 1941. TNA, Records of the Air Ministry, AIR 2/5240.
85. Kathleen Hill interview conducted by Pat Ackerman. CAC, Churchill Oral History Collection, CHOH 1 KHLL – Tape 1, Side 1.
86. Author interview with Gwen Hibbert, 20 June 2024.
87. Mary Churchill to May Hill, 9 June 1944. The Papers of Gwen Hibbert.

BIBLIOGRAPHY

Archives

Birmingham Library and Archive Services, The Michael Hallett/Stefan Lorant Archive
Birmingham University Library, Papers of Neville Chamberlain
Blenheim Palace Archives
Bodleian Archives & Manuscripts
    Archive of Edward Turnour, 6th Earl Winterton
    Archive of Harold Macmillan
    Archive of Shiela Grant Duff
    Conservative Party Archive
    Lawrence Papers
    Papers of Lady Violet Bonham Carter
Bovington Camp Archive Library
British Pathé
Churchill Archives Centre (CAC)
    Churchill Oral History Collection
    Miscellaneous Holdings
    Other Deposited Collections
    The Papers of Adeline, Lady Hankey
    The Papers of Clementine Ogilvy Spencer-Churchill, Baroness Spencer-Churchill of Chartwell
    The Papers of Grace Hamblin
    The Papers of Lady Diana Cooper
    The Papers of Lady Soames
    The Papers of Randolph Churchill
    The Papers of Sarah Churchill
    The Papers of Sir Winston Churchill
Harvard University Archives, Heinrich Brüning Papers
John F. Kennedy Presidential Library, The Personal Papers of Joseph P. Kennedy
John F. Kennedy Presidential Library, Rose Fitzgerald Kennedy Personal Papers

BIBLIOGRAPHY

Magdalen College Oxford, Papers of Jeremy Wilson
National Trust, Oral History Archive
Nuffield College Archives, The Papers of F. A. Lindemann, Viscount Cherwell of
Oxford
Proceedings of the International Churchill Societies
Shapell Manuscript Foundation
The Albert Einstein Archives at the Hebrew University of Jerusalem
The National Archives (TNA)
Cabinet Papers
Captured Records of the German, Italian and Japanese Governments
Records of the Air Ministry
Records of the Foreign Office
Records of the Home Office
Records of the Prime Minister's Office
Records of the Security Service
Records of the War Office

Hansard

5th Series, 1916, Vol. 82
5th Series, 1932, Vol. 270
5th Series, 1932, Vol. 272
5th Series, 1933, Vol. 276
5th Series, 1933, Vol. 280
5th Series, 1934, Vol. 285
5th Series, 1934, Vol. 286
5th Series, 1934, Vol. 295
5th Series, 1935, Vol. 302
5th Series, 1936, Vol. 309
5th Series, 1936, Vol. 312
5th Series, 1936, Vol. 317
5th Series, 1937, Vol. 326
5th Series, 1938, Vol. 332
5th Series, 1938, Vol. 333
5th Series, 1938, Vol. 339
5th Series, 1939, Vol. 345
5th Series, 1939, Vol. 346
5th Series, 1939, Vol. 347
5th Series, 1939, Vol. 350
5th Series, 1939, Vol. 351
5th Series, 1939, Vol. 352
5th Series, 1940, Vol. 356

Government publications

*Documents Concerning German–Polish Relations and the Outbreak of Hostilities
between Great Britain and Germany on September 3, 1939* (His Majesty's
Stationery Office: London: 1939)
Documents on British Foreign Policy, 1919–1939 (His Majesty's Stationery Office:
London: 1949)

BIBLIOGRAPHY

Documents on British Foreign Policy, 1919–1939 (Her Majesty's Stationery Office: London: 1955)

Documents on German Foreign Policy, 1918–1945 (Her Majesty's Stationery Office: London: 1966)

Trials of War Criminals before the Nuernberg Military Tribunals under Control Council Law No. 10 (Government Printing Office: Washington, DC: 1951)

Books

Aldous, R. and S. Lee (eds), *Harold Macmillan: Aspects of a Political Life* (Palgrave Macmillan: London: 1999)

Amery, Leopold, *My Political Life: The Unforgiving Years, 1929–1940* (Hutchinson: London: 1955)

Arthur, Max, *Churchill: The Life – An Authorised Pictorial Biography* (Octopus Publishing Group: London: 2015)

Baigent, Michael and Richard Leigh, *Secret Germany: Stauffenberg and the True Story of Operation Valkyrie* (Skyhorse Publishing: New York: 2008)

Barnes, J. and D. Nicholson (eds), *The Empire at Bay: The Leo Amery Diaries, Volume 2: 1929–45* (Hutchinson: London: 1988)

Beaton, Cecil, *The Glass of Fashion: A Personal History of Fifty Years of Changing Tastes and the People Who Have Inspired Them* (Weidenfeld & Nicolson: London: 1954)

Bedts, Ralph F. De, *Ambassador Joseph Kennedy 1938–1940: An Anatomy of Appeasement* (P. Lang: New York: 1985)

Beloff, Halla, *Camera Culture* (Basil Blackwell: Oxford: 1985)

Bennett, Edward M., *Separated by Common Language: Franklin Delano Roosevelt and Anglo-American Relations 1933–1939* (iUniverse: Bloomington, IN: 2002)

Bennett, Gill, *Churchill's Man of Mystery: Desmond Morton and the World of Intelligence* (Routledge: London: 2007)

Benz, Wolfgang and Barbara Distel, *Terror ohne System: Die ersten Konzentrationslager im Nationalsozialismus 1933–1935* (Metropol: Berlin: 2001)

Blyth, Ronald, *The Age of Illusion: England in the Twenties and Thirties: 1919–1940* (Hamish Hamilton: London: 1963)

Bond, Martyn, *Hitler's Cosmopolitan Bastard: Count Richard Coudenhove-Kalergi and his Vision of Europe* (McGill-Queen's University Press: Montreal: 2021)

Born, Max, *The Born-Einstein Letters: Correspondence between Albert Einstein and Max and Hedwig Born from 1916 to 1955 with Commentaries by Max Born* (Macmillan: London: 1971)

Brackman, Arnold C., *The Last Emperor* (Scribner: New York: 1975)

Brüning, Heinrich, *Briefe und Gespräche 1934–1945* (Deutsche Verlags-Anstalt: Stuttgart: 1974)

Chang, Iris, *The Rape of Nanking: The Forgotten Holocaust of World War II* (Basic Books: New York: 2014)

Christiansen, Arthur, *Headlines All My Life* (Harper: New York: 1961)

Churchill, Randolph S. (ed.), *Into Battle: Speeches by the Right Hon. Winston S. Churchill, P.C., M.P.* (Cassell and Company: London: 1941)

———, *Twenty-One Years* (The Riverside Press: Cambridge: 1965)

Churchill, Sarah, *A Thread in the Tapestry* (Andre Deutsch: London: 1977)

———, *Keep on Dancing* (Coward, McCann & Geoghegan: New York: 1981)

BIBLIOGRAPHY

Churchill, Winston S., *The Story of the Malakand Field Force* (Longmans: London: 1901)

———, *Proceedings at the Unveiling of the Memorial to Lawrence of Arabia, 3 October 1936* (J. Thornton & Son: Oxford: 1937)

———, *While England Slept: A Survey of World Affairs, 1932–1938* (G. P. Putnam's Sons: New York: 1938)

———, *Great Contemporaries* (Thornton Butterworth: London: 1939)

———, *The Second World War, Volume 1: The Gathering Storm* (Cassell & Co.: London: 1950)

———, *Step by Step: Political Writings: 1936–1939* (Bloomsbury Academic: London: 2015)

Churchill, Winston S. (Jnr) (ed.), *Never Give In!: The Best of Winston Churchill's Speeches* (Pimlico: London: 2004)

Citrine, Lord, *Men and Work* (Hutchinson: London: 1964)

Clark, Ronald W., *Einstein: The Life and Times* (Hodder and Stoughton: London: 1973)

Collier, Peter and David Horowitz, *The Kennedys* (London: Secker & Warburg: 1984)

Colvin, Ian Goodhope, *Master Spy: The Incredible Story of Admiral Wilhelm Canaris, Who, While Hitler's Chief of Intelligence, Was a Secret Ally of the British* (McGraw-Hill: New York: 1952)

———, *Chief of Intelligence* (Read Books: London: 2013)

Conradi, Peter, *Hitler's Piano Player: The Rise and Fall of Ernst Hanfstaengl, Confidant of Hitler, Ally of FDR* (Carroll & Graf: New York: 2006)

Cooper, Diana, *The Light of Common Day: Autobiography* (Century Publishing: London: 1984)

Coudenhove-Kalergi, Richard N., *Pan-Europe* (Alfred Knopf: New York: 1926)

———, *An Idea Conquers the World* (Roy Publishers: New York: 1953)

Croft, Henry Page, *My Life of Strife* (Hutchinson: London: 1948)

Davenport-Hines, Richard, *Ettie: The Intimate Life and Dauntless Spirit of Lady Desborough* (Weidenfeld & Nicolson: London: 2008)

Domarus, Max (ed.), *Hitler: Speeches and Proclamations 1932–1945* (Bolchazy-Carducci Publishers: Würzburg: 1990)

Eden, Anthony, *Facing the Dictators: The Memoirs of Anthony Eden* (Cassell: London: 1962)

Einstein, Albert (trans. A. Harris), *The World As I See It* (Covici Friede: New York: 1934)

Faber, David, *Munich, 1938: Appeasement and World War II* (Simon & Schuster: New York: 2009)

Fishman, Jack, *My Darling Clementine: The Story of Lady Churchill* (David McKay Company: New York: 1963)

Floris, Maria, *Bakery: Cakes and Simple Confectionery* (Wine and Food Society: London: 1968)

Fölsing, Albrecht, *Albert Einstein: A Biography* (Viking: London: 1997)

Galante, Pierre, *Operation Valkyrie: The German Generals' Plot against Hitler* (Harper & Row Publishers: New York: 1981)

Garnett, David (ed.), *The Letters of T. E. Lawrence* (Jonathan Cape: London: 1938)

Gervais, Thierry, *The Making of Visual News: A History of Photography in the Press* (Bloomsbury: London: 2017)

BIBLIOGRAPHY

Gilbert, Martin, *Winston S. Churchill: 1922–1939* (Houghton Mifflin: London: 1966)
———, *Churchill: A Photographic Portrait* (Houghton Mifflin Company: Boston, MA: 1974)
———, *The Wilderness Years* (Houghton Mifflin Company: Boston, MA: 1982)
———, *Winston S. Churchill. Companion Volume V. Part 3: The Coming of War, 1936–1939* (Houghton Mifflin Company: Boston, MA: 1983)
———, *Prophet of Truth: Winston S. Churchill, 1922–1939* (Minerva: London: 1990)
———, *Churchill: A Life* (Minerva: London: 1992)
———, *In Search of Churchill* (HarperCollins Publishers: London: 1994)
———, *Churchill and America* (Free Press: New York: 2005)
———, *Kristallnacht: Prelude to Destruction* (HarperPress: London: 2006)
———, *Churchill and the Jews* (Henry Holt & Co.: New York: 2007)
——— (ed.), *The Churchill Documents, Volume 12: The Wilderness Years, 1929–1935* (Hillsdale College Press: Hillsdale, MI: 2012)
——— (ed.), *The Churchill Documents, Volume 13: The Coming of War, 1936–1939* (Hillsdale College Press: Hillsdale, MI: 2012)
Glendon, Mary Ann, *A World Made New* (Random House: New York: 2001)
Gorodetsky, Gabriel (ed.), *The Maisky Diaries: Red Ambassador to the Court of St James's 1932–1943* (Yale University Press: New Haven and London: 2015)
Grant Duff, Shiela, *The Parting of the Ways: A Personal Account of the Thirties* (Peter Owen: London: 1982)
Gray, Annie, *Victory in the Kitchen: The Life of Churchill's Cook* (Profile Books: London: 2020)
Grieser, Dietmar, *Wien: Wahlheimat der Genies* (Heyne: Munich: 1996)
Groot, Gerard J. De, *Liberal Crusader: The Life of Sir Archibald Sinclair* (C. Hurst & Co: London: 1993)
Gunther, John, *Inside Europe* (Harper & Brothers: New York: 1940)
Haigh, R. H., D. S. Morris and A. R. Peters, *The Years of Triumph? German Diplomatic and Military Policy 1933–41* (Barnes & Noble Books: Totowa, NJ: 1986)
Halle, Kay, *Irrepressible Churchill* (The World Publishing Company: Cleveland, OH: 1966)
Hallett, Michael, *The Real Story of Picture Post* (ARTicle Press: Birmingham: 1994)
———, *Stefan Lorant: Godfather of Photojournalism* (Scarecrow Press: Lanham, MD: 2005)
———, *Conversations with Lorant* (Crabapple Publications: Worcester: 2020)
Hanfstaengl, Ernst, *Zwischen Weißem und Braunem Haus* (R. Piper & Co.: Munich: 1970)
———, *Hitler: The Missing Years* (Arcade Publishing: New York: 1994)
———, *Hitler: The Memoir of a Nazi Insider Who Turned against the Führer* (Arcade Publishing: New York: 2011)
Hardwick, Michael and Mollie Hardwick, *Writers' Houses: A Literary Journey in England* (Phoenix House: London: 1968)
Harrod, R. F., *A Personal Memoir of Lord Cherwell* (Macmillan & Co.: London: 1959)

BIBLIOGRAPHY

Hildebrand, Klaus, *The Foreign Policy of the Third Reich* (University of California Press: Berkeley, CA: 1973)

Hinsley, F. H., *Hitler's Strategy* (Cambridge University Press: Cambridge: 1951)

Hitler, Adolf, *Mein Kampf* (Verlag Franz Eher Nachfolger: Munich: 1925)

Höhne, Heinz, *Canaris: Patriot im Zwielicht* (Bertelsmann: Munich: 1976)

Holmes, Alison R. and J. Simon Rofe (eds), *The Embassy in Grosvenor Square: American Ambassadors to the United Kingdom, 1938–2008* (Palgrave Macmillan: Basingstoke: 2012)

Hömig, Herbert, *Brüning – Politiker ohne Auftrag: Zwischen Weimarer und Bonner Republik* (Ferdinand Schöningh: Paderborn: 2005)

Horne, Alistair, *Macmillan 1894–1956: Vol. 1 of the Official Biography* (Membury Press: London: 1988)

————, *Harold Macmillan: The Official Biography* (Penguin Books: New York: 1991)

Hunter, Ian (ed.), *Winston and Archie: The Collected Correspondence of Winston Churchill and Sir Archibald Sinclair* (Politico's: London: 2005)

Hyde, H. Montgomery, *Solitary in the Ranks: Lawrence of Arabia as Airman and Private Soldier* (Atheneum: New York: 1978)

Iklé, Frank William, *German–Japanese Relations, 1936–1940: A Study in Totalitarian Diplomacy* (Bookman Associates: New York: 1956)

Jarman, Thomas L., *The Rise and Fall of Nazi Germany* (New York University Press: New York: 1977)

Jones, Larry Eugene and James N. Retallack (eds), *Between Reform, Reaction, and Resistance: Studies in the History of German Conservatism from 1789 to 1945* (Providence: Oxford: 1993)

Kennedy, John F., *Why England Slept* (Wilfred Funk: New York: 1940)

Lavery, John, *The Life of a Painter* (Cassell: London: 1940)

Lawrence, A. W. (ed.), *T. E. Lawrence by his Friends* (Jonathan Cape: London: 1935)

Leamer, Laurence, *The Kennedy Men: 1901–1963: The Laws of the Father* (Harper Perennial: New York: 2002)

Liddell Hart, B. H., *T. E. Lawrence: In Arabia and After* (Jonathan Cape: London: 1936)

Macdonald, C. A. and Jan Kaplan, *Prague in the Shadow of the Swastika: A History of the German Occupation, 1939–1945* (Quartet Books: London: 1995)

McDonough, Frank, *Neville Chamberlain, Appeasement, and the British Road to War* (Manchester University Press: Manchester: 1998)

Macmillan, Harold, *The Price of Peace: Notes on the World Crisis* (Macmillan and Co., : London: 1938)

————, *Economic Aspects of Defence* (Macmillan and Co., : London: 1939)

————, *Winds of Change, 1914–1939* (Macmillan: London: 1966)

————, *The Blast of War, 1939–1945* (Macmillan: London: 1967)

————, *The Past Masters: Politics and Politicians, 1906–1939* (Macmillan: London: 1975)

Manchester, William, *The Caged Lion: Winston Spencer Churchill, 1932–1940* (Pan Macmillan: London: 1988)

Martin, Hugh, *Battle: The Life Story of the Rt Hon. Winston S. Churchill* (Sampson Low, Marston & Co: London: 1932)

BIBLIOGRAPHY

Medawar, Jean and David Pyke, *Hitler's Gift: The True Story of the Scientists Expelled by the Nazi Regime* (Arcade Publishing: New York: 2012)

Meinertzhagen, R., *Middle East Diary: 1917–1956* (Cresset Press: London: 1959)

Mowrer, Edgar Ansel, *Triumph and Turmoil: A Personal History of our Time* (Weybright and Talley: New York: 1968)

Namier, L. B., *Europe in Decay* (Macmillan & Co.: London: 1950)

Nathan, Otto and Heinz Norden (eds), *Einstein on Peace* (Simon & Schuster: New York: 1960)

Nicolson, Nigel (ed.), *Harold Nicolson: Diaries and Letters, 1930–1939* (Collins: London: 1966)

Nicosia, Francis R. and Lawrence D. Stokes (ed.), *Germans Against Nazism: Nonconformity, Opposition and Resistance in the Third Reich* (Berg Publisher: New York: 1990)

Noakes, J. and G. Pridham, *Nazism 1919–1945: Foreign Policy, War, and Racial Extermination*, Vol. 3 (University of Exeter Press: Devon: 2010)

Norman, Andrew, *T. E. Lawrence: Unravelling the Enigma* (Halsgrove: Tiverton: 2003)

Ogley, Bob, *Biggin on the Bump* (Froglets Publications: Westerham: 1990)

Pakula, Hannah, *The Last Empress: Madame Chiang Kai-shek and the Birth of Modern China* (Simon & Schuster: New York: 2009)

Patch, Jr, William L., *Heinrich Brüning and the Dissolution of the Weimar Republic* (Cambridge University Press: Cambridge: 1998)

Pearson, John, *The Private Lives of Winston Churchill* (Simon & Schuster: New York: 1991)

Petrie, Charles (ed.), *The Life and Letters of the Right Hon. Sir Austen Chamberlain* (Cassell: London: 1939)

Porch, Douglas, *Defeat and Division: France at War, 1939–1942* (Cambridge University Press: Cambridge: 2022)

Rhodes James, Robert (ed.), *Chips: The Diaries of Sir Henry Channon* (Weidenfeld & Nicolson: London: 1967)

—— (ed.), *Winston S. Churchill: His Complete Speeches 1897–1963*, 8 vols (Bowker: New York: 1974)

——, *Robert Boothby: A Portrait of Churchill's Ally* (Viking: New York: 1991)

Roberts, Allen, *Web of Intrigue (Anti-Hitler Opposition)* (Moore Pub. Co.: Durham, NC: 1979)

Roberts, Cecil, *Sunshine and Shadow: Being the Fourth Book of an Autobiography 1930–1946* (Hodder & Stoughton: London: 1972)

Roberts, Geoffrey, *The Unholy Alliance: Stalin's Pact with Hitler* (Indiana University Press: Bloomington, IN: 1990)

Robinson, Andrew, *Einstein on the Run: How Britain Saved the World's Greatest Scientist* (Yale University Press: New Haven and London: 2019)

Roth, Hans Ingvar, *P. C. Chang and the Universal Declaration of Human Rights* (University of Pennsylvania Press: Philadelphia, PA: 2018)

Rowe, David E. and Robert Schulmann (eds), *Einstein on Politics: His Private Thoughts and Public Stands on Nationalism, Zionism, War, Peace and the Bomb* (Princeton University Press: Princeton, NJ: 2013)

Rowse, A. L., *Appeasement: A Study in Political Decline, 1933–1939* (Norton: New York: 1961)

BIBLIOGRAPHY

Sandys, Celia, *Churchill's Little Redhead* (Fonthill: London: 2021)

Scott, William Evans, *Alliance against Hitler* (Duke University Press: Durham, NC: 1962)

Self, Robert C. (ed.), *The Austen Chamberlain Diary Letters: The Correspondence of Sir Austen Chamberlain with his Sisters Hilda and Ida, 1916–1937* (Cambridge University Press: Cambridge: 1995)

—— (ed.), *The Neville Chamberlain Diary Letters, Vol. 4, The Downing Street Years: 1934–1940* (Ashgate: Aldershot: 2000)

Sheean, Vincent, *Between the Thunder and the Sun* (Macmillan & Co.: London: 1944)

Shepardson, Donald E., *Conflict & Diplomacy from the Great War to the Cold War* (P. Lang: New York: 1999)

Shirer, William L., *The Rise and Fall of the Third Reich: A History of Nazi Germany* (Simon & Schuster: New York: 2011)

Simpson, Andrew R. B., *Another Life: Lawrence after Arabia* (Spellmount: Stroud: 2008)

Smith, Amanda (ed.), *Hostage to Fortune: The Letters of Joseph P. Kennedy* (Viking: New York: 2001)

Smith, Clare Sydney, *The Golden Reign: The Story of my Friendship with 'Lawrence of Arabia'* (Cassell & Co.: London: 1949)

Soames, Mary (ed.), *Speaking for Themselves: The Personal Letters of Winston and Clementine Churchill* (Black Swan: London: 1999)

——, *Clementine Churchill* (Doubleday: London: 2003)

——, *A Daughter's Tale: The Memoir of Winston Churchill's Youngest Child* (Doubleday: London: 2011)

Spier, Eugen, *FOCUS: A Footnote to the History of the Thirties* (Oswald Wolff: London: 1963)

Sylvester, A. J., *Life with Lloyd George* (Barnes and Noble: New York: 1975)

Taylor, Blaine, *Hitler's Headquarters: From Beer Hall to Bunker, 1920–1945* (Potomac Books: Washington, DC: 2007)

Thomas, David Arthur, *Churchill: The Member for Woodford* (F. Cass: Ilford: 1995)

Thorpe, D. R., *Supermac: The Life of Harold Macmillan* (Pimlico: London: 2011)

Tilden, Philip, *True Remembrances: The Memoirs of an Architect* (Country Life: London: 1954)

Treviranus, Gottfried R., *Für Deutschland im Exil* (Econ Verlag: Düsseldorf: 1973)

Urbach, Karina (ed.), *European Aristocracies and the Radical Right 1918–1939* (Oxford University Press: Oxford: 2007)

Wallach, Janet, *Desert Queen: The Extraordinary Life of Gertrude Bell, Adventurer, Adviser to Kings, Ally of Lawrence of Arabia* (Anchor Books: New York: 2005)

Weinberg, Gerhard L., *Hitler's Foreign Policy, 1933–1939* (Enigma Books: New York: 2010)

Weitz, John, *Hitler's Diplomat: The Life and Times of Joachim von Ribbentrop* (Ticknor & Fields: New York: 1992)

Werth, Alexander, *France and Munich before and after the Surrender* (Harper and Brothers ublishers: New York: 1939)

Williams, Charles, *Harold Macmillan* (Phoenix: London: 2010)

Willstätter, Richard, *Aus meinem Leben: von Arbeit, Muße und Freunden* (Verlag Chemie: Weinheim: 1949)

BIBLIOGRAPHY

Willoughby, Westel W., *The Sino-Japanese Controversy and the League of Nations* (Johns Hopkins University Press: Baltimore, MD: 1935)

Wilson, Jeremy and Nicole Wilson (eds), *T. E. Lawrence: Correspondence with Bernard and Charlotte Shaw* (Fordingbridge: Castle Hill Press: 2000)

Windsor, Edward, Duke of, *A King's Story: The Memoirs of HRH the Duke of Windsor* (Cassell and Company: London: 1951)

Ziegler, Philip, *King Edward VIII* (HarperCollins: London: 1991)

Articles

Ball, Stuart, 'Churchill and the Conservative Party', *Transactions of the Royal Historical Society*, Vol. 11 (2001)

Black, Naomi, 'Decision-Making and the Munich Crisis', *British Journal of International Studies*, Vol. 6, No. 3, special number on appeasement (Oct. 1980)

Cannadine, David, 'Churchill and the British Monarchy', *Transactions of the Royal Historical Society*, Vol. 11 (2001)

Casey, Steven, 'Franklin D. Roosevelt, Ernst "Putzi" Hanfstaengl and the "S-Project", June 1942–June 1944', *Journal of Contemporary History*, Vol. 35, No. 3 (July 2000)

Ceadel, Martin, 'The King and Country Debate, 1933: Student Politics, Pacifism and the Dictators', *Historical Journal*, Vol. 22, No. 2 (1979)

Chang, P. C., 'Civilisation and Social Philosophies', *Progressive Education Booklet*, No. 9 (1938)

Fox, Robert, 'Einstein in Oxford', *Notes and Records: The Royal Society Journal of the History of Science*, Vol. 72, No. 3 (May 2018)

Glasspool, J. and W. L. Andrew, 'The Exceptional Summer of 1933', *Quarterly Journal of the Royal Meteorological Society* (Jan. 1934)

Hill, C. J., 'Great Britain and the Saar Plebiscite of 13 January 1935', *Journal of Contemporary History*, Vol. 9, No. 2 (Apr. 1974)

Lukes, Igor, 'The Czechoslovak Partial Mobilization in May 1938: A Mystery (almost) Solved', *Journal of Contemporary History*, Vol. 31, No. 4 (Oct. 1996)

Mordfin, Robin I., 'Seeking the Past: Early Chinese Scholars at the Law Schools', *University of Chicago Law School* (Fall 2012)

Nicholas, Mary Ann, 'Review – Picture Post', *British Journalism Review*, Vol. 6, No. 1 (1995)

Robbins, Keith G., 'Konrad Henlein, the Sudeten Question and British Foreign Policy', *Historical Journal*, Vol. 12, No. 4 (Dec. 1969)

Robertson, James C., 'The British General Election of 1935', *Journal of Contemporary History*, Vol. 9, No. 1 (Jan. 1974)

Schwoerer, Lois G., 'Lord Halifax's Visit to Germany: November 1937', *The Historian*, Vol. 32, No. 3 (May 1970)

Soames, Mary, 'Father Always Came First, Second and Third', *Finest Hour: The Journal of the International Churchill Society*, Vol. 116 (Autumn 2002)

Spinks, Charles Nelson, 'The Termination of the Anglo-Japanese Alliance', *Pacific Historical Review*, Vol. 6, No. 4 (Dec. 1937), pp. 321–40

Stone, William T., 'The Briand Project for European Union', *Foreign Policy Associations*, Vol. 6, No. 13 (Sept. 1930)

BIBLIOGRAPHY

Newspapers and magazines

Argus
Atlantic
Belfast Telegraph
Boston Evening Transcript
Bulletin of International News
Chicago Tribune
China Journal
China Mail
China Weekly Review
Civil & Military Gazette
Collier's Weekly
Country Life
Daily Express
Daily Herald
Daily Mail
Daily Mirror
Daily News
Daily Telegraph
Deutscher Reichsanzeiger
Evening Despatch
Evening Express
Evening News
Evening Standard
Hong Kong Telegraph
Illustrated London News
Kent and Sussex Courier
LIFE Magazine
Liverpool Daily Post
Liverpool Echo
New York Times
Northern Echo
Observer
Picture Post
Reuters
Reynold's Newspaper
Sevenoaks Chronicle
Strand Magazine
Sunday Dispatch
Sunday Express
Sunday Graphic
Sunday Mercury
Sunday Pictorial
Tatler
The Times
Time
Victoria Daily Times
Völkischer Beobachter
Windsor Star
Winnipeg Tribune

FURTHER READING

Here is a selection of noteworthy books from the last decade (the duration of my time at Chartwell, to date), which shed further light on the people, subjects, issues and period of the focus of this book:

Bouverie, Tim, *Appeasement: Chamberlain, Hitler, Churchill and the Road to War* (Tim Duggan Books: New York: 2019)

Brendon, Piers, *Churchill's Bestiary: His Life Through Animals* (Michael O'Mara Books: London: 2018)

———, *Churchill's Menagerie: Winston Churchill and the Animal Kingdom* (Pegasus: New York: 2019)

Drake, James and Allen Packwood, *Letters for the Ages: The Private and Personal Letters of Sir Winston Churchill* (Bloomsbury Continuum: London: 2023)

Gray, Annie, *Victory in the Kitchen: The Life of Churchill's Cook* (Profile Books: London: 2020)

Lough, David, *No More Champagne: Churchill and His Money* (Picador: London: 2015)

Purnell, Sonia, *Clementine: The Life of Mrs Winston Churchill* (Viking: New York; Aurum: London, 2015)

Roberts, Andrew, *Churchill: Walking with Destiny* (Allen Lane: London; Viking: New York: 2018)

Sandys, Edwina, *Winston Churchill: A Passion for Painting* (Donning: Virginia Beach, VA: 2015)

Soames, Emma (ed.), *Mary Churchill's War: The Wartime Diaries of Churchill's Youngest Daughter* (Two Roads: London: 2021)

Stelzer, Cita, *Working with Winston: The Unsung Women behind Britain's Greatest Statesman* (Pegasus: New York: 2019)

Vale, J. Allister and John W. Scadding, *Winston Churchill's Illnesses 1886-1965* (Frontline: Barnsley: 2020)

INDEX

Figures are shown by a page reference in *italics*.

INDEX

INDEX

opposition to Indian independence, 2, 3, 23, 79, 83, 86, 95, 211, 250
as a painter, 35, 93, 117–18, 152, 165, 176, 238, *290*
photos of, *5, 14, 178, 220, 239, 290, 300*
political standing, 1–4, 23, 24, 55, 83, 88, 98, 103, 105–6, 110, 113, 125, 152, 157–8, 186, 228–9, 234, 240, 245–6, 265
as Prime Minister, 309, 312
referenced in Hitler's speech, 228
role of Minister of Defence, 107, 110
as Secretary of State for the Dominions and Colonies, 46–7
stock market investments, 87–8, 91, 186, 187
trips to America, 4–5, 131, 145
trips to France, 234–5, 289, *290*
The World Crisis, 50, 66, 70
see also articles (by Churchill); speeches (by Churchill)
Churchill Group, 106–8, 120, 123, 208
Clark, Allan, 127
Clark Kerr, Sir Archibald, 266–7
collective security
Anglo-French pact, 121, 122–4, 163
Churchill's belief in, 117, 155, 183
Macmillan's belief in, 251
Pan-European Union, 167, 169–71, 175–6
Colvin, Ian, 198–9, 201, 202, 225, 232, 274
conscription, 255–6, 262
Cooper, Alfred 'Duff', 255, 256, 296
Cooper, Diana, 62
Cot, Pierre, 155
Coudenhove-Kalergi, Richard
approach to Churchill, 169–71, 174
concerns over Austria, 171, 173, 174
exile from Austria, 181–2, 184, 306–7
Great Contemporaries gifted to, 167, 179, 182, 184
meetings with Churchill, 171, 174, 253–4
Nazi invasion of Austria, 180–1

Pan-Europeanism, 167, 169–70, 175–6
photo, *170*
on a Russia-Germany pact, 253–4
visit to Chartwell, 167, 175–9, 183
Coward, Noel, 292
Crowdy, Dame Rachel, 274
Curtis, Lionel, 61, 67
Cutting, Joyce, 73
Czechoslovakia
British support for, 199–200, 211, 214–16, 220–4
Franco-Soviet-British defence of, 213, 215, 216–19, 221, 222, 245
German occupation, 244–5, 247
Munich Agreement, 224–5, 226, 244, 245
possible invasion on, 185, 190, 193, 209–10, 214–15
pro-German agitation, 209, 212, 240, 243
Sudetenland region, 193, 203, 213, 214, 217, 221–2, 224
see also Grant Duff, Shiela; Kleist-Schmenzin, Ewald von

Dalton, Hugh, 207–8, 209
Deakin, Bill, 117, 153, 166, 178, 289, 292
Desborough, Ettie, 84–5
Disarmament Convention, 45
disarmament/rearmament
Churchill's campaign for rearmament, 55, 67–8, 74, 82–3, 102, 116, 127, 130–1, 133–4
collective security strategies, 117, 155
Hitler's 'Peace Speech', 27–8
rearmament by Nazi Germany, 13, 71, 79, 80, 127, 168–9, 175, 196
unilateral disarmament movements, 14, 19–20, 27, 40
Dowding, Sir Hugh, 255
Dudley Ward, Freda, 62, 126

Eden, Anthony
China's requests for support against Japan, 267–8
the Czechoslovak situation, 224

INDEX